GUSTAV AND ALMA MAHLER

COMPOSER RESOURCE MANUALS
(VOL. 28)

GARLAND REFERENCE LIBRARY
OF THE HUMANITIES
(VOL. 738)

GARLAND COMPOSER RESOURCE MANUALS

General Editor: Guy A. Marco

1. *Heinrich Schütz: A Guide to Research* by Allen B. Skei
2. *Josquin Des Prez: A Guide to Research* by Sydney Robinson Charles
3. *Sergei Vasil'evich Rachmaninoff: A Guide to Research* by Robert Palmieri
4. *Manuel de Falla: A Bibliography and Research Guide* by Gilbert Chase and Andrew Budwig
5. *Adolphe Adam and Léo Delibes: A Guide to Research* by William E. Studwell
6. *Carl Nielsen: A Guide to Research* by Mina F. Miller
7. *William Byrd: A Guide to Research* by Richard Turbet
8. *Christoph Willibald Gluck: A Guide to Research* by Patricia Howard
9. *Girolamo Frescobaldi: A Guide to Research* by Frederick Hammond
10. *Stephen Collins Foster: A Guide to Research* by Galvin Elliker
11. *Béla Bartók: A Guide to Research* by Elliott Antokoletz
12. *Antonio Vivaldi: A Guide to Research* by Michael Talbot
13. *Johannes Ockeghem and Jacob Obrecht: A Guide to Research* by Martin Picker
14. *Ernest Bloch: A Guide to Research* by David Z. Kushner
15. *Hugo Wolf: A Guide to Research* by David Ossenkop
16. *Wolfgang Amadeus Mozart: A Guide to Research* by Baird Hastings
17. *Nikolai Andreevich Rimsky-Korsakov: A Guide to Research* by Gerald R. Seaman
18. *Henry Purcell: A Guide to Research* by Franklin B. Zimmerman
19. *G. F. Handel: A Guide to Research* by Mary-Ann Parker Hale
20. *Jean-Philippe Rameau: A Guide to Research* by Donald Foster
21. *Ralph Vaughan Williams: A Guide to Research* by Neil Butterworth
22. *Hector Berlioz: A Guide to Research* by Jeffrey A. Langford and Jane Denker Graves
23. *Claudio Monteverdi: A Guide to Research* by K. Gary Adams and Dyke Kiel
24. *Carl Maria von Weber: A Guide to Research* by Donald G. Henderson and Alice H. Henderson
25. *Orlando di Lasso: A Guide to Research* by James Erb
26. *Giovanni Battista Pergolesi: A Guide to Research* by Marvin E. Paymer and Hermine W. Williams
27. *Claude Debussy: A Guide to Research* by James Briscoe
28. *Gustav and Alma Mahler: A Guide to Research* by Susan M. Filler

GUSTAV AND ALMA MAHLER
A Guide to Research

Susan M. Filler

GARLAND PUBLISHING, INC. • NEW YORK & LONDON
1989

© 1989 Susan M. Filler
All rights reserved

Library of Congress Cataloging-in-Publication Data

Filler, Susan Melanie, 1947–
    Gustav and Alma Mahler: a guide to research / Susan M. Filler.
      p. cm. — (Garland reference library of the humanities ; vol. 738) (Garland composer resource manuals ; vol. 28)
    Includes bibliographical references.
    ISBN 0-8240-8483-7 (alk. paper)
    1. Mahler, Gustav, 1860–1911—Bibliography. 2. Mahler, Alma, 1879–1964—Bibliography. I. Title. II. Series. III. Series: Garland composer resource manuals ; v. 28.
ML134.M34F54   1989
016.78'092—dc20   89–23369
                                                                CIP

Printed on acid-free, 250-year-life paper
Manufactured in the United States of America

This Book is Dedicated

to the Memory

of

JACK DIETHER

GARLAND COMPOSER RESOURCE MANUALS

In response to the growing need for bibliographic guidance to the vast literature on significant composers, Garland is publishing an extensive series of research guides. This ongoing series encompasses more than 50 composers; they represent Western musical tradition from the Renaissance to the present century.

Each research guide offers a selective, annotated list of writings, in all European languages, about one or more composers. There are also lists of works by the composers, unless these are available elsewhere. Biographical sketches and guides to library resources, organization, and specialists are presented. As appropriate to the individual composer, there are maps, photographs, or other illustrative matters, and glossaries and indexes.

TABLE OF CONTENTS

Introduction   xi

Gustav and Alma Mahler (A Brief Chronology)   xxi

Mahler's Works:

    I. Mature works   xxix
   II. Early works   xxxviii
  III. Editions, transcriptions and completions of
       works by other composers, and spurious works   xliii

Surviving Works of Alma Mahler-Werfel   xlviii

List of Abbreviations   li

Bibliography

  Compendia   3
  Encyclopedia References   9
  Catalogues and Lists   11
  History
    General   19
    Judaism and Antisemitism
      Background History and Culture   24
      Jews in the German-Speaking Countries
        (General)   26
      Jews in Music   28
      Antisemitism (General)   43
      Antisemitism in Music   43
  Visuals   53
    Places   54
    Portraits   57
  Biographies
    Non-eyewitness (with or without studies of works)   58
    Medical/Psychiatric   70
    The "Mahler Circle"   77
    Eyewitness Accounts
      Autobiographies and Biographies   81
      Letters   92
      Essays and Miscellaneous   99
  Mahler's Letters
    Primary   108
    Commentary   114
  Conducting Activities
    General   115

Early Positions	119
Prague	121
Leipzig	122
Budapest	123
Hamburg	124
Vienna	
General	124
Vienna Philharmonic Orchestra	126
Opera	
General	130
Individual Productions	139
New York	
General	143
Metropolitan Opera	143
New York Philharmonic Orchestra	145
Alma Mahler-Werfel	
Biographical/Analytical	
Primary	146
Secondary	150
Literary Influences	
Texts used by Alma Mahler-Werfel	153
Mahler's Symphonic Texts	154
Mahler's Vocal Works	
Des Knaben Wunderhorn	156
Rückert Lieder/Kindertotenlieder	157
Das Lied von der Erde	158
Mahler's Early Works and Their Texts	159
General and Miscellaneous	161
Publishers	
General	164
Bote und Bock	165
Ludwig Doblinger	166
Ernst Eulenberg	167
C. F. Kahnt	167
C. F. Peters	168
B. Schotts Söhne	170
Universal Edition	171
Josef Weinberger	172
Mahler's Place in Musical History	172
Reception/Historiography	189
Media and Criticism	197
Philosophical Views	202

Table of Contents ix

Mahler's Works
  Style
    Form/Harmony/Melody 209
    Orchestration 214
    Program, Nature and Folk 217
  Collective Analyses
    Symphonies and Songs, etc. 222
    Symphonies 227
    Songs 242
      Lieder eines fahrenden Gesellen 247
      Des Knaben Wunderhorn 249
      Rückert settings 249
  Individual Analyses
    Das klagende Lied 250
    Das Lied von der Erde 253
    Symphony no. 1 258
    Symphony no. 2 260
    Symphony no. 3 263
    Symphony no. 4 266
    Symphony no. 5 268
    Symphony no. 6 270
    Symphony no. 7 273
    Symphony no. 8 276
    Symphony no. 9 279
    Symphony no. 10 283
  Other Works
    Klavierquartett 292
    Symphonic Prelude [spurious] 292
    Four Early Symphonies 293
    Scherzo in c minor and *Presto in F major* 294
    Editions of Works by Other Composers
      Weber, *Die drei Pintos* 294
      Retouches
        General 297
        Bach 298
        Beethoven 298
        Bruckner 299
        Schubert 300
        Schumann 300
  Miscellaneous 301

Index of Composers, Authors, Editors, Compilers,
Translators, Contributors, Arrangers, Librettists
and Poets 305
Subject Index 319

INTRODUCTION

Gustav Mahler was recognized in his time as a major conductor, but he did not achieve commensurate reputation as a composer until many years after his death. His works gained a modicum of acceptance through the labors of conductors who had been his colleagues, despite popular and critical ambivalence. With the centennial of Mahler's birth, however, a change in popular reaction to his music in the concert hall became evident, and today the Mahler "boom" is still vital.

However, while audiences became increasingly interested in Mahler's music and composers of the present century acknowledged debts to his style in their own works, musicological study of Mahler's work lagged behind in pace. The need for critical study of his work and the conditions under which he did it has only been recognized comparatively recently.

This problem was particularly unfortunate in view of the importance of Mahler as a personage in his time. He was a linchpin in a circle of intellectual giants who affected the history of creative endeavor to this day. He was born in Bohemia at a time when it was part of the Austrian Empire; he was a Jew who formally converted to Catholicism, but neither he, his friends nor his enemies forgot his Jewish background. While Jews in the Austrian Empire from intellectual to laborer felt the widespread antisemitism existing in the Austrian governmental and social hierarchy every day (and with good reason, since it was strongly entrenched and would culminate in the tragedy of the Third Reich), the Jews of Vienna included some of the greatest luminaries of the intellectual and political revolutions at the turn of this century, such as Mahler, Arnold Schoenberg, Viktor Adler, Ludwig Wittgenstein, Sigmund Freud, Theodor Herzl and Franz Werfel.

It seems incredible that such brilliance could grow so strong in ground which, in retrospect, appeared incapable of nourishing anything but decay, ennui and suicide. Certainly Josef Stalin and Adolf Hitler learned political lessons in Vienna which resulted in terrible consequences not many years later, even as Mahler, Freud, Adler, Wittgenstein, Werfel, Herzl and the composers of the Second Viennese School sought to make positive gains from the old order. We are bound to concede that Vienna was a major center for changes that are with us to this day, for better or worse.

Mahler lived only a limited time in that rarified atmosphere, but he did not live in a vacuum; his music and his writings reveal sensitivity to the world around him and its effect on his own life. Romantic in emotional expression, he was nevertheless grounded in the forms of the classical and baroque periods. His works are based on the forms of sonata, rondo, theme-and-variations, scherzo-and-trio, even ritornello, which he adapted from the examples of Bach, Mozart and Beethoven; yet his gift for melody was his own, and his orchestration was likewise unique. He was influenced by poetry of the "folk" type while simultaneously incorporating elements of Nietzsche and Goethe and German adaptations of exotica from the East; this was a diversity he shared with Schubert, Schumann and Brahms. His vocal style was influenced by the operas of Wagner; but he wrote no operas of his own, confining most of his work to the song and the symphony. He wrote music that melodically creates a sense of déjà vu; but he antagonized audiences and critics of his time (and long after) with harmonic experiments which influenced Schoenberg and his followers in their own revolution.

In short, Mahler was a "Januskopf," a head looking both forward and backward at once; he was therefore misunderstood by the concertgoing public of his time (which misunderstood the work of those who came after him, true to pattern). Yet, although the public was skeptical of his genius as a composer, it recognized his remarkable powers as a conductor. For ten years he was the Director of the Vienna Opera, an institution which has taken, chewed up and spit out more famous conductor-directors than almost any other opera house in history. That he survived in the position for such an extended period--and the incredible span of ten years is the second longest in the history of the house, equalled by Salmhofer and surpassed only by Jahn--testifies to Mahler's artistry, business acumen and, ironically, tenacity.

In his artistic perfectionism he spared neither himself nor others. In that respect he was a dreamer, and his results have enriched posterity. Conversely, however, he was eminently practical; without such practicality he could not have run the leading opera house in Europe for ten years, nor fought his way up the ladder in other houses until he reached that peak. Therefore, in a manner of speaking, he was a man of great stature; his head was in the clouds, but his feet were solidly planted on the ground.

Mahler's wife, Alma, was herself a composer of considerable quality; but her work was neglected even longer than her husband's. While Alma, as a Catholic, was not impeded by the antisemitism that affected Mahler, she carried a different handicap because of her sex. Musicologists have only recently begun to accord the work of female composers the same consideration given to the work of their male counterparts, i.e. concern for quality of composition untempered by societal prejudice inherent in knowledge of the composer's gender. Even

Introduction

today, however, advocates of the work of Alma Mahler must struggle to obtain recognition for the composer without reference to the *femme fatale* known to history.

She was "liberated" in a society that gave women few professional options; she was an intellectual companion to men who would not suffer fools gladly: Mahler, Walter Gropius, Oskar Kokoschka, Franz Werfel, Arnold Schoenberg, Thornton Wilder, Arthur Schnitzler, Max Reinhardt, Thomas Mann and many others. She was physically beautiful, but men were drawn to her by her wit and intelligence, which were more permanently valuable than any conventional sex appeal. Her strong will and sense of herself as focus among all those intellectuals have created enemies for her; yet she exerted influence on men seldom seen in the life of one woman. She observed and recorded history and culture with a sharp critical eye, although she has been accused of distorting reality in her writings.

However, in spite of the limitations in her representation of reality, she was an important commentator on subjects from music to politics, literature to art, medicine to world travel. And she was never dull.

While much has been written about Mahler and more than one might think about Alma, the literature is variable in type and quality. It is impossible to include all existing literature on the subject, in this book or any other; that corpus grows month by month. Thus, in writing this book, my first and most difficult task was that of selection. Not surprisingly, I was affected by the work of predecessors who had trod similar ground, the chief of these being Bruno and Eleonore Vondenhoff and Simon Michael Namenwirth. I salute the work of these scholars, but--while acknowledging their example--I must note that my conception of my task differs somewhat from theirs.

I have chosen to include information in eighteen languages, in order to show the scope of literature on Mahler and Alma in many different forms. Considering that this book is being published in the United States, the inclusion of information in such languages as Russian, Greek, Yiddish, Hebrew and Slovene may appear to be an exercise in eccentricity, if not indeed futility (especially in view of the fact that entries in such languages are small in number by comparison with the compass of literature in German, English and other Western European languages). But my aim has been partially to show that the literature on the subject has taken forms which might even surprise specialists who are familiar with the available literature, and partially to show to those who are familiar with such languages as native speakers that information is available to them, often in forms completely distinct from equivalents in the languages of Western Europe and the United States. Not all literature is of such type as to be automatically included. My selections have followed these guidelines:

(a) Eyewitness accounts of Mahler and Alma's lives by themselves and others (including letters, autobiographies, biographies and essays).
(b) Biographies of Mahler and Alma which do not rank as eyewitness accounts, especially by scholars from the postwar period to the present, which has seen the major development in Mahler studies.
(c) Medico-psychological studies, which present a specialized but substantial subsection of the biographical references.
(d) Eyewitness critical accounts of Mahler's performances reprinted in book form (as opposed to such reviews from periodicals, which are so numerous as to be disconcerting and also rather ephemeral).
(e) Musicological and historical studies placing Mahler and Alma's lives and works in musical and cultural perspective (actually two subjects, since studies of their works inevitably refer to their background).
(f) Individual analyses of works (including introductory critical studies in scores comparable to articles and books) and collections of such analyses.
(g) Literary sources used by Mahler and Alma in their works, especially the vocal settings in song, symphony and cantata form, and critical assessments of these sources, when relevant to their musical connections.
(h) Documentation of the history of the publishers of Mahler and Alma's music.

Likewise, I omitted certain types of sources which appeared to be less relevant to modern use or of lesser permanent value:

(a) Biographies of other composers, except such autobiographies that include eyewitness accounts of Mahler or Alma, on the theory that such biographies--while not necessarily irrelevant--are not central to the subject at hand and are doubtless best handled by specialists to whom their subjects are central.
(b) Obituaries and social notices from periodicals, which share the limitations of the reviews of performances in periodicals as noted above.
(c) Unpublished sources with the exception of completed doc-

Introduction xv

       toral dissertations and a small number of others (although the exclusion of dissertations in progress as of this writing has been a difficult qualification to make).

(d) Program notes from individual performances (although I have included certain collections of such notes documenting cycles of many works of Mahler for the reason that these are comparable to short introductory collections of analyses in book form, unlike individual notes).

(e) General histories of music, except certain books valuable for historical documentation of the musicological reception of Mahler's work.

Of course, not every entry in the bibliography is of equal merit. A difficult choice I was forced to make was whether to cite items which are not reliable sources of information. In electing to include sources that are inferior in factual quality, I suggest that the reader take them at face value for historiographical documentation and no more. A special facet of this problem was the inclusion of many items from the German-speaking countries during the Third Reich. The antisemitic literature on Mahler dated from his lifetime and continued without abatement for at least thirty-five years after his death; it was at a peak during the pseudo-musicology of the Third Reich, in which Mahler's reputation was vilified along with the reputations of other Jewish intellectuals from the Mendelssohns to Heine, from Freud to Schoenberg. The ugly literature written by Nazi adherents has been eschewed by postwar scholars on moral grounds, and with very good reason. My purpose in including such materials in this book has been to show that such contributions, apart from their immorality, were intellectually unsound. I have not yet read a Nazi contribution to the Mahler literature that was really well-reasoned and documented in the manner expected of musicologists today. But, while worthless intellectually, such material constitutes revealing documentation of a stage in the history of the reception of Mahler's work, and it is therefore historiographically necessary for an understanding of the long road Mahler has come in professional reputation.

While I felt the necessity of including such materials for intellectual scrutiny, my personal reaction was at best ambivalent. As an American Jew of the generation following the Holocaust, I had not experienced it personally; but the connection of the Nazi-sponsored literature with the atrocities committed during the period was obvious and hateful. I have continued my work in this difficult area because of my conviction that I live to contribute to the historical record on behalf of those who did not.

Many materials included here may not be easily accessible. I located them in libraries specializing in literature long out of print, or collections of specialized nature assembled without distinction of language. While I have not been able to incorporate into this book the information in my files about locations of rare items, I suggest that my readers make their own quests for some of these esoterica, which round out the picture of Mahler research beyond references routinely cited in major lists and filed in major libraries. My own discoveries of many of these items often resulted in some of the happiest moments in the preparation of this book, proving that research is, in itself, a satisfying if difficult process for those who are emotionally committed to its methods.

A major breakthrough in the history of Mahler research has been provided in the publications of the Internationale Gustav Mahler Gesellschaft of Vienna. I owe much to the Critical Edition, the more recent *Bibliothek der Internationalen Gustav Mahler Gesellschaft* series, and especially the continuing issues of *News About Mahler Research (Nachrichtungen zur Mahler-Forschung)*. The latter publication, besides including listings of Mahler editions, books, articles, meetings and lectures, has recently begun to include short articles of individual interest. I listed many of those articles, as well as depending on the information on outside publications in my own search process. As this publication is issued simultaneously in German and English, my citations in this book take the English forms; but, after comparing the versions in the two languages, I doubt that German-speaking readers will be much at a loss if they investigate such items in the German versions, as the pagination and content are comparable.

The process of compiling information for this book would have been interminable if I had not been assisted by many people and organizations. I owe a major debt to the late Jack Diether, to whom I dedicate this book; I am saddened that he did not see it completed. He was my friend and mentor over a period of fifteen years, from the time of my doctoral research to his own death. His wife Doris has been unsparing in good sense, moral support and sense of humor.

Next, I am greatly indebted to Emmy Hauswirth of the Internationale Gustav Mahler Gesellschaft for her patience, hard work in supplying me with information, and practicality which was indispensable during some rather trying periods. I also owe much to the cooperation of Herta Blaukopf, which has been unique in its quality.

I should also render thanks to Mr. H. Nieman of the Gustav Mahler Stichting Nederland, who extended the courtesy of the Stichting's collection in Wassenaar, Holland, sent copies

Introduction   xvii

of many items which I could not otherwise obtain, gave generously of his own knowledge, and challenged me with many questions which raised my consciousness. Such gratitude is also due to my wise friend, Henry-Louis de la Grange, who opened to me his collection in the Bibliothèque Musicale Gustav Mahler, Paris. This collection was an important source for many items in this book, and although the time I spent there was comparatively brief, it was of rare value due to the expert assistance of the staff, who located many items quickly during a mere few days.

My work took me to many libraries and collections in addition to those mentioned above. In some places I located many items, in others a handful; but I am grateful for the opportunity to have visited them all, since in each one I located information that I had not found elsewhere, and every such discovery was a triumph. In the United States these locations included the Library of Congress, the Ryerson and Burnham Library of the Art Institute of Chicago, the public libraries of the cities of Chicago and Evanston, Illinois, New York, Boston and Seattle, the libraries of the University of Missouri (Kansas City and Columbia campuses), the University of Chicago, the University of Washington (Seattle), the University of Illinois (Champaign-Urbana and Chicago campuses) and the University of South Dakota (Vermillion), the Pierpont Morgan Library (New York), the library of the Institute for Psychoanalysis (Chicago) and the library of the Spertus College of Judaica (Chicago). In Europe my work took me to the British Library, the library of the University of London, and the Wiener Library (London), the archive of the Amsterdam Concertgebouw, the Gemeentemuseum (Den Haag), the Österreichische Nationalbibliothek (Vienna), the Universitätsbibliothek in Heidelberg, the Niedersächsische Staats- und Universitätsbibliothek (Göttingen) and the Bayerische Staatsbibliothek (Munich). I am grateful to the staffs and librarians of these libraries.

Above all, this book owes much of its substance to many hours of work in the Newberry Library (Chicago) and the libraries of Northwestern University, my alma mater (Chicago and Evanston). My work in the latter system really encompassed three libraries: the University Library, the library of the Medical School (where I was saved from being entirely lost by several helpful physicians who probably wondered why I was there at all) and, especially, the Music Library, where Don Roberts' staff watched me stagger around with heavy piles of books which they patiently put away time after time when I had finished with them. I also owe Don Roberts himself a special vote of thanks for producing an uncatalogued Italian book; without his cooperation on that occasion I would have been obliged to return to Munich for it.

For many acts of friendship and professional assistance I am indebted to Alexander Main, Hans Tischler, William Porter and Theodore Karp, whom I am proud to call my friends. To Sue Taylor, Jerry Bruck, Michael Steinberg, John Composono, Frans Bouwman, Robert Becqué and my cousin Barbara Sopkin I owe my gratitude for their patience in listening while I worked out my ideas; whenever I paused for breath they would inject ideas of their own. My fellow author in this series, Theodore Albrecht, and his wife Carol Padgham Albrecht, have given me all of the above and more.

James Zychowicz has provided a constructive example of the professional relations which materially contribute to the mechanics of writing such a book as this. Dr. Stuart Feder, by providing me with copies of his three remarkable articles --which I had not been able to locate elsewhere--proved that practitioners of the medical and musical professions have much to gain from cooperation with each other. And Professor Marius Flothuis has, by admitting me to conversation with him on several occasions, which were all too rare, shown me the perspective of many years in which the study of Mahler and his music has grown from minimal beginnings to its present richness. I am grateful to him personally and professionally.

I would here like to express my respect for a Mahler specialist whom I have not been fortunate enough to meet: Inna Barsova (Moscow), whose untiring work in compiling a list of Russian references on Mahler (not to mention her own contributions to those references) was a touchstone of my own documentation of the wide-ranging Russian contributions to the Mahler literature. The work I did to complement that of Dr. Barsova, while anticipated to some degree by Bruno and Eleonore Vondenhoff, resulted in a realization that our colleagues in the Soviet Union have written more about Mahler than is generally acknowledged by Western scholars. I hope that this book will reach Dr. Barsova and thus inform her that her work and that of her colleagues is not unknown outside the Soviet Union.

Donald Mitchell materially stimulated my ambition to write this book, which was certainly as important as the intellectual labor I have devoted to the project. That is indeed a unique debt.

To Zoltan Roman, who has come to be like an older brother, I owe something that cannot be classified: the knowledge that I could be assured of his objective, thoughtful opinion about any problem which usually revealed perspectives about my own work that I had not recognized at all. To Jeffrey Wasson I gladly acknowledge a debt of faith in my professional growth which goes back to our days in graduate school. To Knud Martner I am equally indebted, although in a different way: our professional cooperation has resulted in my discovery of personal qualities in myself which I recognize through his eyes rather than my own. As for my wise and patient mentor, Kenneth Isaacs, I think that no words are necessary.

Special thanks to my editors, Marie Ellen Larcada, Guy Marco and Barry Brook, who bore with me during the four years it took to write this book and never pushed me to finish prematurely.

Finally, to my family--my parents, my brothers and sisters and their families, and my grandmother--I give my love, which has never been in doubt but was a constant factor from start to finish.

Susan M. Filler

GUSTAV AND ALMA MAHLER

A Brief Chronology

Note: Arabic numerals refer to works listed in the following sections "Mahler's Works" and "Surviving Works of Alma Mahler-Werfel" (see "Works" Column).

I

Gustav Mahler

Chronology

DATE	LIFE	WORKS
1860	Mahler born Kalište, Bohemia, July 7 Mahler moves with parents to Jihlava, December	
1861-70	Jihlava	#21, #25
1870	First public piano recital, Jihlava, October 13	
1871	Goes to gymnasium, Prague	
1871-75	Returns to Jihlava	#22, #32
1874	Brother Ernst dies, April 13	
1875-78	Student at Vienna Conservatory	#20, #23, #24, #26, #27, #29, #30, #31, #39, #46
1878-79	Attends lectures at University of Vienna	#40
1879	Piano tutor Vienna and Hungary	#33
1880	Summer appointment as opera conductor at Bad Hall	#11, #12, #28, #34, #41
1881	Appointment as opera conductor at Laibach (Ljubljana)	
1882	Returns to Vienna	
1883	Appointment as opera conductor at Olomouč, January-March	#36
1883-85	Appointment as second conductor at Kassel Court Theater	#1, #13, #37, #38
1885-86	Appointment as second conductor, Prague Landestheater	
1886-88	Appointment as second conductor, Leipzig Opera	#35, #53
1888-91	Appointment as conductor, Royal Hungarian Opera, Budapest	#2
1889	Father dies February 18 Mother dies October 11	
1891-97	Appointment as conductor, Hamburg Opera	#3, 14

DATE	LIFE	WORKS
1894	Conductor of Hamburg concerts	#49?, #50
1895	Brother Otto commits suicide, February 6	#43
1897	Converts to Catholicism, February 23 Appointment as Kapellmeister, Hofoper, Vienna, April Appointment as Director, Hofoper, Vienna, September 8	
1898	Appointment as conductor, Vienna Philharmonic Orchestra, September	#44
1899-1900	Vienna	#4, #18, #19, #44, #45, #52
1901	Meets Alma Schindler, November	#5, #15, #16, #47
1902	Marries Alma Schindler, March 9 Daughter Maria Anna born, November 3	#5, #15, #16, #43
1904	Daughter Anna Justina born, June 15	#6, #16, #56
1905	Vienna	#7
1906	Vienna	#8, #48
1907	Daughter Maria Anna dies, July 5 Diagnosis of Mahler's cardiac problem, summer Resigns from Hofoper effective December	#17
1908-09	Appointment as conductor, Metropolitan Opera, New York	#9, #17
1909-11	Appointment as conductor, New York Philharmonic Orchestra	#42
1910	Crisis with Alma and consultation with Sigmund Freud, summer	#10, #51
1911	Dies May 11, Vienna	#51

II

Alma Mahler

Chronology   xxvii

DATE	LIFE	WORKS
1879	Alma Schindler born, August 31, Vienna	
1892	Father dies, summer	
1890s	Studies counterpoint with Josef Labor	
1897	Mother marries Carl Moll	
	Alma begins study of composition with Alexander von Zemlinsky, autumn	[#1, #2], #3 (i, iv)
1901	Meets Mahler, November	
	Ceases study with Zemlinsky late in year	
1902	Marries Mahler, March 9	
	Daughter Maria Anna born, November 3	
1904	Daughter Anna Justina born, June 15	
1907	Daughter Maria Anna dies, July 5	
1910	Meets Walter Gropius, summer	
	Resulting marital crisis with Mahler, late summer	
1911	Mahler dies, May 18	#3 (ii, iii)
1912-15	Lives with Oskar Kokoschka	
1915	Marries Walter Gropius, August 18	[#4]
1916	Daughter Manon Gropius born, October 5	
1917	Meets Franz Werfel, autumn	
1918	Son Martin Werfel born, August 1	
1919	Son Martin dies, spring	
1919-29	Leaves Gropius and lives with Werfel	
	Divorced from Gropius in interim	
1929	Marries Werfel, July 6	
1935	Daughter Manon dies, April 22	

DATE	LIFE	WORKS
1938	Leaves Austria, March 13	
	Settles in France with Werfel later in year	
1940	Publishes *Gustav Mahler, Erinnerungen und Briefe* in Amsterdam	
	Leaves France via Spain and Portugal, sails with Werfel to United States	
	Arrives New York October 13	
	Settles with Werfel in Beverly Hills, California, December 30	
1945	Franz Werfel dies, August 26	
1952	Alma moves to New York	
1958	Publishes *And the Bridge is Love* in New York	
1960	Publishes *Mein Leben* in Frankfurt	
1964	Dies New York, December 11	
1988	Anna Mahler dies, London, June 2/3	

MAHLER'S WORKS

I

Mature works

1. *Symphony no. 1*

    Movements: Langsam. Schleppend/Im Anfang sehr gemächlich (D major/d minor)
    Andante allegretto "Blumine" (C major)
    Kräftig bewegt, doch nicht zu schnell/Recht gemächlich [scherzo & trio] (A major)
    Feierlich, und gemessen, ohne zu schleppen (d minor)
    Stürmisch bewegt/Sehr gesangsvoll/Langsam (f minor/D major)
    Date of composition: 1884-88
    Publication data: Wien: Josef Weinberger, 1898/99
    Wien: Universal Edition, 1906
    Bryn Mawr, Pennsylvania: Theodore Presser; London: Faber Music Ltd., 1967 ("Blumine" only)
    Premiere: Budapest, November 20, 1889
    Remarks: the first and second versions published in 1898/99 and 1906 included all movements except the second, which was published as "Blumine" in 1967.

2. *Symphony no. 2*

    Movements: Allegro maestoso (c minor)
    Andante moderato (A^b major)
    In ruhig fliessender Bewegung (c minor)
    Urlicht. Sehr feierlich, aber schlicht [contralto solo] (D^b major)
    Im Tempo des Scherzos/Kräftig/Langsam. Misterioso [soprano & contralto solos & mixed chorus] (c minor/E^b major)
    Date of composition: 1888-94
    Publication data: Leipzig: Friedrich Hofmeister, 1897
    Wien: Josef Weinberger, 1897
    Wien: Universal Edition, 1906
    Premiere: Berlin, March 4, 1894 (mvts. 1, 2 & 3 only)
    Berlin, December 13, 1895 (complete)
    Remarks: Weinberger took over the first version shortly after first publication by Hofmeister,

but apart from the name of the publisher there are no changes between the two scores.

3. *Symphony no. 3*

Movements: *Kräftig. Entschieden* (d minor/F major)
Tempo di Menuetto. Sehr mässig (A major)
Comodo. Scherzando. Ohne Hast (c minor)
Sehr langsam. Misterioso. Durchaus ppp [contralto solo] (D major)
Lustig im Tempo und keck im Ausdruck [contralto solo, women's chorus & children's chorus] (F major)
Langsam. Ruhevoll. Empfunden (D major)
Date of composition: 1895-96
Publication data: Wien: Josef Weinberger, 1902
Wien: Universal Edition, 1910
Premiere: Berlin, November 9, 1896 (mvt. 2 only)
Hamburg, December 7, 1896 (mvt. 2 only)
Budapest, March 31, 1897 (mvt. 2 only)
Berlin, March 9, 1897 (mvts. 2, 3 & 6 only)
Krefeld, June 9, 1902 (complete)
Remarks: the song "*Das himmlische Leben,*" which had been composed in 1892, was planned as the last movement of this symphony in 1895, and was later moved to the position of second movement in 1896; however, it was removed from the work in July/August 1896.

4. *Symphony no. 4*

Movements: *Bedächtig. Nicht eilen* (G major)
In gemächlicher Bewegung. Ohne Hast (c minor)
Ruhevoll (G major)
Sehr behaglich [soprano solo] (G major/E major)
Date of composition: 1899-1900 (first three movements)
1892 (final movement)
Publication data: Wien: Ludwig Doblinger, 1902
Wien: Universal Edition, 1906
Premiere: München, November 25, 1901
Remarks: the last movement of this work had been composed as the song "*Das himmlische Leben*" in 1892 and, after being incorporated into the Third Symphony (see preceding entry), was removed from that work and finally settled

Mahler's Works (I): Mature Works   xxxi

> in its position of last movement in the Fourth Symphony.

5. *Symphony no. 5*

   Movements: *Trauermarsch. In gemessenem Schritt.*
   Streng. Wie ein Kondukt (c# minor)
   Sturmisch bewegt, mit grösster Vehemenz (a minor)
   Scherzo. Kräftig, nicht zu schnell (D major)
   Adagietto. Sehr langsam (F major)
   Rondo-Finale. Allegro (D major)
   Date of composition: 1901-02
   Publication data: Leipzig: C.F. Peters, 1904
   Premiere: Köln, October 18, 1904
   Remarks: all versions of this symphony were published by Peters, which reissued the symphony after Mahler revised it on more than one occasion.

6. *Symphony no. 6*

   Movements: *Allegro energico, ma non troppo* (a minor)
   Scherzo. Wuchtig (a minor/F major)
   Andante moderato (E^b major)
   Finale. Allegro moderato (a minor)
   Date of composition: 1903-04
   Publication data: Leipzig: C.F. Kahnt, 1906
   Premiere: Essen, May 27, 1906
   Remarks: three versions were issued by Kahnt in 1906, necessitated in the first instance by Mahler's decision to reverse the order of the inner movements (placing the andante before the scherzo), in the second instance by revisions in the orchestration. The final version of 1906 remained with the scherzo following the andante, but in the Critical Edition of the work published in 1963 the original order has been restored, on the basis of documentary proof cited by the editor to show that Mahler decided to return the movements to their original order after the third version of 1906.

7. *Symphony no. 7*

   Movements: *Langsam. Allegro* (e minor)
   Nachtmusik. Allegro moderato (c minor)

Scherzo. (Schattenhaft. Fliessend, aber
nicht schnell) (d minor)
Nachtmusik. Andante amoroso (F major)
Rondo-Finale. Allegro ordinario (C major)
Date of composition: 1904-05
Publication data: Berlin: Bote und Bock, 1909
Premiere: Prague, September 19, 1908
Remarks: Mahler made many alterations in the scoring
of this work after initial publication. Some
were noted in a list of "Errata" published
by Bote & Bock after Mahler's death; many
others were incorporated in the Critical
Edition in 1959.

8. *Symphony no. 8*

Movements: Teil 1. Hymnus: "Veni, creator spiritus"
(E^b major)
Teil 2. Schluss-szene aus Goethes "Faust"
(e^b minor/E^b major)
Date of composition: 1906
Publication data: Wien: Universal Edition, 1910-11
Premiere: München, September 12, 1910
Remarks: in addition to orchestra, this work includes
parts for eight vocal soloists (3 sopranos,
2 contraltos, tenor, baritone and bass), two
mixed choruses and children's chorus.

9. *Symphony no. 9*

Movements: Andante comodo (D major)
Im Tempo eines gemächlichen Ländlers. Etwas
täppisch und sehr derb (C major)
Rondo. Burleske. Allegro assai. Sehr
trotzig (a minor)
Adagio. Sehr langsam (D^b major)
Date of composition: 1909
Publication data: Wien: Universal Edition, 1912
Premiere: Wien, June 26, 1912
Remarks: the premiere took place after Mahler's death
and was conducted by Bruno Walter.

10. *Symphony no. 10*

Movements: Adagio (F# major)
Scherzo. Schnelle Viertel (f# minor/F#
major)

                Purgatorio. *Allegretto moderato* (b^b minor/B^b major)
                Scherzo. *Allegro pesante. Nicht zu schnell* (e minor/d minor)
                Finale. *Langsam, schwer* (d minor/F# major)
Date of composition: 1910
Publication data: Wien: Paul Zsolnay, 1924
                New York: Associated Music Publishers, 1951 (first & third movements only)
                Wien: Universal Edition, 1964, 1969 (first movement only)
                München: Walter Ricke, 1967
                London: Faber Music Ltd.; New York: Associated Music Publishers, 1976
Premiere: Wien, October 12, 1924 (first & third movements only)
           London, August 13, 1964 (first performing version by Deryck Cooke)
           London, October 15, 1972 (final performing version by Deryck Cooke)
           Chicago, April 8, 1983 (performing version by Clinton Carpenter)
           Utrecht, November 14, 1986 (first three movements of performing version by Remo Mazzetti)
Remarks: as of this writing, a full premiere of the performing version of Mazzetti has not taken place. Information on the performing version of Joseph Wheeler is difficult to obtain. The Vienna premiere of the first and third movements, which were prepared by Ernst Krenek, was conducted by Franz Schalk. The premieres of the two versions by Deryck Cooke were conducted by Berthold Goldschmidt (1964) and Wyn Morris (1972). The world premiere of the version by Clinton Carpenter was made by the Civic Orchestra of Chicago conducted by Gordon Peters. The partial performance of the version by Remo Mazzetti was conducted by Gaetano Delogu.

11.   *Das klagende Lied*

    Teil 1. Waldmärchen. *Langsam und träumerlich*
    Teil 2. Der Spielmann. *Sehr gehalten*
    Teil 3. Hochzeitsstück. *Heftig bewegt*

Date of composition: 1880-98
Publication data: Wien: Josef Weinberger, 1902 (parts
   2 & 3 only)
   Wien: Universal Edition, before
   September 1911 (parts 2 & 3 only)
   Melville, New York & New York City:
   Belwin-Mills, 1973 (part 1 only)
Premiere: Wien, February 17, 1901 (parts 2 & 3 only)
   Brno, November 28, 1934 (part 1 only)
   Wien, April 8, 1935 (complete)
Remarks: publications by Weinberger and Universal
   covered parts 2 and 3 only, without titles
   cited above. Part 1, "Waldmärchen," was
   published for the first time in the Bel-
   win-Mills score of 1973. As of this writing
   there is no published score of the full three-
   part work. Text by Mahler adapted from
   Ludwig Bechstein and the Grimm brothers.

12. *Lieder und Gesänge*

Heft 1. *Frühlingsmorgen* (Richard Leander)
   Erinnerung (Richard Leander)
   Hans und Grete (Volkslied)
   Serenade aus "Don Juan" (Tirso de Molina)
   Phantasie aus "Don Juan" (Tirso de Molina)
Heft 2. *Um schlimme Kinder artig zu machen*
   Ich ging mit Lust durch einem grünen Wald
   Aus! Aus!
   Starke Einbildungskraft
Heft 3. *Zu Strassburg auf der Schanz'*
   Ablösung im Sommer
   Scheiden und Meiden
   Nicht wiedersehen!
   Selbstgefühl
Date of composition: 1880-92
Publication data: Mainz: B. Schotts Söhne, 1892
Premiere: Prague, April 18, 1886 (I/i & iii)
   Hamburg, April 29, 1892 (II/iii, III/iv)
   Wien, February 15, 1900 (III/v)
   Berlin, December 14, 1907 (II/i, III/ii)
Remarks: dates of premieres of the remaining five
   songs remain uncertain. Mahler wrote all
   fourteen for voice and piano only, although
   a partial draft of "Zu Strassburg auf der
   Schanz'" for orchestra survives in manuscript

and is discussed by la Grange. Texts of all songs in Books 2 and 3 are from *Des Knaben Wunderhorn*.

13. *Lieder eines fahrenden Gesellen*

    Wenn mein Schatz Hochzeit macht
    Ging heut' Morgen über's Feld
    Ich hab' ein glühend Messer
    Die zwei blauen Augen

    Date of composition: 1884
    Publication data: Wien: Josef Weinberger, 1897
    Premiere: Berlin, March 16, 1896
    Remarks: texts of all four songs were by Mahler himself, although the first text is obviously based on an untitled poem from *Des Knaben Wunderhorn*, a connection which has been pointed out by several commentators including la Grange. Mahler wrote alternative versions for voice and piano and voice and orchestra, both published by Weinberger in 1897.

14. *Des Knaben Wunderhorn*

    Der Schildwache Nachtlied
    Verlor'ne Müh'
    Trost im Unglück
    Wer hat dies Liedlein erdacht?
    Das irdische Leben
    Des Antonius von Padua Fischpredigt
    Rheinlegendchen
    Lied des Verfolgten im Turm
    Wo die schönen Trompeten blasen
    Lob des hohen Verstandes

    Der Tamboursg'sell
    Revelge

    Date of composition: 1892-95 (#1-10), 1899-1901 (#11-12)
    Publication data: Wien: Josef Weinberger, c. 1900/1901 (#1-10)
    Wien: Universal Edition, by September 1911 (#1-10)
    Leipzig: C.F. Kahnt, 1905 (#11-12)
    Premiere: Berlin, December 12, 1892 (i, ii)

xxxvi   Mahler Bibliography

              Hamburg, October 27, 1893 (iii, iv, vii)
              Wien, January 14, 1900 (v, ix)
              Wien, January 29, 1905 (vi, viii, xi, xii)
              Wien, February 3, 1905 (x)
     Remarks: the first ten songs were published by Wein-
              berger together with *Urlicht* (see entry on
              Symphony no. 2) and *Es sungen drei Engel*
              (see entry on *Symphony no. 3*), the latter ar-
              ranged for solo voice from the original choral
              version. The last two songs were published
              with the five *Rückert Lieder* by C. F. Kahnt
              as *Sieben Lieder* (see next entry). There is
              no evidence that Mahler considered these
              songs a complete cycle, either in the piano-
              vocal version or the orchestral version, but
              they are now generally considered as a group
              for purposes of performance.

15. *Rückert Lieder*

     Ich atmet' einen Linden Duft
     Liebst du um Schönheit
     Blicke mir nicht in die Lieder!
     Ich bin der Welt abhanden gekommen
     Um Mitternacht

     Date of composition: 1901-02
     Publication data: Leipzig: C.F. Kahnt, 1905
     Premiere: Wien, January 29, 1905 (i, iii-v)
     Remarks: the date of the premiere of *Liebst du um
              Schönheit* is unknown beyond the composer's
              private presentation of that song to his
              wife in the summer of 1903 in Maiernigg. Re-
              cent scholarship has shown that Mahler or-
              chestrated only four of these songs; *Liebst
              du um Schönheit* was evidently orchestrated
              by Max Puttmann. This song stands aside
              from the others by virtue of the ambiguity
              surrounding performances in Mahler's life-
              time and the facts of orchestration. The
              five songs were published with *Revelge* and
              Der Tamboursg'sell (see preceding entry) as
              Sieben Lieder. All above conditions of pub-
              lication, orchestration and performance
              strongly reinforce the impression that the
              composer did not consider these songs to be
              a cycle.

16. **Kindertotenlieder**

> Nun will die Sonn' so hell aufgeh'n
> Nun seh' ich wohl, warum so dunkle Flammen
> Wenn dein Mütterlein
> Oft denk' ich, sie sind nur ausgegangen
> In diesem Wetter
>
> Date of composition: 1901-04
> Publication data: Leipzig: C. F. Kahnt, 1905
> Premiere: Wien, January 29, 1905
> Remarks: Mahler wrote these songs in piano-vocal and piano-orchestral versions. Unlike the other five Rückert songs, they are definitely meant to be a cycle. Texts from Rückert's collection of hundreds of poems of the same name.

17. **Das Lied von der Erde**

> Das Trinklied vom Jammer der Erde (Li Tai Po)
> Der Einsame im Herbst (Chang Tzi)
> Von der Jugend (Li Tai Po)
> Von der Schönheit (Li Tai Po)
> Der Trunkene im Frühling (Li Tai Po)
> Der Abschied (Mong Kao Jen/Wang Wei)
>
> Date of composition: 1907-08
> Publication data: Wien: Universal Edition, 1911
> Premiere: München, November 20, 1911
> Remarks: the premiere was conducted by Bruno Walter, Mahler having died six months earlier. Mahler regarded this work as a symphony, although he did not number it in the succession of the other symphonies. The original Chinese texts (one for each of the first five movements, two for the last movement) had been chosen from *Die chinesische Flöte* of Hans Bethge, who had taken many liberties with his translation; Mahler made yet further changes and actually added text at the end of the final movement.

18. **Scherzo in c minor**

> Date of composition: c. 1900
> Publication data: none (unpublished)

xxxviii   Mahler Bibliography

Premiere: none
Remarks: Susan M. Filler has made a performing version
           of this draft, which was left by Mahler in
           short score with several preliminary sketches.
           As of this writing her version remains un-
           published and unperformed although in orchest-
           ral version. Filler posited the theory that
           this work was drafted at about the time that
           Mahler was composing the *Presto in F major*
           (see following entry) and that Mahler in-
           tended both movements to be components of a
           symphony envisaged about the time of the
           Fourth or Fifth Symphonies, which did not
           reach full fruition. The manuscript is in
           the Wiener Stadtbibliothek after having been
           sold to the city of Vienna by Hans Molden-
           hauer.

19.   *Presto in F major*

      Date of composition: c. 1900
      Publication data: none (unpublished)
      Premiere: none
      Remarks: see remarks in previous entry, Filler having
                 connected this work with the *Scherzo in c
                 minor* chronologically. Mahler drafted this
                 manuscript in the key of G major but wrote a
                 verbal note to indicate that he intended to
                 transpose it to F major. The manuscript is
                 in the Pierpont Morgan Library, New York.
                 Filler has made a performing version for
                 orchestra which, like her performing version
                 of the *Scherzo in c minor*, remains unpub-
                 lished and unperformed as of this writing.

                                II

                            Early works

20.   *Piano Quartet in a minor*

      Nicht zu schnell (a minor)
      Scherzo (g minor)

      Date of composition: 1876
      Publication data: Hamburg: Hans Sikorski, 1973

Premiere: Iglau, September 12, 1876 (*Nicht zu schnell* only)
Remarks: the scherzo remained unfinished; the facsimile and transcription of the manuscript of this movement published by Sikorski with the first movement shows that the scherzo would have been in g minor.

21. *Polka with Introductory Funeral March*

    Date of composition: c. 1867
    Publication data: none (lost)
    Premiere: none
    Remarks: cited by Natalie Bauer-Lechner.

22. *Pieces for Piano*

    Date of composition: before 1875
    Publication data: none (lost, possibly not written down)
    Premiere: Baden, 1875?
    Remarks: cited by la Grange "jouées par Mahler à Julius Epstein à Baden"; la Grange also questions if these pieces were ever written down.

23. *Suite for Piano*

    Date of composition: 1875-78?
    Publication data: none (lost)
    Premiere: 1878?
    Remarks: cited by Natalie Bauer-Lechner as winner of a prize at the Conservatory in Vienna.

24. *Nocturne for [Violon]cello [and piano]*

    Date of composition: 1876-78?
    Publication data: none (lost)
    Premiere: unknown
    Remarks: cited by Natalie Bauer-Lechner.

25. *"Die Türken haben schöne Tochter"* [song]

    Date of composition: c. 1867
    Date of publication: none (lost)
    Premiere: unknown
    Remarks: text by Gotthold Ephraim Lessing. Cited by Natalie Bauer-Lechner.

26. *Song [title unknown]*

   Date of composition: unknown (1875-78?)
   Publication data: none (lost)
   Premiere: unknown
   Remarks: cited by Ludwig Karpath, who mentions that this song was written for a competition at the Conservatory in Vienna.

27. *Zwei Lieder*

   Es fiel ein Reif in der Frühlingsnacht
   Im wunderschönen Monat Mai

   Date of composition: 1875-80?
   Date of publication: none (uncompleted, in manuscript)
   Premiere: none
   Remarks: cited by Natalie Bauer-Lechner. Texts by Heinrich Heine.

28. *String Quartet (?)*

   Date of composition: c. 1880
   Publication data: none
   Premiere: unknown
   Remarks: cited by Alma Mahler-Werfel; however, la Grange expresses some doubt of the existence of this work.

29. *Piano Quartet (no. 2?) or Quintet*

   Date of composition: 1878
   Publication data: none (lost)
   Premiere: Wien, 1878 ("chez Theodor Billroth," according to la Grange)
   Remarks: cited by Natalie Bauer-Lechner. This manuscript was apparently sent to Russia for a competition and was lost.

30. *Piano Quintet*

   Date of composition: 1876
   Publication data: none (lost)
   Premiere: Iglau, September 12, 1876
   Remarks: cited by Natalie Bauer-Lechner, who also noted that the first movement received a prize at the Conservatory in Vienna before the first public performance in Iglau.

31. *Piano Quintet*

   Date of composition: 1878
   Publication data: none (lost)
   Premiere: Wien (Conservatory), July 11, 1878 (scherzo
             movement only)
   Remarks: cited by Natalie Bauer-Lechner. Probably unfinished.

32. *Herzog Ernst von Schwaben [opera]*

   Date of composition: before 1875
   Publication data: none (lost)
   Premiere: none
   Remarks: probably unfinished. Cited by Mahler in his
            letters and by Guido Adler. Text by Josef
            Steiner after Uhland.

33. *Die Argonauten [opera]*

   Date of composition: 1879-80
   Publication data: none (lost)
   Premiere: none
   Remarks: unfinished. Cited by Natalie Bauer-Lechner,
            Guido Adler and Paul Stefan-Gruenfeldt. Text
            by Mahler or Josef Steiner after Grillparzer.

34. *Rübezahl [opera]*

   Date of composition: 1880-90
   Publication data: none
   Premiere: none
   Remarks: libretto by Mahler still in existence today,
            no music known (lost or never composed).
            Cited by Alma Mahler-Werfel, Guido Adler,
            Paul Stefan-Gruenfeldt, Natalie Bauer-Lechner
            and Richard Specht, and in Mahler's letters.

35. *Opera [title unknown]*

   Date of composition: 1887-88
   Publication data: none (lost)
   Premiere: none
   Remarks: cited by Natalie Bauer-Lechner as a collaborative project of Mahler and Carl von Weber.
            Could she have been in error with this for
            Mahler's work on *Die drei Pintos* (see no. 53
            below)?

36. Prelude with Chorus

   Date of composition: 1883?
   Publication data: none
   Premiere: Kassel, June 23, 1884
   Remarks: cited by la Grange. For the jubilee of the actor Karl Häser.

37. Der Trompeter von Säkkingen [incidental music]

   Date of composition: 1884?
   Publication data: none
   Premiere: Kassel, June 23, 1884
   Remarks: cited by la Grange ("musique d'accompagnement pour des 'tableaux vivants' illustrant le poème de Joseph Vikor von Scheffel"). Surviving music includes:

   Ein Ständchen am Rhein
   Die erste Begegnung
   Das Maifest am Bergsee
   Trompeten-Unterricht in der Geissblattlaube
   Der Überfall im Schlossgarten
   Liebesglück
   Wiedersehen in Rom

   Diether and Mitchell have cited connections between this music and the *Blumine* andante (see entry on *Symphony no. 1* above).

38. Das Volkslied [incidental music]

   Date of composition: 1885?
   Publication data: none
   Premiere: Kassel, April 20, 1885
   Remarks: cited by la Grange ("poème avec lieder, choeurs et tableaux vivants, de Salomon Hermann Mosenthal"). Surviving music in eleven sections cited in full by la Grange, including notable folk texts like *Ännchen von Tharau*, *Gaudeamus igitur* and *Die Loreley*.

39. Two Symphonies

   Date of composition: 1876-78
   Publication data: none (lost)
   Premiere: unknown

Mahler's Works (II): Early Works									xliii

>	Remarks: the first of these two works was, according to Natalie Bauer-Lechner, presented for a competition at the Conservatory in Vienna. The second work is said by Bauer-Lechner to have been in three movements and to have been in a minor. Were these the works cited by Marion von Weber many years later in a conversation in Dresden with Mengelberg?

40. *Nordic Symphony [or Suite]*

    Date of composition: 1878-82
    Publication data: none (lost)
    Premiere: none
    Remarks: cited by Guido Adler and Paul Stefan-Gruenfeldt, and in Mahler's letters.

41. *3 Lieder*

    Im Lenz
    Winterlied
    Maitanz im Grünen

    Date of composition: February 19 and 27 and March 5, 1880 respectively
    Publication data: none (in manuscript)
    Premiere: Radio Brno, September 30, 1934
    Remarks: for tenor and piano. Premiered by Zdenek Kittel (tenor) and Alfred Rosé (piano). Manuscript in the collection of Alfred Rosé. The last song is undoubtedly an early version of *Hans und Grethe* (see *Lieder und Gesänge*, Heft 1, above). The texts are Mahler's own.

III

Editions, Transcriptions and Completions of Works by Other Composers, and Spurious Works

42. Bach, Johann Sebastian. *Suite aus seinen Orchesterwerken*

    Ouverture (from *Suite no. 2*)
    Rondeau (from *Suite no. 2*)
    Badinerie (from *Suite no. 2*)

Air (from *Suite no. 3*)
Gavottes I and II (from *Suite no. 4*)

Publication data: New York: G. Schirmer, 1911
Premiere: New York, November 25, 1909
Remarks: Mahler conducted this suite at its premiere from altered piano (continuo).

43. Beethoven, Ludwig van. *Symphonies*

Symphony no. 5
Symphony no. 9

Publication data: none (published scores of works with Mahler's handwritten retouches)
Premiere: Hamburg, March 11, 1895 (*Symphony no. 9*)
Wien, April 15, 1902 ("*Ihr stürtzt nieder, Millionen*" from *Symphony no. 9*)
Remarks: these two works are rescorings of previously completed works for Mahler's own use, and they were never published with his annotations and alterations. The originals with his handwritten markings are in the library of the University of Southampton.

44. Beethoven, Ludwig van. *Overtures*

Coriolan
Egmont
Die Weihe des Hauses
Leonore no. 2

Publication data: none
Premiere: Wien, November 6, 1898 (*Coriolan*)
[Wien, December 3, 1899] (*Die Weihe des Hauses*)
Remarks: all of these four overtures were conducted by Mahler on many occasions during his career, but only the first has been extensively discussed in the literature and is therefore possible to date beyond doubt in terms of his alterations, which were never published. The tentative date of the premiere of this version of *Die Weihe des Hauses* is based on data cited by Knud Martner, as Mahler conducted that work in Vienna during the season 1899-1900 and repeated it only in New York.

45. Beethoven, Ludwig van. *Streichquartett f-moll, op. 95*

    Publication data: none
    Premiere: Wien, January 15, 1899
    Remarks: string quartet rescored by Mahler for string orchestra.

46. Bruckner, Anton. *Symphonie nr. 3*

    Publication data: Wien: Theodor Rättig, 1878
    Premiere: none
    Remarks: arrangement for piano four hands in collaboration with Rudolf Krzyzanowski. This was Mahler's first publication.

47. Bruckner, Anton. *Symphonie nr. 5*

    Publication data: none
    Premiere: Wien, February 24, 1901
    Remarks: original substance altered by rescorings and cuts. For Mahler's own use, as in the case of the Beethoven symphonies (see no. 43).

48. Mozart, Wolfgang Amadeus. *Le Nozze de Figaro*

    Publication data: Leipzig: C.F. Peters, 1907
    Premiere: Wien, March 30, 1906
    Remarks: the contribution by Mahler was a recitative which he wrote into the "Judgement Scene" in collaboration with Max Kalbeck.

49. Schubert, Franz. *Symphonie nr. 9*

    Publication data: none
    Premiere: unknown
    Remarks: original substance altered by rescorings as in the case of the works of Beethoven and Bruckner noted above. For Mahler's own use.

50. Schubert, Franz. *Der Tod und das Mädchen [quartet]*

    Publication data: London: Josef Weinberger, 1984
    Premiere: Hamburg, November 19, 1894 (*andante* only)
    New York, May 6, 1984 (complete)
    Remarks: string quartet rescored by Mahler for string orchestra.

51. Schumann, Robert. *Symphonies*

   Symphony no. 1
   Symphony no. 2
   Symphony no. 3
   Symphony no. 4

   Publication data: none
   Premiere: [Wien, January 15, 1899] *(Symphony no. 1)*
   [New York, November 22, 1910] *(Symphony no. 2)*
   [New York, January 31, 1911] *(Symphony no. 3)*
   [Wien, January 14, 1900] *(Symphony no. 4)*
   Remarks: these rescorings of works by Schumann were never published but exist in scores with Mahler's handwritten alterations at the University of Southampton. The dates of premiere above are based upon Knud Martner's data and the present author's own deductions about the circumstances of Mahler's conducting career. The *Symphony no. 3* with his retouches was recorded by Carlo Maria Giulini in the 1960s.

52. Schumann, Robert. *Manfred [overture]*

   Publication data: none
   Premiere: [Wien, November 11, 1900]
   Remarks: rescoring of Schumann as in the case of the symphonies (see no. 51). Date of premiere presumptively based upon Knud Martner's data and the present author's deductions surrounding Mahler's conducting career.

53. Weber, Carl Maria von. *Die drei Pintos [opera]*

   Date of composition: 1888 (completed by Mahler)
   Publication data: Leipzig: C.F. Kahnt, 1888
   Premiere: Leipzig, January 20, 1888
   Remarks: the most well-known work Mahler did on the score of another composer, this project entailed the editing of the eight numbers completed by Weber, the selection and rescoring of other works of Weber as numbers in the opera, and the composition of two numbers based upon themes by Weber from the materi-

als he himself had left behind. Mahler's librettist/collaborator in this enterprise was the composer's grandson, Captain Carl von Weber.

54. Weber, Carl Maria von. *Euryanthe [opera]*

   Publication data: Wien: Universal Edition, n.d. (orchestral score)
   Leipzig: C.F. Peters, 1904 (piano--vocal score)
   Premiere: Wien, January 19, 1904
   Remarks: Mahler modified both text and music in his production of this work, cutting some parts, restoring others which Weber himself had deleted, according to his letters to Max Kalbeck.

55. Weber, Carl Maria von. *Oberon [opera]*

   Publication data: Wien: Universal Edition, 1914
   Premiere: Köln, [January] 1913
   Remarks: new libretto arranged from the original by Mahler and Gustav Brecher, dating from c. 1906. Premiered and published after Mahler's death. The Köln premiere was conducted by Brecher.

Spurious Work

56. *Sinfonisches Präludium für Orchester*

   Publication data: Hamburg: Sikorski, 1981
   Premiere: Berlin, March 19, 1981
   Remarks: theorized by Albrecht Gürsching (who edited the published score), Paul Banks and Donald Mitchell to be an early work of Mahler dating from about 1876, but later proved by Rudolf Stephan not to be by Mahler. Other theories suggest Bruckner or Rudolf Krzyzanowski as possible composers.

SURVIVING WORKS OF ALMA MAHLER-WERFEL

1. *Aus dem Cyclus:* "Mütter" *von Rainer Maria Rilke*

   [Leise weht ein erstes Blühn von den Lindenbäumen]
   [Kennst du meine Nächte?]

   Date of composition: c. 1899-1901
   Publication data: none (in manuscript)
   Premiere: New York, June 10, 1981
   Remarks: these two songs for voice and piano have not been published but survive in manuscript. The New York performance of 1981 was the first on historical record traced by the present author, who edited the two songs for that performance. The text of the first song is from *Advent*, a cycle of poems published by Rilke in 1898. The text of the second song has not been traced in the published works of Rilke and its attribution to him is therefore speculative. The present author has dated the two songs partially from the publication date of the first poem as noted above, partially from the signature of the composer on the title page as "Alma M. Schindler," her maiden name.

2. *Fünf Lieder*

   Die stille Stadt (Richard Dehmel)
   In meines Vaters Garten (Otto Erich Hartleben)
   Laue Sommernacht (Otto Julius Bierbaum)
   Bei dir ist es traut (Rainer Maria Rilke)
   Ich wandle unter Blumen (Heinrich Heine)

   Date of composition: unknown (c. 1900/1910?)
   Publication data: Wien: Universal Edition, 1910
   Premiere: unknown
   Remarks: these five songs were apparently written before Alma married Mahler and, by her account in her biography of Mahler, revised for publication in the summer of 1910. In the same book she refers to a premiere of one song by Frances Alda in New York in the winter of 1910-11 but does not specify the song. Modern performances in the United States by the New York Mahlerites have included individual

songs from this set. *Laue Sommernacht* was identified in the score published in 1910 as a text of Gustav Falke, but Knud Martner has correctly identified it with *Gefunden* by Bierbaum.

3. *Vier Lieder*

   Licht in der Nacht (Otto Julius Bierbaum)
   Waldseligkeit (Richard Dehmel)
   Ansturm (Richard Dehmel)
   Erntelied (Gustav Falke)

   Date of composition: 1901 (*Licht in der Nacht, Erntelied*), 1911 (*Waldseligkeit, Ansturm*)
   Publication data: Wien: Universal Edition, 1915
   Premiere: unknown
   Remarks: the first and last of these songs were apparently written before Alma's marriage to Mahler and revised at the time of composition of the two middle songs in 1911. The dates of the four songs are given in the original print of 1915, and the possibility of extensive revision of the two earlier songs is supported by study of their manuscripts, of which a film is on deposit in the New York Public Library (Toscanini Memorial Archive).

4. *Fünf Gesänge*

   Hymne (Novalis)
   Ekstase (Otto Julius Bierbaum)
   Der Erkennende (Franz Werfel)
   Lobgesang (Richard Dehmel)
   Hymne an die Nacht (Novalis)

   Date of composition: 1915 *(Der Erkennende)*; others unknown
   Publication data: Wien: Josef Weinberger, 1924
   Premiere: Wien, [September] 1924
   Remarks: these five songs were composed for voice and piano, like the other songs listed above. The composer herself dates *Der Erkennende* to 1915 in her autobiography; the other four songs, while not dated, may also have been

composed after Mahler's death, unlike the songs listed in the previous entries. The performance of 1924 is documented in the Viennese press as consisting of three songs for voice and orchestra, which have been confirmed by Knud Martner as matching three of the songs in this group for voice and piano; however, as of this writing, the present writer lacks information about which three songs were thus introduced and the identity of the orchestrator. Modern performances of individual songs from this group have been given in the United States at concerts of the New York Mahlerites, and *Ekstase* and *Der Erkennende* were included in a recital at the 1980 Ravinia Festival.

Note: all songs in the three published groups listed under entries 2, 3 and 4 above were reprinted by Universal Edition in 1984. *Der Erkennende* was also reprinted in *Historical Anthology of Music By Women* (Indiana University Press, 1987).

The composer refers to many songs which she had composed before her marriage to Mahler which were never published and were destroyed in manuscript in the bombing of Vienna during World War II. The actual number of these songs has not been possible to document, the only surviving manuscript sources of her songs being the two songs in entry no. 1 (evidently in private hands, although copies are in the possession of collectors including the Internationale Gustav Mahler Gesellschaft and the present writer) and the four songs in entry no. 3, for which a film (not the original manuscript) is located in the New York Public Library in the Toscanini Memorial Archive.

The composer also refers in her autobiography to other works written when she was studying with Robert Gound, Josef Labor and Alexander von Zemlinsky, and prior to that period. These works were evidently in instrumental forms (specific mention of a movement of a sonata being made). These works do not appear to have survived.

LIST OF ABBREVIATIONS

AfMw	Archiv für Musikwissenschaft
BzMw	Beiträge zur Musikwissenschaft
CD	Chord and Discord
diss.	dissertation
DMT	Dansk Musik Tidsskrift
ed.	edited/editor
hrsg.	herausgegeben
IGMG	Internationale Gustav Mahler Gesellschaft
JAMS	Journal of the American Musicological Society
Mf	Die Musikforschung
MGG	Die Musik in Geschichte und Gegenwart. Hrsg. von Friedrich Blume. Kassel: Bärenreiter, 1949-68. 14 vols.
ML	Music and Letters
MLA Notes	Music Library Association Notes
MQ	Musical Quarterly
MT	Musical Times
NaMR	News About Mahler Research (Nachrichtungen zur Mahler-Forschung)
New Grove	New Grove Dictionary of Music and Musicians. Ed. by Stanley Sadie. London: Macmillan, 1980. 20 vols.
19th C Mus	Nineteenth Century Music
N Riv Mus It	Nuova Rivista Musicale Italiana
OeMZ	Österreichische Musikzeitschrift
Riv Mus It	Rivista Musicale Italiana
23	Drei und Zwanzig
vols.	volumes

Reproduced from Alfred Roller, *Die Bildnisse von Gustav Mahler* (Leipzig, Wien, Zurich: E.P. Tal, 1922).

Courtesy Internationale Gustav Mahler Gesellschaft (Vienna).

Gustav and Alma Mahler

COMPENDIA

1. *Der Anbruch.* Gustav Mahler. Vol. 12 no. 3 (März 1930).
   Entire issue devoted to Mahler comprising six articles on various aspects of Mahler's standing in musical history (as composer and conductor) and his *modus operandi* on its own merits. Most contributors from Mahler's own circle, if not from among his closest friends. Individual articles cited in appropriate sections of bibliography below.

2. *L'Approdo Musicale.* No. 16/17 (1963).
   Includes four major articles on various aspects of Mahler's work as composer, chronology of his life and works, chronology of performances at the Hofoper in Vienna in which he was involved, select bibliography and discography. Dated but still useful. Individual articles cited in appropriate locations elsewhere in this bibliography.

3. *L'Arc.* No. 67. Mahler. Aix-en-Provence: Mistral à Cavaillon, [1976]. 80 pp.
   Comprises ten essays tending toward studies of Mahler as composer with the changing status of his worth in the passage of time. See individual articles by subject elsewhere in this bibliography.

4. Carner, Mosco. *Of Men and Music: Collected Essays and Articles.* London: Joseph Williams, 1944. 182 pp.
   This book includes the following essays of interest to Mahler specialists: "Mahler in his Letters (A Psychological Study)" (pp. 101-05), "Mahler's Visit to London" (pp. 106-10), "Form and Technique of Mahler's 'Song of the Earth'" (pp. 111-14), "Mahler's Re-Scoring of the Schumann Symphonies" (pp. 115-28) and "Judaism in Music" (pp. 10-13). The essays are reprinted from various periodicals including *Music Review* and *Monthly Musical Record.* These essays are decidedly radical

for their time, covering various subjects in connection with Mahler as a person and composer; the author was bold enough to espouse Mahler's cause during a period when Mahler's music was rarely heard in England. His discussion of Mahler as a Jew in the last essay cited above has rarely been mentioned in the literature but is a worthy model for all such discussions by Jew and non-Jew alike.

5. *Colloque Internationale Gustav Mahler 25. 26. 27. Janvier 1985*. Paris: Société Européene des Arts Graphiques, 1986. 119 pp. ISBN 2-905296-01-1. Reproduces papers presented at the French Mahler colloquium of January 1985, including eleven essays in French and three in English. Individual articles are cited in appropriate sections of this bibliography below.

6. *Feuilles musicales et courrier suisse du disque*. Numéro spécial consacré à Gustave Mahler, à l'occasion du prochain centième anniversaire de sa naissance. Vol. 12 no. 8 (Octobre 1959).
Full issue published in Lausanne, devoted to Mahler, earliest of the contributions to the Mahler centenniel celebration. Includes four articles devoted to various aspects of Mahler the composer, three of which are original in French, the fourth translated from an earlier source in German. Cited individually in appropriate sections of this bibliography.

7. *Gustav Mahler*. Tübingen: Rainer Wunderlich, 1966. 236 pp.
Includes eight essays reprinted from various earlier sources, some by Mahler's associates, considering various aspects of Mahler's life and work as conductor and composer. The individual essays are cross-referenced in this bibliography by their original sources prior to this reprinting.

8. *Gustav Mahler Kolloquium 1979: ein Bericht*. Österreichischen Gesellschaft für Musik Beiträge '79-81. Kassel, Basel, London: Bärenreiter, 1981. 126 pp.
A reproduction of papers included in the 1979 Vienna Mahler colloquium (June 10-16). Participants included Kurt Blaukopf, Carl Schorske, Constantin Floros, Zoltan Roman, Inna Barsova, Rudolf Stephan and Peter Revers. While wide-ranging in content, the various

papers show a tendency toward subjects relating to
Mahler as a man in his time, emphasizing his relations with other creative intellectuals in music, literature, art and psychiatry. See individual citations
below under various sections of this bibliography.

9. *Gustav Mahler: the Composer, the Conductor and the
   Man. Appreciations by Distinguished Contemporary
   Musicians.* New York: Society of Friends of Music,
   1916. 36 pp.
   This society had a long record (1913-31) for introducing unusual repertoire to New York, and in 1916 it
   sponsored the first New York performance of Mahler's
   Symphony no. 8 (conducted by Leopold Stokowski), on
   the occasion of which this little symposium was published. Among the seventy contributors participating
   were Amy Marcy Cheney Beach, Pablo Casals, George
   Whitefield Chadwick (whose *Melpomene Overture* had been
   conducted by Mahler in one of his last concerts in New
   York in February 1911), Clara Clemens, Ossip Gabrilowitsch, Paul Draper (whose mother had been a member
   of the committee with which Mahler had worked during
   his tenure with the New York Philharmonic Orchestra),
   Rudolf Ganz, Percy Grainger, Daniel Gregory Mason,
   Theodore Spiering and Josef Stransky. While not of
   lasting musicological value, this book shows the widespread contacts Mahler hade made during his time in
   the United States and includes many personal reminiscences.

10. Kolleritsch, Otto, hrsg. *Gustav Mahler: Sinfonie und
    Wirklichkeit.* Studien zur Wertungsforschung, 9.
    Graz: Universal Edition für Institut für Wertungsforschung, 1977. 216 pp. ISBN 3-7024-0124-5.
    Series of fifteen essays, eleven focusing on various
    aspects of Mahler's work, tending to favor subjects
    which show his historical influence over discussions
    of individual compositions. Essays cited individually in appropriate sections of this bibliography below.

11. Mengelberg, Curt Rudolf, hrsg. *Das Mahler-Fest Amsterdam: Vorträge und Berichte.* Wien, Leipzig:
    Universal Edition, 1920. 71 pp.
    Published shortly after the Mahler Festival in Amsterdam conducted by Willem Mengelberg. Falls into two
    basic sections: essays based on lectures delivered

by the editor and others who had known Mahler personally (including Guido Adler, Paul Stefan-Gruenfeldt and Richard Specht) which are listed individually in other sections of this bibliography; and twenty-three press notices from various newspapers which had covered the Festival, in German, French, Italian and English.

12. *Der Merker.* Vol. 3 (1. März-Heft 1912).

    A memorial issue entirely devoted to reminiscences by Mahler's close friends, and his own letters and poems. More biographical than musicological, discussing the man's life rather than his works. Also illustrated with photographs, sketch and facsimile materials of Mahler, his house in Toblach and a portion of a letter. See individual entries elsewhere in this bibliography.

13. *Moderne Welt.* Gustav-Mahler-Heft. Vol. 3 no. 7 (1921).
    Comprises fourteen short essays focusing particularly on Mahler as operatic conductor. Several of these reports are contributed by his singers and other collaborators who worked with him and observed him in rehearsal and performance. Handsomely illustrated with photographs, line drawings, paintings and score facsimiles. Individual entries are cited elsewhere in this bibliography.

14. *Musica.* Robert Schumann-Gustav Mahler Heft. Jahrgang 4, Heft 6 (Juni 1960).
    Includes four articles on various aspects of Mahler's life and work as composer and conductor. This issue is divided between articles on Schumann and Mahler in observance of their 150th and 100th-year anniversaries respectively. Would have been excellent opportunity to include discussion of Mahler's work with Schumann symphonies (not to mention influence of Schumann's style on Mahler's), but none of the individual essays considers these subjects. The articles are individually cited below in this bibliography.

15. *Die Musik.* Vol. 10 no. 8 (Zweites Juniheft 1911).

    Collection of reflections on Mahler as composer, conductor and man, written shortly after his death by insiders who had known him and worked with him personally. See individual essays under various sections of this bibliography following.

16. *Musikblätter des Anbruch.* Gustav-Mahler-Heft. Vol. 2, no. 7/8 (April 1920).
    Comprises thirteen articles, many written by Mahler's friends, ranging over subjects both biographical and musical, on Mahler as composer and as conductor-director. Occasion for special issue was Amsterdam Mahler cycle of May 1920. Also includes Mahler's remarks on composition quoted by Natalie Bauer-Lechner (pp. 306-09) and two pages of the manuscript of the Tenth Symphony published for the first time. See individual citations of contributions elsewhere in this bibliography.

17. *Musik und Bildung.* Gustav-Mahler-Heft. Vol. 5 no. 11 (November 1973).
    Comprises twelve essays on various subjects, the sum total rather uneven. See individual entries for assessment of their value in other parts of this bibliography.

18. *Österreichische Musikzeitschrift.* Gustav-Mahler-Sonderheft. Vol. 15 no. 6 (Juni 1960).
    Essays on the occasion of the centennial of Mahler's birth, including contributions by Erwin Ratz, Erwin Mittag, Erik Werba, Hermann Ullrich, Friedrich Wildgans and Carmen Weingartner-Studer. Primarily concerned with Mahler as a person in the context of his time and in connection with other musical professionals. Individual essays are cited in various sections of this bibliography.

19. *Österreichische Musikzeitschrift.* Vol. 34 no. 6 (Juni 1979).
    Comprises five articles devoted to the present state of Mahler scholarship, published on the occasion of the 1979 Vienna Mahler Colloquium (but in no way duplicating the contributions to that colloquium cited under no. 8 above). Individual articles cited in other portions of this bibliography.

20. Ruzicka, Peter, hrsg. *Mahler: eine Herausforderung.* Wiesbaden: Breitkopf und Härtel, 1977. 212 pp.
    Comprises twelve essays concerned overall with recep-

tion of Mahler's works in our time by audiences, other musicians and scholars. Most of these articles are reproduced from earlier sources and are individually cited in their original forms below with cross-references to this symposium; the few contributions newly written for this book are so noted in their individual citations.

21. Stahmer, Klaus Hinrich, hrsg. *Form und Idee in Gustav Mahlers Instrumentalwerk*. Taschenbücher zur Musikwissenschaft, 70. Hrsg. von Richard Schaal. Wilhelmshaven: Heinrichshofen, 1980. 276 pp. ISBN 3-7959-0299-1.
Comprises five extensive essays discussing aspects of Mahler's compositional style, with special reference to the *Symphony no. 1* and the *Symphony no. 9*. Individual contributions are cited in the sections of this bibliography devoted to those two works.

22. Stefan-Gruenfeldt, Paul, hrsg. *Gustav Mahler: ein Bild seiner Persönlichkeit in Widmungen*. München: R. Piper, 1910. 95 pp.
Group of thirty essays, poems and letters by Mahler's friends and colleagues, compiled as a celebratory offering for his fiftieth birthday. Primarily devoted to views of Mahler's historical influence as conductor and director rather than analysis of his work as composer, which was characteristic for his lifetime. Entries are too numerous to list individually in this bibliography, but the most important ones are cited below where appropriate.

23. Stein, Erwin. *Orpheus in New Guises: the Music of Mahler, Schoenberg, Webern, Berg, Britten*. London: Rockliff, 1953. vii, 167 pp.
This collection of essays includes six dealing with various aspects of Mahler's work as composer and interpreter of works by other composers. Five are English translations of articles in German which Stein had published in various books and journals in the 1920s. Most of the translations were made by Hans Keller. They are cross-referenced in this bibliography in the English versions of this book as well as the original German versions.

24. Stephan, Rudolf, hrsg. *Mahler-Interpretation: Aspekte zum Werk und Wirken von Gustav Mahler.* Mainz, London, New York, Tokyo: B. Schotts Söhne, 1985. 190 pp. ISBN 3-7957-1788-4.
Based on the 1979 Mahler Symposium in Nordrhein-Westfalen, including nine papers on various aspects of Mahler's music which are individually cited elsewhere in this bibliography.

ENCYCLOPEDIA REFERENCES

25. Barsova, Inna. "Gustav Maler." *Muzykal'naya entsiklopediya.* Moskva: Izdatel'stvo "Sovetskaya Entsiklopediya," 1976, vol. 3, columns 413-20.
The leading discussion of Mahler's life and music in Russian reference sources. Shows remarkable insight and originality and is an invaluable source of information on Russian literature on Mahler, improved on only in Barsova's unpublished list of sources of 1978/1979 (see no. 35).

26. Broeckx, Jan L. "Gustav Mahler." *Algemene muziek encyclopedie.* Ed. by J. Robijns and Miep Zijkstra. Haarlem: Lenaerts/Motus Contrarius/De Haan, 1982, vol. 6, pp. 168-73.
Dutch encyclopedia article by author who had earlier written comprehensive study of *Das Lied von der Erde* (see no. 879). While not as detailed as similar articles in *Grove* and *MGG,* it is notable for thoughtfully chosen selective bibliography.

27. Engel, Gabriel. "Gustav Mahler." *International Cyclopedia of Music and Musicians.* Ed. by Bruce Bohle. Tenth Edition. New York, Toronto: Dodd, Mead; London: J. M. Dent & Sons, 1975, pp. 1309-12.
Summary of Mahler's life and work by major American Mahler partisan. Useful but limited in view of time of publication, especially on comparison with Redlich in *MGG* and Mitchell and Banks in the sixth edition of *Grove.*

28. la Grange, Henry-Louis de. "Mahler." *Encyclopédie de la musique.* Paris: Fasquelle, 1958-61, vol. 3, pp. 132-36.
Remarkably detailed summary of Mahler's life and work in French, obviously abstract for the extended work

29. Mitchell, Donald and Paul Banks. "Gustav Mahler." *New Grove*, vol. 11, pp. 505-31.
Extensive account incorporating major literature and updating history of Mahler research since the previous edition of *Grove* before the "boom" at the time of the centenniel. Bibliography detailed but difficult to use as it is arranged chronologically rather than alphabetically. This article has been twice reprinted and updated, first in *New Grove Turn of the Century Masters: Janacek, Mahler, Strauss, Sibelius* (London: Macmillan, 1985, pp. 79-181, ISBN 0-333-38541-1) and in monograph form in 1986 (121 pp.).

30. Redlich, Hans. "Gustav Mahler." *MGG*, vol. 8, columns 1490-1500.
Remarkably detailed account of Mahler's life and summary of his works considering the time in which it was published (before the "Mahler Boom" had really taken hold). Useful bibliography details all major writings on Mahler to that date. The most useful summary study of the period from Mahler's death to the centenniel, still valuable even today after great expansion of the Mahler literature in the interim.

31. Restagno, Enzo. "Gustav Mahler." *Dizionario enciclopedico universale della musica e dei musicisti*. Le biografie, 4. Dir. da Alberto Basso. Torino: Unione Tipografico-Editrice Torinese (UTET), 1986, pp. 573-83.
Remarkably detailed Italian encyclopedia reference on Mahler's life and work, with nearly comprehensive list of works and rather selective but very well-chosen bibliography.

32. Rognoni, Luigi. "Gustav Mahler." *Enciclopedia della musica*. Milano: Giulio Ricordi, 1964, vol. 3, pp. 74-76.
Discusses Mahler's life and works in general terms. Apparently aimed at Italian audience, this encyclopedia article is shorter and less detailed than the later equivalent by Restagno (see no. 31) but is nonetheless reliable in its content.

33. Walter, Bruno. "Gustav Mahler." *Universal Jewish Encyclopedia: An Authoritative and Popular Presentation of Jews and Judaism Since the Earliest Times.* Ed. by Isaac Landman. New York: Universal Jewish Encyclopedia, Inc., 1939-43, vol. 7, pp. 282-84.
Useful summary of Mahler's life and work by one of his closest friends and colleagues. Despite "Jewish" context, Walter makes no attempt to explore the sensitive issue of Judaism in Mahler's life and work. Primarily published as counter to Nazi tactics of silence or vilification of that time.

CATALOGUES AND LISTS

34. *Ausstellung: Gustav Mahler und seine Zeit--Katalog.* Wien: Direktion der Wiener Festwochen, 1960. 112 pp.
Catalogue of the centennial exhibition on Mahler held in conjunction with the Wiener Festwochen. Divided into five sections focusing on Mahler as Director of the Hofoper, composer and person, as well as the time in which he lived and his associates. Listings particularly heavy on photographs and manuscript documents. Early example of exhibition catalogue which has now mushroomed into a trend; although lacking visual illustration still a model of its type.

35. Barsova, Inna. "Mahler-Bibliographie." Unpublished typescript. In Russian. 13 pp.
Lists publications in the Russian language about Mahler and his music covering the period 1902-78. Includes books, dissertations, articles and reviews. In the archives of the Internationale Gustav Mahler Gesellschaft. Transliterated with editorial annotations by Susan M. Filler.

36. "Bibliography of Books on Mahler." *CD* 2 (1948): 79-80.
Early bibliography limited by the comparatively modest number of books on the subject at the time of publication, but valuable because multilingual.

37. *Denkschrift zu den Meisteraufführung Wiener Musik: Veranstaltet von der Gemeinde Wien, 26. Mai - 13. Juni 1920.* Wien: Österreichische Staatsdruckerei,

1920. 87 pp. Published for a major exhibition celebrating music in Vienna. Essays by many important people including Kalbeck, Tietze, Bittner, Graf, Orel and Weingartner. Includes a poem, *Requiem: Erinnerung aus Gustav Mahlers Fünfte Symphonie seinem Andenken gewidmet,* by Martina Wied, on pp. 47-51, and a woodcut of Mahler's grave by M. Vera Frieberger-Brunner. Book covers subjects from "Viennese Music" to the Second Viennese School.

38. Fülöp, Peter. *The Discography of Mahler's Works.* Studia Musicologica Academiae Scientiarum Hungaricae, 26. Budapest: Akadémiai Kiadó, 1984. 200 pp. (pp. 219-418).
Very different discography from those of Smoley and Weber (see no. 55 and no. 61 below), of lasting value, giving full details of record labels, participants and dates, supplementary information including annotators and supplemental materials. Blessedly free of opinionated commentary on the quality of performances and recordings! Cross-referenced by performers and record labels.

39. Grasberger, Franz, hrsg. *Die Handschriften der Meister: Berühmte Werke der Tonkunst im Autograph--Gestaltung und Katalog.* Wien: Gesellschaft der Musikfreunde, [1966]. 286 pp.
Catalogue of an exhibition of musical manuscript materials by the Musikverein from May 22 to June 20, 1966. In Part 5, *Strauss bis Bartók,* there is a facsimile page from the fair copy of Mahler's *Symphony no. 4.* The listings of the Mahler manuscripts from the exhibition cover pp. 198-201.

40. *Gustav Mahler: un homme, une oeuvre, une époque: Musée d'Art Moderne de la Ville de Paris 24. Janvier - 31. Mars 1985.* Paris: Association Gustav Mahler/ Bibliothèque Nationale, 1985. 223 pp. ISBN 2-905296-00-3.
Catalogue of an exhibition in the Musée d'Art Moderne de la Ville de Paris arranged by the Association Gustav Mahler and the Bibliothèque Nationale. Introduction and other sections contributed by Henry-Louis de la Grange, with other contributors including Jean-Michel Nectoux and Danielle Gutmann. Handsomely illustrated with photographs, facsimiles and line drawings. In-

dividual entries to the items in the exhibition give
considerable information for reference/historical purposes.

41. Hadamowsky, Franz und Alexander Witeschnik, hrsg. *Ju-
bilaümausstellung: 100 Jahre Wiener Oper am Ring.*
Wien: Aktionskomitee 100-Jahrfeier der Wiener Staatsoper, 1969. 278 pp.
Catalogue of an exhibition celebrating the centennial
of the Vienna Opera, prominently featuring Mahler and
his successors including close friends Bruno Walter
and Richard Strauss.

42. Hilmar, Ernst. "Mahleriana in the Wiener Stadt- und
Landesbibliothek." *NaMR,* no. 5 (June 1979): 3-18.
Lists sources of Mahler's music in the municipal library of Vienna, including manuscripts, proofs, early
prints and letters. Differentiates between Mahler's
own works and sources by other composers with which
Mahler worked as a conductor. Important as documentation of the holdings of this library, but even more
important for commentary on the history of the sources.

42a. *Ein Jahrhundert Wiener Musikleben: aus der Geschichte
der Gesellschaft der Musikfreunde in Wien 1812-1912
--Führer durch die Ausstellung.* Wien: Gesellschaft
der Musikfreunde, 1912. 28 pp.
Catalogue of an exhibition celebrating a century of
musical history in Vienna. Mahler is represented in
listings no. 286-89, two of which are documents from
his time at the Conservatory as a student, the third
a "Plakett von Th. Isnenghi, 1912" (not further described) and the fourth the fair copy of *Wer hat dies
Liedel erdacht.* Actually not bad for Vienna only a
year after Mahler's death.

* Keller, Otto. "Gustav Mahler-Literatur." *Musik* 10
(1911): 369-77.
Full citation under no. 15 above. Surveys literature
on Mahler published to the time of his death. Supple-
mented by Arthur Seidl in *Musik* 10 (Erste Augustheft
1911) (see no. 52 below).

43. Lelieveld, K. *Catalogus Gustav Mahler tentoonstelling:
Den Haag (1. - 22. Juni 1974).* Den Haag: Muziekan-
tiquariat Lelieveld, 1974. 44, xvii pp.
Catalogues an exhibition devoted to Mahler in The Hague

in 1974. This exhibition focused on books and articles on Mahler and documentation including portraits. Especially valuable for its information on Dutch Mahler scholarship.

44. Loewenberg, Alfred. *Annals of Opera, 1597-1940.* Cambridge: W. Heffer and Sons, 1943; second ed.: Genève: Societas Bibliographica, 1955 (corrected and revised by Frank Walker); third ed., Totowa, New Jersey: Rowman and Littlefield, 1978 (introduction by Edward J. Dent). 1. ed., xxiii, 879 pp. 2. ed., xxv pp., 1756 columns in 2 vols. 3. ed., xxv pp., 1756 columns in 1 vol. ISBN 0-87471-851-1 (3. ed. only).
See columns 702-03 for discussion of Mahler's production of Weber's *Oberon* and columns 1130-31 for discussion of Weber's *Die drei Pintos*. Strictly factual statistics concerning operas, arranged chronologically by premiere. Mahler's productions in Vienna are cited in several instances, the most important being the version of *Oberon*; the factual data on the Leipzig premiere of *Die drei Pintos* agrees in all essential details with accounts in the press in 1888.

45. *Mahler e Trieste.* Civico Museo Teatrale di Fondazione Carlo Schmidl, 15. - 30. maggio 1981. [Trieste]: Civici Musei di Storia ed Arte, 1981. 16 pp.
Catalogue of little-known exhibition on Mahler in Trieste in 1981, focusing on rehearsals and performance of Mahler with the Orchestra of the Trieste Philharmonic Society in November/December 1905 which included works of Beethoven and Mozart as well as Mahler's *Symphony no. 5*. Documented with memorabilia from the performance as well as letters from Mahler to Alma and contemporary coverage of the concert in the press.

46. Mahler, Gustav. *Verzeichnis der Werke.* Wien: IGMG, 1959. 14 pp.
Somewhat dated today but still useful as an introductory listing of Mahler's symphonies and vocal works. Omits any mention of Mahler's versions of works by other composers and his own poems, but does include valuable information on the publishers, score numbers and resources required for performance.

47. *Mahler tentoonstelling 13. - 30. November. Muziekcentrum Vredenburg Utrecht.* Den Haag: Lelieveld, 1986. 187 pp.
Catalogue of Mahler exhibition in Utrecht held in con-

junction with the Symposium on Mahler's *Symphony no. 10* sponsored by the University of Utrecht. Exhibition includes many articles unique to the history of Mahler performance in the Netherlands from his lifetime to the present.

48. Martner, Knud. *Gustav Mahler im Konzertsaal: eine Dokumentation seiner Konzerttätigkeit, 1870-1911*. Kopenhagen: Privatdruck, 1985. vi, 195 pp.
    Exhaustive and unique source of information covering the history of Mahler as concert conductor and pianist, from his debut at the age of ten to his last concert in New York in early 1911. Programs listed in chronological order, with details including soloists, locations of concerts, repertoire. Heavily illustrated with facsimiles of programs, posters and newspaper announcements. Separate indices by composer/work, types of works performed, names of assisting artists and cities of performances. Indispensable.

49. Namenwirth, Simon Michael. *Gustav Mahler: a Critical Bibliography*. Wiesbaden: Otto Harrassowitz, 1987. 3 vols. ISBN 3-447-02731-2.
    Extensive bibliography of secondary sources on Mahler and his music. Differs from earlier catalogues by Vondenhoff (see no. 59 and no. 60 below) in its organization and in the inclusion of annotations to many of the items in the bibliography. Includes a great deal of useful information for the Mahler specialist, but is weakened by several factors: first, inaccessible organization of information only partially alleviated by indexing in the third volume; second, opinionated coverage in the annotations, which are often so rambling as to be akin to short essays; third, complete lack of annotation in many cases in which author has not consulted the sources themselves; fourth, less than optimum usage of the English language in which author has written the book; five, arbitrary omission of many important sources in the literature because of author's stated decision to confine himself to references in languages with which he himself is familiar. Despite these factors, this book--used best in conjunction with those by Vondenhoff--is indispensable to Mahler research and should become a necessary acquisition of any major library.

50. Sakata, Kenichi. "Mahler-Literature in Japanese."

NaMR, no. 3 (July 1978): 11-14.
Lists books and articles relating to Mahler in Japanese, covering a time span from the 1920s to the 1970s. Some discussion of the nature of the limited number of books, but no commentary on the content of the articles, most of which are in *Ongaku Geijutsu* and *Record Geijutsu.* Since the publication of this list, a new book has been published in the Japanese language, *Gustav Mahler: Road to Contemporary Music,* by Namio Shibata (Iwanami, 1984, 208 pp.), as well as Japanese translations of several German books on Mahler.

51. Schultz, Klaus. *Mahler-Ansichten--Zu den Veranstaltungen im Kultur-Forum Bonn Center: Mahler 1975 (Vorträge, Diskussionen, Hörversuche, Interpretationsvergleiche usw.) 11. - 14. Dezember.* Konzeption Diether Schnebel. Bonn: Kulturamt der Stadt Bonn, 1975. 44 pp.
Documents the Mahler symposium and associated events in Bonn of 1975. Briefer than some later catalogues of symposia and exhibitions in other cities.

52. Seidl, Arthur. "Gustav Mahler-Literatur: Nachlese." *Musik* 10 (1. Augustheft 1911): 154-58.
Complements and supplements earlier list of literature compiled by Otto Keller (see above).

53. Seltsam, William. *Metropolitan Opera Annals: A Chronicle of Artists and Performers.* New York: H.W. Wilson, 1947. xvi, 751 pp.
First supplement (1957), xiii, 115 pp. (1947-57)
Second supplement (1968): xiii, 126 pp. (1957-66)
Third supplement, Clifton, New Jersey: Published for the Metropolitan Opera Guild by James T. White, 1978. xi, 208 pp. (by Mary Ellis Peltz, covering 1966-76).
Exhaustive documentation of the history of the Metropolitan Opera, chronological, giving names of artists, dates of programs, repertoire and representative press reports. No editorial prose or interpretation, but so thoroughly packed with facts as to be indispensable to interpretive studies.

54. Silbermann, Alphons. *Lübbes Mahler Lexikon.* Bergisch Gladbach, West Germany: Gustav Lübbe, 1986. 352 pp. ISBN 3-7857-0416-6.
Reference dictionary listing Mahler's compositions,

places of his activity as conductor and composer, important associates, friends and family members, and musicoliterary concepts that influenced him. Useful for brief reference in individual cases for profiles, but not for in-depth research. Bibliography near end of book decidedly weighted in the direction of German language sources at the expense of sources in other languages. List of works by Mahler perfunctory and incomplete showing that author was perhaps not current in his own knowledge of the literature.

55. Smoley, Lewis, comp. *The Symphonies of Gustav Mahler: a Critical Discography*. Discographies, 23. New York, Westport, Connecticut and London: Greenwood Press, 1986. xv, 191 pp. ISBN 0-313-25189-4.
Discography aimed at audio buffs covering the symphonies and *Das Lied von der Erde*. Useful as source of data about recording labels, dates and participants, but seriously marred by subjective assessments of performances and technical audio quality. Best viewed as example of the futility of popular criticism, since no reader will agree completely with author's views and audio buffs are notoriously individualistic in their preferences. Obsolete in any case since more entries to recorded literature are released every month.

56. Stephan, Rudolf. *Gustav Mahler: Werk und Interpretation. Autographe, Partituren, Dokumente*. Köln: Arno Volk, 1979. 120 pp. ISBN 3-87252-118-7.
Catalogue of an exhibition of Mahler sources at the Heinrich Heine Institut, Düsseldorf, from October 1979 to January 1980. Especially favors scores, both published and manuscript types, including Mahler's own compositions and those of other composers with whose works he worked. Heavily illustrated with facsimiles of many of the materials in the exhibition. Also includes brief essays placing the items in the exhibition in the context of Mahler's life and work.

57. *Traum und Wirklichkeit: Wien 1870-1930*. Hrsg. vom Historischen Museum der Stadt Wien unter der Leitung von Robert Waissenberger. Salzburg, Wien: Residenz, 1985. 801 pp.
An exhaustive catalogue of the ninety-third special exhibition of the Historisches Museum der Stadt Wien im Karlsplatz 5, 28. März - 6. Oktober 1985. Documents music, art, literary and other intellectual endeavors

during the time in question and shows how rich Vienna was as a cultural source in the period. Of particular interest is the essay "Gustav Mahlers Heimat" by Herta Blaukopf (pp. 126-30).

58. Turner, J. Rigbie. "Nineteenth-Century Autograph Music Manuscripts in the Pierpont Morgan Library: A Check List." *19th C Mus* 4 (1980): 157-83.
A listing of such manuscripts in two parts, in which Mahler manuscripts owned and deposited in the Pierpont Morgan Library are listed in Part 2. The entire bipartite article was published as a monograph by the Pierpont Morgan Library in 1982. Very informative in view of the growing number of Mahler manuscripts in this collection.

59. Vondenhoff, Bruno und Eleonore Vondenhoff. *Gustav Mahler Dokumentation: Sammlung Eleonore Vondenhoff. Materialen zu Leben und Werk*. Publikationen des Instituts für Österreichische Musikdokumentation, 4. Hrsg. von Franz Grasberger. Tutzing: Hans Schneider, 1978. xxii, 676 pp.
Lists many secondary sources documenting the lives and works of Mahler and Alma, ranging from newspaper, journal and magazine articles to books. Particularly strong in newspaper coverage from Mahler's own time. Weak in score sources. Heavily slanted toward German-language sources. Difficult to use because of awkward organization and inadequate indexing, but indispensable.

60. Vondenhoff, Bruno und Eleonore Vondenhoff. *Gustav Mahler Dokumentation: Sammlung Eleonore Vondenhoff. Materialen zu Leben und Werk. Ergänzungsband*. Publikationen des Instituts für Österreichische Musikdokumentation, 9. Hrsg. von Günter Brosche. Tutzing: Hans Schneider, 1983. 327 pp. ISBN 3-7952-0397-X.
Supplementary volume to no. 59. Updates information included in that volume and adds new materials. Shares the strengths and weaknesses of the main volume, with the added problem that this volume means little without tandem use of its predecessor. The two volumes together, however, are a major, necessary source.

61. Weber, J.F. *Mahler*. Discography Series, 9. Utica, N.Y.: n.p., 1971. 38 pp.
Lists known recordings of works of Mahler to 1971, divided according to works and arranged in chronological

order under each title. Includes names of conductors, orchestras, pianists and vocal soloists, dates of release of each recording, labels and numbers. Refers to relevant articles in *Schwann, Stereo Review, High Fidelity* etc., reviews, occasional references to authors of program notes.

HISTORY

General

62. Barea, Ilsa. *Vienna*. New York: Alfred A. Knopf, 1966. 381 pp.
 Insider's view of Vienna from the Renaissance to World War I. Informative, surveys history, politics, art, literature and music; reliable, scholarly yet readable, a mosaic view of a unique phenomenon.

63. Crankshaw, Edward. *Vienna: the Image of a Culture in Decline*. New York, London: Macmillan, 1938, 1976. ix, 253 pp.
 History of Viennese society in decay as seen through the eyes of an observer on the streets. Concentrates on familiar landmarks from the Ring to Stefansdom, from Schönbrunn to the Prater. Critical, affectionate and current as well as historically grounded.

64. Drage, Geoffrey. *Austria-Hungary*. London: John Murray, 1909. xix, 846 pp.
 Current in its time for study of day-to-day administration in agriculture, industry, commerce and finance in the Empire. Fascinating discussion of the "racial question" referring to the Jews and other minorities including Magyars, Slovaks and Croats. Extensive and well documented with quotations from the constitution, laws, conventions and statutes.

65. Grunfeld, Frederic V. *Prophets Without Honor: A Background to Freud, Kafka, Einstein and Their World*. New York: Holt, Rinehart and Winston, 1979. xiii, 349 pp. ISBN 0-03-017871-1.
 A study of the rich intellectual and social developments in the Austrian Empire at the turn of this century and beyond, especially in the Jewish intelligentsia. Mahler figures prominently as Director of the Opera and as composer and intellectual indicator of his day.

66. Janik, Allen and Stephen Toulmin. *Wittgenstein's Vienna*. New York: Simon and Schuster, 1973. 314 pp. ISBN 0-671-21360-1 (hardbound), 0-671-21725-9 (paper). Rich, well-documented study of intellectual Vienna in the time of the Wittgenstein family, Mahler, the Second Viennese School, the Sezession, Freud and Herzl. Particularly notable for its emphasis on the seeds of intellectual revolution among the Jewish thinkers and creators in Vienna.

67. Johnson, William M. *The Austrian Mind: an Intellectual and Social History, 1848-1938*. Berkeley, Los Angeles, London: University of California Press, 1972. xv, 515 pp. ISBN 0-520-01701-3. A major study of Austrian intellectual and cultural life from the revolutions of 1848 to the *Anschluss*. Covers the period when Mahler, Herzl, Freud, the Second Viennese School, the Wittgensteins and the major artists and architects were drawn to the Empire, later to the Republic. Considers the effect of changing political conditions on the intellectuals, especially Jews and their enemies. A German version of this book, *Österreichische Kultur- und Geistesgeschichte: Gesellschaft und Ideen im Donauraum 1848 bis 1938* (transl. by Otto Grohma) was published in Vienna in 1974.

68. Morton, Frederic. *A Nervous Splendor: Vienna 1888/1889*. Boston, Toronto: Little, Brown and Co., 1979; New York: Penguin Books, 1980, 1981, 1984. x, 340 pp. ISBN 0-316-58532-7 (hardbound), 0-1400-5667-X (paper). A survey of life in Vienna during the year of 1888-89, written in novelistic style but researched historically and culturally with unusual care. Central figure is the Archduke Rudolf and the life he leads during the year in question up to his suicide at Mayerling; but Mahler, Freud, Herzl and other intellectual luminaries play major secondary roles, although--during the year in question--Mahler was not in Vienna but in Budapest.

69. Nebehay, Christian Michael. *Ver sacrum 1898-1903*. Wien: Tusch, 1975. 321 pp. English version (with same title, transl. by Geoffrey Watkins) New York: Rizzoli, 1977. 329 pp. ISBN 0-8478-0115-2. Richly illustrated selection of artistic work from major Austrian artistic periodical which included work

of many in Mahler and Alma's circle (Klimt, Moll, Moser and Roller). Also involves literary influences from same circle including Bahr, Rilke, Bierbaum and Dehmel. Unfortunately does not include much information on music during the period, but does point out Mahler's influence on the movement as a personal friend and colleague of many of the contributors.

70. Palmer, Francis H.E. *Austro-Hungarian Life in Town and Country*. Our European Neighbors. Ed. by W.H. Dawson. New York, London: G.P. Putnam's Sons, 1903, 1984. vii, 301 pp.
    Account of daily life, historical, cultural and personal, in the time of the Dual Monarchy, contemporary with Mahler's tenure at the Hofoper in Vienna. Informative for the average reader in its time, historical document as recent reprint.

71. Petermann, Reinhard E. *Wien im Zeitalter Kaiser Franz Josephs I*. Wien: R. Lechner (Wilhelm Muller), 1908. 411 pp.
    Substantial study of Vienna at the time of the Emperor Franz Josef, written toward the end of the Emperor's long reign. Worth observing as a study made on the spot at the time, if not wholly objective in viewpoint; more extensive in coverage than most from that period.

72. Pollak, Michael. *Vienne 1900: une identité blessée*. Collection Archives, 94. [Paris]: Gallimard/Juillard, 1984. 215 pp.
    Cogent account in French of Vienna coming of age at the turn of the century--politically, intellectually and culturally. Liberally documented with archival quotations from the great intellectual and political writings of the time (in translation) including Herzl, Schnitzler and Bahr. See especially section "L'impossible harmonie: l'antisémitisme," pp. 75-107.

73. Redl, Renate. "Berta Zuckerkandl und die Wiener Gesellschaft: ein Beitrag zur österreichischen Kunst- und Gesellschaftskritik." Ph.D. diss., Universität Wien, 1978. 307 pp.
    Study of intellectual Vienna in Mahler's time as seen by Berta Szeps-Zuckerkandl, who was a mutual friend of Mahler, Alma and others on the scene at the turn of the century. Refers to Zuckerkandl's own writings and those of others commenting on Vienna at that time.

74. Schorske, Carl E. *Fin-de-siècle Vienna: Politics and Culture.* New York: Alfred A. Knopf, 1980; New York: Vintage Books (Division of Random House), 1981. xxx, 378 pp. ISBN 0-394-74478-0.
Surveys Viennese cultural and intellectual life at the turn of this century through the medium of individual seminal figures in literature (Hofmannsthal, Schnitzler), architecture (Wagner), politics (Lueger, Schönerer and Herzl), psychiatry (Freud), art (Klimt and Kokoschka) and music (Schoenberg). Relates the work of these men to the societal norms in Vienna in their time and makes connections between them and their predecessors and followers.

75. Spiel, Hilde. *Vienna's Golden Autumn: From the Watershed Year 1866 to Hitler's Anschluss, 1938.* New York: Weidenfeld and Nicolson, 1987. 248 pp. ISBN 1-55584-136-8.
Loving but melancholy study of Vienna from the Austro-Prussian War to the *Anschluss,* in the tradition of Bahr, Specht and Zweig as literatus insiders. Less concerned with politics as such than with their effect on the creative people in the city. Demonstrates the pivotal role of the Jews from Mahler, Schoenberg and Wellesz in music to Salten, Werfel, Hofmannsthal and Schnitzler in letters. Occasionally inaccurate in detail, but in many ways more informative and well-written than other histories by outsiders better documented. Gains from extending time span forward to 1938, especially in discussion of the Jews.

76. Waissenberger, Robert, hrsg. *Wien 1890-1920.* Freiburg: Office du Livre, S.A., 1984. 276 pp. English version: *Vienna 1890-1920.* New York: Rizzoli, 1984. 276 pp.
Richly illustrated coffee-table book documenting intellectual, cultural and political Vienna during the period when Mahler and his circle affected those events. Mahler figures prominently, especially in essay "Gustav Mahler," pp. 214-17.

77. Weigel, Hans. *"Ad absurdum": Satiren, Attacken, Parodien aus drei Jahrzehnten.* Graz, Köln, Wien: Styria, 1980. 296 pp.
A savage view of intellectual and social life in the Austrian Empire as illustrated by commentary and caricature reproduced from contemporary sources. Indis-

pensable as the voice of the "opposition" for comparison with conventional sources.

78. Wunberg, Gotthart, hrsg. *Die Wiener Moderne: Literatur, Kunst und Musik zwischen 1890 und 1910.* Unter Mitarbeit von Johannes J. Braakenburg. Universal-Bibliothek, 7742. Stuttgart: Reclam, 1981. 725 pp. ISBN 3-15-007742-7, 3-15-027742-6.
Selections of writings of great intellectuals in Vienna at the twenty years around the turn of the century. See *Gustav Mahler* by Schoenberg (pp. 596-97), a memorial piece later included in *Style and Idea*; Mahler's own poem *Die Nacht blickt mild* (p. 598) and "Siegfried im Opernhaus" by Karl Kraus (pp. 599-600), an appraisal of Mahler's first performance of *Lohengrin* (NOT *Siegfried!*) in the Hofoper.

79. Zeman, Z[bynek] A.B. *Twilight of the Habsburgs: the Collapse of the Austro-Hungarian Empire.* Library of the Twentieth Century. New York: American Heritage Press, 1971. 127 pp. ISBN 07-072798-8 (hardbound), 07-072799-6 (paper).
Richly illustrated brief study of Vienna from the late nineteenth century to World War I. Valuable more for its visual illustrations than its text, which is limited and rather simplistic, this book gives overview of the society with its politics, culture and intellectual achievement.

80. Zweig, Stefan. *Die Welt von Gestern: Erinnerung eines Europäers.* Stockholm: Bermann-Fischer, 1944; Frankfurt am Main: Suhrkamp, 1947; Berlin, Frankfurt am Main: G.B. Fischer, 1962; Frankfurt am Main, Hamburg: Fischer-Bücherei, 1973. 317 pp.
An eyewitness account of the incredibly diverse and rich intellectual flowering in Europe (especially Vienna) in the early twentieth century, as observed by one of its most brilliant lights. Zweig wrote this book in exile because of the Nazi policy. Versions in English (*The World of Yesterday: an Autobiography by Stefan Zweig*, New York: Viking Press; London, Toronto: Cassell, 1943; Lincoln, Nebraska: University of Nebraska Press, 1964) and French (*Le Monde d'Hier*, Paris: Albin Michel, 1945) were released closely with the German version; the English version has actually attained wider circulation than the German version through its many reprints.

Judaism and Antisemitism

Background History and Culture

* Bonnet, Jacques and François Latraverse. "Une Message Impérial." *L'Arc* 67: 64-79. Full citation under no. 3 above. Surveys Viennese intellectual achievement in the reign of Franz Josef, with particular emphasis on the work of the Jews from the Wittgensteins to Freud to Mahler.

81. Carsten, Francis Ludwig. *Fascist Movements in Austria: from Schönerer to Hitler*. SAGE Studies in Twentieth Century History, 7. London, Beverly Hills: SAGE Publications, 1977. 356 pp. ISBN 0-8039-99925 (hardbound), 0-8039-98570 (paper).
German version: *Faschismus in Österreich: von Schönerer zu Hitler*. München: Wilhelm Fink, 1977. 373 pp. ISBN 3-7705-1480-7.
Study of Fascist, pan-German and antisemitic political movements in Germany and Austria from Schönerer and Lueger to the Anschluss. Heavily documented with excerpts from archival sources.

82. Damon, Lindsay Todd. "Austrian Antisemitism." *The Nation* 70 (1900): 453-55.
An on-the-spot account of the Jewish community in Austria and its contributions to the political and cultural life of the country; then an account of day-by-day antisemitic laws and customs which separated Jews from the general population and made them political whipping boys. Rare, objective observation published in its time.

83. Glockemeier, Georg. *Zur Wiener Judenfrage*. Leipzig, Wien: Johannes Gunther, 1936. 127 pp.
Historical and statistical study of the Jews in Vienna, one of the last written from non-Nazi point of view before the *Anschluss* and the barrage of Nazi-oriented studies. Useful background with tabular and bibliographic data.

84. Hantsch, Hugo. *Die Nationalitätenfrage im alten Österreich: das Problem der konstruktiven Reichsgestaltung*. Wiener historische Studien, 1. Wien: Herold, 1953. 124 pp.
Brief but immediate and well-documented study of racial-national movement in Austria from the Empire to the

Judaism & Antisemitism (Background)

Third Reich. More of an insider's view than Kann (see no. 88 below), perhaps less objective but valuable because personal.

85. Jenks, William Alexander. *Vienna and the Young Hitler.* New York: Columbia University Press, 1960; New York: Octagon Books, 1976. 252 pp. ISBN 0-374-94206-4.
    Chronicles Hitler's sojourn in Vienna from 1907 to 1913, documenting his "education" in the political thought he later adopted as legal policy in the Third Reich. As this was the Vienna which made Mahler's life miserable due to inbred antisemitism, the study is pertinent as the story of a society in decay as the ground for later mass murder.

86. Jones, J. Sydney. *Hitler in Vienna, 1907-1913: Clues to the Future.* New York: Stein and Day, 1982. xi, 350 pp. ISBN 0-8128-2855-0.
    German version: *Hitlers Weg begann in Wien, 1907-1913.* Transl. by Sylvia Eisenburger. Wiesbaden: Limes Verlag, 1983. 351 pp.
    Surveys Vienna in the first and second decades of the twentieth century, drawing parallels between the young Adolf Hitler and other men of that time, including Mahler, in terms of sociocultural background and interests.

87. Kann, Robert A. "German-Speaking Jewry During Austria-Hungary's Constitutional Era." *Jewish Social Studies* 10 (1948): 239-56.
    Summarizes the position of Jews in the Dual Monarchy as influenced by antisemitic propaganda of Lueger and the Christian Socialists and the reactions of Jewish leaders including Dr. Josef Bloch, publisher of *Österreichische Wochenschrift*.

88. Kann, Robert A. *The Multinational Empire: Nationalities and National Reform in the Habsburg Monarchy, 1848-1918.* New York: Columbia University Press, 1950. 2 vols.
    Exhaustively documented study of race and nationalism in the Austrian Empire, readable style but scholarly basis. Indispensable, accessible for discussion of atmosphere influencing intelligentsia of many fields during the time Mahler was one of their number.

89. Pulzer, Peter G.J. *The Rise of Political Anti-Semi-*

tism in Germany and Austria, 1867-1938. New York: John Wiley and Sons, 1964. xiv, 364 pp.
Traces the use of antisemitism as a political tool in the German-speaking countries during Mahler's lifetime and up to the Anschluss. Well-documented study of the economic and political conditions affecting the legal status of the Jews. Especially important study of Lueger and Schönerer's tactics in Vienna during Mahler's time.

90. Rosensaft, Menachem Z. "Jews and Antisemites in Austria at the End of the Nineteenth Century." *Leo Baeck Institute Yearbook* 21 (1976): 57-86.
Documented summary of pro- and antisemitic political trends in Austria at the time Mahler lived, with special attention to the platforms of Lueger and Schönerer.

91. Smith, Bradley F. *Adolf Hitler: His Family, Childhood and Youth.* Stanford: The Hoover Institution on War, Revolution and Peace/Stanford University, 1967, 1968, 1972, 1975. 180 pp.
Chiefly valuable to Mahler specialists for its extensive bibliography of sources covering Austria at the turn of the century.

92. Whiteside, Andrew. *Austrian National Socialism Before 1918.* The Hague: Martinus Nijhoff, 1962. 143 pp.
Short but useful study of the political conditions in Austria in the late nineteenth and early twentieth centuries which laid the foundation for the Nazi movement. Covers the conditions in Vienna, especially, which influenced the "education" of the young Hitler, especially emphasizing the effects of the work of Karl Lueger and Georg von Schönerer.

Jews in the German-Speaking Countries (General)

93. Goldhammer-Sahawi, Leo. *Die Juden Wiens: eine statistische Studie.* Wien, Leipzig: R. Löwit, 1927. 70 pp.
Statistical-cultural-economic study of the Jewish community of Vienna by journalist-author who continued the work of Theodor Herzl as President of the Zionist organization in Austria. Good background for life of Jews observed by author during residence in Vienna

at the period when Mahler was Director of the Hofoper and immediately following.

94. Grünwald, Max. *The Jews of Vienna*. Philadelphia: Jewish Publication Society, 1936. xxiv, 557 pp.
Exhaustive historical-cultural-statistical study of the Jewish community in Vienna, a rare source in English in its time period when most such studies were in German. Pro-semitic, well documented in contrast to Nazi contributions to literature a few years later.

95. Grunberger, Richard. *The Twelve-Year Reich: a Social History of Nazi Germany, 1933-1945*. New York: Holt, Rinehart and Winston, 1971. vi, 534 pp. ISBN 0-03-076435-1 (hardbound), 0-03-048226-7 (paper).
Previously published in England as *A Social History of the Third Reich*. This is a critical study of intellectual endeavor during the Third Reich and how it was affected by Nazi policies. While Chapter 27, "Music" (pp. 406-20) is particularly relevant to musicologists as an objective commentary realizing perspective to Nazi musicology, the chapters on education in the Third Reich are also useful to historians of the teaching of music in the Nazi schools on all levels. With Wulf's *Die Musik im Dritten Reich* (see no. 187, below), the best available source as a basis of intensive study of the Nazi literature on music in general and music by Jewish composers in particular.

96. Kaznelson, Siegmund, hrsg. *Juden im deutschen Kulturbereich: ein Sammelwerk*. 3. Auflage. Berlin: Jüdischer Verlag, 1962. xx, 1060 pp.
Originally published in 1934, second edition 1959. Exhaustive survey of the contributions of Jews to the cultural-intellectual life of the German-speaking countries, in which both Mahler (see especially pp. 155-58, 194-97, 881 and 907) and Franz Werfel (pp. 47-48 and 50) are prominently discussed. Meant as response to Nazi allegations of Jewish "cultural parasitism" when first published in 1934, later expanded and updated in subsequent editions.

97. Mayer, Sigmund. *Die Wiener Juden: Kommerz, Kultur, Politik 1700-1900*. Wien, Berlin: R. Löwit, 1918. xii, 531 pp.
History of the Jewish community in Vienna from 1700 to 1900, documenting activity in politics, business and

culture. Straightforwardly chronological narrative, very extensive although not documented in a scholarly manner.

98. Rozenblit, Marsha L. *The Jews of Vienna, 1867-1914: Assimilation and Identity.* SUNY Series in Modern Jewish History. Ed. by Paul E. Hyman and Deborah Dash Moore. Albany, N.Y.: State University of New York Press, 1983. xvii, 284 pp. ISBN 0-87395-844-6 (hardbound), 0-87395-845-4 (paper).
Exhaustive statistical study of the Jews in Vienna during Mahler's time, exploring the controversy between assimilationists and nationalists and surveying the socioprofessional lives of the majority. Points out the futility of the actions of assimilationists in view of the prevailing antisemitic attitude of the Austrian society. Emphasizes conversion and intermarriage of Mahler and others as examples. Extensive bibliography of other sources on the subject.

99. Tietze, Hans. *Die Juden Wiens: Geschichte--Wirtschaft --Kultur.* Leipzig, Wien: E.P. Tal, 1933. 301 pp.
Chronicles the history of the Jews of Vienna from the Middle Ages to the early twentieth century. Shows the face of the community by an insider and notes achievements of individuals in finance, medicine, politics and culture. The section "Die Ära des Nationalismus" profiles Mahler, Freud, Herzl and others in the context of the political movements in Vienna in their time.

Jews in Music

100. Batka, Richard. "Das Jüdische bei Gustav Mahler." *Kunstwart* 23 (2. Juliheft 1910): 97-98.
An early discussion of Mahler as "Man on the Margin" between Jewish and German creative standards in music, addressing rationally the "theories" proposed by Rudolf Louis (see no. 170 below). By a musicologist/critic who was a frequent observer of Mahler as conductor and composer.

101. Berl, Heinrich. "Gustav Mahler." *Das Judentum in der Musik.* Stuttgart, Berlin, Leipzig: Deutsche Verlagsanstalt, 1926, pp. 153-67.
Considers question of Judaism in the style of Mahler's music with particular reference to other musicologists

including Arno Nadel, Max Brod and Paul Bekker. Places Mahler in historical perspective with other Jewish composers. Pro-semitic, an answer to the Nazis before they even came to power.

102. Berl, Heinrich. "Zum Problem einer jüdischen Musik, I: Gustav Mahler." *Der Jude* 7 (1923): 309-20. Discusses the "assimilated" Jewish composer and his contribution to the overall profile of Jews in music. See also Berl's book *Das Judentum in der Musik* (no. 101 above), for which this essay is an early germ seed. Concludes that Mahler was heir to Jewish sociocultural influence without necessarily showing Jewish stylistic characteristics in his compositional techniques.

103. Bloch, Ernst. "Philosophie der Musik." *Geist der Utopie*. Berlin: Paul Cassirer, 1923, pp. 43-193. French version: *L'Esprit de l'Utopie*. Traduit par Anne-Marie Lang et Catherine Piron-Audard. Paris: Gallimard, 1977. 344 pp.
Section "Strauss, Mahler, Bruckner" (pp. 82-89 of the original German version of this book) was also published as an article in *Die Musik* 15 (1923), pp. 664-70. Discusses the three composers and their roles in the history of Germanic music, considering the question of "Jewish" vs. "German" character of their music. Along the way, Bloch overturns the prevailing opinions of what is Jewish or German in music characteristic of that time, even suggesting that the character of Mahler's music is more German than Jewish, that of Bruckner and Strauss the opposite! The section "Melismatische Depeschen aus fernem Hauptquartier" from this essay was reprinted in *Gustav Mahler* (1966), pp. 59-60 (see no. 7, above).

104. Brod, Max. *Gustav Mahler: Beispiel einer deutschjüdischen Symbiose*. Von Gestern zum Morgen, 13. Frankfurt am Main: Ner Tamid, 1961. 30 pp.
An argument for Mahler as an "assimilated Jewish composer," counterweight to the extensive corpus of Nazi literature which attempted to isolate Mahler for purposes of political propaganda. Well thought out and relevant. Influential in connection with other discussions of Mahler's sociohistorical background and how it affected his work.

105. Brod, Max. "Gustav Mahlers jüdische Melodien." *Anbruch* 2 (1920): 378-79.
Brief, early essay on the "Jewish" character of melody in Mahler's works; later, in other writings, Brod seems to have altered his theories and concentrated on Mahler's Jewish identity as a social rather than strictly musical phenomenon.

106. Brod, Max. *Die Musik Israels*. Tel Aviv: Zionist Educational Dept., 1951. Rev. Ausgabe mit einem 2. Teil von Yehuda Walter Cohen ("Werden und Entwicklung der Musik in Israel") Kassel: Bärenreiter, 1976. 164 pp. ISBN 3-7618-0513-6.
English version: *Israel's Music*. Transl. by Toni Volcani. Tel Aviv: WIZO Zionist Education Dept., 1951. viii, 62 pp.
Discussion of Mahler in the context of music among Jews, by a Jewish nationalist who argued for Jewish character of Mahler's music—ironic reply to the Nazis who argued the same thing to discredit Mahler.

107. Brod, Max und Felix Weltsch, hrsg. *Zionismus als Weltanschauung*. Moravska Ostrava, Czechoslovakia: R. Färber, 1925. 185 pp.
Includes two essays by Brod in this collection, "Gustav Mahlers IX. Symphonie" (pp. 108-11) and "Zum Problem der jüdischen Musik" (pp. 96-107).

108. Cohen, Maxwell Tillman. *The Jews in Music*. New York: Order of Sons of Zion, 1939. 22 pp.
Brief discussion of Jews as composers and performers, written as counter-argument to the ideas advanced at that period by the Nazis. Lucid, but unfortunately limited in scope, therefore not as effective as other pro-semitic essays written at that time.

109. Engel de Janosi, Joseph (*pseud., J.E. de Sinoja*). *Das Antisemitentum in der Musik*. Zürich, Leipzig, Wien: Amalthea, 1933. 285 pp.
An extended, thoughtful discussion of antisemitism in musical circles in the nineteenth century, with particular emphasis on rebuttal to theories promulgated by Wagner vis-à-vis his relations with Mendelssohn and Meyerbeer. A voice of reason about Jews in musical culture in general, published deliberately as answer to antisemitic junk pouring out of Germany at same time. Well documented for its time and position in

contrast to Nazi ephemera, not to mention Wagner's original essay *Das Judentum in der Musik* (see no. 185, below).

109a. Filler, Susan M. "Mahler as a Jew in the Literature." *Dika Caecilia: Essays for Dika Newlin, November 22, 1988.* Ed. by Theodore Albrecht. Parkville, Missouri: Park College, 1988, pp. 65-85.
Explores the pro- and antisemitic literature profiling Mahler from the standpoint of his Jewish identity as person and composer. Considers the limited question of his musical style with reference to the wider question of Mahler's entire Jewish personal orientation, and summarizes the background and views of those who supported or vilified Mahler with respect to their own connections with him and his music. Beginning of an extensive study of the history of Mahler's role in the writings of Jews and antisemites from his lifetime to the present.

110. Fischer, Theodor. "Aus Gustav Mahlers Jugendzeit." *Deutsche Heimat* 7 (1931): 264-68.
Contribution to controversy about Mahler's background as German, Bohemian or Jew, opting for pro-German point of view. Motivated by changing ethnic patterns after political shifts following World War I, but a minority view hotly contested by the Nazis a few years later. Might have carried more weight if written closer to time of of author's original friendship with Mahler when both were young, but outdated by time of writing.

111. Fraenkel, Josef, ed. *The Jews of Austria: Essays on their Life, History and Destruction.* London: Vallentine Mitchell, 1967, 1970. xv, 585 pp. ISBN 0-853-03000-6 (1967 ed.), 0-853-03045-6 (1970 ed.).
Series of thirty-four essays on various aspects of the history of the Jewish community in Austria from the Renaissance to the Nazi era, with particular emphasis on their professional contributions and sociopolitical status from the last half of the nineteenth century forward. Of special interest are "Jews in Austrian Music" by Peter Gradenwitz (pp. 17-24), "Three Austrian Jews in German Literature: Schnitzler, Zweig, Herzl" by Harry Zohn (pp. 67-82), "Jews in Austrian Journalism" by Richard Grunberger (pp. 83-96), "Jewish Women in Austrian Culture" by Hilde Spiel (pp. 97-110),

"Seeds of a Noble Inheritance" by O.O. Dutch (pp. 177-93), "Prag--Wien--Erinnerungen" by Max Brod (pp. 241-42) and "The Development of Political Antisemitism in Austria" by P[eter] G.J. Pulzer (pp. 429-44). All these essays view Mahler and many of his close associates in Vienna at the turn of the century and underscore his socioprofessional ties to the Jewish community even after his own conversion to Catholicism.

112. Goldblatt, David. "Would the World Benefit by the Assimilation of the Jew? The Jewish Contribution to Music." *Jewish Forum* 9 (1926): 551-54.
    Discusses the problem of the Jewish musician in a society of assimilation, not from the point of view of a historian of music but of the Jews. Author was known as a Jewish nationalist who published books and articles from the first decade of this century to his death in the 1940s. Most of his known contributions to the literature dealt with Jewish identity in linguistic and societal contexts, but this is a rare occasion when he applied his arguments to the area of music as an expression of the Jews as a people. Cited in the musical literature only by Sendrey and seldom noted, but worth study.

113. Gradenwitz, Peter. "Gustav Mahler and Arnold Schoenberg." *Leo Baeck Institute Year Book*. London: East and West Library, 1960, pp. 262-84. Reprinted N.P.: Ktav, 1976, pp. 241-65.
    Compares and contrasts Mahler and Schoenberg in their attitudes to their identity as Jews, less in terms of compositional style than in their philosophical search for the answer. Gradenwitz suggests that, while Mahler and Schoenberg both questioned the meaning of their Jewish status, Schoenberg found an answer satisfactory to him whereas Mahler did not. A sympathetic study coming as a welcome counterbalance to the earlier barrage of Nazi hate literature condemning both composers.

114. Gradenwitz, Peter. *Ha-Musikah be-Yisrael*. . . . [The Music of Israel from its Beginning to the Present Day.] Jerusalem: Rubin Mass, 1945. 198 pp. Second ed. 1955, 254 pp.
    English version: *The Music of Israel: Its Rise and Growth Through 5000 Years*. New York: W.W. Norton, 1949. 334 pp.

German version: *Die Musikgeschichte Israels: von den biblischen Anfängen bis zum modernen Staat.* Übersetzung aus dem Englischen. Kassel, New York: Bärenreiter, 1961. 240 pp. ISBN 3-7618-0524-X.
History of music among the Jews, including liturgical, folk and concert and opera music, tracing influences from the cultures among which it lived. The music of Mahler is discussed as a phenomenon of the time and society in which he wrote his works rather than scanned for "Jewish" traits in the melodies--a wise course. Discussion of Mahler in the German version of this book, the most current, is primarily found on pp. 116-19, 125-33.

115. Gradenwitz, Peter. "Musik der Juden--Jüdische Musik." *Jüdische Rundschau* 39 (1934): March 16, p. 9; April 5, p. 14; August 17, p. 9.
Discusses the distinction between music of a "Jewish" character and music "by Jews" who are "assimilated," i. e. Jewish nationalism vs. Jewish cosmopolitanism as manifested in musical terms. Particularly important as this discussion was published at a time when Nazi writers were denying such distinctions and condemning all Jewish musical professionals regardless of individual orientation.

* Hajdu, André. "Réflexion sur la judaité de Gustav Mahler." *Colloque 1985*: 101-07.
Full citation under no. 5 above. Considers Mahler as a Jew in the antisemitic climate of the time and place in which he lived, and the emotional effect of that atmosphere on his compositions.

116. Heskes, Irene, comp. *The Resource Book of Jewish Music: a Bibliographical and Topical Guide to the Book and Journal Literature and Program Materials.* Musical Reference Collection, 3. Westport, Connecticut and London: Greenwood Press, 1983. xiv, 302 pp. ISBN 0-313-23251-2.
Selective annotated bibliography covering many subjects from Jewish liturgical and folk music to the lives and work of Jewish composers and musicologists. Includes books, articles and musical collections. Information about Mahler best used in conjunction with Sendrey's earlier monumental *Bibliography of Jewish Music* (see no. 140 below).

117. Holde, Artur. *Jews in Music: From the Age of Enlightenment to the Present.* London: Peter Owen; New York: Philosophical Library, 1959. xi, 364 pp. See Chapter 7, "Composers," especially pp. 75-81, and Chapter 17, "The Ideological Conflict: Antagonism against Jewish Music and Musicians," pp. 292-308. In these chapters/subsections, Holde discusses Mahler as heir to the society which fostered Jewish assimilation (*not* as Jewish nationalist) and the antisemitic movement in musical circles from Wagner to the Third Reich. Thoughtful. Good select bibliography.

118. Holländer, Hans. "Gustav Mahler." *MQ* 17 (1931): 449-63. Translated by Theodore Baker. Outlines Mahler's life and work and discusses how one fed into the other; attempts denial of "Jewish influence" even on Mahler's character and circumstances, and ignores the musical connection with Mahler's Jewish identity (if any).

119. *The Jews of Czechoslovakia: Historical Studies and Surveys.* Philadelphia: Jewish Publication Society of America; New York: Society for the History of Czechoslovak Jews, 1968-84. 3 vols. Monumental compendium of essays on the history of the Jewish community in Bohemia, Moravia and Czechoslovakia, from the Austrian Empire to post-World War II. Many of the contributors are scholars whose names are cited elsewhere in this bibliography for other work in this field, as specialists in music, literature, history and law. The following essays are of special interest: (Volume I), "The Jews between Czechs and Germans in the Historic Lands, 1848-1918" by Ruth Kestenberg-Gladstein (pp. 21-71) and "Music" by Paul Nettl (pp. 539-58), as well as "Participation in German Literature" by Harry Zohn (pp. 468-522). In Volume II is a single essay, "Realism and Romanticism: Observations on the Jewish Intelligentsia of Bohemia and Moravia" by Felix Weltsch (pp. 440-54). The first two essays in Volume I and the one in Volume II are variously concerned with the sociopolitical conditions in which Mahler and other musical and nonmusical professionals functioned; the essay by Nettl covers the period from the late nineteenth century to the post-World War II reconstruction. The essay by Zohn not only gives valuable information on the work of Franz Werfel but on other important writers well known to literary and musical historians

of the period, including Kafka, Teweles, Stefan and Brod. Volume III includes an essay "Terezín," by Zdenek Lederer (pp. 104-64) which, while not focusing on the musical aspects of life in the camp during the Third Reich, provides considerable information in that connection as a basis for extended research which has since been taken up by Karas (see no. 122 below). The essay on Terezín covers a time period somewhat later than the other essays in the previous volumes, a fact which is characteristic of the contributions in the third volume in general; while not involved with Mahler and his associates, it is relevant to the subject as a continuation of the story of musical endeavor in the country as handed down from one generation to the next (and the leaders of this endeavor left surviving relatives whose names today come full circle in their contribution to present-day Mahler literature).

120. Kahan, Salomon. *La emoción de la música*. México D.F.: Editorial Independencia, 1936. 336 pp.
Curious history of music from Bach to Chávez composed of series of brief essays rambling in various directions, including biographical sketches of composers and performers, analyses of individual works and surveys of musical types in sociohistorical context. Two essays are of interest to Mahler specialists: "Gustavo Mahler, compositor con problemas cósmicos" (pp. 139-42), which surveys the emotional impact of Mahler's works and how his personality influenced them, and "Compositores hebreos de la historia de la música" (pp. 253-62), a pro-semitic study of Jewish composers with special attention to Mendelssohn, Meyerbeer, Rubinstein, Mahler, Schoenberg and Bloch.

121. Kaiser, Joachim. "Jüdische Komponisten--Tradition und Vorurteil." *Porträts deutsch-jüdischer Geistesgeschichte*. Hrsg. von Thilo Koch. Köln: DuMont Schauberg, 1961, pp. 127-53.
Considers Jewish composers, especially of the "emancipated" era, with special attention to Mahler and Schoenberg and the society in which they lived and built their careers. Couched in series of essays by various writers chronicling the assimilated Jew in society from Moses Mendelssohn to Sigmund Freud.

122. Karas, Joža. *Music in Terezín 1941-1945*. New York: Beaufort Books (in association with Pendragon Press),

1985. xxvii, 223 pp. ISBN 0-8253-0287-0.
A landmark study of music performed in a major concentration camp established by the Nazis. Demonstrates that the inmates of Terezín (Theresienstadt) actively sought to perform music banned officially in the Third Reich, including music of Mahler. This book should be the cornerstone for further research into the lives of musicians proscribed and imprisoned by the Nazis, which included relatives and colleagues of Mahler who sought to promulgate his music under nearly hopeless conditions.

123. Landau, Anneliese. *The Contribution of Jewish Composers to the Music of the Modern World*. Cincinnati: National Federation of Temple Sisterhoods, 1946. 84 pp. Rev. ed. New York: National Federation of Temple Sisterhoods, 1966. 94 pp.
Lists seventy-two Jewish composers of the nineteenth and twentieth centuries in six sections intended for adult study sessions. Mahler is discussed in Section I, "The Great Heritage of Romanticism" (pp. 7-9, 11-12, 13-14 and 15-16), which include a short essay, proposed subjects for discussion, bibliography and discography respectively. Mahler is also cited in the essay on Schoenberg (pp. 31-35) in section III, "The Modern School." Author well known for extensive writing on Jewish music and musicians in Berlin periodicals 1928-38, including "Gustav Mahler, der Unzeitgemässe" in *Almanach des Kulturbundes Deutscher Juden* (1935). In 1938 she contributed an essay to *Musica Hebraica* (published by the World Center for Jewish Music in Palestine); she emigrated shortly after to the United States, where she continued her writings in American and Brazilian periodicals. This book is, therefore, the culmination of many years of writing short pieces on Jewish music and musicians, which qualifies author as a working educator in the cause of Jewish musicians.

124. Lang, Paul Henry. "Background Music for *Mein Kampf*." *Saturday Review of Literature* 28 (January 20, 1945): 5-9.
Discusses the embodiment of antisemitism and German nationalism in the works and life of Wagner and draws direct line of these principles and their application by the Nazis. Cynical view of Wagner as prophet of destructional values and his effect on succeeding generations of musical and political thought, especially relevant at time of publication near end of Nazi era.

125. Lea, Henry A. *Gustav Mahler: Man on the Margin.* Modern German Studies, 15. Bonn: Bouvier Verlag Herbert Grundmann, 1985. viii, 157 pp. ISBN 3-416-01881-8.
Concise study of Mahler as "transitional" man and musician under the conditions of his time, and after. Heavily documented from existing musical and historical literature. Essential reading.

126. Lea, Henry. "Mahler: German Romantic or Jewish Satirist?" *Jews and Germans from 1860 to 1933: the Problematic Symbiosis.* Ed. by David Bronsen. Heidelberg: Carl Winter Universitätsverlag, 1979, pp. 288-305. ISBN 3-533-02640-X, 3-533-02641-8.
Precursor of same author's book cited above as no. 125. Focuses on Mahler's "marginal" Jewish-German status as an emotional phenomenon. Sensitive, pointed and concise, benefits from observation of Jews in historical context at time of Mahler and later.

127. Lea, Henry A. "Mahler: Man on the Margin." *Views and Reviews of Modern German Literature: Festschrift for Adolf D. Klarmann.* Ed. by Karl S. Weimar. Munich: Delp, 1974, pp. 92-104. ISBN 3-7689-0124-6.
Precursor of same author's book cited above as no. 125. Study of Mahler as Jewish-Czech-Austrian phenomenon. Companion germ-seed with no. 126 above.

128. Levy, Simon. *Das Judentum in der Musik: eine kritisch-historische Betrachtung.* Erfurt: Gutenberg-Druckerei Stolzenberg, 1930. 62 pp.
Direct rebuttal to Wagner's attacks in *Das Judentum in der Musik*, taking up not only his points on Jewish musicians of his time but carrying them forward to Mahler and Schoenberg. Not a musical analysis but a philosophical discussion referring to other musicologists' views (especially Paul Nettl, Heinrich Berl etc.).

129. List, Kurt. "Mahler: Father of Modern Music--He Led the Break with Romanticism." *Commentary* 10 (July 1950): 42-48.
Studies Mahler as a musico-cultural *Januskopf*, a product of his society (Jewish identity in the Austrian Empire) and considers the effect of his environment on the style of his music. Limited, but an interesting ground for later writers including Eric Werner and Peter Gradenwitz, who explored the subject extensively.

130. Nadel, Arno. "Jüdische Musik." *Der Jude* 7 (1923): 227-36.
   Attempts a definition of Jewish music from pro-semitic point of view, a focus of all of this writer's research over a period of twenty years. Interesting comparison with Brod et al. Author continued his research into the 1940s and was said to have successfully concealed his papers when taken to Auschwitz and gassed in 1943.

131. Newlin, Dika. "Alienation and Gustav Mahler." *Reconstructionist* 25 (May 15, 1959): 21-25.
   Early discussion of Mahler as "man on the margin"--Jew caught between German and Bohemian and thus living precariously while not reaping any benefit from his Jewish identity. Discusses his position as Jew while a student in Vienna, then considers influence of both Jewish and Christian friends in his conversion, finally considers his crisis of conscience in the maintenance of ties with his Jewish identity. Questions of faith in his music are also discussed, especially with reference to the *Symphony no. 2* and the *Symphony no. 8* (in terms of both texts and musical forms, including the chorale-like setting of *Urlicht*) and the *Symphony no. 8* as "Missa sine Domine" as proposed by Reik. Concludes that the critical controversy about Mahler's work has been more emotional than objective with special reference to the antisemitic arguments of Rudolf Louis and the defensive rebuttals of Specht. Advocates tracing Jewish melodic types in Mahler's music, referring to Eric Werner's argument for Hasidic connection of the main melody in *Ablösung im Sommer*. Summation that religious conflict is actually an enriching factor in Mahler's music.

132. Ocadlik, Mirko. "Sila židovstvi v hudbě." [The influence of Judaism in music.] *Kalendař česke-židovský* 48 (1927-28): 86-92.
   Discussion in Czech about "Jewish" musical traits in the works of Mahler, Bizet (whose *wife* was Jewish) and Schoenberg. Well-intentioned, but doubtful if it succeeds in light of major stylistic differences among composers profiled.

133. Ravina, Menashe [Manasseh Rabinowitz]. "Gustav Mahler." *Musika'im me-Yisrael*. [Musicians of Israel.] Tel Aviv: Hegeh, 1942, pp. 41-47.
   Discussion in Hebrew of Mahler as composer and conductor in the framework of his Jewish identity. In seven

sections devoted to various subjects, the earlier ones considering his work as conductor (especially from Budapest through Hamburg and finally Vienna), the last section touching on his compositions. This is the last of five biographical sketches on musicians of Jewish background, the other four being Mendelssohn, Offenbach, Anton Rubinstein and Joseph Joachim. By musicologist-composer who published actively in Palestine/Israel during the 1930s and 1940s, answering the poison with which German-language writers were flooding the market at that time. Modest, but an early example of a trend which has mushroomed since that time, and published at a time when there was little literature about Mahler in any language but German.

134. Reich, Willi. "Musik und Rasse." *23*, no. 8/9 (23. Februar 1933): 19-29.
Early rebuttal to Richard Eichenauer's book of the same name (see no. 157 below) which had been published in the previous year. Daring, as was characteristic of everything author did as editor of *23*; only known direct answer to Eichenauer's bad book, refreshing compared to citations by German musicologists who appeared to depend on Eichenauer's arguments to a ridiculous degree.

135. *Richard Wagner und das Judentum: ein Beitrag zur Kulturgeschichte unserer Zeit, von einem Unparteiischen.* Elberfeld: Sam. Lucas, 1869. 16 pp.
Rebuttal to Wagner's essay *Das Judentum in der Musik*, refuting Wagner's racial-musical theories. Early, anonymous entry in debate pursued through and beyond Mahler's time to the Nazi era, embraced by associates of Mahler and Alma on both sides.

136. Ringer, Alexander. "Jewish Music--Old Problems, New Dilemmas." *Proceedings of the World Congress on Jewish Music (Jerusalem, 1978)*. Ed. by Judith Cohen. Tel Aviv: Institute for the Translation of Hebrew Literature, 1982, pp. 251-64. ISBN 965-255-016-7.
Reconsiders the question of criteria by which music is considered "Jewish," especially with reference to "assimilated" Jewish composers including Mendelssohn, Mahler and Schoenberg. Worth comparing with the theories advanced by Max Brod in *Mahler: Beispiel einer deutsch-jüdischen Symbiose* (see no. 104 above).

137. Rothmüller, Aron Marko. *Die Musik der Juden: Versuch einer geschichtlichen Darstellung ihrer Entwicklung und ihres Wesens*. Zürich: Pan Verlag, 1951. xii, 193 pp.
English version: *The Music of the Jews: An Historical Appreciation*. Transl. by H.S. Stevens. New York: A.S. Barnes; New York: Beechurst Press, 1954, 1960. xv, 254 pp. London: Valentine, Mitchell and Co., 1953. Revised ed. South Brunswick: T. Yoseloff, 1967. 320 pp.
Considers the question of Jewish identity among composers from Biblical times to the middle of the twentieth century. In Chapter 12, "Judaism in Music," focus is especially directed on the so-called "assimilated" composers of the nineteenth and early twentieth centuries, including Mendelssohn, Mahler and Schoenberg, and whether their music shows any "Jewish" characteristics. Author concludes that Mahler's music is not "Jewish" in style.

138. Sachs, Joseph. "Gustav Mahler." *Beauty and the Jew*. London: Edward Goldston, 1937, pp. 225-36.
Strange and very interesting subjective assessment of Mahler as man and Jew with reference to the creation of symphonic music in the Beethoven line. Not wholly uncritical of Mahler as composer, but ultimately positive and unique, neither technical nor maudlin. Within the context of Jewish conceptions of life and self-expression (music, art, dance and literature), conditioned by Nietzschean and Wagnerian philosophy of the nineteenth and early twentieth centuries.

139. Salesky, Gdal. *Famous Musicians of a Wandering Race: Biographical Sketches of Outstanding Figures of Jewish Origin in the Musical World*. New York: Bloch, 1927. xiv, 463 pp.
Revised ed.: *Famous Musicians of Jewish Origin*. New York: Bloch, 1949, 1951. xvi, 716 pp.
Includes basic summary of Mahler's life and works (pp. 100-06). Not entirely free of factual error but useful for laymen in its time when such summaries were rather rare and usually negative anyway.

140. Sendrey, Alfred. *Bibliography of Jewish Music*. New York: Columbia University Press; London: Geoffrey Cumberlege, 1951. Reprinted New York: Kraus Reprint Co., 1969. xii, 404 pp.

Comprehensive factual listings on Jewish music and literature on the subject, including music, composers and librettists. Covers classical, liturgical and folk music. Indispensable to study of Mahler and sections on literature concerning Jewish composers of classical music, and antisemitic propaganda from the Nazi era and earlier. Bibliography includes both books and articles, including sigla indicating the source of the listing located by Sendrey himself. A monumental source.

141. Stein, Leon. "Jewish Creativity in Music." *Reconstructionist* 42 (April 1976): 13-18.
Surveys the Jewish composer and his various roles in the history of music, whether as assimilationist (Mendelssohn, Mahler and Schoenberg) or as Jewish nationalist (Bloch and Sulzer). A cogent answer to Nazi propaganda against Jews in music, based on an unbiased view of the Jew in historical perspective, with the advantage of the passage of time since the Nazi era.

142. Stein, Leon. *The Racial Thinking of Richard Wagner*. New York: Philosophical Library, 1950. xiv, 252 pp.
An objective, thoughtful view of German nationalism and antisemitism from the lifetime of Wagner to the Third Reich, showing how the concepts affected the work of many composers in the German-speaking world. Indispensable as a rational perspective placing antisemitic hate literature from Wagner to the Third Reich where it belongs, by an American composer and historian of music in society.

143. Stuckenschmidt, Hans Heinz. "Musik unter Hitler." *Forum* 9, no. 108 (Dezember 1962): 510-13, & 10, no. 109 (Januar 1963): 44-48.
Surveys the musical orientation of the Third Reich, including music cancelled by Nazi censors as well as music passed for performance and publication. Mahler's name comes up in connection with music banned.

144. Tramer, Hans. "Ungenannte und umgetaufte: Gustav Mahler und seine Zeit." *Bulletin für die Mitglieder der Gesellschaft des Leo Baeck Instituts*, Nr. 10 (1960): 130-50.
A serious discussion of the prevailing climate in the Jewish community in the Austrian Empire during Mahler's

time and about the phenomenon of conversion as a response to that climate. This discussion of Mahler's particular case was preceded by a brief article in the preceding number of the same periodical, "Österreichisches Judentum," which set the stage for the present article.

145. Weisser, Albert. *Bibliography of Publications and Other Resources on Jewish Music.* New York: National Jewish Music Council, 1969. 117 pp.
Useful as a limited resource on secondary sources about Jews in music. Best used in tandem with superior *Bibliography of Jewish Music* of Sendrey (see no. 140 above), as update information covering the seventeen years between the two publications.

146. Werner, Eric. "Felix Mendelssohn--Gustav Mahler: Two Borderline Cases of German-Jewish Assimilation." *Yuval* 4 (1982): 240-64.
A history of Jewish assimilation in romantic and postromantic Germany, from Abraham Mendelssohn (the father of the composer) to the beginning of the Nazi period, with special attention to comparison and contrast between Felix Mendelssohn and Gustav Mahler. More concerned with the societal dilemma among Jewish musicians than with individual examples of "Jewish" style, this article represents one area of emphasis in the two-pronged research of this author, who is considered to be among the most influential of historians of Jewish music. An early example of this focus in the works of Werner was the essay "Gustav Mahlers Weg" in *Jüdische Rundschau* (18. Mai 1934). The other emphasis in the work of this author, which is concretely concerned with Jewish musical style, has been represented by "Typologie der Themen in der Wunderhorn-Symphonie Gustav Mahlers" (*Musicologica Austriaca*, 1985) and "Identity and Character of Jewish Music" (*Proceedings of the World Congress on Jewish Music, Jerusalem, 1978*). Werner's opinions are definitive and probing whether he is concerned with the societal history of Jews in music or analyzing examples of music for Jewish character.

Antisemitism (General)

147. Dreyer, Ernest Adolf, hrsg. *Deutsche Kultur im neuen Reich: Wesen, Aufgabe und Ziel der Reichskulturkammer.* Berlin: Schliessen, 1934. 138 pp.
    Best taken as fullbodied charter guidelines of the seven departments in the Reich Chamber of Culture, the first of which was the Reichsmusikkammer. The section covering the Music Department (pp. 45-57) includes three essays from its officials of which Richard Strauss was one. Rather more informative documentation than booklet by Irkowsky (see no. 166 below).

148. Dühring, Eugen. *Die Judenfrage als Frage der Racenschädlichkeit für Existenz: Sitte und Cultur der Völker.* Karlsruhe, Leipzig: H. Reuther, 1886. viii, 164 pp.
    Third edition, originally published as *Die Judentum als Rassen-Sitten- und Culturfrage* in 1881. Ersatz scientific observations of the Jews as "inferior race" and their role as such in society, culture, politics etc. Brief discussion of Jews in art, literature and music. Negative curiosity only useful as documentation of the atmosphere in which Mahler grew up and built his career, and as predecessor to deluge of Nazi junk.

Antisemitism in Music

149. Blessinger, Karl. *Mendelssohn, Meyerbeer, Mahler: Drei Kapitel Judentum in der Musik als Schlüssel zur Musikgeschichte des 19. Jahrhunderts.* Berlin: Bernhard Hahnefeld, 1939. 94 pp.
    Revised version: *Judentum und Musik: ein Beitrag zur Kultur- und Rassenpolitik.* Berlin: Bernhard Hahnefeld, 1944. 146 pp.
    Typical Nazi attempt to re-educate musical taste during the tenure of the Third Reich. Singles out Mendelssohn, Meyerbeer and Mahler for special opprobrium, ignoring established theories of continuity in music history in favor of critical dismissal on the basis of the composers' Jewish background. Untrustworthy, useful only as documentation of the function of Nazi musicologists in the changing taste in the course of musical history.

150. Blessinger, Karl. "Musik und Judentum." *Die Musik* 33 (1940): 48-52.

Nazi propaganda, a condensation of the theories posited a year earlier in *Mendelssohn, Meyerbeer, Mahler*; represents something of an interim stage between the first version of the book and its expanded and revised version of 1944 (see no. 149 above).

151. Blume, Friedrich. "Musik und Rasse: Grundfragen einer musikalischen Rassenforschung." *Die Musik* 30 (1938): 736-48.
Precursor study of author's book *Das Rasseproblem in der Musik* published a year later (see no. 152 below). This rather extensive essay itself raises questions about the Nazis' racially biased theories of the history of music which other German musicologists did not consider relevant, and it should therefore be considered of more permanent interest than other German-Austrian musicological literature of the era.

152. Blume, Friedrich. *Das Rasseproblem in der Musik*. Wolfenbüttel, Berlin: Georg Kallmeyer, 1939. 86 pp.
Development of germ-seed planted by author in his article "Musik und Rasse" a year earlier (see no. 151 above). Discusses prevailing theories of racial influence on music with reference to earlier literature by Eichenauer, Moser, Müller-Blattau and others. Ultimately makes more sense than any of the others. Emphasizes positive aspects of German music without controversial judgements on proscribed non-Aryan music.

153. Bücken, Ernst. *Die Musik der Nationen*. Kroners Taschenausgabe, 131. Leipzig: A. Kroner, 1937. x, 494 pp.
Attempts to draw contrasts between Jewish and Aryan composers for the benefit of education in German musicgoing public during the Third Reich. Discussion of Mahler on pp. 438-41 unsatisfactory propaganda.

154. Bücken, Ernst. "Sinfonie und sinfonische Dichtung." *Führer und Probleme der neuen Musik*. Köln am Rhein: P.J. Tonger, 1924, pp. 20-54.
Relates Mahler as symphonist to the nineteenth-century programmatic tradition of Brahms, Bruckner, Liszt and Strauss as composers of symphonies and symphonic poems. The discussion of Mahler, on pp. 34-40, focuses on him as the "racial" recipient of conflicting traditions: intellectualism, iron, nervous energy, triviality, and ultimately concludes that he stands as only a minor

figure in comparison with other composers cited. Ultimately this discussion is unrealistic and is valuable only as a historical document showing the general assessment of Mahler in the generation after his death. Author continued down the same path in his later writings (see no. 153 above for an example).

155. Damisch, Heinrich. "Die Verjudung des österreichischen Musiklebens." *Der Weltkampf* 15 (1938): 255-61.
Antisemitic propaganda documenting the role of Jews in the history of Austrian music--composers, conductors, musicologists and soloists. Mahler and his circle figure prominently in this critical condemnation. Useful only as historical document illustrating changes of public taste with respect to Mahler's music from period to period.

156. Ehlers, Paul. "Die Musik und Adolf Hitler." *NZfM* 106 (1939): 356-62.
Portrays the guidelines adopted by the Nazi Party which affected musical consumption in the Third Reich, showing Hitler's tastes as a touchstone for selection of composers whose works were acceptable (Wagner, Strauss, Bruckner) and those whose works were banned (Mahler, Mendelssohn, Schoenberg, Hindemith). Unreliable as an index of musical value but fascinating as a study of distorted thinking insofar as it affects objective musical judgment.

157. Eichenauer, Richard. *Musik und Rasse*. München: J.F. Lehmann, 1932. 286 pp. 2. ed. 1937, 323 pp.
A prime example of Nazi taste in music, showing not only the bias in musical judgement affecting performance and publication of music during the Third Reich, but also the manner in which the Nazis rewrote musical history to conform with their views of musical quality. Eichenauer was more distinguished for his service to the SS than to the musical community, which is also a trenchant comment on the sort of people dictating musical taste in that period.

158. Friedrich, Julius. "Der Jude als Musikfabrikant." *Die Musik* 28 (1936): 428-30.
Politically biased study arguing that Jewish composers including Mendelssohn, Mahler and others did not write original music of value but "stole" music from German composers or wrote music that was worthless. Utterly

unreliable in terms of musical value but worth observing in historical context and comparing with unprejudiced nonpolitical assessments of music by Jews.

159. Fritsch, Theodor. "Das Judentum in der Musik." *Handbuch der Judenfrage: die wichtigen Tatsachen zur Beurteilung des jüdischen Volkes.* Leipzig: Hammer, 1939, pp. 313-27.
History of the Jews by a Nazi, predictably biased and inaccurate; section on music lists Jewish composers, conductors, performers, musicologists and others with the intention of "purifying" German musical culture by exclusion of all Jewish musical influence. Suspect in any case as author quotes unreliable forebears including Eichenauer as support for his views.

160. Frotscher, Gotthold. "Aufgaben und Ausrichtung der musikalischen Rassenstilforschung." *Rasse und Musik.* Hrsg. von Guido Waldmann. Berlin-Lichterfelde: Chr. Friedrich Nieweg, 1939, pp. 102-12.
Practical plan for promulgation of the Nazi view of music in the educational system of the Third Reich, systematically introducing the tenets basic to teaching the superiority of German composers and the inferiority of Jewish composers including Mahler. Useful as historical document only, in combination with Eichenauer and other books used as texts in the German and Austrian schools of the period.

161. Ganzer, Karl Richard. *Richard Wagner und das Judentum.* Forschungen der Judenfrage, 3. Hamburg: Hanseatische Verlagsanstalt, 1938. 36 pp.
Draws the obvious connection between Wagner's antisemitic essays and their embellishment during the Third Reich. Useful only as documentation of changing attitudes in the public affecting reaction to music of Mahler and other Jewish composers.

162. Gerigk, Herbert. "10 Jahre nationalsozialistisches Musikleben." *Die Musik* 35 (1943): 104-05.
Summary of the results of the Nazi policies in music over ten years, covering the major trends in programming and education and the 'Aryanization' movement.

163. Girschner, Otto. "Juden in der Musik." *Repetitorium der Musikgeschichte.* 11. Auflage. Köln: P.J. Tonger, 1941, pp. 350-411.

This book was a basic musical resource tool of encyclopedic scope, extensively revised in many different editions. The ninth edition, the first to be published during the Nazi era, introduced this essay which was included in all subsequent editions. The essay, as might be expected, is really a plain listing of Jewish composers, performers and musicologists useful for furthering the Nazi purpose of elimination of such persons --whether alive or dead--from German musical life. The length of this article is, in itself, a salient comment on the importance of the Jews in German musical life.

164. Gräner, Georg. "Deutsche und undeutsche Musik." *Die Musik* 26 (1933): 90-93.
Attempts to formulate guidelines for distinction between music by German and non-German composers according to theories of Nazi musicologists. Unconvincing as a theory of musico-historical style, but useful as a historical document showing the manner in which music of Jewish composers was systematically condemned by the Nazis through formulation of guidelines for their purposes. Particularly sad example of the change of views by single musicologist as this author was responsible for good early analysis of *Das Lied von der Erde* (see no. 801 below).

165. Grunsky, Karl. *Richard Wagner und die Juden*. München: Deutscher Volks Verlag, 1920. 96 pp.
Early warning sign of the propaganda which flooded the market during the Nazi era. Relies heavily on Wagner's nationalist and antisemitic literature and applies his theories to literature as well as music. While Mahler is not cited, the discussions of earlier Jewish composers are an obvious predecessor for Blessinger, Eichenauer and others.

166. Irkowsky, Rudolf. *Judentum und Musik: Liste der jüdischen Komponisten als Unterlage für die Säuberungsaktion auf dem Gebiete der Musik*. Linz: Gauleitung der NSDAP Oberdonau, n.d. 16 pp.
Bare-bones list of Jewish composers and performers compiled by nonmusician technocrat for purposes of quick reference in purging process of concert programs etc. Makes other such references including Rock and Bruckner, Stengel and Gerigk and Moser look positively erudite by comparison. Not dated, but probably from early period after the *Anschluss* of 1938.

167. Josewsky, Erwin. "Musik." *Rassenpolitische Unterrichtspraxis*. Hrsg. von Ernst Dobers und Kurt Higelke. Leipzig: Julius Klinkhart, 1938, pp. 311-38.
Introduces methods of teaching music in the schools according to Nazi principles. Briefly considers subject matter adopted and avoided in the classroom.

168. Landau, Ludwig. "Das jüdische Element bei Gustav Mahler." *Der Morgen* 12 (Mai 1936): 67-73.
Nazi trash, best taken as a counterpoint to the sympathetic commentary on Mahler's Jewish identity by Gradenwitz and Brod, in the continuing debate about how "Jewish" Mahler and his music really are.

169. Litterscheid, Richard. "Mendelssohn, Mahler und wir." *Die Musik* 28 (1936): 413-17.
Attempts to show why Mahler and Mendelssohn should be rejected as composers because they were "un-German." A short but deadly study useful only in the context of changing historical opinions concerning Mahler and Mendelssohn's music.

170. Louis, Rudolf. *Die deutsche Musik der Neuzeit*. München: Georg Müller, 1912. 337 pp.
Originally published as *Die deutsche Musik der Gegenwart* in Leipzig and München in 1909. Unsympathetic view of Mahler as composer or conductor, completely misjudging him; assesses him as heir to Bruckner but criticizes him as a failure because of his Jewish background. Useful only as documentation of prevailing attitude about Mahler in his time and immediately after, precursor of later Nazi attacks.

171. Mersmann, Hans. *Eine deutsche Musikgeschichte*. Potsdam, Berlin: Sans-Souci, 1934. xi, 523 pp.
Includes a short essay of which half is devoted to *Das Lied von der Erde* (showing an obvious attempt to inflate the prose with musical example). Brief discussion shows both the influence of the Nazi ideology and the tradition of labelling Mahler banal, empty and weak. Final assessment that Mahler appears to be the "runt of the German litter," comparable treatment being accorded to all Jewish composers discussed in this book.

172. Moser, Hans Joachim. *Musik Lexikon*. Berlin, Schöneberg: Max Hesse, 1935, 2. ed., 1943; Hamburg: Hans

Sikorski, 1951 (3. ed.), 1955 (4. ed.), 1964 (Ergänzungsband). 1. ed., 1005 pp.; 3. ed., 1354 pp.; 4. ed., 2 vols. comprising viii, 1482 pp. Ergänzungsband, viii, 287 pp.
Shows remarkable changes of content from edition to edition, obviously dependent on political fluctuations including the author's affiliation with the Nazi movement, the later growth in popularity of Mahler's music after World War II, etc. Perfunctory even in later editions compared with articles in British and French encyclopedias of same period, and virtually meaningless compared with Redlich's article in *MGG* ten years later.

173. Prieberg, Fred K. *Musik im NS-Staat.* Frankfurt am Main: Fischer Taschenbuch Verlag, 1982. 449 pp. ISBN 3-596-26901-6.
Narrative-style survey of musical life and official policy in the Third Reich, documenting the inclusion and exclusion of music and musicians with extensive quotations from archival sources. Differs from Wulf's *Die Musik im Dritten Reich* (see no. 187 below) in manner of approach to subject (Wulf having relied on heavy documentation with discreet editorial commentary) but equally valuable.

174. Raabe, Peter. *Die Musik im dritten Reich: Kulturpolitische Reden und Aufsätze.* Regensburg: Gustav Bosse, 1935. 93 pp.
Comprises five essays on various aspects of musical life according to the principles of the Nazi Party. Three, "Die Musik im dritten Reich," "Nationalismus, Internationalismus und Musik," and "Kultur und Gemeinschaft," are concerned with the principles of "German" and "un-German" music and the methods of application of these principles, focusing on exclusion of music by Jewish composers and the basis for such exclusion. While the principles are suspect, they are worth studying for the sake of historical perspective.

175. Rock, Christa Maria und Hans Brückner. *Judentum und Musik: mit dem ABC jüdischer und nichtarischer Musikbeflissener.* 2. Auflage. München: Hans Brückner, 1936. 248 pp. 3. Auflage bearbeitet und erweitert von Hans Brückner, 1938. 304 pp.
Lists blacklisted composers and performers for the purposes of defining the musical ideals advanced by the Nazis. Most entries are brief with little detail, but

some--including the entry on Mahler--are much more extensive. Unreliable in terms of content and viewpoint but worth observation for historical interest.

176. Rosenfeld, Paul. "Mahler." *Musical Portraits: Interpretations of Twenty Modern Composers.* New York: Harcourt, Brace and Howe, 1920; London: Kegan Paul, Trench and Trubner, 1922, pp. 205-22. Reprinted Freeport, New York: Books for Libraries Press, 1968.
Unsympathetic, shortsighted and often antisemitic critique of Mahler as man and composer, useful only as historical document exemplifying general public opinion of Mahler in the years following his death. Translate this into German and advance it fifteen years and it could almost have served as Nazi propaganda; at the very least, it is direct heir to theories proposed by Rudolf Louis.

177. Schmidt, Heinrich. "Die drei 'Grossen' M. (F. Mendelssohn, G. Mahler, G. Meyerbeer): zum Thema 'Die Juden in der Musik'." *Rheinische-Westfälische Zeitung,* Essen, 31. Mai 1943 (Nr. 267), p. 3.
Superficially tied to Blessinger's theories as expressed in no. 149. This article was published too long after the revised edition of Blessinger's book was issued to qualify as a simple review; Schmidt was presumably trying to make his own contribution to the Nazi cause. Very sad comedown from his fine dissertation of 1929 (see no. 727 below).

178. Schumann, Otto, hrsg. *Meyers Konzertführer: Orchestermusik und Instrumentalkonzerte.* Leipzig: Bibliographisches Institut, 1937, 1938. 541 pp.
Nazi-influenced account of various composers in chronological order, varying widely in depth and length according to the status of the composers and their works in the Nazi policies. Account of Mahler on pp. 384-86 is brief and dismisses his work without details about individual works or any musical examples, which appears the more unfortunate when compared with chapters on composers like Wagner, Bruckner and Strauss.

179. Schumann, Otto. "Neue Musik und Judentum." *Geschichte der deutschen Musik.* Leipzig: Bibliographisches Institut, 1940, pp. 386-95.
Added as an appendix to an established history of German music, for the purposes of Nazi propaganda, this

essay draws connections between Jewish composers including Mahler and Schoenberg and the "modernistic" trends in music condemned by the Nazis as "cultural bolshevist." Unreliable as musical valuation but important in historical context.

180. Sonner, Rudolf. "Kultur--Rasse--Musik." *Die Musik* 28 (1936): 402-07.
 Exemplifies the racial theories of the Nazis and applies them to qualitative judgement of the works of German and "un-German" composers. Sorts composers into categories for inclusion and exclusion of their works in concert programming. Biased, of course, as all Nazi propaganda on music was, in favor of composers including Wagner, Strauss, Orff and Bruckner, and against Mendelssohn, Mahler, Schoenberg and Hindemith among others; but important as an example of historical didactic criticism.

181. Stengel, Theophil und Herbert Gerigk. "Gustav Mahler." *Lexikon der Juden in der Musik: Veröffentlichungen des Instituts der NSDAP zur Erförschung der Judenfrage*. Berlin: Bernhard Hahnefeld, 1940, columns 168-71.
 Entry in a list of Jewish performers and composers compiled for purposes of furthering Nazi propaganda. Most entries in this dictionary are of brief duration, but the selection on Mahler and those on certain other major Jewish figures in music are unusually long, showing that the authors were making special efforts to discredit them. Of documentary historical interest only.

182. Storck, Karl. "Das Problem Mahler." *Die Musik der Gegenwart*. Sonderausgabe des 12. Buches der "Geschichte der Musik." 3. Auflage. Stuttgart: Muth'sche Verlagshandlung, 1919, pp. 144-57.
 Originally published in *Geschichte der Musik* (1904), later in 3rd ed. (1918), vol. 2, pp. 384-97. Various updatings between the different editions have not altered the fact that this is a shortsighted rehash of the German-vs.-Jewish arguments current in musical circles at least since the time of Wagner. While not dismissing Mahler entirely, Storck regards him as the product of his "race" in terms of musical value, i.e., an interpreter, not a creator, a fault which he considers common to all Jews in music. Self-righteous nonsense in the guise of scholarly assessment.

183. Trienes, Walter. *Musik im Gefahr: Selbstzeugnisse aus der Verfallszeit, ausgewählt und erläutert.* Von deutscher Musik, 53/54. Regensburg: Gustav Bosse, 1939. 146 pp.
Argues for the Nazi theory of music as an indicator of "racial purity."

184. *Verzeichnis jüdischer und nichtarischer Komponisten.* Graz: Gaupropagandaamt Steiermark, 1938. 32 pp.
List of composers on the Nazi blacklist, including Mendelssohn, Mahler and others. Basic, apparently compiled for use in redesigning programs in accordance with the Nazi guidelines; little propaganda, as this list speaks for itself. No credit given to author/compiler, which suggest that list was made by bureaucrat rather than musical professional (see similar list by Irkowsky, no. 166 above, for comparable example).

185. Wagner, Richard [pseud., Karl Freigedank]. "Das Judentum in der Musik." *NZfM* 33 (1850): 101-07, 109-12.
Expanded version under author's own name in *Gesammelte Schriften und Dichtungen.* Vol. 5. Leipzig: C.F.W. Siegel (R. Linnemann), 1907, pp. 66-85.
Notorious "political" document which set the tone for a widely held view of Jewish composers as cultural stepchildren. Adopted by nonmusicians through the period of the Third Reich and applied to qualitative judgement of the works of composers including Mendelssohn and Meyerbeer (who had been Wagner's inspiration when he wrote the original essay), Mahler and Schoenberg (who had not existed when the essay was written but were dragged into the controversy by extension of the principles after Wagner's time).

186. Welter, Friedrich. *Musikgeschichte im Umriss vom Urbeginn bis zur Gegenwart: mit besonderer Berücksichtigung der deutschen Musik seit 1900.* Lehrmeister-Bücherei, 1275/81. Leipzig: Nachmeister und Thal, 1939, 1943. 344 and 352 pp. respectively.
Nazi junk, purporting to be history of music, with obvious German nationalist bias. Discussion of Mahler on pp. 276-82 predictably negative as in all instances of German Jewish composers. Somewhat like Eichenauer's *Musik und Rasse* (see no. 157 above) but comparatively late as Eichenauer had arrived on the ground floor.

187. Wulf, Joseph, hrsg. *Musik im Dritten Reich: eine Doku-*

mentation. Gütersloh: Sigbert Mohn, 1963; Frankfurt-am-Main, Berlin, Wien: Ullstein, 1983. 501 pp. ISBN 3-548-33032-0.
A documentary collection of materials from the archives of the Third Reich and publications in musicological periodicals and books illustrating the musical policies adopted by the Nazis. Carefully compiled. An excellent introduction giving information not only about the policies but about the people who promulgated them. Also a source of bibliographic documentation useful for researchers who wish to pursue the subject beyond the scope of this book. Invaluable.

188. Ziegler, Hans Severus. *Entartete Musik: eine Abrechnung.* Düsseldorf: Völkischer Verlag, 1939. 32 pp. Second edition. Illustrated "little guide" to work of Jewish composers and other "undesirables" including conductors and musicologists, from the late nineteenth century to the date of publication. Singles out serial composers who followed Mahler (especially Schoenberg and Krenek), jazz exponents (Weill), Hindemith, and conductors including Klemperer, musicologists including Bekker. Although this is Nazi propaganda, it is cited by Erwin Kroll in "Verbotene Musik" (*Vierteljahreshefte für Zeitgeschichte,* Juli 1959) as a documentary source of the policies dictating Nazi selection in musical taste. Kroll in turn is cited by Grunberger *post factum* (see no. 95 above) giving this material importance as historical evidence in spite of its miniscule size.

VISUALS

189. Blaukopf, Kurt. *Mahler: sein Leben, sein Werk und seine Welt in zeitgenössischen Bildern und Texten.* Mit Beiträgen von Zoltan Roman. Wien: Universal Edition, 1976. 287 pp.
English version: *Mahler: A Documentary Study.* With contributions by Zoltan Roman. Transl. by Paul Baker, Suzanne Flatauer, P.R.J. Ford, Daisy Loman and Geoffrey Watkins. London: Thames and Hudson; New York, Toronto: Oxford University Press, 1976. 280 pp. ISBN 0-19-519877-8.
Mahler's life documented visually (photographs, caricatures, facsimiles, woodcuts and archival documents)

Places

190. Faltis, Viktor. *Grinzing 1900*. Austriaca 26718. Augsburg: Wilhelm Goldmann, 1981. 143 pp. ISBN 3-442-26718-8.
 First published in 1973 (Wien, München, Zürich: Fritz Molden). A study of the Viennese suburb of Grinzing at the time Mahler lived in Vienna, seen through the eyes of a child growing up. While Mahler himself plays no role in this story, the atmosphere of life in Vienna at the turn of the century is vividly portrayed with the hindsight of an adult recalling after many years. Illustrations show that Grinzing has changed little from the time Mahler was buried in its cemetery to the present.

191. Fuchs, Anton. *Alban Berg, Gustav Mahler, Johannes Brahms, Hugo Wolf, Anton Webern: auf ihren Spuren in Kärnten*. Klagenfurt: Kärntner Druck- und Verlagsgesellschaft, 1982. 83 pp.
 Documents in word, picture and facsimile the time and work spent by the above composers in Carinthia, "of sacred memory." The chapter on Mahler (pp. 21-35) covers his house and "Komponierenhäuschen" at Maiernigg-am-Wörthersee, making an interesting comparison with *Gustav Mahler on Wörthersee* published four years later (see no. 194 below).

192. *Gustav Mahler in Steinbach am Attersee: Documents, Reports, Photographs*. Wien: IGMG, [1985]. 18 pp.
 Simultaneously issued in German and English, this is a brief study of Mahler's work in the summers of 1893-96. Cites documents including several of Mahler's letters from the period, the biography by Natalie Bauer-Lechner and Bruno Walter's *Gustav Mahler* (see no. 298 and no. 325 respectively). Gives new details about the construction of the "Schnützelputz-Häusel" which Mahler used for composition during the four summers he and his sisters spent at Steinbach, and gives a brief his-

tory of the house since Mahler's time. Beautifully illustrated with photographs and facsimiles.

193. *Gustav Mahler in Toblach*. Wien: IGMG; Toblach: Gustav Mahler Komitee, [1981]. 28 pp.
Documents Mahler's work in Toblach during the summers of 1908-10. Divided into three sections: (a) quotations from Mahler's letters to various correspondents from Toblach during the three summers (notably his wife and Bruno Walter), (b) a brief account of Mahler's day-by-day routine while at Toblach by Marianna Trenker, the adopted daughter of the family which owned the property, and (c) an article "Die Toblacher 'Trilogie'" by Ugo Duse, who discusses the composition of *Das Lied von der Erde*, the *Symphony no. 9* and, briefly, the *Symphony no. 10* (although the coverage of that work suffers from bias against the concept of the complete work in five movements). Illustrated richly with photographs and facsimiles from Mahler's draft orchestral score of *Das Lied von der Erde* and a letter to Trenker. Simultaneously issued in Italian *(Mahler a Dobbiaco)* by the Convegno Gustav Mahler, as well as in the above German publication.

194. *Gustav Mahler on Wörthersee: Documents, Reports, Photographs*. Klagenfurt: Kulturamt der Landeshauptstadt Klagenfurt; Wien: IGMG, [1986]. 24 pp.
Simultaneously issued in German and English, this is a study of the work Mahler accomplished during the summers from 1900-07. Cites documents including several of Mahler's letters and the biography by his wife. Essays by Herta Blaukopf and Rudolf Stephan place in perspective the purchase of the land in Maiernigg-am-Wörthersee where Mahler built his house and the *Komponierenhäuschen* and the work he accomplished in the *Symphony no. 5, Symphony no. 6* and *Symphony no. 7*. Well illustrated with photographs and facsimiles.

195. *Gustav Mahler und Wien*. Stuttgart, Zürich: Belser, 1976. 168 pp.
English version: *Gustav Mahler in Vienna*. Transl. by Anne Shelley. Ed. by Sigrid Wiesmann. New York: Rizzoli, 1976; London: Thames and Hudson, 1977. 168 pp. (1976), 165 pp. (1977). ISBN 0-8478-0039-3.
Minimal prose among various essays contributed by Pierre Boulez, Friedrich C. Heller, Henry-Louis de la Grange, Marcel Prawy, Wolf Rosenberg, Gottfried Scholz, Hilde

Spiel and Sigrid Wiesmann. Focus instead on much visual documentation (photographs, facsimiles etc.) illustrating Mahler's tenure in Vienna. Little or no editorializing by contributors, almost a pure source; much more than a book to be visually admired, this source set the example for later books documenting other times and places in Mahler's life.

196. Heinisch, Eduard Christoph. *Grüsse vom Attersee: eine Auswahl alter Ansichtskarten vom Attersee und aus Vöcklabruck.* Linz: Oberösterreichischer Landesverlag, 1981. 75 pp. ISBN 3-85214-301-2.
Pictures the country in which Mahler wrote large parts of the *Symphony no. 2* and *Symphony no. 3* and many of the *Des Knaben Wunderhorn* songs. Most of the illustrations are reproduced from post cards distributed in Mahler's time (the 1890s) or shortly thereafter.

197. "Mahler's Flat in Vienna." *NaMR*, no. 7 (August 1980): 14-15.
Surveys the layout of Mahler's home in Vienna in the Auenbruggergasse, where he lived (first with his sisters, later with his wife and daughters) from 1898-1909. A sketch by Alma Mahler is here published for the first time, showing the major expanse of the apartment.

198. Nebehay, Christian Michael. *Wien speziell--Musik um 1900: wo finde ich Berg, Brahms, Mahler, Schönberg, Hauer, Wolf, Bruckner, Strauss, Zemlinsky, Webern. Leben und Werk/Gedenk- und Wirkungsstätten/Museen und Sammlungen in Wien.* Wien: Christian Brandstätter, 1984. viii, 192 pp. ISBN 3-85447-102-5.
Surveys the "musical ghosts" in and around Vienna which today recall the lives of the major composers in the late nineteenth and early twentieth centuries. Pinpoints places of interest in connection with each composer, and illustrates with portraits, facsimiles and photographs of places frequented by each. May seem as if meant for laymen and students, but of major interest to musical professionals interested in the cultural-social scene in Vienna in the time in question compared with earlier studies by Josef Bergauer (*Das klingende Wien: Erinnerungsstätten berühmter Tondichter*, Wien: Johannes Günther, 2. Auflage 1946, 187 pp.) and Hugo Ellenberger ("Gustav Mahler" in *Wiener Musikgedenkstätten: Wanderungen und Betrachtungen*, Wien, München: Österreichischer Bundesverlag, 1960, pp. 62-63). Un-

like these earlier works, which gave only brief information intended to be spoon-fed to pedestrians walking around the city without any sort of visual illustration, Nebehay profiles each composer in his own section; the information on Mahler is found on pp. V/1-24, and the sections on Berg, Schoenberg, Wolf, Bruckner, Strauss, Zemlinsky and Webern are also worth noticing.

199. Powell, Nicolas. *The Sacred Spring: the Arts in Vienna 1898-1918*. Greenwich, Connecticut: New York Graphic Society; London: Studio Vista, 1974. 224 pp. ISBN 0-8212-0619-2.
Akin to Schorske but concentrates on visuals to equal extent with text. Gives equal balance to architecture, visual arts and music in Vienna at turn of century, showing connections between intelligentsia in various specialties. Section on Mahler, "Mahler and the Vienna School," is on pp. 206-12; other sections concerned with Alma on pp. 33, 117-19, 135-38, 171-73, 207-09.

200. Sachs, Edwin O., and E.A.E. Woodrow. *Modern Opera Houses and Theatres*. London: B.T. Batsford, 1897-98. 3 vols.
Extremely oversized but wonderful essay discussions, with architects' drawings and photographs of major opera houses in many different European cities. Gives specifications for buildings, stages, seats etc. The Hofoper in Vienna is discussed in both vols. 1 and 2, and there are also brief sections on the houses in Prague and Budapest.

Portraits

201. Roller, Alfred. *Die Bildnisse von Gustav Mahler*. Leipzig, Wien, Zürich: E.P. Tal, 1922. 85 pp.
To this day one of the best single sources of pictures of Mahler. Arranged chronologically from 1865 to 1911. No caricatures, but photographs, artists' portraits, busts and death masks, plus a few photographs of "his" places and his grave. Roller gives a brief commentary for each entry referring to its place in Mahler's life and style, based on his own experience of Mahler as man and artist. A year before this book was published Roller had written an article "Wie Mahler aussah" in *Bohemia* (März 1921) which was probably an advance study

for the portraiture as seen through the eyes of the artist.

202. Storck, Karl. *Musik und Musiker in Karikatur und Satire: eine Kulturgeschichte der Musik aus dem Zerrspiegel.* Oldenburg in Grossherzogtum: Gerhard Stalling, 1910. 396 pp.
A priceless and irreverent view of music and musicians which will convulse even the most straitlaced historian. Includes pictures, descriptions, poems and even musical works unduplicated by other sources. Caricature materials on Mahler on pp. 57, 74-75, 100 and 377.

BIOGRAPHIES
(With or Without Studies of Works)

Non-Eyewitness

* Barsova, Inna. "Mahler und Dostojewski." *Gustav Mahler Kolloquium 1979*: 65-75.
Full citation under no. 8 above. Compares emotional/philosophical views of life by Mahler and Dostoevskii. See also Curtis Swanson's treatment of subject (no. 247 below).

203. Blaukopf, Kurt. *Gustav Mahler oder der Zeitgenosse der Zukunft. Glanz und Elend der Meister.* Wien, München, Zürich: Fritz Molden, 1969; München: Deutsche Taschenbuch Verlag, 1973. 326 pp. (1969 ed.), 290 pp. (1973 ed.).
English version: *Gustav Mahler.* Transl. by Inge Goodwin. New York: Praeger; London: Allen Lane, 1973; New York: Limelight Editions, 1985. 279 pp. ISBN 0-87910-029-X.
A major study of Mahler's life and music by one of the most important Mahler specialists since World War II. The importance of this book can be gauged by the fact that--in addition to the English translation noted above--versions in French, Hungarian, Swedish and Japanese have been published.

204. Dernoncourt, Sylvie. *Mahler.* Transl. by Felipe Ximenez de Sandoval. Madrid: Espasa Calpe Co. Músicos de nuestro tiempo, 1979. 111 pp.
Originally written in French and apparently translated

Biographies (Non-Eyewitness)

into Spanish for publication purposes. Takes some departure from Sopeña's *Estudios sobre Mahler* (see no. 246 below) but includes more than Sopeña allowed in biographical data and analysis of individual works.

205. Duse, Ugo. *Gustav Mahler.* Torino: G. Einaudi, 1973. xii, 394 pp.
Decidedly substantial, well annotated. Separate sections devoted to Mahler's life, works (songs, symphonies), appendices (Mahler's texts in German and Italian, life chronology, list of works, bibliography and discography). Marred only by incomplete treatment of the *Symphony no. 10.*

206. Duse, Ugo. *Gustav Mahler: introduzione allo studio della vita e delle opere.* Istituto di Storia della Musica dell'Università di Palermo. Padova: Marsilio Editori, 1962. viii, 270 pp.
Surprisingly detailed and current Italian study of life and works of Mahler, considering the time in which it was written, showing familiarity with major Mahler literature but not without originality of opinion insofar as discussions of the works are concerned. Limited by lack of musical examples even in individual analyses of the symphonies, *Das klagende Lied* and *Das Lied von der Erde* and including little individual analysis of the songs.

207. Engel, Gabriel. *Gustav Mahler: Song-Symphonist.* New York: Bruckner Society of America, 1932. 125 pp. New ed., with preface by Jack Diether, New York: David Lewis, 1970. 136 pp.
Early informal biography of Mahler based on interpretation of his letters. Some information has been reinterpreted by critical biographers, but this book served an important purpose at a time when literature on Mahler in English was lacking.

208. Floros, Constantin. *Gustav Mahler.* Wiesbaden: Breitkopf und Härtel, 1977-85. 3 vols.: (I) *Die geistige Welt Gustav Mahlers in systematische Darstellung.* 240 pp. ISBN 3-7651-0126-5. (II) *Mahler und die Symphonik des 19. Jahrhunderts in neuer Deutung.* 433 pp. ISBN 3-7651-0127-3. (III) *Die Symphonien.* 336 pp. ISBN 3-7651-0210-5.
A far-reaching study of Mahler as a symphonist in the context of nineteenth-century musical history, with

extensive systematic consideration of Mahler's sociohistorical background and its effect on his life and work. Essential to understanding of Mahler as a product of his age. The single limitation is a tendency to favor German literature to the exclusion of sources in other languages in connection with consideration of foregoing Mahler literature.

209. Gartenberg, Egon. *Mahler: the Man and His Music.* London: Collier Macmillan Publishers; New York: Schirmer Books, 1978. x, 406 pp. ISBN 0-02870-840-7. A "popular" biography of Mahler focusing on his life and work in the perspective of the history and culture of the Austrian Empire. Unfortunately compromised in value by many serious errors and simplistic generalizations. Best avoided by the general reading public and useless to specialists.

210. Gedeon, Tibor and Miklós Mathe. *Gustav Mahler.* Budapest: Zeneműkiadó Vállalat, 1965. 377 pp. Very substantial Hungarian biography of Mahler with special emphasis on his tenure in Budapest at the Royal Hungarian Opera.

211. Holländer, Hans. "Gustav Mahler's Jeugd." *De Muziek* 3 (1929): 212-17. Early Dutch study of Mahler's youth, from life with his parents and siblings to the years of education in Vienna. Only known Dutch source by this author who usually wrote in German and English periodicals.

212. Holländer, Hans. "Gustavo Mahler." *Riv Mus It* 40 (1936): 482-99. Early Italian essay outlining Mahler's life and work as composer and conductor. No musical examples or real documentation from letters or other archival sources, but reliable in terms of factual content considering the time in which it was published. With no. 211 above, rare contribution to Mahler literature from this author who usually wrote in German or English periodicals.

213. Holländer, Hans. "Neue Beiträge zu den frühen Lehrjahren Gustav Mahlers (Zum 70. Geburtstag am 7. Juli 1930)." *Schweizerische Musikzeitung* 70 (1930): 559-62. Comparable to no. 211 which had been published a year earlier, but in German and concentrating on Mahler's

education in Vienna, less on his family life.

214. Hutschenruijter, Wouter. *Mahler*. Beroemde Musici, Deel 6. 's-Gravenhage: J. Philip Kruseman, 1927. 107 pp.
Early Dutch reference, including biography, discussions of the first nine symphonies and *Das Lied von der Erde*, and some information about the nonsymphonic works. Includes chapters on Mahler the person and his career as conductor. Almost everything cited from earlier sources is translated into Dutch (except direct quotations of the German texts of Mahler's vocal works), and there are some inaccuracies in factual material; also there are no musical examples, but there is a great deal of illustration with plates and facsimiles.

215. Kennedy, Michael. *Mahler*. The Master Musicians Series. London: J.M. Dent and Sons, Ltd., 1974, 1977. x, 196 pp. ISBN 0-460-03141-4 (hardbound), 0-460-02161-3 (paper).
An important general study of Mahler's life and work which makes a happy blend of information for the general reader and for the specialist. Extraordinarily detailed for its comparatively short length, it shows an excellent and up-to-date grasp of scholarship to the time of publication, and remains a timeless asset to Mahler scholarship to the present date.

216. Kernkamp, H. F. "Gustav Mahler." *Elseviers geillustreerd Maandschrift* 91 (1936): 312-19.
Early essay biography of Mahler in Dutch for the general reader in that language.

217. la Grange, Henry-Louis de. *Gustav Mahler: Chronique d'une vie*. Paris: Fayard, 1979-84. 3 vols.: (I) *Les chemins de la gloire (1860-1900)*. 1158 pp. ISBN 2-213-00661-X. (II) *L'Age d'or de Vienne (1900-1907)*. 1285 pp. ISBN 2-213-01281-4. (III) *Le génie foudroyé (1907-1911)*. 1365 pp. ISBN 2-213-01468-X.
Supersedes the English versions of vol. I of this biography (see no. 218 below), now available complete in three volumes for the first time in this French version. A major resource on Mahler's life, drawing on unpublished sources available to few other researchers and accounting for Mahler scholarship in many countries over a period of many years. Not without flaws in its factual information, concentrating on biograph-

ical data over musical analysis, but essential to any Mahler specialist's collection as a unique item.

218. la Grange, Henry-Louis de. *Mahler*. Vol. I. Garden City, New York: Doubleday, 1973. xxiii, 982 pp. ISBN 0-385-00524-5. Revised ed. London: Gollancz, 1974. xxiii, 987 pp.
Volume I only of projected two. First published in English, later revised and superseded by the French edition in three volumes (see no. 217 above). To be superseded by a new English edition in four volumes, with extensive revisions which are expected to supersede the French version in its turn.

219. Libermann, Arnoldo. *Gustav Mahler o el corazon abrumado: brusqueda en quatro movimientas*. Madrid: Altalena Editores, 1982. 181 pp. 2. ed., 1984. 170 pp. ISBN 84-7475-109-8.
For the general Spanish reader only. Superficial, no documentation of any kind, no evidence of referral to other sources in the literature.

220. Loeser, Norbert. *Gustav Mahler*. Componisten-Serie, 15. Haarlem, Antwerpen: Gottmer, 1950, 1968. 209 pp.
Dutch biography of Mahler, one of a series of composer biographies presumably intended for the general reader. Concentrates on Mahler's life and its historical background rather than his musical works.

221. Loschnigg, Franz. "The Cultural Education of Gustav Mahler." Ph.D. diss., University of Wisconsin, 1976. 559 pp.
Thorough, sensitive study of Mahler's childhood and youth, discussing the socioeconomic conditions in which he grew up and was educated. Especially valuable for its study of the Jewish milieu in the Austrian Empire.

222. Martner, Knud. "Gustav Mahler in Iglau." *OeMZ* 42 (April 1987): 179-82.
Overview of Mahler's early life in his parents' home in Iglau to the time of his departure for the Conservatory in Vienna. Set against a backdrop of other essays in the same issue about the history of music in Moravia. Truncated from author's original conception, but nevertheless valuable information on a somewhat neglected subject.

223. Mathis, Alfred. "Gustav Mahler: Composer-Conductor." *The Listener* 39 (February 5, 1948): 236.
A popularized view of Mahler's two main professional hats.

224. Matter, Jean. *Conaissance de Mahler: documents, analyses et synthèses*. Lausanne: Éditions l'Age d'Homme, 1974. 428 pp.
Both biographical and critical with special emphasis on analysis of Mahler's music, not always formal but substantial (e.g., aspects of nature, the programmatic elements, the use of humor and triviality, and the 'Jewish' question of musical style). Biographical aspects of this study include discussion of Mahler's work as conductor and his relations with other composers including Bruckner, Strauss and the Second Viennese School. Sources include letters, vocal texts, and reviews (in French translation). Interesting attempt which may or may not come off successfully.

225. Matter, Jean. *Mahler: Le démoniaque*. Lausanne: Éditions Foma, 1959. 219 pp.
Curious and interesting study of Mahler as man and creator through the influence of the world around him, especially nature. Not concerned with Mahler's social background, education or relations with fellow musical professionals, rather with his psychological identification with pantheistic nature and the effect of such orientation on the style of his works.

226. McCaldin, Denis. *Mahler*. Novello Short Biographies. Sevenoaks, Kent: Novello, 1981. 32 pp.
Brief but literate biography for educated public, referring to Mahler's compositions in appropriate spots, as well as his work as conductor. Includes short bibliography and chronological list of works. Similar to same author's monograph on Stravinsky in same series.

227. Mengelberg, Curt Rudolf. *Gustav Mahler*. Breitkopf und Härtels Musikbücher: Kleine Musikerbiographien. Leipzig: Breitkopf und Härtel, 1923. 72 pp.
Monograph biography of Mahler complementing Dutch study done by same author at time of the 1920 Amsterdam Mahler festival, the earlier source concentrating primarily on the works performed at the Festival, the later one on the composer's life. A short section from this monograph, "Mahlers Weg," was published in *Musikblätter*

des Anbruch 5 (Mai 1923): 134-35.

228. Mikheeva, Lyudmila. *Gustav Maler 1860-1911: kratkiy ocherk zhizni i tvorchestva.* [Gustav Mahler 1860-1911: brief essay on his life and work.] Popularnaya Monografiya. Leningrad: Muzyka, 1972. 94 pp.
Basic introduction to Mahler's life and compositions for general Russian readers, unfortunately weakened by complete lack of musical examples and severe limitations on other illustrative material. Author had contributed to Russian Mahler literature for over ten years when this book was published; most recently she had written "Tematicheskiye svyazi i zamysel I-IV Simfoniy Malera" [Subject/thematic connections and designs of Mahler's First through Fourth Symphonies] in *Voprosy teorii estetiki muzyki* [Problems of theory and musical aesthetics], ed. by Lev Nikolaevich Raaben (Leningrad: Muzyka, 1969).

229. Mitchell, Donald. "Some Notes on Gustav Mahler." *CD* 2 (1950): 86-91.
Discussion of Mahler from societal point of view, especially in the "crisis" atmosphere of the late nineteenth century musical community. Sharply differs from the partisans of the "Bruckner-Mahler" connection, arguing that Bruckner and Mahler (also Wagner) resemble each other only superficially and that each bore his own role in the social musical environment of their time.

229a. Müller, Karl-Josef. *Mahler: Leben--Werke--Dokumente.* Mainz: B. Schotts Söhne; München: Robert Piper, 1988. 643 pp. ISBN 3-7957-8264-3 (Schott), 3-492-18264-X (Piper).
Extensive biography of Mahler with author's own writing interspersed with many quotations from contemporary documentation by Mahler and his associates. Heavily illustrated with portraits and facsimiles, less heavily with musical examples. Excerpt quotations documented but no documentation for provenance of visual examples. Organized into short sections roughly in chronological order but widely varying in subject. Bibliography heavily weighted toward German language sources. Not for all tastes.

230. Neisser, Arthur. *Gustav Mahler.* Musiker-Biographien, 35. Leipzig: Philipp Reclam, 1918. 128 pp.

Surprisingly objective and detailed study in two parts, the first five chapters tracing Mahler's life and work as conductor, the last seven surveying his compositions from the Conservatory in Vienna until his death. Even includes details about the (then unknown) *Symphony no. 10*.

231. Nejedlý, Zdeněk. *Gustav Mahler*. Praha: Státní Nakladatelstvi Krásné Literatury, Hudbi a Umění, 1958. 88 pp.
Originally published in 1913 ("Psano roku 1912, rok po Mahlerove smrti Vyslo v. Hudebnim sborniku I, 1913"). Brief early Czech biography of Mahler by influential liberal musicologist, humanist, statesman and writer. Opinionated early champion of Mahler.

232. Nemeth, Amade. *Gustav Mahler eletenek kronikaja*. [A chronicle of Gustav Mahler's life.] Life Chronicles of Great Musicians, 18. Budapest: Zenemükiado, 1984. 300 pp.
Detailed Hungarian biography of Mahler, one of a series of composer biographies presumably oriented toward the general reader interested in Mahler's life more than detailed analysis of his works.

233. Newlin, Dika. *Bruckner, Mahler, Schoenberg*. New York: King's Crown Press, 1947, 1953. x, 293 pp. Revised ed. New York: W.W. Norton, 1978; London: Marion Boyars, 1979. x, 308 pp. ISBN 0-7145-2658-4.
German version: *Bruckner-Mahler-Schönberg*. Übersetzt von Carl Nemeth und Hugo Zelzer. Wien: Bergland, 1954. 303 pp.
Originally the author's Ph.D. diss. (Columbia University, 1945, 293 pp.). Revolutionary study of the three composers, written at a time when none of them were popular with either audiences or musical professionals. Traces the continuity of Viennese musical trends through the connections between the three as men and composers (from the point of view of the author who had herself studied composition with Schoenberg). Daring in its match of Bruckner with Mahler and Schoenberg, which was contrary to the musical history being written at the same time in the German-speaking countries where the composers had lived and worked. The first dissertation on any of these composers in the United States (and the first on Schoenberg anywhere), this book has

stood the test of time and is immensely valuable in its revised edition today.

234. Perez de Arteaga, Jose L. *Mahler*. Biblioteca Salvat de Grandes Biografias, 98. Barcelona: Salvat, 1986. 200 pp. ISBN 84-345-8145-0, 84-345-8243-0.
Basic introduction to Mahler's life and works, better than earlier Spanish sources, probably aimed at Spanish readers with basic knowledge of music and its history, but too general for specialists.

235. Principe, Quirino. *Mahler*. Milano: Rusconi, 1983. 1028 pp.
The most extensive of the Italian biographical references on Mahler, owing considerable to French and English versions of la Grange. Recent citations refer to an edition of 1986 (682 pp.).

236. Pugliese, Giuseppe. *Gustav Mahler . . . 'Il mio tempo verra'*. Milano: Nuove Edizioni, 1976, 1977. 410 pp.
Essentially a history of Mahler's works in performance rather than a biography, an interesting approach. Author later built on this premise in a lecture "Per una Storia dell'Interpretazione delle Sinfonie di Gustav Mahler: Appunti e riflessioni" [For a history of the interpretations of the symphonies of Gustav Mahler: Notes and reflections], at the 1981 Music Week in Memoriam Gustav Mahler in Toblach.

237. Ratz, Erwin. "Persönlichkeit und Werk: Gustav Mahler zum 100. Geburtstag." *OeMZ* 15 (1960): 282-91.
Summarizes Mahler's life and salient characteristics of his works.

* Ratz, Erwin. "Von Leben und Werk." *Gustav Mahler* (1966): 71-89.
Full citation under no. 7 above. Summarizes Mahler's life and works, concentrating primarily on the symphonies; marred by author's personal prejudice against the performing versions of the *Symphony no. 10*.

238. Raynor, Henry. *Mahler*. The Musicians. Genl. ed.: Geoffrey Hindley. London: Macmillan, 1975. 112 pp. ISBN 0-333-14579-8.
Surprisingly accurate information for a "coffee-table book," concentrating more on Mahler's life and his com-

positional style rather than pointed analyses of individual works. Profusely illustrated with pictures from Mahler sources and also from ballet productions based on Mahler's music, a rather neglected area.

239. Redlich, Hans Ferdinand. *Bruckner and Mahler.* Master Musicians. London: J.M. Dent and Sons, Ltd., 1955; New York: Farrar, Straus and Cudahy, 1963. xi, 300 pp. ISBN 0-460-03125-2.
Critically surveys Mahler's life, times and work. With *Bruckner-Mahler-Schoenberg* of Newlin (see no. 233 above) an important early biography and musical study, still useful despite the advances of other research since its publication. Shows the effect of many years of study somewhat rare among serious musicologists before the centenniel. See especially pp. 109-231, 273-90.

240. Reeser, Eduard. "Mahler." *Caecilia en de muziek* 93 (1936): 274-78.
Written on the occasion of the twenty-fifth anniversary of Mahler's death, in Dutch; an early contribution from a major Dutch scholar to the Mahler literature even to the present day.

241. Rutters, Herman. *Gustav Mahler.* Mannen en vrouwen van beteekenis levens- en karakterschetsen. Baarn: Hollandia-Drukkerij, 1919. 59 pp.
Short early Dutch monograph, concentrating more on biographical information for the general public than on assessment of Mahler's compositions for musical professionals. Mitchell cites English translation published in 1953 without giving details.

242. Schreiber, Wolfgang. *Gustav Mahler in Selbstzeugnissen und Bilddokumenten.* Rowohlts Monographien. Reinbek bei Hamburg: Rowohlt Taschenbuch Verlag, 1971. 190 pp. 680-ISBN-3-499-50181-3.
Traces Mahler's life and work relying directly on photographs, reproductions of manuscripts and published scores, facsimiles of posters, books, programs and letters, and quotations from Mahler's letters and literary sources. Among the appendices is an unusually detailed bibliography in proportion to the size of this book.

243. Seckerson, Edward. *Mahler: His Life and Times.* Tunbridge Wells, England: Midas Books; New York: Hip-

pocrene Books, 1982. 150 pp. ISBN 0-85936-152-7 (English printing), 0-88254-662-7 (American printing).
Reasonable biography of Mahler without much discussion of his works; good as introduction to the general public. Straightforward, not heavily documented although Seckerson does refer to other sources on many occasions.

244. Šíp, Ladislav. *Gustav Mahler*. Hudební Profily, 23. Praha: Editio Supraphon, 1973. 223 pp.
Primarily biography with some discussion of Mahler's works integrated. Makes no attempt to be comprehensive but stands out as a good introduction to the subject in Czech. Substantial, well illustrated with plates and musical examples. Includes list of works, very brief bibliography and rather more extensive discography. Gives somewhat more proportionate weight to Mahler's early years than more "comprehensive" biographies.

245. Sollertinskiy, Ivan Ivanovich. *Gustav Maler*. Leningrad: Gosudarstvennoye Muzykal'noye Izdatel'stvo, 1932. 75 pp.
Limited study of Mahler and his work, first in the Russian language. One of a series of basic composer profiles written by this author, under the auspices of the Leningrad Philharmonic Orchestra.

246. Sopeña Ibáñez, Federico. *Estudios sobre Mahler*. Madrid: Servicio de Publicaciones del Ministerio de Educación y Ciencia, 1976. 113 pp. ISBN 84-3690027-8.
Light compendium giving a brief summary of Mahler's life chronology, short discussions of his works, and--inexplicably--an extended discussion of Visconti's view of Mahler in the film *Death in Venice*. For the general public only; not useful to scholars.

* Stein, Erwin. "Mahler." *Orpheus in New Guises*: 5-14.
Full citation under no. 23 above. Studies the man and his works focusing on the first nine symphonies and *Das Lied von der Erde*. A preliminary to the essays which follow it in this book, essential to their understanding. Views Mahler and his works positively ahead of its time in England.

247. Swanson, Curtis. "Mahler and Dostoevski." *CD* 2 (1946): 67-70.
Compares the two creative geniuses as "soul brothers" and considers Mahler's attitude to Dostoevski's work and its effect on his own cynical view of man's duality and suffering. Interesting comparison with later discussion by Barsova.

248. Tarazona, Andrés Ruiz. *Gustav Mahler: el cantor de la decadencia.* Colección músicos, 2. Madrid: Real Música, 1974. 79 pp. ISBN 84-387-0000-2.
Brief Spanish biography of Mahler, less challenging in theoretical questions of Mahler's music than earlier study by Sopeña (see no. 246 above).

249. Vignal, Marc. *Mahler.* Collection "Solfèges," 26. Paris: Éditions du Seuil, 1966. 187 pp.
A brief introduction to Mahler's life and music in the French language. A Spanish edition was published in 1974 and re-released in 1977 (Madrid: Editorial Castellote). For nonspecialists only.

250. Werfel, Franz. "Gustav Mahler." *CD* 2 (1946): 49-50.
Short study, not biographical but consideration of the personality of Mahler the man as it influenced his musical works. Lent interest by author's status as Mahler's successor vis-à-vis Alma, and his friendship with others in the Mahler circle. Published posthumously.

251. Wessely, Othmar. "Anton Bruckner und Gustav Mahler." *OeMZ* 32 (1977): 57-67.
Prudently eschews comparison between the works of the two composers and instead concentrates on comparison and contrast of their lives in the context of the milieu in the Austrian Empire they shared. Considers their differing personalities but leaves untouched the subject of their different faiths.

252. Wessem, Constant von. *Gustav Mahler.* Arnhem: Van Loghum Slatterus, 1920; Amsterdam: Seyffardt, 1926. 113 pp.
Most extensive and general of Wessem's writings on Mahler, full biography in Dutch expanding on earlier short specialized studies of individual works (see no. 834 below for an example).

253. Wessling, Berndt Wilhelm. *Gustav Mahler: ein prophetisches Leben.* Hamburg: Hoffmann und Campe, 1974. 367 pp. Later published in paperback form as *Gustav Mahler: Prophet der neuen Musik.* Heyne Biographien, 75. München: [Heyne], 1980. 303 pp.
At best a flight of fancy, based heavily on interview with Alma Mahler-Werfel; undocumented, repeating observations of others or else citing "new" material without substantiation which makes it highly suspect. Unreliable, possibly false.

254. Zaccaro, Gianfranco. *Gustav Mahler: studio per un' interpretazione.* I musicisti. Firenze: Santoni; Milano: Accademia, 1971. 250 pp.
A basic introduction to the life of Mahler and his works in Italian. Comprises three parts. The first section deals with the life of Mahler, the second with his musical works, and the third with a brief study of Mahler's position in his time (a sort of catchall). For newcomers who want an easy beginning to the subject.

Medical/Psychiatric

255. Allemandou, André. "Gustav Mahler: essai de pathographie." Thèse de Médicine, Université de Paris VI, 1980. 127 pp.
A medico-psychiatric study drawing extensively on sources from Mahler's letters to the writings of his wife and associates. Refers to an earlier thesis, "Gustave Mahler, quelques Réflexions à propos de la vie et de l'oeuvre d'un obsessionel" completed in Paris in 1969.

* Babin, Pierre. "Gustave Mahler, un enfant malade." *Colloque 1985*: 57-61.
Full citation under no. 5 above. Assesses Mahler and the "Holy Mary" complex mentioned by Freud with reference to his sexual relations with Alma and the crisis of 1910.

256. Christy, Nicholas P., Beverly M. Christy and Barry C. Wood. "Gustav Mahler and his Illnesses." *Transactions of the American Clinical and Climatological Association* 82 (1970): 200-17.

A major study in a neglected area by a physician who --contrary to the prevailing trends in such studies-- concentrates on Mahler's physical health rather than his mental health. Argues conclusively that Mahler had inherited his cardiac problems from his mother and describes what might have been done by his physicians to treat him if he had lived in the present time with surgical techniques and antibiotics. Based on accounts of Mahler's physicians (Joseph Fraenkel, Emanuel Libman and George Baehr) during the final months in New York.

257. Collins, Dean T. "Gustav Mahler's Summer of 1910." *Bulletin of the Menninger Clinic* 46, no. 3 (1982): 255-79.
Account of Mahler's psychiatric situation at the time of the composition of the Tenth Symphony and the marital crisis with Alma in the summer of 1910. Marred by inaccuracies in biographical background but interesting from point of view of psychosocial insight into the creative process.

258. Crandall, John W. "Gustav and Alma Mahler: a Marriage Destroyed by Love." *Medical Aspects of Human Sexuality* 20 (January 1986): 118-19.
A semi-popular version of Crandall's article "A Study in Pathological Nurturance: the Marriage of Gustav Mahler" (see no. 259 below).

259. Crandall, John W. "A Study in Pathological Nurturance: the Marriage of Gustav Mahler." *Clinical Social Work Journal* 9 (1981): 91-100.
Studies the psychiatric concept of "pathological nurturance" and how it applies to the problems experienced by Mahler and his wife, stressing especially the foundation which led to the marital crisis in the summer of 1910. More sympathetic to Alma than to Mahler, although it draws on the famous consultation between Mahler and Sigmund Freud that summer and apparently does not draw on Alma's unpublished diary as a counterbalance. Abbreviated version of this article published in 1986 (see no. 258 above).

260. Diether, Jack. "Gustav Mahler and Orgonomy." *Journal of Orgonomy* 8 (1974): 216-24.
A relatively early study of Mahler's music as a process parallel to biological/sexual experience of human

life, especially as it affected his own life. Short but thought-provoking, perhaps influential in light of other studies written by J. Sydney Jones, Frederic Morton and Carl Schorske.

261. Diether, Jack. "Mahler and Psychoanalysis." *Psychoanalysis and Psychoanalytic Review* 45 (Winter 1958-59): 3-14.
Describes the marital crisis between Mahler and Alma in the summer of 1910 and Mahler's consultation with Sigmund Freud, with a difference from the similar literature contributed by psychiatrists and psychologists on the same subjects: refers to Mahler's musical works as evidence of his problems both medically and psychiatrically more extensively and more accurately than is generally found in other literature. Refers not only to the "death syndrome" in the last two symphonies and *Das Lied von der Erde*--which other writers have done--but involves discussion of the *Symphony no. 5* and the *Symphony no. 8* and *Lieder eines fahrenden Gesellen*.

262. Feder, Stuart. "Gustav Mahler Dying." *International Review of Psychoanalysis* 5 (1978): 125-48.
First of three studies by this author (see no. 263 and no. 264 for later ones). Emphasis more psychological than musical. Studies Mahler's brush with death during his illness of 1901 (which is worth comparing with treatment of the same subject in Kravitt's "Mahler's Dirges for his Death" cited as no. 268 below), his personal attitudes about death as a result of the experience and of the preponderance of death in his family during his youth. Considers his marriage and fatherhood in similar context, and views his wife's affair with Walter Gropius as a crisis from which Mahler was saved by his creative work in terms of self-identity.

263. Feder, Stuart. "Gustav Mahler: the Music of Fratricide." *International Review of Psychoanalysis* 8 (1981): 257-84.
Last of this author's trio of essays focusing on Mahler from the view of psychological motivations for his life and work. In this essay Feder considers Mahler's relations with his brothers and sisters, the many deaths among them, and his assumption of the paternal role for the survivors after his parents' death. Explores

the concept of fratricide in *Das klagende Lied* and its connection with symbols in other works from Mahler's early period. This article presents a strong contrast with Newlin's "Mahler's Brother Syndrome" (cited below as no. 273) in conceptual terms, and is worth noting although it refers less to strictly musical subject matter because of its audience than if it had been published in a musicological journal.

264. Feder, Stuart. "Gustav Mahler um Mitternacht." *International Review of Psychoanalysis* 7 (1980): 11-26.
   Second of three essays by Feder in this journal, representing a midground between the others (see no. 262 and no. 263 above); considers the song "Um Mitternacht" as an example of Mahler's concept of time, life and death. Compares the song to other works Mahler wrote before and after in this context. Grows out of "Gustav Mahler Dying" in its discussion of Mahler's ideas about death, and foreshadows "The Music of Fratricide" in its concern with Mahler's relations with others including his brothers and sisters and his friends.

265. Graf, Max. *From Beethoven to Shostakovich: the Psychology of the Composing Process*. New York: Philosophical Library, 1947. Reprinted New York: Greenwood Press, 1969. 474 pp.
   Quasi-psychological implications of the compositional process by a musicologist of the Viennese school, somewhat original when compared with such sources by psychiatrists which outnumber this. The major composers discussed include not only Mahler but Bach, Beethoven, Brahms, Berlioz, Bruckner, Handel, Haydn, Mozart, Schubert, Schumann and Wagner; secondary discussions include Meyerbeer, Mendelssohn, Reger, Schoenberg, Stravinsky and Wolf, resulting in widely divergent conclusions according to the individual composers discussed.

266. Kerner, Dieter. "Gustav Mahler." *Krankheiten grosser Musiker*. Stuttgart, New York: Friedrich-Karl Schattauer, 1963, 1967, vol. 2, pp. 175-86. Revised ed. 1973-74, vol. 1, pp. 239-58.
   Medicopsychological study of the composer by professional physician rare in the German literature. While not as technical as other articles on this subject by

David Levy (see no. 270 below) and Nicholas Christy (see no. 256 above), this study offers a rounded view of Mahler's medical and psychological history including documentation from his own words and the observations of his associates.

267. Kerner, Dieter. "Gustav Mahlers Ende." *NZfM* 122 (1961): 188-90.
   Summarizes Mahler's final illness, although with less technical medical information than that used by Christy nine years later. Predecessor sketch to full chapter in *Krankheiten grosser Musiker* cited above under no. 266.

268. Kravitt, Edward F. "Mahler's Dirges for his Death: February 24, 1901." *MQ* 64 (1978): 329-53.
   Focuses on Mahler's actual experiences of death, not only with his brothers and sisters, his parents and his daughter Maria, but his own near-death in early 1901; traces transmutation of actual experiences into certain musical works, especially the *Kindertotenlieder*. Refers to medical evidence in articles by Nicholas Christy and Stuart Feder as well as musical sources and biographical material, especially from Alma Mahler-Werfel and la Grange. Unusual approach to subject from musicologist rather than physician.

269. Kuehn, John L. "Encounter at Leyden: Gustav Mahler Consults Sigmund Freud." *Psychoanalytic Review* 52 (1965): 345-65.
   Discusses Mahler's consultation with Freud in format of case study report: introductory statement of purpose of essay, survey of Mahler's biography and cultural background, circumstances necessitating the consultation, survey of Mahler's "premorbid" personality, summary of the clinical problem and the techniques used by Freud in the consultation. Marred by inaccurate factual background, but stimulating, breaking psychiatric ground not found in most references of this kind since Freud's own account (see no. 307 below).

270. Levy, David. "Gustav Mahler and Emanuel Libman: Bacterial Endocarditis in 1911." *British Medical Journal* 293 (20-27 December 1986): 1628-31.

Considers the question of Mahler's last illness taking up where Christy left off, i.e. clinically presenting evidence of Mahler's cardiac history and documenting subacute bacterial endocarditis from the medical records of the physicians Emanuel Libman and George Baehr who attended Mahler with Dr. Fränkel. Presented as a case study abstracted from existing records in the National Library of Medicine in Bethesda, Maryland. Specialized for medical readers and not accessible to most musical professionals, but a rare document in the growing study of medical problems among performing and creative artists.

* McGrath, William J. "Mahler and Freud: the Dream of the Stately House." *Gustav Mahler Kolloquium 1979*: 40-51.
Full citation under no. 8 above. Explores parallels between Mahler and Freud, apparent from their mutual background recognized even before their meeting in 1910.

271. Mitchell, Donald. "Mahler and Freud." *CD* 2 (1958): 63-68.
Study of Mahler's consultation with Freud and the personal conditions that emerged from the insights gained in the experience. Touches on the influence of the character on the music he wrote, without overplay.

272. Mooney, William E. "Gustav Mahler: A Note on Life and Death in Music." *Psychoanalytic Quarterly* 37 (1968): 80-102.
Psychoanalytic study of Mahler's choices of subjects relating to death in his music, and the personality background behind those choices.

273. Newlin, Dika. "The 'Mahler's Brother Syndrome': Necropsychiatry and the Artist." *MQ* 66 (1980): 296-304.
Disputes "necropsychiatry" practiced on any works of Mahler, contravening the movement among psychiatrists and psychologists to treat Mahler as a "case study" after his death, based on interest in Mahler's consultation with Freud in 1910. Directly addresses Diether's "Notes on Some Mahler Juvenilia" (cited below under no. 772) and urges return to analysis of music *qua* music. Based on paper presented at 1978 meeting of American Musicological Society.

274. Pollock, George H. "Psychoanalysis of the Creative Artist: Presentation on Gustav Mahler to Chicago Psychoanalytic Society." *Chicago Psychoanalytic Society Fifth Regional Conference Reports* (1974): 82-142.
Pollock's presentation on Mahler is on pp. 91-116. This is a transcript of a lecture given during a workshop at the CPS 1974 meeting. While inaccurate in some biographical details, Pollock's discussion is an interesting perusal of Mahler's concepts of death as formed by his own experiences, and how the concepts affected his music. Discussion by other participants in the workshop including Charles Kligerman and Maria Piers offers perspective to Pollock's views.

275. Reik, Theodor. *The Haunting Melody: Psychoanalytic Experiences in Life and Music*. New York: Farrar, Straus and Young, 1953; New York: Grove Press, 1960. Reprinted New York: Da Capo Press, 1982. 376 pp. ISBN 0-306-76138-6.
A fantastical study of the relation between emotion and music, told in the first person by a somewhat controversial practitioner of the art of psychoanalysis. The chapter "Freud and Mahler" is interesting as a comparison piece to the account given by Ernest Jones (see no. 307). Editions of this book were also released in French (*Variations Psychoanalytiques sur un Theme de Gustav Mahler*, Paris: Editions Denoël, 1972) and Spanish (*Variaciones psicoanalíticas sobre un tema de Mahler*, Madrid: Ediciones Taurus, 1975).

276. Reik, Theodor. "Sigmund Freud and Gustav Mahler." *Revista psicoanalítica* 1 (1944): 315-18.
Published in Buenos Aires, this brief essay on Mahler's consultation with Freud in 1910 may be considered a forerunner to *The Haunting Melody* (see no. 275).

* Rousseau, Jacqueline. "Ach, du lieber Augustin. . . ." *L'Arc* 67: 3-11.
Full citation under no. 3 above. Surveys the crisis between Mahler and Alma in the summer of 1910 and Mahler's consultation with Freud, and compares the two men with reference to writings of Reik and Jones.

277. Still, Robert. "Gustav Mahler and Psychoanalysis." *American Imago* 17 (1960): 217-40.
Views Mahler as obsessional neurotic, fostered by sex-

ual conflict in his family life when he was a child. Considers relations not only with his brother Ernst and how they may have affected his conception of *Das klagende Lied,* but also his attitude to his parents and his other siblings, thus offering theories later developed by Feder.

The "Mahler Circle"

278. Banks, Paul. "The Early Social and Musical Environment of Gustav Mahler." Ph.D. diss., St. John's College, Trinity, 1980. 372 pp.
 Exhaustive account of Mahler's early life from his birth in Kalište to the end of his student career in Vienna in 1878. Draws extensively on primary Austrian government papers and accounts from Mahler's associates. Outlines the lives and works of Mahler's fellow students including Wolf, Rott and Krzyzanowski. Compare with Max Brod with reference to the Jewish question, which is treated in somewhat limited fashion in this case, despite serious study of the legal position of the Jews in the Austrian Empire in Mahler's time.

279. Banks, Paul. "Hans Rott, 1858-1884." *MT* 125 (September 1984): 493-95.
 Surveys the life and most important works of Mahler's close friend and fellow-student at the Conservatory in Vienna. Focuses particularly on the *Symphony in E major* and the *Quartet in c minor.* Worth reading in conjunction with Mitchell's *Gustav Mahler: the Early Years* (cited as no. 776, revised edition) and la Grange (see no. 217) as well as Banks's dissertation cited as no. 278.

280. Bernet-Kempers, Karel Philippus. "Mahler und Willem Mengelberg." *Bericht über den Internationalen Musikwissenschaftlichen Kongress Wien Mozartjahr 1956, 3. bis 9. Juni. . . .* Hrsg. von Erich Schenk. Graz, Köln: Hermann Böhlaus Nachfolger, 1958, pp. 41-46.
 An early essay on the relationship of Mahler and Mengelberg, the Dutch tradition with Mahler's music. Cites statistics on performances of Mahler's works in the Netherlands to the time of writing. Also considers the scores of Mahler's works from Mengelberg's private collection which bear Mengelberg's annotations and some by Mahler, in connection with the biographical background of the works' composition.

* Blaukopf, Kurt. "Hindernisse beim Zeichen von Mahlers Bild." *Musik und Bildung* 5 (1973): 588-90.
  Full citation under no. 17 above. Shows Mahler through the eyes of his associates and their disciples of the next generation to the time of writing.

* Blaukopf, Kurt. "Mahler und die Secession." *Gustav Mahler Kolloquium 1979*: 7-15.
  Full citation under no. 8 above. Discusses Mahler's personal relations with members of the Secession artistic group and their effect on his productions at the Hofoper in Vienna.

281. Bottenheim, Sam. *Geschiedenis van het Concertgebouw.* Amsterdam: Joost van den Vondel, 1948-50. 3 vols.
     Exhaustive study of the Concertgebouw, its members, conductors, staff, repertoire and functions.

* Deliège, Celestin. "Mahler/Schoenberg-Berg: Confrontation." *L'Arc* 67: 51-63.
  Full citation under no. 3 above. Three-part study of Mahler and the composers of the Second Viennese School, focusing on (a) Mahler's personal relations with Schoenberg, Berg and Webern, (b) the concept of musical form as influenced by common factors working on Mahler and Schoenberg, and (c) the influence of Mahler's *Symphony no. 6* on the early compositions of Berg.

282. Flothuis, Marius. "Gustav Mahler's 'Eckermann.'" *NaMR*, no. 19 (March 1988): 15-20.
     The "Eckermann" in question is Natalie Bauer-Lechner, and this essay adds to the new edition of Bauer-Lechner's memoir of Mahler Professor Flothuis's pointed observations on her transmission of Mahler's opinions of his works and those of others (including Bach, Beethoven, Weber, Schubert and Schumann). These observations are made from the perspective of changing musicological values between Mahler's time and the present. They should be understood as personal views complementing not only Mahler and Bauer-Lechner but the editorial work of Knud Martner in the new edition.

283. Graf, Max. "Bruno Walter und Gustav Mahler." *OeMZ* 3 (1948): 100-03.
     Surveys relationship between Mahler and Walter from their first meeting in Hamburg to the premiere of *Das Lied von der Erde* after Mahler's death. Cites dates

and sources as foundations for assessment of their professional and personal closeness.

284. Harris, Donald. "A Mahler Enthusiast by Name of Alban Berg." *NaMR*, no. 7 (August 1980): 13.
    A brief study of Berg's work on behalf of Mahler's music, especially as a conductor. Lists performances of Mahler's music conducted by Berg by date and place as well as by work.

285. Kuret, Primož. "Gustav Mahler i Anton Krisper." [Gustav Mahler and Anton Krisper.] *Mužikoloski zbornik* 17, no. 2 (1981): 77-85.
    Traces the friendship between Mahler and Krisper when both were students in Vienna and discusses six letters Mahler wrote to Krisper in 1879-80, documenting his professional plans. Suggests that Krisper was responsible for persuading Mahler to take position in the theater in Laibach (Ljubljana). In Slovene with English summary.

286. Mahler, Arnošt. "Mahler--Schoenberg--Zemlinsky." *Musica* 29 (1975): 125-27.
    Discusses the musical and personal relations between the three composers, giving particular attention to Zemlinsky as the least known of the three and surveying the literature available documenting their relations and the time in which they lived and wrote their works.

287. Mitchell, Donald. "Gustav Mahler and Hugo Wolf." *CD* 2 (1948): 40-46.
    Compares and contrasts Mahler and Wolf as men, with discussion of their early lives and especially their relationship during their student days in Vienna. Comparison between them at all rather revolutionary at the time this article was published, but fascinating.

288. Newlin, Dika. "Arnold Schoenberg's Debt to Mahler." *CD* 2 (1948): 21-26.
    Traces Mahler's relations with Schoenberg on personal level and his influence on Schoenberg's musical style (tonality and scoring particularly). See also Diether, "Mahler and Atonality" (no. 619 below), which debates issue of one-sided influence as proposed by Newlin vs. cross-fertilization in both directions.

289. Paap, Wouter. "Mengelberg en Mahler." *Willem Mengelberg*. Introduction by Paul Cronheim. Amsterdam, Brussels: Elsevier, 1960, pp. 47-55.
Discusses professional and personal relations between the two conductors in the general context of essays dealing with Mengelberg's life and work. Brief, later fleshed out by publication of the correspondence between Mahler and his Dutch colleagues (see no. 391 below), but step in the right direction early in growth of Mahler studies.

290. Reilly, Edward R. "Mahler and Guido Adler." *MQ* 58 (1972): 436-70.
Early study of the long relationship between Mahler and the great Austrian musicologist beginning with their student days and continuing to Mahler's death. Precursor to same author's book *Gustav Mahler and Guido Adler: Records of a Friendship* (see no. 293 below), drawing on Adler's book *Gustav Mahler* which would be translated in its entirety as part of Reilly's study.

* Rexroth, Dieter. "Mahler und Schönberg." *Sinfonie und Wirklichkeit*: 68-80.
Full citation under no. 10 above. Surveys the personal and cross-musical relations between Mahler and Schoenberg with special attention to Mahler's influence on Schoenberg's early works.

291. Schneider, Gunter. "Egon Wellesz über Gustav Mahler: zum 100. Geburtstag von Egon Wellesz." *OeMZ* 12 (1985): 637-45.
Based on the author's lecture at the 1984 music week in memoriam Gustav Mahler at Toblach. Surveys Wellesz's early career in Vienna and his relations with Mahler, referring to Wellesz's own published references to Mahler's life and work. Reasonable summary, but worth more if fleshed out with Wellesz's own articles in many Austrian, German, American, British and Israeli periodicals, as well as *Die neue Instrumentation* and his joint autobiography with his wife.

* Schorske, Carl E. "Mahler and Klimt: Social Experience and Artistic Evolution." *Gustav Mahler Kolloquium 1979*: 16-28.
Full citation under no. 8 above. Logical continuation of Blaukopf's essay in same book, this time focusing

on Mahler's particular relations with Gustav Klimt.

* Stefan, Paul. "Mahler und das Theater." *Anbruch* 12 (1930): 96-98.
Full citation under no. 1 above. Surveys Mahler's work as conductor and producer at the Hofoper in Vienna. Later developed in author's book *Die Wiener Oper* (see no. 467 below). This essay spotlights the collaboration between Mahler and Alfred Roller.

* Stefan, Paul. "Mahlers Freunde." *Musikblätter des Anbruch* 2 (1920): 287-89.
Full citation under no. 16 above. Contrast to essay "Mahlers Feinde" by Specht in same issue of journal. Gives credit to Mahler's supporters including Adler, Walter, Bülow, Strauss and others, both personal and professional. A rare recognition to those who stood by Mahler despite conditions varying over time.

292. Türcke, Berthold. "The Mahler Society: a Project of Schoenberg and Mengelberg." *Journal of the Arnold Schoenberg Institute* 7 (1983): 28-92.
Exhaustively documented story of the plans formulated by Schoenberg and Willem and Curt Rudolf Mengelberg for the establishment of a "Mahler Bund" in 1920; unfortunately the plan was never realized because of divergent concepts in organization and statutes. Original correspondence and archival documents in German and translations in English.

* Weingartner-Studer, Carmen. "Gustav Mahler und Felix Weingartner." *OeMZ* 15 (1960): 308-10.
Full citation under no. 18 above. Discusses the relations between Mahler and Weingartner, illustrated by selections from letters they exchanged. Argues against the prevailing opinion of antipathy and rivalry between Mahler and his successor at the Hofoper.

Eyewitness Accounts

Autobiographies and Biographies

293. Adler, Guido. *Gustav Mahler*. 2. Auflage. Wien, Leipzig: Universal Edition, 1916. 106 pp. Reprinted in Reilly, Edward R. *Gustav Mahler und Guido Adler: zur Geschichte einer Freundschaft*. Bibliothek der

IGMG. Wien: Universal Edition, 1978. 69 pp. ISBN 3-7024-0127-X.
English version: *Gustav Mahler and Guido Adler: Records of a Friendship*. Cambridge: Cambridge University Press, 1982. viii, 163 pp. ISBN 0-521-23592-8.
An important personal account of Mahler and his works by a close friend, a great musicologist. The edition by Edward Reilly includes commentary on the friendship between the two men which was not well documented by impartial observers prior to its publication; it counterbalances the negative aspects in the account of Adler by Mahler's wife.

294. Bahr, Hermann. *Selbstbildnis*. Berlin: S. Fischer, 1923. 309 pp.
Autobiography of the great Viennese literatus, depicting not only his own life but a whole portrait of the time in which he lived and the people he knew, including Mahler and Anna Bahr-Mildenburg. Also includes many observations on literary forebears of Bahr from Plato through Goethe, Eichendorff and Heine, and references to colleagues and contemporaries.

295. Bahr, Hermann. *Tagebuch: 1905/1906 bis Herbst 1908*. Berlin: Paul Cassirer, 1909. 268 pp.
Earliest of several diaries by Bahr, giving a detailed account of life in Vienna through the eyes of a literary linchpin. On-the-spot view of Mahler and his circle, among many figures passing across the author's stage.

296. Bahr, Hermann. *Tagebuch 1918*. Tagbücher, 2. Innsbruck, Wien, München: Verlagsanstalt Tyrolia, 1919. 305 pp.
Second diary of Bahr, written some years after Mahler died but still valuable as a picture of life in Vienna as changed by World War I, along with candid portraits of those in the intellectually elite circles.

297. Bahr-Mildenburg, Anna. *Erinnerungen*. Wien, Berlin: Wiener Literarische Anstalt, 1921. 230 pp.
Eyewitness account of Mahler, who worked with the author in Hamburg and Vienna, in the context of her autobiography. See especially the sections "Meine erste Proben mit Gustav Mahler" (pp. 11-24), "Erinnerung an Mahler" (pp. 24-33), and "Aus Briefen Gustav Mahler" (pp. 33-43), which latter section was an early

Eyewitness Accounts (Biographies) 83

        alternative source for a selection of Mahler's letters. Not always completely flattering, but honest and worth comparison with accounts by Alma Mahler-Werfel, Natalie Bauer-Lechner and Bruno Walter.

298. Bauer-Lechner, Natalie. *Erinnerungen an Gustav Mahler.* Hrsg. von H.J. Killian. Eingeleitet von Paul Stefan. Leipzig, Wien, Zürich: E.P. Tal, 1923. ix, 187 pp. Revised ed.: *Gustav Mahler in der Erinnerungen von Natalie Bauer-Lechner.* Mit Anmerkungen von Knud Martner. Hamburg: Karl Dieter Wagner, 1984. 239 pp. ISBN 3-921029-92-9.
English version: *Recollections of Gustav Mahler.* Transl. by Dika Newlin. Ed. and annotated by Peter Franklin. London: Faber Music Ltd.; New York: Cambridge University Press, 1980. 250 pp. ISBN 0-521-23572-3.
Invaluable portrait of Mahler as man and musician by a close friend who observed him from day to day up to the time of his marriage. Early edition of 1923 considerably truncated, but expanded and annotated to update in later editions based upon the author's unpublished diary.

299. Clemens, Clara. *My Husband Gabrilowitsch.* New York, London: Harper and Bros., 1938. Reprinted New York: Da Capo Press, 1979. v, 351 pp. ISBN 0-306-79563-9.
Includes a sensitive account of Gabrilowitsch's relations with Mahler, illustrated with a long quotation from Gabrilowitsch's diary and the full text of his letter to Krehbiel after Mahler's death. The text of the letter is also separately printed as *An Open Letter to the Music Critic of the New York Tribune* (München: A. Schmid Nachf., 1911, 11 pp.).

300. Damrosch, Walter. *My Musical Life.* New York: Charles Scribner's Sons, 1923, 1926; London: George Allen and Unwin, 1924. viii, 376 pp.
Less a source of firsthand anecdotes about Mahler than a keen observation of musical life in the United States (especially New York) at the time of Mahler's tenure there and later. Damrosch as a conductor seems to wear blinkers when discussing Mahler's compositions.

301. Farrar, Geraldine. *Such Sweet Compulsion: the Autobiography of Geraldine Farrar.* New York: Greystone Press, 1938. xii, 303 pp. Reprinted New York: Da

Capo Press, 1970. xvi, 303 pp. ISBN 0-306-71863-4. Essentially a great singer's view of her own life and work, but less self-centered than most, giving interesting views of her singer-colleagues, conductors, and other collaborators. Recognizes Mahler as a great operatic conductor in Europe and at the Met, and offers a brief but positive view of him as a person who had worked with Farrar.

302. Foerster, Josef Bohuslav. *Der Pilger: Erinnerungen eines Musikers.* Einleitende Studie und Auswahl für die deutsche Ausgabe von F. Pala. Prag: Artia, 1955, 1959. 765 pp.
Extremely detailed memoirs of Mahler's colleague-composer. Wide-ranging, includes portrait of Mahler in the chapter "Hamburg 1893-1903," valuable for complement to writing of Pfohl (see no. 314 below).

303. Grünfeld, Heinrich. *In Dur und Moll: Begegnungen und Erlebnisse aus 50 Jahren.* Leipzig, Zürich: Grethlein, 1923. 280 pp.
Autobiography of the cellist with whose family Mahler lived for a time while attending school in Prague. Briefly mentions Mahler as routine subject, probably with the humor of hindsight.

304. *Gustav Mahler: Im eigenen Wort--im Wort der Freunde.* Hrsg. von Willi Reich. Zürich: Die Arche, 1958. 95 pp.
Compilation of quotations by and about Mahler as man and musician, taken from his own letters and the accounts of those who knew him, including Alma Mahler-Werfel, Natalie Bauer-Lechner, Bruno Walter and many others. Useful although since superseded in many ways by publication of the full texts of many of these references.

305. Gutheil-Schoder, Marie. *Erlebtes und Erstrebtes: Rolle und Gestaltung.* Wien, Leipzig: Rudolf Krey, 1937. 58 pp.
Contains an eyewitness account of Mahler at work in the Hofoper in Vienna, valuable from one of his most important sopranos (although somewhat dimmed by the passage of time).

306. Halban, Desi, hrsg. *Selma Kurz: die Sängerin und ihre Zeit.* Unter Mitarbeit von Ursula Ebbers. Stuttgart, Zürich: Belser, 1983. 208 pp.

Biography of one of Mahler's greatest sopranos, by her daughter. Affords an insider's view of Vienna from the time of Mahler forward, showing the circle which focused around the Hofoper from Mahler to Bruno Walter.

307. Jones, Ernest. *Sigmund Freud: Life and Work.* London: Hogarth Press, 1953-57. 3 vols.
Abridged version: *The Life and Work of Sigmund Freud.* Ed. and abridged by Lionel Trilling and Steven Marcus. Introduction by Lionel Trilling. New York: Basic Books, 1953-57. 3 vols.
A major study of Freud's work by a close friend. Jones had the benefit of information from Freud's own mouth, and among Freud's revelations was one that concerned his consultation with Mahler in the summer of 1910. Versions of the abridged edition have been published in German (*Das Leben und Werk von Sigmund Freud*, Bern, Stuttgart: Hans Huber, 1962), Spanish (*Vida y obra de Sigmund Freud*, Barcelona: Anagrama, 1970, 1981) and Italian (*Vita e opere di Freud*, transl. by A. and M. Novelletto, Milano, 1967), although the original unabridged version in English should be preferred whenever possible.

308. Karpath, Ludwig. *Begegnung mit dem Genius: Denkwürdige Erlebnisse mit Johannes Brahms--Gustav Mahler--Hans Richter--Max Reger--Puccini--Mascagni--Leoncavallo und vielen anderen bedeutenden Menschen: unbekannte Briefe und Abbildung.* 2. Aufl. Wien, Leipzig: Fiba, 1934. 412 pp.
Dedicated to Alma Mahler Werfel. The first portion of the book, pp. 9-189, is extensively devoted to Mahler's tenure in Vienna and his effect on the Hofoper. No commentary on Mahler as composer, but good positive eyewitness account of the conductor and the man.

309. Karpath, Ludwig. *Lachende Musiker: Anekdotisches von Richard Wagner, Richard Strauss, Liszt, Brahms, Bruckner, Goldmark, Hugo Wolf, Gustav Mahler und anderen Musikern.* München: Knorr und Hirth, 1929. 132 pp.
Lighthearted anecdotes about various musical giants of the late nineteenth and early twentieth centuries, recounted by one who knew many of the subjects personally. One anecdote on Mahler, "Welcher Zahn ist es?" (pp. 55-56), compares essentially in all respects with account of visit to a dentist in Alma Mahler-Werfel's

biography of Mahler. See also the introduction to the book by Leo Slezak, which recounts still another incident involving Mahler with Karpath himself.

310. Klemperer, Otto. "Meine Erinnerungen an Gustav Mahler." *Meine Erinnerungen an Gustav Mahler und andere autobiographische Skizzen.* Freiburg im Breisgau, Zürich: Atlantis, 1960, pp. 5-12.
English version: *Minor Recollections.* Transl. by J. Maxwell Brownjohn. London: Dennis Dobson, 1964. 124 pp.
Klemperer's recollections of Mahler as conductor and friend are a brief but invaluable source of eyewitness information about Mahler the man, ranking with the accounts of Bruno Walter, Guido Adler and Natalie Bauer-Lechner as affectionate yet objective studies. A Russian version of this essay, "Moi vospominaniya o Gustava Malere i drugiye avtobiograficheskiye nabroski" (in *Ispolitel'skoye iskusstvo zarubezhnykh stran,* vol. 3) is mentioned by Inna Barsova and dates from 1967.

311. Lebrecht, Norman, [ed.]. *Mahler Remembered.* London, Boston: Faber and Faber, 1987. xxx, 322 pp. ISBN 0-571-15009-8, 0-571-14692-9 PbK.
Collection of personal reminiscences of Mahler from friends and enemies, generally translated from various original languages including French and German as well as English originals. Arranged in roughly chronological order to document Mahler's life and work. Divided into six sections: "Songs of a travelling apprentice (1860-88)," "Resurrection (1889-97)," "The heavenly life (1897-1902)," "Songs on the death of children (1902-07)," "I am lost to the world (1907-11)," and "Epilogue: My time will come." These titles should be taken only semi-literally, although borrowed from Mahler himself, as the works to which they refer are points of focus for the sections but not overweening themes. Useful source book for English-speaking readers, more of a kaleidoscope than an in-depth study. Useful editorial summaries preceding many of the selections giving information about the people who offered the reminiscences, from Mahler's wife to his colleagues and collaborators to his critics.

312. Mann, Thomas. *Tagebücher.* Frankfurt: S. Fischer, 1977-82. 5 vols.
English version: *Diaries, 1918-1939.* Transl. by Rich-

ard and Clara Winston. Selection and Foreword by Hermann Kesten. New York: H.N. Abrams, 1982. vii, 471 pp. ISBN 0-8109-1309-6.
Wide-ranging and very informative view of Mann's life and his observations on the lives and work of his contemporaries and colleagues from Mahler and Alma to Werfel, Bahr and Hauptmann, to Freud, to Hitler. The five volumes of the German original cover the years 1918-21, 1933-34, 1935-36, 1937-39 and 1940-43 respectively; the English version is much truncated.

313. Mengelberg, Willem. *Gedenkboek 1895-1920*. 's-Gravenhage: Martinus Nijhoff, 1920. xiv, 289 pp.
Mengelberg's personal and musical recollections, including an intimate portrait of Mahler as colleague and discussion of performances of his works in Amsterdam. Published at the time of Mengelberg's silver jubilee with the Concertgebouw which was celebrated with the famous Mahler cycle entirely conducted by Mengelberg. Fresh, current, day-by-day account.

314. Pfohl, Ferdinand. *Gustav Mahler: Eindrücke und Erinnerungen aus den Hamburger Jahren*. Hrsg. von Knud Martner. Hamburg: Verlag der Musikalienhandlung Wagner, 1973. 86 pp. ISBN 3-921029-15-5.
Documentation illustrating Mahler's tenure in Hamburg --letters, recollections and on-the-spot information. Ranks with Bauer-Lechner (see no. 298 above) as worthy documentation of Mahler in mid-career.

315. Rachmaninoff, Sergei. *Rachmaninoff's Recollections told to Oskar von Riesemann*. Transl. from the German manuscript by Dolly Rutherford. London: George Allen and Unwin; New York: Macmillan, 1934. 272 pp.
Includes Rachmaninoff's account of his work with Mahler and the New York Philharmonic Orchestra on the Third Concerto (see especially pp. 158-60). An eyewitness view of Mahler's working methods with the orchestra by a fellow musical professional who admired Mahler as a conductor; shows Mahler's problems with the orchestra as well as his disciplinary tactics.

316. Schiedermair, Ludwig. *Gustav Mahler: eine biographisch-kritische Würdigung*. Moderne Musiker. Leipzig: Hermann Seemann Nachf., 1900. 38 pp.
Qualifies as the first known published biography of Mahler, although limited to monograph form. Written

during his lifetime, this is a sort of predecessor to later compendium of essays on the symphonies by this author and others (see no. 801 below).

317. Slezak, Leo. *Meine Lebensmärchen*. München: Piper, 1948, 1962. 207 pp.
Autobiography of one of the great singers of the Vienna Opera, giving refreshingly candid views of his friends and collaborators including Mahler. A little too self-centered to be objective, but nonetheless fascinating. Discussions of Mahler on pp. 102-08, 115-16, 122-23 and 143.

318. Slezak, Leo. *Meine sämtlichen Werke*. Berlin: E. Rowohlt, 1922. 263 pp. Reprinted with *Der Wortbruch* in 1925 and 1927 (323 pp.).
English version: *Song of Motley, Being the Reminiscences of a Hungry Tenor*. London: W. Hodge, 1938. 302 pp.
Includes an affectionate and admiring portrait of Mahler (pp. 247-57 of the first edition) by the great tenor who worked with him in both Vienna and New York.

319. Smyth, Ethel Mary. *Impressions that Remained: Memoirs*. London: Longmans Green, 1919. 2 vols. New York: Alfred A. Knopf, 1946. xxxv, 509, xi pp. Reprinted New York: Da Capo Press, 1981. xxxvi, 510, xi pp. ISBN 0-306-76107-6.
Irreverent, honest and utterly disarming. Includes a rather different view of Mahler vis-à-vis his relations with the Webers in Leipzig at the time of his work on *Die drei Pintos*, which shows Mahler in a rather amazing cynical way. Da Capo Press edition contains an introduction by Ernest Newman and a new introduction by Ronald Crichton.

320. Specht, Richard. *Gustav Mahler*. Modern Essays, 52. Berlin: Gose und Tetzlaff, 1905, 1912. 59 pp.
First monograph of Specht, later superseded by full-fledged biography of Mahler (see no. 321 below). Current while Mahler was still alive, benefits from the author's knowledge of Mahler as insider.

321. Specht, Richard. *Gustav Mahler*. Berlin, Leipzig: Schuster und Loeffler, 1913; Stuttgart, Berlin: Deutsche Verlagsanstalt, 1918, 1925. 1st ed., 388 pp.; 2nd ed., 295 pp. (1918), 327 pp. (1925).

Earliest full-length biography of Mahler, expanded from monograph published during Mahler's lifetime (see no. 320 above). Author benefitted from his personal knowledge of Mahler, expanding and revising as new information and opinions affected the situation. 1925 edition notable for addition of material on the *Symphony no. 10*.

322. Stefan, Paul. *Das Grab in Wien: eine Chronik 1903-1911*. Berlin: Erich Reiss, 1913. 146 pp.
Affectionate view of music in Vienna and sometimes elsewhere from 1903-11, by a friend of Mahler who was writing from season to season. While semi-novelistic, this book is very informative. Mahler is the hero of this quasi-novel, which concludes with his death and "Das Grab in Wien"--his grave.

323. Stefan, Paul. *Gustav Mahler: eine Studie über Persönlichkeit und Werk*. München: R. Piper, 1910, 1912, 1913, 1920, 1981. 153 pp. (1920 ed., 172 pp.).
English version: *Gustav Mahler: a Study of His Personality and Work*. Transl. by T.E. Clark. New York: G. Schirmer, 1913. viii, 128 pp.
Well-rounded early book on Mahler, concerned with both the man's life and background and his compositions, most of which are presented individually and with personal thought and care. Originally published while Mahler was still alive, revised after his death.

324. Strauss, Richard. *Betrachtungen und Erinnerungen*. Hrsg. von Willi Schuh. Zürich: Atlantis, 1949, 1952. 206 pp. Revised ed.: Zürich: Atlantis, 1957, 1981. 262 pp. ISBN 3-7611-0636-X.
English version: *Recollections and Reflections*. Transl. by L.J. Lawrence. Ed. by Willi Schuh. London, New York: Boosey and Hawkes, 1953. Reprinted Westport, Connecticut: Greenwood Press, 1974. 173 pp. ISBN 0-8371-7366-3.
Various aphorisms on music and musicians, not an autobiography, but drawn from author's experiences. Collected from sources dating from 1892 to 1949. Mahler wanders through the book in roles of friend, colleague, conductor and composer; the brief "Gustav Mahler" on page 114 shows Strauss's sincere appreciation.

325. Walter, Bruno. *Gustav Mahler*. Wien, Leipzig, Zürich: Herbert Reichner, 1936; Berlin, Frankfurt am Main: S. Fischer, 1957. 114 pp. Later updated edition

Gustav Mahler: ein Porträt. Nachwort von Ekkehard Kroher. Taschenbücher zur Musikwissenschaft, 72. Hrsg. von Richard Schaal. Wilhelmshaven: Heinrichshofen, 1981. 131 pp. ISBN 3-7959-0305-X. English versions: (a) Gustav Mahler. Transl. by James Galston. With a biographical essay by Ernst Krenek. London: Kegan Paul, Trench, Trubner, 1937; New York: Greystone Press, 1941; New York: Vienna House, 1973. xi, 236 pp. ISBN 0-8443-0035-7. (b) Gustav Mahler. Transl. supervised by Lotte Walter Lindt. New York: Alfred A. Knopf, 1958. Reprinted New York: Da Capo Press, 1970. 236 pp. ISBN 0-306-71701-8. This biography ranks with those by Alma Mahler-Werfel, Natalie Bauer-Lechner and Guido Adler in value as eyewitness accounts of Mahler by those close to him. In objectivity this book surpasses the biography by Mahler's wife, although it was written many years after Mahler's death without benefit of a journal for reference as Alma Mahler-Werfel had had. Foreshadowed by "Persönliche Erinnerungen an Gustav Mahler" (*Der Tag*, Vienna, 17. November 1935) and author's contributions to special issue of *Der Merker* (1912) and *Gustav Mahler: ein Bild seiner Persönlichkeit in Widmungen*, the book's importance can be measured by the fact that--in addition to the two English versions, of which the one by Galston is the superior--translations have been published in Spanish (Madrid: Alianza Editorial, 1983), French (Paris: Collection Pluriel, 1979, in the series "Le Libre de Poche") and Czech (*Gustav Mahler: Portrét*, published with *Dopisy Gustava Mahlera*, ed. by Alma Mahler, transl. by Frantiska Pekelska, Praha: Svobodné Slovo-Melantrich, 1958, 1965, 197 pp.) which latter edition predated Bartos's edition of the letters cited below as no. 380.

326. Walter, Bruno. *Thema und Variationen: Erinnerungen und Gedanken*. Stockholm: Bermann-Fischer, 1947; Frankfurt: S. Fischer, 1973. 502 pp.
In contrast to Bruno Walter's biography of Mahler, which concentrated entirely on Mahler the man, conductor and composer, this book places Mahler in the perspective of his influence on Bruno Walter's life. This book also draws a sharply defined picture of artistic life in Vienna and in the musical community in southern California at the time Walter emigrated to the United States after the Nazis came to power. Versions of this book have been published in English (*Theme and

Variations: an Autobiography, New York: Alfred A. Knopf, 1946, 1947, reprinted Westport, Connecticut: Greenwood Press, 1980), Dutch (Amsterdam: Von Ditmar, 1947) and Russian (Moscow, 1958).

327. Weingartner, Felix [von]. *Lebenserinnerungen*. Wien, Leipzig: Wiener Literarische Anstalt, 1923; Zürich, Leipzig: Orell Füssli, 1928-29. 2 vols. English version: *Buffets and Rewards: a Musician's Reminiscences*. Transl. by Marguerite Wolff. London: Hutchinson, 1937. 383 pp.
Weingartner's autobiography includes personal reminiscences of his relations with Mahler which he considered poor at the time of the change of directorship at the Hofoper in Vienna. Personal prejudice mars this account.

328. Wellesz, Egon und Emmy Wellesz. *Egon Wellesz: Leben und Werk*. Hrsg. von Franz Endler. Wien, Hamburg: Paul Zsolnay, 1981. 293 pp.
Eyewitness account of the Vienna of Wellesz's youth, when Mahler was a central influence in his circle, as well as the conditions after the rise of the Third Reich which caused Wellesz to emigrate to England. As a member of Schoenberg's circle, Wellesz was an acute observer of Mahler, with whom he worked, and his positive eyewitness account must be considered along with those in the letters of Schoenberg and Berg (see no. 333 below).

329. Winter, Josefine von. *50 Jahre eines Wiener Hauses*. Wien: Wilhelm Braumüller, 1927. iii, 104 pp.
Modest account of life in Vienna, based on author's personal journal (which included musical and personal observations of Mahler and others). Somewhat truncated from the original journal but still of interest. Excerpts from the original journal were published in the German and English issues of *NaMR*, no. 11 (March 1983): 3-7.

330. Zichy, Géza. *Aus meinem Leben: Erinnerungen und Fragmente*. Stuttgart: Deutsche Verlagsanstalt, 1911-20. 3 vols.
Autobiography of Mahler's major collaborator at the Royal Hungarian Opera in Budapest. Extensive, covering the major portion of author's life and providing detailed portraits of many important associates besides Mahler. Personal, not heavily documented.

331. Zuckerkandl, Bertha. *Österreich intim: Erinnerungen 1892-1942*. Hrsg. von Reinhard Federmann. Frankfurt, Berlin, Wien: Propyläen, 1970. 228 pp.
English version: *My Life and History*. Transl. by John Sommerfeld. New York: Alfred A. Knopf, 1939. viii, 324 pp.
An observation of Austrian musical, literary, artistic, political and medical life in a series of essays by a close friend of Mahler and Alma who had many contacts among the greatest intelligentsia of her time. Less a historical study than a portrait of a society through the day-to-day workings of a woman who was herself a linchpin. See especially essays "Gustav Mahler" (pp. 38-43), "Gespräch mit Alma" (pp. 67-69), "Mahlers Abschied" (pp. 70-74) and "Franz Werfel" (pp. 171-72).

Letters

332. Berg, Alban. *Briefe an seine Frau*. Hrsg. von Helene Berg. München, Wien: Albert Lange/Georg Müller, 1965. 666 pp.
English version: *Letters to his Wife*. Ed., transl. and annotated by Bernard Grun. New York: St. Martin's Press; London: Faber and Faber, 1971. 456 pp.
One of the best firsthand sources documenting life in the musical community of Vienna, by the composer who was a touchstone in that community from Mahler's time until his own death. Valuable accounts spread over time, showing Mahler, Alma, Werfel, Anna and their entire circle. The English edition omits eighty-one of the original 569 letters, but is heavily annotated and includes supplementary material not found in the German original.

333. Berg, Alban and Arnold Schoenberg. *The Berg-Schoenberg Correspondence: Selected Letters*. Ed. [and transl.] by Juliane Brand, Christopher Hailey and Donald Harris. New York, London: W.W. Norton, 1987. xxvii, 497 pp. ISBN 0-393-01919-5.
Broad selection in English translation of correspondence between Berg and Schoenberg covering the period from 1911 to 1935. Divided into three time periods (1906-15, 1916-25 and 1926-35) roughly corresponding to Schoenberg's professional periods in Berlin and elsewhere and, more subjectively, to the development of the relationship between the two men in stages. Sub-

jects cover music, politics, daily living and many others. Although correspondence begins shortly after Mahler's death, his work and influence on the younger composers are documented everywhere in this correspondence, as is the relationship of both Berg and Schoenberg and their wives to Alma Mahler-Werfel. This is a valuable eyewitness portrait of life in the German-speaking countries and in the United States in the generation after Mahler when his influence was beginning to be felt, almost as good as a double autobiography.

334. Bruckner, Anton. *Gesammelte Briefe*. Neue Folge, gesammelt und hrsg. von Max Auer. Regensburg: Gustav Bosse, 1924. 408 pp.
Covers time span from 1852 to Bruckner's death in 1896 with appendix of letters written to Bruckner by others. Mahler is mentioned in several of Bruckner's letters, as well as being the writer of one in the appendix; he is also mentioned in a letter to Bruckner written by Wilhelm Zinne.

335. Bülow, Hans von. *Briefe und Schriften*. Hrsg. von Marie von Bülow. Leipzig: Breitkopf und Härtel, 1895-1908. 8 vols.
Includes an eyewitness account of Mahler by a major elder colleague conductor; valuable taken in tandem with the letters which passed between Bülow and Richard Strauss (see no. 347 below). Especially important as illumination of Mahler's tenure in Hamburg.

336. Busoni, Ferruccio Benvenuto. *Briefe an seine Frau*. Hrsg. von Friedrich Schnapp. Mit einem Vorwort von Willi Schuh. Erlenbach, Zürich, Leipzig: Rotapfel, 1935. xxvi, 404 pp.
English version: *Letters to his Wife*. Transl. by Rosamond Ley. London: E. Arnold, 1938. Reprinted New York: Da Capo Press, 1975. 319 pp. ISBN 0-306-70732-2.
Includes firsthand view of Mahler's tenure in New York and an early account of his first meeting with Busoni in England in 1903, also observations on Mahler's works.

337. Dehmel, Richard. *Ausgewählte Briefe aus den Jahren 1902 bis 1920*. Berlin: S. Fischer, 1923. 528 pp.
Dehmel's letters cover a wide range of recipients including his family and colleagues (Max Brod, Gustav Falke, Hugo von Hofmannsthal, Armin Knab, Detlev von

Liliencron, Oskar Loerke, Thomas Mann and Stefan Zweig). Chronologically arranged, they cover a wide range of topics from family matters to life, music, literature and politics. Letter no. 430 to Robert Scheu brings up Mahler among other names of international intelligentsia by country; it is dated February 1, 1905.

338. Diepenbrock, Alphons. *Brieven en documenten*. Ed. by Eduard Reeser. Utrecht: Vereniging voor Nederlandse Muziekgeschiedenis, 1962–
Multivolume set in progress. Letters and essays of Mahler's Dutch colleague Diepenbrock, in which Mahler figures as recipient and subject of discourse in both letters and essays.

339. Mahler, Alma. *Gustav Mahler: Erinnerungen und Briefe*. Amsterdam: Allert de Lange, 1940. 480 pp. Rev. Ausgabe (hrsg. von Donald Mitchell) Frankfurt am Main, Berlin: Ullstein/Propyläen, 1971. 392 pp. ISBN 3-549-17445-4.
English version: *Gustav Mahler: Memories and Letters*. Transl. by Basil Creighton. New York: Viking Press, 1946; Seattle, London: University of Washington Press, 1968. vi, 277 pp. Revised ed. (ed. by Donald Mitchell) London: John Murray, Ltd., 1968, 1969; New York: Viking Press, 1969; Seattle, London: University of Washington Press, 1971. 3rd ed. (further enlarged with new appendix and chronology by Knud Martner and Donald Mitchell) London: John Murray, 1973; Seattle, London: University of Washington Press, 1975, 1979. Editions of 1968, 1969 and 1971, xl, 369 pp. 1973 ed., xl, 393 pp. Edition of 1975/1979, xliii, 399 pp. ISBN 0-295-95378-0.
A firsthand portrait of Mahler through the eyes of his wife, complemented by his letters to her. Passage of time has resulted in reassessment of Alma Mahler's opinions and attitude toward Mahler, and the alterations have not always been favorable to her objectivity; nevertheless, this is an important source, and the later editions beginning with 1968 include materials not in the original editions published in Alma Mahler's lifetime which offer perspective in the light of recent Mahler scholarship. The original editions in English and German are the basis of editions in Swedish (*Gustav Mahler: Kompositören och människan*, transl. by Emanuel Lillieroth, Stockholm: Natur och Kultur, 1948, 300 pp.), Italian (1961), Czech (1962)

and Russian (1964). Revised editions based on the English and German versions beginning in 1968 include *Gustav Mahler: Minnen från ett Aktensap* (Stockholm: Natur och Kultur, 1977, xvi, 207 pp.), *Mahler: Memoires et Correspondance* (transl. by Natalie Godard, preface by Henry-Louis de la Grange, Paris: Editions Jean-Claude Lattès, 1980); *Gustav Mahler: recuerdos y cartas* (Madrid: Ediciones Taurus, 1978); and *Gustav Mahler: ricordi e lettere* (transl. by Laura Dallapiccola, ed. by Luigi Rognoni, Milano: Il Saggiatore, 1976, xiv, 409 pp.).

340. Mann, Thomas. *Briefe*. Hrsg. von Erika Mann. Frankfurt am Main: S. Fischer, 1961-65. 3 vols.
English version: *Letters of Thomas Mann, 1889-1955*. Selected and transl. by Richard and Clara Winston. New York: Alfred A. Knopf, 1971. xlv, 690, xxiv pp. Original edition covers 1889-1936, 1937-47 and 1948-55 respectively in the three volumes. A rich, remarkable view of German-Austrian literary, artistic, musical and political life by a great man. The text of Mann's famous letter to Mahler after the premiere of the *Symphony no. 8* is in volume I, and all three volumes include many references to Mahler, Alma, Franz Werfel and many others from their circle. A unique and special view of individuals in a society observed by a man who was a linchpin of that society.

341. Pfitzner, Hans Erich. *Reden, Schriften, Briefe: Unveröffentliches und bisher Verstreutes*. Hrsg. von Walter Abendroth. Berlin-Frohnau, Neuwied/Rhein: Hermann Luchterhand, 1955. 336 pp.
Curious compilation in three parts: (a) essays and aphorisms by Pfitzner on various musical subjects, (b) autobiography, *Eindrücke und Bilder meines Lebens* (originally published Hamburg & Bergedorf: Stromverlag, 1948), covering Pfitzner's early life and career, and (c) selected letters. Brief assessment of the Mahlers and their circle at the time of the Vienna premiere of *Rose vom Liebesgarten* under Mahler is in second section of book.

342. Rolland, Romain et Richard Strauss. *Correspondance. Fragments de journal*. Cahiers Romain Rolland, 3. Avant-Propos de Gustave Samazeuilh. Paris: Editions Albin Michel, 1951. 243 pp.
English version: *Richard Strauss and Romain Rolland:*

Correspondence. Together with Fragments from the Diary of Romain Rolland and Other Essays and an Introduction by Gustave Samazeuilh. Ed. by Rollo Myers. Berkeley: University of California Press, 1968. xvi, 239 pp.
Interesting contemporary view of Mahler by two great men of their time. Rolland, while apparently not personally acquainted with Mahler, was intelligent enough to recognize his importance. Information on Mahler is dispersed through the two men's letters and Rolland's essays.

343. Schalk, Franz. *Briefe und Betrachtungen.* Veröffentlicht von Lili Schalk. Hrsg. von der Internationalen Bruckner-Gesellschaft. Mit einem Lebensabriss von Victor Junk. Wien, Leipzig: Musikwissenschaftlicher Verlag, 1935. 91 pp.
Interesting personal description of musical life during Mahler's time by a colleague, as well as correspondence from Bruckner. Falls between the time of the subjects' student days and their work at the Hofoper in Vienna a generation later.

344, Schnitzler, Arthur. *Briefe.* Frankfurt-am-Main: S. Fischer, 1981-84. 2 vols.
Multivolume series in progress. The two volumes published as of this writing cover Schnitzler's letters from 1875-1912 (vol. 1), 1913-31 (vol. 2). The first volume was edited by Therese Nickl and Heinrich Schnitzler, the second by Peter Michael Braunwarth, Richard Miklin, Susanne Pertlik and Heinrich Schnitzler. Valuable on-the-spot observations of Mahler (vols. 1-2), Alma, their daughter Anna and Franz Werfel (vol. 2 only), as Schnitzler was an insider to the circle. ISBN 3-10-073528-5 (vol. 1), 3-10-073530-7 (vol. 2).

345. Schoenberg, Arnold. *Briefe.* Hrsg. von Erwin Stein. Mainz: B. Schotts Söhne, 1958. 309 pp.
English version: *Letters.* Transl. by Eithne Wilkins and Ernst Kaiser. Selected and ed. by Erwin Stein. New York: St. Martin's Press, 1965; London: Faber and Faber, 1964. 309 pp. ISBN 0-571-10514-9.
Selection of Schoenberg's letters from 1910-51. Obviously valuable eyewitness accounts of Mahler and Alma who were recipients of several letters and discussion of Mahler's works. The German and English editions differ considerably in content, since some letters or-

iginally in English had been omitted from the German version and were restored to the English version. See also Hans Gal. *In Dur und Moll: Briefe grosser Komponisten von Orlando di Lasso bis Arnold Schoenberg.* Frankfurt-am-Main: G.B. Fischer, 1966, where one letter is reproduced on pp. 546-47.

346. Strauss, Richard und Franz Schalk. *Ein Briefwechsel.* Hrsg. von Günter Brosche. Veröffentlichungen der Richard-Strauss-Gesellschaft München, 6. Tutzing: Hans Schneider, 1983. xxvi, 423 pp. ISBN 3-7952-0365-1.
    Correspondence covers the period from 1897-1929, most of it falling into the period 1918 onwards. Primarily concerned with musical affairs and personages in Vienna, in which the shadow of the departed Mahler is acknowledged and appreciated by both men, especially Strauss. Editing by Brosche discreet with marginal annotations clarifying identity of personages mentioned in letters.

347. Strauss, Richard und Hans von Bülow. "Hans von Bülow--Richard Strauss: Briefwechsel." *Richard Strauss Jahrbuch 1954.* Hrsg. von Willi Schuh und Franz Trenner. Bonn: Boosey and Hawkes, 1953, pp. 7-88.
    English version: *Correspondence of Hans von Bülow and Richard Strauss.* Transl. by Anthony Gishford. Ed. by Willi Schuh and Franz Trenner. London, New York: Boosey and Hawkes, 1953. 104 pp.
    Covers music in the 1880s and 1890s especially in Leipzig, including Mahler's work on Weber's *Die drei Pintos.*

348. Wagner, Cosima und Richard Strauss. *Briefwechsel.* Hrsg. von Franz Trenner unter Mitarbeit von Gabriele Strauss. Veröffentlichungen der Richard-Strauss-Gesellschaft München, 2. Tutzing: Hans Schneider, 1978. xvi, 312 pp. ISBN 3-7952-0258-2.
    Includes interesting account of Mahler's accession to the directorship of the Hofoper in Vienna which Cosima Wagner had opposed while Strauss supported it. This collection consists of 223 letters (177 between Strauss and Cosima, 20 between Strauss and Siegfried Wagner and 26 involving other family members). Span of time covers 1889-1940.

349. Walter, Bruno. *Briefe 1894-1962.* Hrsg. von Lotte Walter Lindt. Geleitwort von Wolfgang Stresemann. Frankfurt am Main: S. Fischer, 1969. xv, 461 pp.

Includes eyewitness personal observations of Mahler (who was also recipient of the letter "Hochverehrter, teurer Freund" about June 1910, reprinted by Paul Stefan in no. 22 above). Several letters addressed to Alma Mahler-Werfel, and many others about Franz Werfel and others in their circle. Widespread commentary about Mahler's work likewise. More comprehensive and immediate than author's autobiography or his biography of Mahler in many ways.

* Walter, Bruno. "Hochverehrter, teurer Freund!" *Gustav Mahler: ein Bild seiner Persönlichkeit in Widmungen:* 82-88.
Full citation under no. 22 above. Reprints a congratulatory letter on Mahler's fiftieth birthday, in which his friend and colleague casts retrospective survey over their relationship in professional and personal terms. Later reprinted in collection of Bruno Walter's letters (see no. 349 above).

350. Wolf, Hugo. *Briefe an Heinrich Potpeschnigg.* Hrsg. von Heinz Nonveiller. Stuttgart: Union Deutsche Verlagsgesellschaft, 1923. 239 pp.
Comprises 230 letters covering period 1890-98. Among other subjects, Mahler's inception at the Hofoper in Vienna and his plans for production of Wolf's *Corregidor* are mentioned frequently in the period May 1897 to February 1898. Somewhat contrasting picture to the one drawn by Mahler's wife.

351. Wolf, Hugo. *Briefe an Melanie Köchert.* Hrsg. von Franz Grasberger. Tutzing: Hans Schneider, 1965. xx, 241 pp.
Covers most of Wolf's long relationship with his mistress which extended from their first meeting in 1879 to his death in 1903, during which period he inscribed all of his song manuscripts to her. Mahler is mentioned several times in the course of this correspondence, notably--as in other correspondence from Wolf-- in connection with Mahler's appointment in Vienna and the plans for *Corregidor*.

352. Wolf, Hugo. *Briefe an Oskar Grohe.* Hrsg. von Heinrich Werner. Berlin: S. Fischer, 1905; Leipzig: Breitkopf und Härtel, 1911. 316 pp.
Comprises 211 letters covering period 1890-98 to Grohe and his wife. Mahler is mentioned in connection with

his appointment to the Hofoper in Vienna and his first performances there, especially Wagner operas; however, there is no discussion of the plans to produce *Corregidor*, which leaves a slight contrast between this group of letters and those to Potpeschnigg and Köchert.

353. Wolf, Hugo. *Ein Persönlichkeit in Briefen: Familienbriefe*. Hrsg. von Edmund Hellmer. Leipzig: Breitkopf und Härtel, 1912. v, 159 pp.
Comprises 106 letters, most from Wolf to his parents and siblings, covering much of his life from youth until 1898. Interspersed with brief editorial commentary tracing the course of Wolf's life. Mahler is twice mentioned on very different occasions: in a letter of 1879 when he and Wolf were sharing quarters as students in Vienna; and in 1897 at the time of Mahler's appointment to the Hofoper in Vienna when *Corregidor* was considered for production.

Essays and Miscellaneous

* Adler, Guido. "Ein Freundeswort." *Gustav Mahler: ein Bild seiner Persönlichkeit in Widmungen*: 3-6.
Full citation under no. 22 above. Brief essay summarizing the long friendship between Mahler and the great musicologist.

* Adler, Guido. "Gustav Mahlers Persönlichkeit." *Mahlerfest Amsterdam*: 17-20.
Full citation under no. 11 above. Perhaps the most personal of the contributions to the Mahler Festival in Amsterdam, an affectionate reminiscence closely related to Adler's biography of Mahler published four years previously but with some additional views including observations on the sonata-allegro form in the *Symphony no. 8*.

* Adler, Guido. "Zum Mahler-Fest in Amsterdam." *Musikblätter des Anbruch* 2 (1920): 255-56.
Brief dedicatory essay commemorating Mahler and giving send-off to Amsterdam Mahler Festival scheduled for that May. Full citation under no. 16 above.

354. Bahr, Hermann. "Mahler." *Bilderbuch*. Wien, Leipzig: Wila, 1921, pp. 59-69.

Profile of Mahler's work in Vienna by a major literary compatriot, observer of the Viennese scene, and, incidentally, husband of Mahler's operatic collaborator Anna Bahr-Mildenburg.

355. Bahr, Hermann. *Wien. Städte und Landschaften*, 6. Stuttgart: Carl Krabbe, 1906. 136 pp.
An insider's portrait of Vienna, its history, politics, musical and literary tradition, highlighting major personages in these areas. Critical yet affectionate; makes no attempt to be comprehensive but shows the life of a city through the eyes of a major literary commentator. Originally (and significantly) banned by the censors in Vienna.

* Bahr-Mildenburg, Anna. "Die Mahler-Zeit der Wiener Oper: Erinnerungen von Wiener Künstlers--aus Briefen Mahlers." *Moderne Welt* 3 (1921): 13-14.
Full citation under no. 13 above. Something of a concentrated summary of author's discussion of Mahler in her *Erinnerungen* of same year (see no. 297 above). Quotes extensively from Mahler's letters to author. A misnomer as the real subject of this essay is the relationship between her and Mahler 1896-97 which was really before the "Mahler-Zeit" in Vienna.

356. Batka, Richard. *Aus der Opernwelt: Prager Kritiken und Skizzen*. München: Callwey, 1907. viii, 204 pp.
Collection of reviews and essays on opera and its proponents in Prague, by a major critical supporter of Mahler's work. Ranges over a considerable time, having been reprinted from Batka's timely contributions to the periodical literature; fresh and immediate, an on-the-spot observation of the period which included Mahler's tenure in Prague.

357. Batka, Richard. *Die moderne Oper*. Prag: Verlag der Lese- und Redehalle der deutschen Studenten in Prag, 1902. 16 pp. Reprinted in *Kranz: Gesammelte Blätter über Musik* (Leipzig: Lauterbach und Kuhn, 1903), pp. 243-70.
A bird's eye summary of opera since Wagner from a critic who saw performances of good and bad alike in his long stint as critic in Prague and followed Mahler's work as conductor and composer long past Mahler's tenure in that city. Useful background along with Korngold and Hanslick for on-the-spot critical observation of opera done

Eyewitness Accounts (Essays)

        in the time when Mahler was conducting it.

*   [Bauer-Lechner, Natalie.] "Aus einem Tagebuch über Mahler." *Der Merker* 3: 184-88.
Full citation under no. 12 above. Unsigned in this issue, but identifiable on comparison with Natalie Bauer-Lechner's book *Erinnerungen an Gustav Mahler* (see no. 298 above) published eleven years later.

358. Behn, Hermann. "Gustav Mahler." *Musikwelt* 8 (1928): 239-47.
Personal reminiscences of Mahler by a lawyer and composer who was a close friend especially during the Hamburg era, closely involved with performance and publication of the *Symphony no. 2.*

*   Casella, Alfredo. "Festrede." *Mahler-Fest Amsterdam*: 21-25.
Full citation under no. 11 above. A serious consideration of "where music stood" since Wagner and where Mahler figures in the grand scheme of things therein. Also a recollection of the author's relationship with Mahler, the premiere of the *Symphony no. 8* in Munich in 1910, and a grateful salutation to Mengelberg as pioneer of the new effort on Mahler's behalf, especially since World War I. In French, by contrast with the other essays in this symposium; Italian version translated by Paolo Gallarati in *N Riv Mus It* 6 (January-March 1972): 93-97.

359. Clémenceau, Paul. "Gustav Mahler und Rodin." *Kunstauktion* 4 (13. Juli 1930): 9.
Eyewitness account of the meeting between Mahler and Rodin and their cooperation as artist and subject at the time Rodin made his famous bust of Mahler. Written by husband of Sophie Szeps (sister of Berta Szeps-Zuckerkandl) who was brother of Georges Clémenceau, responsible for introducing Mahler and Rodin. Berta Szeps-Zuckerkandl had written "Paul Clémenceau spricht über Gustav Mahler: wie Rodins Mahler-Büste entstand" in *Deutsche La Plata Zeitung* (13. Juli 1929), but this is a true eyewitness account rather than discussion at second hand as in the earlier article.

*   Decsey, Ernst. "Stunden mit Mahler." *Die Musik* 10 (1911): 352-56.
Full citation under no. 15 above. An informal portrait

of Mahler from day to day with friends and co-workers, at the Opera, in the cafes and on vacation in the summer. Really allows Mahler to draw his own portrait in speech. This article was the first of a two-part study; the second part was published in *Die Musik* 10 (Erste Augustheft): 143-53.

360. Diepenbrock, Alfons. *Ommegangen: verzammelte opstellen.* Amsterdam: Van Munster's Uitgevers-Maatschappij, 1924. 211 pp.
Essays of Mahler's Dutch colleague published following his death in 1921; focuses on many aspects of music including firsthand description of Mahler himself and analyses of certain of Mahler's compositions. Since superseded by the collected edition of Diepenbrock's essays and letters in multivolume set edited by Reeser (see no. 338 above).

* "Erinnerungen an Gustav Mahler." *Musikblätter des Anbruch* 2 (1920): 291-300.
Full citation under no. 16 above. Personal recollections of Mahler by Josef Bohuslav Foerster, Max Steinitzer and Emil Nikolaus von Reznicek.

361. Foerster, Josef Bohuslav. "Aus Mahlers Werkstatt: Erinnerungen." *Der Merker* 1 (1910): 921-24.
Author's personal recollections of Mahler during Hamburg period, spotlighting the early part of 1894 when Mahler was preparing production of *Fidelio* at the Opera and finishing the *Symphony no. 2*. Especially important for eyewitness account of Bülow's funeral and Mahler's inspiration by the *Auferstehungsode*. Compare this brief account with later one in *Der Pilger* (see no. 302 above) after Mahler's death.

* Gutheil-Schoder, Marie. "Mahler bei der Arbeit." *Der Merker* 3: 165.
Full citation under no. 12 above. An eyewitness account of Mahler as operatic director by one of his most famous sopranos, with special reference to production of *Figaro* in which author herself sang the role of Susanna.

* Gutheil-Schoder, Marie. "Mahleriana." *Moderne Welt* 3 (1921): 14-15.
Full citation under no. 13 above. Recollections of author's work with Mahler at the Hofoper in Vienna fo-

cusing particularly on his working methods rather than on individual production as in preceding entry from *Der Merker*.

362. Heuberger, Richard. *Im Foyer: Gesammelte Essays über das Opernrepertoire der Gegenwart*. 2. Auflage. Leipzig: Hermann Seemanns Nachfolger, 1901. viii, 303 pp.
Collected essays on opera in Vienna (primarily at the Hofoper, some at the Theater an der Wien) from 1890-1900 by a major critic and sometime composer. Observant in chronicling the background of his subjects, commenting on stories, music and productions. Productions cited in which Mahler was involved include *Dalibor* (pp. 244-51), *Die Bohème* (pp. 259-64--the version by Leoncavallo, not the one by Puccini), *Der Barenhäuter* (pp. 265-74) and *Der Dämon* (pp. 275-85).

* Karpath, Ludwig. "Gustav Mahler in Amerika." *Moderne Welt* 3 (1921): 33-35.
Straightforward account of Mahler's work in the United States and his final illness and death. Anti-American in point of view, painting dark picture of Mahler's work in the United States; prejudiced and unsatisfactory. Full citation under no. 13 above.

* Klemperer, Otto. "Erinnerungen." *Gustav Mahler* (1966): 61-70.
Full citation under no. 7 above. Personal recollections of Mahler by Klemperer, including the story of Mahler's assistance in the early days of Klemperer's career and how Mahler behaved professionally and personally during the time from Hamburg to Vienna and his death.

* Kurz, Selma. "Mein Entdecker." *Moderne Welt* 3 (1921): 15.
Full citation under no. 13 above. Brief but interesting summary of Mahler's work with the author, from the date he hired her and thus began her career. Sympathetic, more concerned with Mahler as a human being to work with than with the famous conductor.

363. Mahler, Gustav. "The Influence of the Folk Song on German Musical Art: from an Interview with the Eminent Composer and Director Gustav Mahler." *Etude*, May 1911: 301-02.

Off-the-cuff remarks by Mahler on "Assimilating Good Music in Childhood," "Plagiarism?" "Haydn's Appreciation of the Folk-Song," "Beethoven's Incomparable Melodies" and "A Grave Question for America." Fascinating view of the composer and conductor in his own words, rare in comparison to his letters. Cited by Zoltan Roman in connection with Mahler's historical awareness of composers before his own time.

364. Moldenhauer, Hans und Rosaleen Moldenhauer. "Gustav Mahler und Moriz Rosenthal." *Orchester* 30 (1982): 430-32.
First publication of the *Mahleriana* manuscript of the Polish pianist Moriz Rosenthal, who was a classmate of Mahler at the University in Vienna and saw Mahler later on other occasions when Mahler was established as Director of the Hofoper. Manuscript apparently dates from about 1888 according to the Moldenhauers, who had acquired it for the archive and here provide introduction placing the account in historical perspective.

* Neitzel, Otto. "Gustav Mahler und das Amsterdamer Concertgebouw." *Musikblätter des Anbruch* 2 (1920): 256-62.
Full citation under no. 16 above. Summarizes author's contacts with Mahler including premiere of the *Symphony no. 8* and Mahler's work and other history with the Concertgebouw which became major champion of Mahler's music (and other 'risky' repertoire) when other orchestras would not take such risks.

365. Pfitzner, Hans Erich. *Vom musikalischen Drama: Gesammelte Aufsätze*. München, Leipzig: Süddeutsche Monatshefte, 1915. 253 pp.
See especially the essay "Die 'Symbolik' in der Rose vom Liebesgarten" (pp. 188-97), which forms part of the chapter "Zur Grundfrage der Operndichtung." Not only explores the symbolism of the work, which was premiered in Vienna by Mahler, but discusses the history of its performance 1900-14.

366. Pringsheim, Klaus. "My Recollections of Gustav Mahler." *CD* 2 (1958): 114-16.
Brief but fascinating account of relationship between Mahler and a young assistant conductor who later proved a major influence in the growing popularity of Mahler's music in Japan.

367. Ritter, William. "Souvenirs sur Gustav Mahler." *Schweizerische Musikzeitung* 101 (1961): 29-39.
Personal recollections of Mahler covering the period from 1900-11, concerned with performances of his works which he himself conducted in many cities; also sketches the relationship between the two men. Written in June 1945, perhaps limited by the lapse of memory over time, but affectionate portrait.

368. Rosé, Alfred. "From Gustav Mahler's Storm and Stress Period." *Canadian Music Journal* 1 (Winter 1957): 21-24.
Brief description of Mahler's life during the summers of 1893-96 at Steinbach-am-Attersee, told by his nephew, who incorporated information received from his mother, Mahler's sister Justine, and his own observations from visits to the area. Preceded by an earlier German article, "Intimes aus Gustav Mahlers Sturm- und Drangperiode: wie die Zweite und Dritte Symphonie in Steinbach-am-Attersee entstanden ist (1893 bis 1896)," which appeared in *Neues Wiener Journal* (August 19, 1928) and *Vossische Zeitung* (December 29, 1928).

369. Schiedermair, Ludwig. "Richard Strauss und Gustav Mahler." *Musikalische Begegnungen: Erlebnis und Erinnerung*. Köln: Staufen, 1948, pp. 41-46.
A personal point of view of the two composer-conductors who were friends of each other and acquaintances of the author.

* Schönberg, Arnold. "Prager Rede." *Gustav Mahler* (1966): 11-58.
Full citation under no. 7 above. Reproduces the famous lecture given by Schoenberg in Prague on March 25, 1912, discussing Mahler as a compositional influence on his friends and colleagues. Considers Mahler's symphonies individually but gives short shrift to the *Symphony no. 10* since the author was not familiar with it at the time of the lecture.

370. Schoenberg, Arnold. *Style and Idea: Selected Writings of Arnold Schoenberg*. Ed. by Leonard Stein. Transl. by Leo Black. New York: St. Martin's Press, 1975. 559 pp. ISBN 0-571-09722-7.
First issued in 1950 (New York: Philosophical Library), but greatly expanded and newly edited in this edition. Several essays in the first edition were translated by Schoenberg's student Dika Newlin. Schoenberg's essay,

"Gustav Mahler," on pp. 449-72 of the new edition, is well known; among the new additions also worth noting are "Gustav Mahler: In Memoriam" (pp. 447-48, which had originally been published in *Der Merker* 3, pp. 182-83, cited as no. 12 above), and "Two Speeches on the Jewish Situation" (pp. 501-05). Editions in German (*Stil und Gedanke/Aufsätze zur Musik*, Frankfurt: S. Fischer, 1976) and French (*Le Style et l'Idée*, Paris: Buchet Chastel, 1977) have also been published; the German edition comprises volume I of *Gesammelte Schriften*. A major reference by a devoted friend and colleague of Mahler. Special and unique.

* Seidl, Arthur. "Zu Gustav Mahlers Gedächtnis: eine nichtgehaltene Rede." *Der Merker* 3: 192-95.
Full citation under no. 12 above. Author's recollections of Mahler spanning the period 1896-1910, informal compared to many other such eyewitness accounts. Shows Mahler in a variety of situations (many controversial) in performance, in conversation with friends, etc.

* Slezak, Leo. "Gustav Mahler." *Moderne Welt* 3 (1921): 16-17.
Full citation under no. 13 above. Excerpted from the author's *Meine sämtlichen Werken* (see no. 318 above). Here as companion to accounts of Mahler by three great sopranos Mildenburg, Kurz and Gutheil-Schoder.

* Specht, Richard. "Gustav Mahler." *Die Musik* 10 (1911): 335-41.
Full citation under no. 15 above. Reminiscences of Mahler as man from a friend and collaborator who published analyses of many of the symphonies and earliest major biographies.

371. Specht, Richard. "Mahler als Dirigent." *Kunstwart* 23 (2. Juliheft 1910): 94-97.
Eyewitness portrait of Mahler as operatic conductor by insider who saw many of his performances in Vienna. Original and immediate during Mahler's lifetime. Special attention to Mahler's work with operas of Wagner.

* Specht, Richard. "Mahlers Feinde." *Musikblätter des Anbruch* 2 (1920): 278-87.
Full citation under no. 16 above. Blistering indictment of Mahler's enemies and the problems they caused

during his tenure in Vienna and after, with praise for contrast afforded in Amsterdam by Mahler cycle conducted by Mengelberg. Most devastating attack since Gabrilowitsch's *Open Letter* to Krehbiel (see no. 299).

* Stefan, Paul. "Gustav Mahlers Kindheit, erste Jugend und Lehrjahre." *Die Musik* 10 (1911): 342-51.
Full citation under no. 15 above. Surveys Mahler's life from Kalište to the Conservatory in Vienna. Major statement for its time when little was known or documented about Mahler's early years.

* Stehmann, Gerhard. "Gustav Mahlers Proben." *Moderne Welt* 3 (1921): 17-19.
Full citation under no. 13 above. Remarkable view of Mahler in his shirt sleeves during rehearsal, beginning with Hamburg and Mahler's first meeting with Bruno Walter (which essentially confirms Walter's own account in *Gustav Mahler* cited above as no. 325) to Vienna. Quotes directly from Mahler's off-the-cuff remarks to his singers. Particular reference to *Tristan*. Unromantic and blunt, but shows how Mahler did his work by any and all means.

372. Stransky, Josef. "Begegnungen mit Gustav Mahler."
Signale für die musikalische Welt 69 (1911): 1027-32.
Memorial essay sketching Mahler's relations (professional and personal) with the author, the Czech conductor who had directed the Czech Philharmonic and ultimately succeeded Mahler with the New York Philharmonic. Reproduces in facsimile and typed transcription Mahler's letter to Stransky postmarked March 8, 1898.

373. Walter, Bruno. "Bruckner and Mahler." *Hallé* 7 (October/November 1947): 1-9.
Compares and contrasts Bruckner and Mahler as men and composers, based on author's experience of the works of both, his friendship with Mahler and his Viennese experiences with Bruckner's compatriots. Also published in *C&D* 2 (1960): 41-49.

* Walter, Bruno. "Mahlers Weg: ein Erinnerungsblatt."
Der Merker 3: 166-71.
Full citation under no. 12 above. An affectionate portrait of Mahler as man and composer, profiling his friendship with author and assessing Mahler's changing compositional orientation over time from the romantic-

ism of the first period to the classical philosophism of the middle period, to the vision of the future in the late works.

374. Wellesz, Egon. "Anfänge der 'Neuen Musik' in Wien." *OeMZ* 25 (1970): 312-15.
An eyewitness view of musical circles in Vienna, including not only Mahler but Schoenberg and his students, Guido Adler, the Rosé quartet and Zemlinsky. Surveys musical events c. 1904-21.

375. Wellesz, Egon. "Erinnerungen an Gustav Mahler und Arnold Schönberg." *Orbis musicae*, no. 1 (Summer 1971): 72-82.
Among other articles written by Wellesz concentrating on his own experiences of musical life in Vienna, this remembrance stands out by virtue of its context as well as its content. His memories of the two composers are here presented in a periodical dedicated to "Mediterranean subjects and as an East-West musical forum" with Jewish emphasis, published in Tel Aviv. This makes it special from a writer who was himself an assimilated Jew but who usually published his books and articles in German- or English-language forums.

376. Wellesz, Egon. "Reminiscences of Mahler." *Score*, no. 28 (January 1961): 52-57.
An affectionate personal recollection of Mahler, focusing on his achievement at the Hofoper in Vienna, the originality of his own compositions, and his human character which--according to the author--made a major thrust forward for Schoenberg and those who followed.

MAHLER'S LETTERS

Primary

377. Bata, András and Ágnes Gádor, eds. "Tizenegy kiadatlan Mahlerlevél a Zeneművészeti főiskola Kőnyvtárában." [Eleven unpublished Mahler letters at the Music Academy.] *Magyar zene*, no. 1 (1980): 86-108.
Reproduces in full eleven letters from Mahler to Ed. von Mihalovich, in German and in Hungarian translation with annotations by the editors. Time span covered by these letters is 1891-1904. Letters are published here for the first time, originals being in

*   Duse, Ugo. "Mahler nella parola viva del compositore: estratti de lettere, programmi, testimonianze." *L'Approdo musicale*, no. 16/17: 120-35.
    Full citation under no. 2 above. Mahler on his own works as extracted from his letters and translated into Italian.

*   Fähnrich, Hermann. "Gustav Mahler: der Mensch und Musiker in der Darstellung von Alma Mahler-Werfel." *Musica* 1960: 359-62.
    Full citation under no. 14 above. Considers Mahler as man and musician through the eyes of his wife, documented by quotations from the writings of both.

*   "Gustav Mahler: ein Selbstporträt in Briefen." *Der Merker* 3: 172-81.
    Full citation under no. 12 above. An early publication of Mahler letters predating the first book collection by thirteen years. Includes eleven letters covering the period from 1878 to 1910. Recipients include Julius Epstein, Richard Batka, Friedrich Löhr and Bruno Walter among others. Wide range of musical and personal subjects.

378. Holländer, Hans. "Unbekannte Jugendbriefe Mahlers." *Die Musik* 20 (1928): 807-13.
    This article and a second one published by Holländer in the same year ("Unbekannte Briefe aus Gustav Mahlers Jugend" in the *Neues Wiener Journal*) spotlight Mahler's youth through publication, for the first time, of letters Mahler wrote to his friends in the 1870s. This article includes six letters dating from 1879-80 from Mahler to Anton Krisper. Holländer gives some historical background on Krisper which is worth comparing with the later treatment by Kuret (see no. 285 above). Also published here are two Mahler poems, "Ballade vom blonden und braunen Reitersmann" (which formed the basis of the *Waldmärchen* section of *Das klagende Lied*) and "Vergessene Liebe." The letters are first of their kind, not having been included in the 1925 edition of the letters edited by Alma Mahler.

379. Klemm, Eberhardt. "Zur Geschichte des Fünften Sinfonie von Gustav Mahler: der Briefwechsel zwischen Mahler und dem Verlag C.F. Peters und andere Dokumente."

Jahrbuch Peters 1979: Aufsätze zur Musik. Hrsg. von Eberhardt Klemm. Leipzig: Edition Peters, 1980, pp. 9-16.
Exhaustively documents the history of the publication of the Symphony no. 5 by C.F. Peters in 1904, citing the extensive correspondence between Mahler and Henri Hinrichsen, the director of the house. Covers an important area of Mahler's history as a letter-writer not cited in other sources of the extant letters.

* Löhr, Friedrich. "Zwei Jugendbriefe--von Mahler und über ihn." Musikblätter des Anbruch 2 (1920): 301-05.
Full citation under no. 16 above. Publishes for the first time Mahler's letter to Löhr of November 28, 1885/December 3, 1885 from Prague, and offers contrast background with account of Mahler's activities in Prague as director of opera and concerts.

380. Mahler, Gustav. Briefe 1879-1911. Hrsg. von Alma Maria Mahler. Berlin, Wien, Leipzig: Paul Zsolnay, 1925. xiv, 495 pp. Hildesheim, New York: Georg Olms, 1978. 494 pp. New ed. (edited by Mathias Hansen) Leipzig: Philipp Reclam, 1981, 1985. 431 pp. Revised ed. compiled by Herta Blaukopf: Briefe. Bibliothek der IGMG. Wien, Hamburg: Paul Zsolnay, 1982. xx, 459 pp. ISBN 3-552-0330-0.
English version: Selected Letters. Transl. by Eithne Wilkins, Ernst Kaiser and Bill Hopkins. Enlarged, ed. and with new Introduction, Illustrations and Notes by Knud Martner. London: Faber and Faber; New York: Farrar, Straus and Giroux, 1979. 480 pp.
Czech version: Dopisy. Pameti, korespondence, dokumenty. [Letters, correspondence, documents.] Ed. by Vydal Frantisek Bartos. Praha: Státní Hudebni Vydavatelství, 1962. 412 pp.
Russian version: Pis'mo. Vospominaniye. Sostavleniye, vstupitel'n'iy stat'ya i primechaniya. [Letters. Recollections. Compositions, Introduction, Articles and Notices.] Perevod s nemetskogo S. Osherova. [Transl. from the German by S. Osherova.] Ed. by Inna Barsova. Moskva: Muzyka, 1964. 635 pp. Second edition, 1968, 606 pp.
Each new edition of Mahler's letters makes a step forward in the critical study of chronology and contextual meaning in his correspondence, which is his single most important literary contribution, tantamount to

the autobiography he never wrote. In addition to the editions in the original German, which reflect the changing conditions of Mahler research from the generation after his death to the "Boom" in critical Mahler research, editions in other languages each contribute something to the total picture besides attempts to make Mahler's correspondence available to different language groups. The edition in English, while a collaborative project insofar as the translation itself is concerned, is especially notable for extensive chronological revisions, annotations and additional material introduced by Knud Martner which affords perspective unknown to most other editions and renders this edition indispensable. The Czech edition was for many years the only alternative besides the original German edition of 1925, and was more definitive than that edition because it included materials not found in the German version until later revisions. The Russian edition, while based essentially on the edition of 1925, is valuable for the long introductory essay by Barsova. A circumscribed selection in French, *Lettres à Alma* (transl. by M. and R. d'Asfeld, Paris: Éditions Francis van de Velde, 1979), is devoted to the letters Mahler addressed to his wife; it is of limited usefulness because of its lesser scope than that of the other editions and is best used in conjunction with Alma's biography of Mahler.

381. Mahler, Gustav. *Unbekannte Briefe*. Hrsg. von Herta Blaukopf. Mit Beiträgen von Kurt Blaukopf. Bibliothek der IGMG. Wien: Paul Zsolnay, 1983. 257 pp.
English version: *Mahler's Unknown Letters*. Ed. by Herta Blaukopf. Transl. by Richard Stokes. London: Gollancz, 1986. 241 pp. ISBN 0-575-03644-3.
Letters of Mahler not included in any previous collection, with introductory essays by specialists including Edward Reilly, Rudolf Stephan, Zoltan Roman, Kurt and Herta Blaukopf, Eduard Reeser and Marius Flothuis. Grouped by recipients of the letters, among whom were Oskar Fried, Leo Slezak, Cosima Wagner, Justine Mahler-Rosé and Hermann Behn.

382. Mahler, Gustav. "Ein Brief Mahlers an Bruckner." *Musikblätter des Anbruch* 5 (Mai 1923): 137-38.
First publication of a short letter from Mahler to Anton Bruckner dated Hamburg, April 16, 1982. Subject of letter primarily Mahler's performance of *Te Deum*

on the day before he wrote this letter. Reproduced in Max Auer, *Bruckner* (Amalthea Verlag).

383. Mahler, Gustav. "Briefe Gustav Mahlers an Ferruccio Busoni." *BzMw* 19 (1977): 212-15. Edited by Jutta Theurich, who accompanied these five letters with a short essay discussing the history of the friendship between Mahler and Busoni. The letters present problems of dating but appear to date mainly from 1894 (except the last one which is probably from 1906). Subjects discussed are primarily musical/performance oriented.

384. Mahler, Gustav. "Zwei Briefe von Gustav Mahler an Richard Batka." *Die Musik* 15 (1923): 262-64. First publication of two letters from Mahler to the Prague critic-musicologist, the first dating from 1896, the second undated. Mahler's own outline of his life and work to that time is of great interest, focusing more on his compositions up to and including the *Symphony no. 3* than on his life circumstances. No editorial commentary included, which allows the letters to speak for themselves.

385. Mahler, Gustav und Richard Strauss. *Briefwechsel 1888-1911*. Hrsg. von Herta Blaukopf. Bibliothek der IGMG. München: R. Piper, 1980. 260 pp. ISBN 3-492-02559-5. München: Wilhelm Goldmann; Mainz: B. Schott's Söhne, 1984. 232 pp. ISBN 3-442-33037-8. English version: *Gustav Mahler/Richard Strauss: Correspondence 1888-1911*. Ed. by Herta Blaukopf. Transl. by Edmund Jephcott. Chicago: University of Chicago Press; London: Faber and Faber, 1984. 172 pp. ISBN 0-226-05767-4. Newly edited and much more extensive than any previous sources citing correspondence between the two composers. Versions have also been published in Spanish (*Gustav Mahler-Richard Strauss correspondencia 1888-1911*, transl. by J. Martinez Aragon, Madrid: Altalena Editores, 1982) and in Japanese (transl. by Satoshi Tsukakoshi, Tokyo: Orion Press, 1980). A supplement to these letters is provided in Edward Reilly, "An Addendum to the Mahler-Strauss Correspondence," *19th C Mus* 12 (Summer 1988): 23-26, which quotes in full four letters from Strauss to Mahler, in the original German and in English translation; these letters date from 1890 to 1901.

386. Martner, Knud und Robert Becqué. "Zwölf unbekannte Briefe Gustav Mahlers an Ludwig Strecker." *AfMw* 34 (1977): 287-97.
Critically edited and annotated letters from Mahler to the director of B. Schotts Söhne, dating from 1891-92. Subjects range over performance and publication of Mahler's works to that point, including the *Lieder und Gesänge* (which was published by Schott at that time), the five-movement version of the *Symphony no. 1*, and the *Symphony no. 2*.

387. Mengelberg, C[urt] Rudolf. "Gustav Mahler an Willem Mengelberg: ein Blatt zeitgenössischer Musikgeschichte." *Neue Musik-Zeitung* 41 (1920): 234-36.
First publication of a selection of Mahler's letters to Mengelberg, comprising seven letters dating from 1903 to 1908. Discussing mostly musical matters including Mahler's compositions and conducting engagements, the letters are illustrated with photographs and a facsimile of the fifth letter (1906). Some commentary by Mengelberg's nephew offering historical perspective to the correspondence. See also *Gustav Mahler und Holland* listed below under no. 391, for full collection of Mahler's correspondence with Mengelberg and also Diepenbrock and Messchaert.

388. Moldenhauer, Hans. "Unbekannte Briefe Gustav Mahlers an Emil Hertzka." *NZfM* 135 (1974): 544-49.
Reproduces in full, for the first time, ten letters from Mahler to the director of Universal Edition, covering the period from 1909-11. Most letters are from New York, some from Toblach and Rome. Primarily concerned with publication problems affecting Mahler's works. Illustrated with some facsimiles of the original letters.

389. Mueller von Asow, Erich H. "Ein ungedruckter Brief Mahlers." *OeMz* 12 (1957): 63-64.
First publication of a letter from Mahler to Staegemann dating from 1889. Subject primarily friends (including one of the Krzyzanowski brothers, perhaps Rudolf) and family (Justine, Alois and Otto). Mueller von Asow adds commentary on the content of the letter placing it in historical perspective.

390. Nettl, Paul. "Mahler as Musicologist." *Saturday Review* 41 (April 26, 1958): 40-41.

Cites complete in translation a letter Mahler wrote to a Miss Witt (Gisela Tolney-Witt, probably the same as Gisela Selden-Goth) which shows that Mahler was well-educated and decidedly opinionated on the subject of musical history and musicology as it was viewed in his time. A neglected area of Mahler studies which should be seriously explored as a facet of Mahler's conception of his own music in historical context.

391. Reeser, Eduard, hrsg. *Gustav Mahler und Holland: Briefe.* Bibliothek der IGMG. Wien: Universal Edition, 1980. 119 pp. ISBN 3-7024-0145-8.
Beautifully edited collection of letters from Mahler to his Dutch colleagues, including Mengelberg, Diepenbrock, Messchaert, and letters from various of his colleagues to others in which Mahler and his works form a part of the subjects discussed. Also includes two writings about Mahler by Diepenbrock (a discussion of the *Symphony no. 4* and an obituary) plus a list of Mahler performances in the Netherlands.

392. Stephan, Rudolf. "Mahlers letztes Konzert in Berlin: unbekannte Briefe Mahlers." *Festschrift Rudolf Elvers zum 60. Geburtstag.* Hrsg. von Ernst Herttrich und Hans Schneider. Tutzing: Hans Schneider, 1985, pp. 491-503.
Comprises fifteen telegrams and letters documenting the organization of Mahler's concert in Berlin of February 14, 1907 (not an orchestral concert but a *Liederabend* of Mahler songs with the composer at the piano accompanying the baritone Johannes Messchaert). Time span from April 15, 1906 to early February 1907. There are four letters and telegrams from Johannes Messchaert, nine from Mahler and two from Mahler's secretary Alois Przistaupinsky, all addressed to Herwarth Walden, the organizer of the concert. The letters and telegrams, here published for the first time, tell their own story about the selection of the repertoire for the concert and the arrangements; Stephan judiciously adds little of his own and then only for historical perspective.

Commentary

393. Altmann, Wilhelm. "Urteile Gustav Mahlers über Ton-

setzer und Dirigenten." *Allgemeine Musikzeitung* 57 (1930): 720-22.
Author paints a portrait of Mahler's opinions about his contemporaries (composers and conductors) and their repertoire, especially operatic, with direct quotations from Mahler's letters. Among subjects are composers as diverse as Brahms and Smetana, conductors including Nikisch, Bülow and Richter, and operas from many countries, primarily of Mahler's own time.

394. Biba, Otto. "New Mahleriana in the Archives of the Gesellschaft der Musikfreunde, Vienna." *NaMR*, no. 18 (October 1987): 7-11.
Lists correspondence of Mahler and others in his circle with historical implications for his life, which have been acquired by the Gesellschaft der Musikfreunde between 1982 and 1987. Quotes and abstracts correspondence from Mahler, Wolf, Alma Mahler-Werfel, Zemlinsky and others.

395. Wittenberg, J.J. "Gustav Mahler in de spiegel van zijn schrift." *Nederlands tijdschrift voor grafologie* 10 (1960): 59-73.
Apparently based on a paper "Die Schrift Gustav Mahler's als Projektion seines Weltbildes" read on August 2, 1958 at the Fourth International Congress for Projective Methods in Psychodiagnostics, Brussels. Original manuscript about sixteen or seventeen pages. A study in Dutch concerning itself with Mahler's view of the world around him as expressed in his writings.

CONDUCTING ACTIVITIES

General

* Bienenfeld, Elsa. "Mahler, der Dirigent." *Moderne Welt* 3 (1921): 6-7.
Full citation under no. 13 above. Critical view of Mahler's conducting techniques with visual illustrations including silhouettes by Otto Böhler, reference to repertoire and scoring of works he conducted in different stages of his career. Focuses especially on his work as operatic conductor.

* Blaukopf, Kurt. "Gustav Mahler und die tschechische

Oper." *OeMz* 34 (1979): 285-88.
Full citation under no. 19 above. Discusses Mahler's involvement with operas of Smetana, Dvořák and Janaček, with extensive quotation from contemporary Czech musicians' letters.

* Gutmann, Emil. "Gustav Mahler als Organisator." *Die Musik* 10 (1911): 364-68.
Full citation under no. 15 above. Surveys "Mahler in charge" as conductor and administrator, particularly with reference to preparations for the premiere of the *Symphony no. 8*.

396. Harcourt, Eugène d'. *La musique actuelle en Allemagne et en Autriche-Hongrie: conservatoires, concerts, théâtres.* Paris: F. Durdilly (C. Hayet, succ^r)/ Librairie Fischbacher, 1908. 565 pp.
Detailed study of musical life in fifteen cities of Germany, Austria, Hungary and Bohemia. Tables and data in other forms offering hard statistics on conservatory education, concerts and theatrical performances. Visual illustrations of opera houses and concert halls in both photographs and line drawings. Mahler is heavily covered in the chapter on Vienna and frequently mentioned in other chapters on cities where he had conducted including Hamburg, Prague, Budapest, Leipzig and Munich. Data and illustrations directly gathered and author gives information in a fresh and personal way.

397. Herzfeld, Friedrich. *Magie des Taktstocks: die Welt der grossen Dirigenten, Konzerte und Orchester.* Berlin: Ullstein, 1953. 207 pp.
History of the conducting profession from the classical period to the post-World War II reorganizations. Begins as chronological account and then changes to national groups in the last portion of the book covering the postwar period. Account of Mahler's work covers both opera and concert, essentially in the chapter "Unser Jahrhundert" (pp. 63-74).

398. Keener, Andrew D. "Gustav Mahler as Conductor." *ML* 66 (1975): 341-55.
Traces Mahler's career as conductor, especially of opera, to a lesser extent of concerts, showing his stature among his contemporaries and also devoting considerable comment to his alterations in his own and others' works in the historical context of such practices.

Conducting Activities

399. Krebs, Carl. *Meister des Taktstocks.* Berlin: Schuster & Loeffler, 1919. 229 pp.
Study of Mahler as conductor of concerts and opera, briefly summarizing his career as conductor from the early positions in provincial houses through Vienna, is mainly centered on pp. 185-87. Discussed in the context of directorial/conductorial activity in the houses of the German-speaking world. Actually the book begins in the medieval period, but concentrates primarily on the period from the mid-nineteenth century forward.

400. Lert, Ernst J.M. "The Conductor Gustav Mahler." *CD* 1 (1938): 10-28.
Rare psychological study of the art of the conductor and where Mahler fits into the conventions of the role in his physical movements, professional behavior toward his colleagues and collaborators, and interpretational concepts.

401. Mikorey, Franz. *Grundzüge einer Dirigierlehre: Betrachtungen über Technik und Poesie des modernen Orchesterdirigierens.* Leipzig: C.F. Kahnt, 1917. 72 pp.
A "conductor's manual" relying less on technical directions about movement than on penetration to basic questions about musical emotion, by a contemporary of Mahler who conducted repertoire similar to Mahler's. Draws examples from Mozart and Beethoven to Wagner in time span. Unfortunately no examples from works of Mikorey himself, including the *Sinfonia Engiadina* which is rumored to have been based on Mahler's last symphony. Second edition of book published later in 1917.

* Mittag, Erwin. "Gustav Mahler als Dirigent." *OeMz* 15 (1960: 294-96.
Full citation under no. 18 above. Discusses Mahler as conductor among other major conductors of his time, documented by contemporary eyewitness accounts of his performances.

402. Schonberg, Harold. "Gustav Mahler." *The Great Conductors.* New York: Simon and Schuster, 1967, pp. 223-35.
A study of Mahler in the context of the history of conducting. Unusual in its concentration on Mahler as a

conductor to the total exclusion of his work as composer, considering him in comparison with other conductors in his time and later. A German version of this book, *Die grossen Dirigenten* (München: List, 1973) is probably not as useful as the original edition in English.

403. Seidl, Arthur. *Moderne Dirigenten*. Berlin, Leipzig: Schuster und Loeffler, 1902. 48 pp.
Brief accounts of major conductors at the turn of the century, including Mahler (see especially pp. 43-47), Strauss and Nikisch. Unusual assessment of Mahler as conductor during his lifetime, being in book form instead of the day-to-day articles and reviews of performances common in Mahler's time.

* Stefan, Paul. "Gustav Mahler und das Theater." *Mahler-Fest Amsterdam*: 25-28.
Full citation under no. 11 above. Summarizes Mahler's work as operatic conductor and director, covering his positions held successively from 1880 (Bad Hall) to 1907 (departure from Vienna). Critically positive, but would have benefitted from brief discussion of Mahler's work in New York in addition to above.

* Stefan, Paul. "Richard Wagner und Mahler." *Der Merker* 3: 189-91.
Full citation under no. 12 above. Surveys Mahler as conductor of Wagner operas in Prague, Leipzig, Budapest, Hamburg and Vienna. Less a study of detail in production than an assessment of Mahler's motivations affecting his long involvement with Wagner's works. Ironic when compared with Nazi assessments a generation later.

404. Stompor, Stephan. "Gustav Mahler als Dirigent und Regisseur: ein Beitrag zur Geschichte der Operninterpretation." *Jahrbuch der Komischen Oper Berlin* 8 (1968): 110-40.
Shows Mahler as operatic conductor/director in Budapest, Hamburg, Vienna and New York, documented by his own statements and those of his collaborators. Concerned with Mahler's ideas about opera and how they influenced his rehearsal and performance standards. A Czech version of this article, "Gustav Mahler jako dirigent a režisér," appeared in *Hudební rozhledy* 25 (1972): 459-67.

405. Weissman, Adolf. "Mahler." *Der Dirigent im 20. Jahrhundert*. Berlin: Propyläen, 1925, pp. 66-79.
History of conductors focusing particularly on the nineteenth century to the early twentieth, each chapter focusing on one major conductor and describing his career and conducting style in perspective of his peers. Chapter on Mahler more pointed than similar account by Herzfeld in 1953 (see no. 397 above).

406. Woolridge, David. *Conductor's World*. New York, Washington: Praeger, 1970. xiv, 379 pp.
Considers Mahler the conductor in the context of the history of the conducting profession, contrasting him with Artur Nikisch, Hans Richter, Richard Strauss and other major conductors of his time, especially on pp. 103-13. Acknowledges Mahler's stature as a conductor without being sidetracked by any consideration of his work as a composer, a rare approach noted also by critic Schonberg (see no. 402 above).

Early Positions

407. Cvetko, Dragotin. "Gustav Mahlers Saison 1881/1882 in Laibach." *Musik des Ostens: Sammelbände für historische und vergleichende Forschung*. Hrsg. von Fritz Feldmann. Johann-Gottfried-Herder-Forschungsstelle für Musikgeschichte, 5. Kassel: Bärenreiter, 1968, pp. 74-83. ISBN 3-7618-0157-2.
A rare account of Mahler's work in an early position as conductor in the provincial theater of Laibach (Ljubljana), Yugoslavia. Covers the main events of the season with emphasis on Mahler's relations with Anton Krisper, his repertoire, and the critical response.

408. Kučerová, Dagmar. "Gustav Mahler a Olomouč." *Hudební věda* 4 (1968): 267-40.
An extensive account of Mahler's work at the provincial opera house of Olmütz (Olomouč), Moravia in 1883. Almost unique treatment of a neglected subject.

409. Mahler, Arnošt. "Gustav Mahler und seine Heimat." *Mf* 25 (1972): 437-48.
See also: "Gustav Mahler a Cechy." *Hudební rozhledy* 26 (1973): 85-90.
These two articles cover essentially the same premise

(the first in German, the second in Czech): Mahler's work in his native country, including his conducting stints in Olomouc and Prague, and his strong interest in music by Czech composers whose works he programmed especially in Prague, Hamburg and New York. Heavy documentation by contemporary accounts, especially Adler and Foerster, concerning Mahler's youth in Bohemia and its long-term effect on his work as conductor.

410. Schaefer, Hans Joachim. *Gustav Mahler in Kassel.* Kassel: Bärenreiter, 1982. 98 pp. ISBN 3-7618-0685-X. Documents the events during Mahler's tenure at the opera house in Kassel, showing both Mahler's activity as conductor (albeit confined to operatic repertoire, a sphere recently expanded by Knud Martner with data on non-operatic repertoire) but information about Mahler's compositions during that period, especially *Lieder eines fahrenden Gesellen.* Richly illustrated and well documented with primary sources. Apart from being foreshadowed by Schaefer's article "Gustav Mahlers Wirken in Kassel" in *Musica* (see next entry) and his participation in *Theater in Kassel* (see no. 411 below), this book was also preceded by "Mahler in Cassel" (*Opera* 28, August 1977, pp. 734-41); Schaefer allowed his research on this period in Mahler's life to mature over many years.

* Schaefer, Hans Joachim. "Gustav Mahlers Wirken in Kassel." *Musica* 1960: 350-57. Full citation under no. 14 above. Chronicles Mahler's tenure in Kassel (1883-86) with many quotations from contemporary sources including Mahler's own letters and newspaper notices. First steps toward Schaefer's book on the subject (see no. 410 above).

411. *Theater in Kassel: aus der Geschichte des Staatstheaters Kassel von den Anfängen bis zur Gegenwart.* Beiträge von Christiane Engelbrecht, Wilfried Brennecke, Franz Uhlendorff, Hans Joachim Schaefer. Kassel: Bärenreiter, 1959. 247 pp. ISBN 3-7618-0368-0. Essentially straightforward narrative with many visual illustrations of artists and fair proportion of quotations from archival sources. See especially the chapter "Chronik des Kasseler Musiktheaters von 1814-1944" by Uhlendorff, pp. 65-102, for coverage of Mahler's tenure in Kassel.

Prague

412. Lébl, Vladimír. "Gustav Mahler als Kapellmeister des Deutschen Landestheaters in Prag." *Hudební věda* 12 (1975): 351-69.

    Detailed discussion of Mahler's tenure in the Opera in Prague, drawing heavily on documentation from the time including correspondence between Mahler and Angelo Neumann, press notices of the time, and records of the repertoire at the house during Mahler's tenure.

413. Ludvová, Jitka. "Gustav Mahler in Prague in May 1908." *Hudební věda* 23 (1986): 255-62.
    In Czech. Centers on single concert of the Czech Philharmonic conducted by Mahler on May 23, 1908, including study of the score and parts used for Beethoven's *Coriolan Overture* and *Symphony no. 7* discovered in the archive of the orchestra by author. Also considers rehearsals and critical reaction to the concert itself. Little or no attention to overtures of Smetana and Wagner also performed in that concert according to Martner.

414. Ludvová, Jitka. "Německý hudební život v Praze 1880-1939." [German music life in Prague, 1880-1939.] *Uměnovědne studie* 4 (1983): 174-83.
    Views the cross-mating of Czech and German musical influences in Prague from Mahler's time to the Nazi occupation of Czechoslovakia. Differs from earlier sources on same subject (e.g. Nejedly, Quoika, Fischer and Arnošt Mahler) in reversing the emphasis from Czech folk influences on German-speaking composers to German influences on Czech composers and musical life.

415. Nettl, Paul. "Gustav Mahler in Prag: ein Beitrag zur Geschichte der deutschen Oper und Musikkritik in Prag." *Sudetendeutsches Jahrbuch*, 2. Hrsg. von Otto Kletzl. Augsburg: Johannes Slauda, 1926, pp. 53-60.
    Important early assessment of Mahler's achievement in opera during his tenure in Prague, documented through the information about productions of German opera and critical reception in Mahler's time.

* Neumann, Angelo. "Mahler in Prag." *Gustav Mahler:*

ein Bild seiner Persönlichkeit in Widmungen: 7-9.
Full citation under no. 22 above. Retrospective on
Mahler's tenure at the Opera in Prague by the Intendant of the house with whom Mahler had worked (and who
died in the year this essay was published). The essay
may well be a summary of Neumann's observations on
Mahler first published in Prager Erinnerungen in 1908.

416. Rosenheim, Richard. *Die Geschichte des deutschen
Bühnen in Prag 1883-1918: mit einem Rückblick 1783-
1883.* Prag: Heinrich Mercy Sohn, 1983. 234 pp.
Study of German repertoire on the stages of Prague including the time when Mahler conducted opera there and
surveying earlier influences during the preceding century.

417. Wenig, Jan. *Sie waren in Prag: Mozart, Beethoven, C.
M. von Weber, Berlioz, Chopin, Richard Wagner, Franz
Liszt, Tschaikowski, Grieg, Charpentier, Gustav Mahler.* Praha: Supraphon, 1971. 246 pp.
Survey of music in the history of the city of Prague
from the time of Mozart to Mahler's tenure at the Opera. Little known but an important alternative source
because it covers a rare subject compared to the flood
of sources on the history of music in Vienna.

Leipzig

418. Hempel, Gunter. "Gustav Mahler in Leipzig." *Musik und
Gesellschaft* 17 (1967): 784-85.
By means of two letters from the time of Mahler's tenure in Leipzig (one from the orchestra sketching his
difficult manner of enforcing his professional standards, the other from his director, Max Staegemann,
defending him), a nutshell view of Mahler's work in
Leipzig is provided.

419. Schulze, Friedrich Karl Alfred. *Hundert Jahre Leipziger Stadttheater: ein geschichtlicher Rückblick.*
Leipzig: Breitkopf und Härtel, 1917. viii, 275 pp.
Centennial study of the Opera in Leipzig, including
the time when Mahler conducted there; primarily useful
as in-house source of repertoire and personnel data.

* Steinitzer, Max. "Mahler in Leipzig." *Gustav Mahler:*

ein Bild seiner Persönlichkeit in Widmungen: 10-15.
Full citation under no. 22 above. Retrospective on
Mahler's tenure at the Opera in Leipzig by a major
critic and musicologist who was an early supporter of
Mahler as conductor and composer.

Budapest

* Hirschfeld, Ludwig. "'Walküre'-Abend unter Mahler."
   Moderne Welt 3 (1921): 25-29.
   Full citation under no. 13 above. Reprinted from *Jupiter in der Wolke* (Berlin: B. Harz, 1906). Concentrates entirely on *Walküre* at the Opera in Budapest, from the opening of the doors to the audience to the reports of the critics. A rare eyewitness account of a single operatic performance conducted by Mahler beyond the critical coverage in periodicals of the time.

420. Jemnitz, Alfred. "Gustav Mahler als königlicher ungarischer Hofoperndirektor: ein Beitrag zur Lebensgeschichte des Künstlers." *Auftakt* 16 (1936): 7-11, 63-67, 183-88.
   Serialized three-part study of Mahler's tenure at the Royal Hungarian Opera, from his appointment in 1888 to his resignation in 1891. Draws heavily on documentation from Mahler's letters and accounts by his contemporaries for information on production, repertoire, collaborators and critical coverage. Analyzes reasons for Mahler's departure after short tenure and considers the harm to his compositional schedule afforded by his work as conductor.

421. Kadar, Jolán[tha]. *A nemzeti szinház százéves története.* [The centennial history of the National Theater.] Magyarország újabbkori történétenek forrásai. Budapest: Magyar Történelmi Társulat, 1938-40. 2 vols.
   Volume 2 published in 1938, volume 1 in 1940. Centenniel history of the National Theater in Budapest. Best consulted in conjunction with same author's *History of German Theater in Pest and Buda* (see next entry); both cover time of Mahler's tenure in Budapest at the Royal Hungarian Opera, as well as the work of his colleagues including Geza Zichy and Sandor Erkel.

422. Kadar, J[olántha]. *A Pésti és Budai német színészet története.* [The history of German theater in Pest and Buda.] Német philologiai dolgozatok, 29. Budapest: n. pub., 1914-23. 316 pp.
This reference, along with same author's *Centennial History of the National Theater* (see preceding entry), documents the tradition of German drama and opera in Hungary, including the time when Mahler was director of the Royal Hungarian Opera in Budapest.

* Roman, Zoltan. "The Royal Hungarian Opera under Mahler." *Gustav Mahler Kolloquium 1979*: 52-64.
Full citation under no. 8 above. Documented overview of Mahler's tenure in Budapest (1888-91). Only known discussion of this type in English.

Hamburg

423. Chevalley, Heinrich. *Hundert Jahre Hamburger Stadt Theater.* Hrsg. von der Hamburger Stadt-Theater Gesellschaft. Hamburg: Broschek, 1927. 257 pp.
Centennial volume covering history of the Hamburg Opera from 1827 to 1927. Constructed as a series of essays devoted to the intendants of the house with some quotations from archival sources and limited visual documentation. Great detail about Mahler in the chapter "Pollini (1873-1897)," pp. 31-158.

424. Scharberth, Irmgard. "Gustav Mahlers Wirken am Hamburger Stadttheater." *Mf* 22 (1969): 443-56.
Surveys Mahler's work in Hamburg as conductor, drawing heavily on contemporary sources including Mahler's letters and archival documents cited by Chevalley (see preceding entry).

Vienna

General

* Bahr, Hermann. "Mahler als Direktor." *Musikblätter des Anbruch* 2 (1920): 275-76.
Full citation under no. 16 above. Profiles Mahler as musical director and general powerhouse during his ten-

ure in Vienna where he had been observed by author as seasoned commentator on intellectual endeavor and society in Vienna.

* Bahr, Hermann. "Mahler und das deutsche Theater." *Gustav Mahler: ein Bild seiner Persönlichkeit in Widmungen*: 17-21.
Full citation under no. 22 above. Critiques Mahler's work in German opera, possibly influenced by author's marriage that year to Anna Bahr-Mildenburg who was one of Mahler's most important collaborators in that repertoire.

425. Betti, Adolfo. "La vita musicale a Vienna (Note retrospettive sulla stagione 1897-98)." *Riv Mus It* 6 (1899): 119-58.
Surveys a year of musical activity in Vienna in eight sections: (a) Introduction, (b) "Hans Richter e i 'Concerti filarmonici,'" (c) "Antonio Bruckner e la sua 'Terza sinfonia,'" (d) "Riccardo Strauss e i suoi poemi sinfonici 'Don Giovanni' e 'Zarathustra,'" (e) "Richard von Perger e i 'Gesellschafts-Concerte,'" (f) "Gustavo Mahler e l''Hof-Operatheater,'" (g) "Concerti vari," (h) conclusion. The sixth section (pp. 146-54) is devoted less to Mahler himself than to his innovative programming at the Hofoper, discussing productions of Smetana's *Dalibor*, Tchaikowsky's *Eugene Onegin* and Leoncavallo's *Bohème* in special detail with respect to plots, literary-historical background and production quality. The complete article was also published in monograph form in the same year (Torino: Fratelli Bocca, 1899).

* Burckhard, Max. "Der Fall Mahler als Politikum." *Gustav Mahler: ein Bild seiner Persönlichkeit in Widmungen*: 44-50.
Full citation under no. 22 above. Studies the effect of politics on Mahler's work in Vienna. By his counterpart at the Burgtheater, who met him through mutual contact with Alma, and who doubtless had a unique insider's view of such politics himself.

426. Graf, Max. *Legend of a Musical City*. New York: Philosophical Library, 1945. Reprinted Westport, Connecticut: Greenwood Press, 1971. 302 pp. ISBN 0-8371-2128-0.
German version: *Legende einer Musikstadt*. Wien: Österreichische Buchgemeinschaft, 1949. 476 pp.

Insider's account of music in Vienna, especially from Beethoven to the beginning of the Third Reich. Chapter "Modern Music in Vienna" focuses on Mahler, Strauss and Schoenberg. Positive advocacy of Mahler's musical experimentations from longtime supporter of his work; not scholarly, but crammed with information and fresh even today. Illustrations by Carry Hauser in German edition.

427. Gutmann, Albert. *Aus dem Wiener Musikleben: Kunstlererinnerungen 1873-1908.* Wien: Hofmusikalienhandlung A.J. Gutmann, 1914. 151 pp.
Informative vignettes depicting musical life in Vienna by an insider who was there. Although no single essay is devoted to Mahler, he is discussed in various essays on Richard Strauss, Alice Barbi, Brahms and Hellmesberger. Not scholarly, but entertaining and current to Mahler's time.

Vienna Philharmonic Orchestra

428. Boese, Helmut und Alois Franz Rottensteiner. *Botschaft der Musik: die Wiener Philharmoniker.* Wien, München: Österreichischer Bundesverlag für Unterricht, Wissenschaft und Kunst, 1967. 118 pp.
History of the Vienna Philharmonic Orchestra with texts in German, English and French, covering Mahler's tenure with the orchestra in chronological context with other conductors and music directors.

429. Effenberger, Rudolf. *71, die in die Augen stechen: Wiener Philharmoniker Symphoniker und Symphonikerinnen in Karikatur und Reim.* Wien: n. pub., c. 1930. 80 pp.
Satirical look at the Vienna Philharmonic Orchestra by affectionate insider. Refreshing compared to anniversary volumes and humorless inside reports that could see no wrong; akin only to Witeschnik (see no. 442 below) and therefore almost unique.

430. Freyenfels, Jodok. "Mahler und der 'fesche Pepi': eine Konfrontation der Elemente." *NZfM* 132 (1971): 178-83.
Traces the crisis of 1903 between Mahler and Hellmesberger and its effect on the Vienna Philharmonic Orchestra.

Conducting Activities (Vienna): VPO   127

431. Graf, Max. "Gustav Mahler." *Wagner-Probleme und andere Studien*. Wien: Wiener Verlag, 1911, pp. 122-34.
    More circumscribed than some of Graf's other essays on Mahler's work, concentrating particularly on Mahler as conductor of the Vienna Philharmonic Orchestra, especially vis-à-vis other conductors including Hans Richter. Concludes that Mahler and Richter were complementary in their techniques.

432. Jerger, Wilhelm, hrsg. *Festschrift zur Jahrhundert-Feier der Wiener Philharmoniker 1842-1942*. Mit Beiträge von Richard Strauss, Wilhelm Furtwängler, J. Marx, Gerhard Hauptmann, E.G. Kolbenheyer, J. Weinheber, M. Mell, H. von Srbik und A. Wolfram. Wien: Universal Edition, 1942. 47 pp.
    Brief monograph celebrating the centennial of the Vienna Philharmonic Orchestra with contributions by insiders of large and small reputation. Suspect, as it was published during Nazi period, content politically biased and scope narrow; useful mainly for historiographical documentation.

433. Jerger, Wilhelm. *Die Wiener Philharmoniker: Erbe und Sendung*. Wien: Wiener Verlagsgesellschaft, 1942, 1943. 101 pp.
    Brief history of the Vienna Philharmonic from its inception to the Nazi administration, written by its intendant. Substance suspect as slanted in favor of Nazi ideology; useful mainly as historical documentation of changing views of the orchestra and its conductors, including Mahler, who is discussed on pp. 57-58.

434. Korngold, Julius. "Das Jubiläum der Wiener Philharmoniker." *Signale für die musikalische Welt* 68 (1910): 679-82.
    Summary of the history of the Vienna Philharmonic Orchestra from its inception in 1860 (and earlier before formalization, as far back as 1833) to the fiftieth anniversary at the time of writing. Written by major Vienna critic of *Neue Freie Presse* who consistently championed Mahler as composer and conductor, including here.

435. Kralik, Heinrich von. *Die Wiener Philharmoniker und ihre Dirigenten*. 4. Auflage. Wien: Wilhelm Frick,

1960. 242 pp.
Originally published in 1938 as *Die Wiener Philharmoniker: Monographie eines Orchesters* and subsequently as *Das grosse Orchester: die Wiener Philharmoniker und ihre Dirigenten* in 1952. Each edition of this book consists basically of a series of essays outlining the history of the Vienna Philharmonic and its conductors as seen through series of incidents in the performance roster. The first version covers the period from Otto Nicolai in the 1840s to the *Anschluss*, while the two later versions include the post-World War II period as well as the war itself. The following essays cover Mahler's tenure with the orchestra: "Gustav Mahler," "Beethoven-Problem," "Die Neunte Symphonie," "Pariser Reise" and "Affären." Factual account of the history of the orchestra by an insider for many years, but little documentation of the information cited other than visual illustrations of the history of the orchestra and its conductors. Curiously emotionless view of Mahler's influence in the orchestra considering that this book was first published during Nazi period, later by same publisher after end of war.

436. Kraus, Hedwig und Karl Schreinzer. *Statistik der Wiener Philharmoniker 1842-1942*. Wien: Universal Edition, 1942. 2 vols. in one. 255 pp.
Statistical survey of the first hundred years of the Vienna Philharmonic Orchestra, not without reference value, but suspect as politically slanted toward ideology of Nazi period (which may account for comparatively limited citation of Mahler in connection with the orchestra). See especially pp. 74-75, 104, 212-13.

437. Mittag, Erwin. *Aus der Geschichte der Wiener Philharmoniker*. Wien: Gerlach und Wiedling, 1950. 136 pp. English version: *The Vienna Philharmonic*. Transl. by J.R.L. Orange and G. Morice. Vienna: Gerlach und Wiedling, 1950. 125 pp.
Apart from a short chapter on Mahler's work with the Philharmonic as a conductor, this book is a good, if rather brief, source of information on the history of the performance of his music by that orchestra under such colleagues as Bruno Walter who conducted the orchestra after Mahler's death. Inclined to gloss over the negative aspects of the history of the orchestra but well grounded with information obtained from orchestra insiders.

438. Perger, Richard von. *Die Wiener Philharmoniker: Denkschrift zur Feier des 50jährigen ununterbrochenen Bestandes der Philharmonischen Konzerte in Wien (1860-1910).* Wien: C. Fromme, 1910. 131 pp.
Fiftieth-anniversary commemoration of the Vienna Philharmonic Orchestra by an insider, offering chronological discussion through information about its personnel. Mahler's tenure is extensively covered (see pp. 37-43, 73-75, 80, 86-88, 99 and 121), remarkable in view of the fact that he was still alive when this book was published.

439. Schönfeldt, Christl, hrsg. *Die Wiener Philharmoniker.* Österreich-Reihe, 25/26. Wien: Bergland, 1956. 112 pp.
Documentary history of the Vienna Philharmonic Orchestra, introducing letters and archival papers covering the history of the orchestra from its inception to the beginning of the Karajan era. At least one letter from Mahler to the orchestra is cited in this book. An English version was issued by the same publisher in 1957 (Österreich-Reihe, 27/28).

440. Weigel, Hans. "Die Wende." *Das Buch der Wiener Philharmoniker.* Salzburg: Residenz, 1967, pp. 53-60.
Celebrates the 125th anniversary of the Vienna Philharmonic Orchestra, tracing orchestra's history through its conductors. Richly illustrated concentrating especially on portraiture. Text represents affectionate insider's view shared with the general reader, informative if not scholarly.

441. Werba, Robert. "Mahlers Mozart-Bild: die Philharmonischen Konzerte." *Wiener Figaro: Mitteilungsblatt der Wiener Mozartgemeinde* 44 (Oktober 1977): 22-25.
Fourth in Werba's series of articles covering Mahler's Mozart performances in Vienna, this one standing out by virtue of documenting concert performances of the last two symphonies of Mozart with the Vienna Philharmonic rather than opera productions at the Hofoper. These performances took place in 1898 and 1899 respectively. As in other articles in the series (see nos. 483-90 below), this entry includes excerpts from critical notices of the time.

442. Witeschnik, Alexander. "Fin de siècle: Gustav Mahler." *Musizieren geht übers Probieren, oder Viel*

Harmonie mit kleinen Dissonanzen: die Geschichte der Wiener Philharmoniker in Anekdoten und Geschichten. Wien, Berlin: Paul Neff, 1967, pp. 59-76.
Views Mahler in the context of the history of the Vienna Philharmonic and its conductors, documented by anecdotes concerning incidental moments during rehearsal and performance. A personal view by insiders including members of the orchestra itself. Within the individual chapters the content is episodic, but this book is still interesting as a collective view of a major Viennese institution and the importance of the conductors who worked with the orchestra in its long history.

Opera

General

443. *80 Jahre Wiener Oper 1869-1949*. Wien: Renaissance Verlagsgesellschaft, 1949. 99 pp.
Eighty-year anniversary volume tracing history of the Vienna Opera from its inception to post-World War II. Modest, probably due to postwar economic limitations, but an improvement in content over Nazi-inspired and -controlled sources only a few years preceding.

444. Bauer, Anton. *Opern und Operetten in Wien: Verzeichnis ihrer Erstaufführungen in der Zeit von 1629 bis zur Gegenwart*. Graz: H. Böhlaus Nachf., 1955. xii, 156 pp.
Lists operas and operettas performed in Vienna 1629-1955, classified alphabetically by title (entries including genre of opera, name of theater, composer, author of libretto and date of Viennese premiere), with cross-references by composer, librettist/editor/translator and chronology. Limited by failure of cumulation combining all sorts of cross-references in single index.

445. Beetz, Wilhelm. *Das Wiener Opernhaus 1869 bis 1945*. Zürich: Central European Times, 1949, 1955. 262 pp.
Begins with a brief history of opera in Vienna prior to the opening of the Hofoper in 1869, then covers the history of the house until the bombing of 1945. Includes exhaustive lists of personnel classified by position and chronology, from Director to cloakroom

attendant. Repertoire is exhaustively listed by librettists etc., titles, numbers of performances according to seasons. Chronological lists of important world and Viennese premieres. Many photographs concentrating on the building itself and sets used in performances rather than people. Invaluable.

446. Deutsch, Otto Erich und Rudolf Klein. "Das Repertoire der höfischen Oper, der Hof- und der Staatsoper." *OeMz* 24 (1969): 369, 379-421.
    Exhaustive chronological list of operatic repertoire in Vienna from 1631 to 1968. Dates, theaters, titles and composers included.

447. Farga, Franz. *Die Wiener Oper von ihren Anfängen bis 1938*. Wien: Franz Göth, 1947. 324 pp.
    Covers history of Vienna Opera from its inception to the *Anschluss*, focusing on singers, directors, conductors and production coordinators of various types. The tenure of Mahler is covered in Chapter 28 (pp. 282-92) and Chapter 29 (pp. 293-304) along with the period immediately following; view of Mahler and Roller's collaboration benefits from perspective of time. Many photographic illustrations, especially of singers.

448. Fröhlich, Heinrich, hrsg. *Jahrbuch des K.K. Hofoperntheater in Wien*. Wien: Im Selbstverlag des Herausgebers, 1891-1907. [13 vols.]
    An invaluable source of information about personnel at the Hofoper while Mahler was director. Covers all personnel from Mahler to the corps-de-ballet, the technical employees and the musical staff. Also details the repertoire in each season. Volumes 4-13 (covering the period 1898-1907) are of special interest since they cover Mahler's tenure year by year.

449. Graf, Max. *Die Wiener Oper*. Wien, Frankfurt-am-Main: Humboldt, 1955. 384 pp.
    Includes several essays, "Erlebnisse mit Gustav Mahler" (pp. 81-99), "Gustav Mahler im Kaffeehaus" (pp. 77-80) and "Gustav Mahler: Persönlichkeit und Werk" (pp. 74-77). These essays show different aspects of Mahler as man, seen through his life during tenure as director of the Hofoper. The book in general is a personal view of the major figures in the history of the Opera, and the studies of Mahler place him in the context of the history of the house.

450. Haas, Robert Maria. *Die Wiener Oper.* Wien, Budapest: Eligius, 1926. 70 pp., 59 plates.
Divided into two sections: first a prose history of opera in Vienna from the seventeenth century to the post-World War I era; second, illustrative plates mostly representing decorative art on operatic subjects and settings. Mahler's tenure at the Hofoper is covered on pp. 64-68. Considerable factual information, unfortunately no source documentation beyond the plates.

451. Hadamowsky, Franz, bearb. *Die Wiener Hofoper (Staatsoper), 1811-1974.* Wien: Brüder Hollinek, 1975. xvi, 669 pp. ISBN 3-85119-077-7.
This book constitutes the second volume of *Die Wiener Hoftheater (Staatstheater): ein Verzeichnis der aufgeführten und eingereichten Stücke mit Bestandsnachweisen und Aufführungsdaten.* It is the most exhaustive listing of cumulative information about the Vienna Opera to date, listing (a) alphabetical cumulation of operas and ballets performed, with composers, dates of world and Vienna premieres, and publishers of scores, (b) index of personnel, and (c) chronological ordering of Vienna premieres from 1811 to 1973. Indispensable. reference without editorial interference which lets the information speak for itself. Monumental.

452. Hirschfeld, Robert. "Oper in Wien." *Zeitschrift der internationalen Musikgesellschaft* 1 (1899-1900): 264-67.
Brief summary of opera in Vienna by a major critic of Mahler's time, focusing on the period 1857-1900. Concentrates especially on conductors and repertoire, giving Mahler pride of place compared to his predecessors.

453. Kitzwegerer, Liselotte. "Alfred Roller als Bühnenbilder." Ph.D. diss., Universität Wien, 1959. 329 pp.
Study of the major effect of Alfred Roller on Viennese opera production during and after his time. Chapter 3, "Alfred Roller-Gustav Mahler," on pp. 78-108, is of especial interest.

454. Klein, Rudolf. *Die Wiener Staatsoper: ein Führer durch das Haus und seine hundertjähriges Geschichte.* Wien: Elisabeth Lafite, 1967, 1969. 80 pp.

English version: *The Vienna State Opera: an Account of the Opera House and its Hundred Years' History.* Transl. by Richard Rickett. Vienna: Elisabeth Lafite, 1967. 80 pp.
Brief centennial study of the Vienna Opera, covering its conductors and major singers, including Mahler, in chronological context. Brief summary for nonprofessional audience, stepping-stone to other more detailed sources for professional historians.

455. Kralik, Heinrich [von]. *Das Opernhaus am Ring.* Wien: Brüder Rosenbaum, 1955. 195 pp.
Series of short essays comprising a chronological history of the Vienna Opera from its inception to the post-World War II reopening. Not documented in a scholarly way, but solid information from inside sources, with unique illustrations from set designs and costume sketches to portraits of directors, singers and dancers. The Mahler era is profiled in the essays "Gustav Mahler" (pp. 41-44), "Mahlers Ensemble" (pp. 44-49), "Neuer Darstellungsstil" (pp. 49-50), and "Alfred Roller" (pp. 51-53).

456. Kralik, Heinrich [von]. *Die Wiener Oper.* Wien: Brüder Rosenbaum, 1962. 189 pp.
English version: *The Vienna Opera.* Transl. by Richard Rickett. Vienna: Brüder Rosenbaum, 1963. 189 pp.
Akin to Kralik's earlier *Das Opernhaus am Ring* (see preceding entry), this book is a series of essays on the history of the Vienna Opera from its inception through the tenure of Herbert von Karajan.

457. Pirchan, Emil, Alexander Witeschnik und Otto Fritz. *300 Jahre Wiener Operntheater: Werk und Werden.* Hrsg. mit Förderung des Bundestheaterverwaltung. Wien: Fortuna, 1953. 321 pp., 233 plates.
Exhaustive three-part study of the history of opera in Vienna from early Baroque to the post-World War II division of the Staatsoper in interim quarters. There are several sections of interest to Mahler specialists: "Von Gustav Mahler bis Richard Strauss" (pp. 188-202) and detailed lists of productions by date and composer in Part Three are the most important. Photographic section at end of book primarily devoted to building specifications, sets and costumes rather than to individuals.

458. Prawy, Marcel. "Neues Hören, neues Sehen: Das Dezen-

nium Gustav Mahlers 1897-1907." *Die Wiener Oper: Geschichte und Geschichten.* Wien, München, Zürich: Fritz Molden, 1969, pp. 63-75. Later paperback edition in 3 vols. [München]: Wilhelm Goldmann, [1981].
English version: "New Sounds--New Sights: Gustav Mahler's Ten Years at the Helm, 1897-1907." *The Vienna Opera.* New York, Washington, D.C.: Praeger, 1970, pp. 63-75.
Surveys Mahler's tenure at the Hofoper in terms of its effect on the policies and reputation of the house. More popular than scholarly in effect, but valuable as a personal view by an insider familiar with the institution over many years; proves that the effect of Mahler's work were felt in the house for many years after his departure.

459. Przistaupinsky, Alois, hrsg. *50 Jahre Wiener Operntheater: eine Chronik des Hauses und seine Künstler in Wort und Bild, der aufgeführten Werke, Komponisten und Autoren vom 25. Mai 1869 bis 30. April 1919.* Wien: Im Selbstverlag des Verfassers, 1919. 130 pp.
Documents the first fifty years of the Vienna Opera by pictures, lists of repertoire with production specifications, house personnel; compiled from inside by the man who had been Mahler's secretary during his tenure there. Little editorial commentary, allows the data to speak for itself.

460. Reich, Willi. "Ein heiteres Dokument aus der Wiener Mahler-Zeit." *Festschrift Otto Erich Deutsch zum achtzigsten Geburtstag.* Hrsg. von Walter Gerstenberg, Jan LaRue und Wolfgang Rehm. Kassel: Bärenreiter, 1963, pp. 257-58.
Originally published in *L'Approdo Musicale*, no. 16/17 (see no. 2 above). Not really an original article, but citation of a discovery made by Reich, i. e. the rules laid down by Mahler for attendees at the Hofoper, photographically reproduced following a letter from Reich to Deutsch announcing the discovery.

* Roller, Alfred. "Mahler und die Inszenierung." *Musikblätter des Anbruch* 2 (1920): 272-75.
Republished in *Moderne Welt* 3 (1921): 4-5.
Full citations under both no. 13 and no. 16 above. An insider's view of Mahler as reformer in opera production, by his chief artistic collaborator. The repub-

lication in *Moderne Welt* represents a sort of contextual view to the pieces by Mahler's singers in the same issue.

* Roller, Alfred. "Mahler und die Opern-Inszenierung." *Gustav Mahler: ein Bild seiner Persönlichkeit in Widmungen*: 13. Full citation under no. 22 above. Short commentary on Mahler's innovations in opera production. Not the same as preceding entry representing later article in *Musikblätter des Anbruch* and *Moderne Welt*.

461. Rozenshil'd, K[onstantin Konstantinovich]. "Iz Malerovskikh vremen." [In Mahler's times.] *Sovetskaya muzyka* 31 (January 1967): 78-89, (March 1967): 87-97.
German version: "Zu Mahlers Zeiten." *Sowjetwissenschaft, Kunst und Literatur* 15 (1967): 1306-19.
Part of a series "Poeziya i muzyka y nachale 900kh Godov v Avstrii: Glavy iz knigi" [Poetry and music at the beginning of the 900th year in Austria: chapters from books]. Portrait of musical activity in Mahler's era, focusing on his work at the Hofoper and his involvement with other musical professionals including singers, composers and conductor-colleagues. Unusual subject in Mahler literature in Russian.

462. Scanzoni, Signe. *Wiener Oper: Wege und Irrwege. Ein Bericht*. Stuttgart: Wilhelm Frick, 1956. 102 pp.
Chatty nontechnical view of opera in Vienna for those who prefer accounts of conductors and singers from backstage. Author also wrote *Richard Strauss und seine Sänger: eine Plauderei über das Musiktheater in der Wind gesprochen* (München: Walter Ricke, 1961), which apparently continues subject on a more specific but not more technical level.

* Seligmann, A.F. "Silhouetten aus der Mahler-Zeit." *Moderne Welt* 3 (1921): 10-12. Full citation under no. 13 above. Primarily devoted to the visual background of Mahler's work as conductor in Vienna (buildings and sets).

463. Specht, Richard. *Das Wiener Operntheater von Dingelstedt bis Schalk und Strauss: Erinnerung aus 50 Jahren*. Wien: Paul Knepler (Wallishaussersche Buchhandlung), 1919. 126 pp.

Modest prose history of the first fifty years of the Vienna Opera, in which Mahler and his vocal collaborators are prominently discussed (see especially pp. 37-52, 75-79 and 103-12). Not heavily documented like other sources, but authoritative as Specht was a longtime observer and supporter of Mahler. Many photographic illustrations.

464. Stauber, Paul. *Vom Kriegsschauplatz der "Wiener Hofoper": das wahre Erbe Mahlers. Kleine Beiträge zur Geschichte der Wiener Hofoper nebst einem Anhang: Dokumente zum Fall Hirschfeld.* Wien: Huber und Lahme Nachf., 1909. 67 pp.
A study of Mahler's achievement at the Hofoper, published shortly after his departure and emphasizing how much Mahler's history and contacts in Vienna had contributed to his success. Well documented with statistics.

465. Stefan, Paul. *Gustav Mahlers Erbe: ein Beitrag zur neuesten Geschichte der deutschen Bühne und das Herrn Felix von Weingartner.* München: Hans von Weber, 1908. 72 pp.
History of Mahler's achievement at the Hofoper, emphasizing his and Roller's reforms in production and choosing individual examples of productions, published shortly after Mahler's departure. Not heavily documented but valuable as insider's view, contrasting with study by Stauber (see preceding entry).

466. Stefan, Paul. "Magie des Künstlers: Gustav Mahler." *Das neue Haus: ein Halbjahrhundert Wiener Opernspiel und was voranging.* Wien, Leipzig: Ed. Strache, 1919, pp. 52-63.
Affectionate fiftieth anniversary commemmoration of the Vienna Opera, almost a private publication in orientation as only an insider can be. Divided into two sections: first, earlier opera in Vienna before 1869; second, history of the Hofoper/Staatsoper for its first fifty years chronologically by director. Not documented heavily but shows inside view of Mahler at work comparable only to Specht in same year (see no. 463 above).

467. Stefan, Paul. *Die Wiener Oper: ihre Geschichte von den Anfängen bis in die neueste Zeit.* Wien: Augarten, 1932. 102 pp.

The most extensive of Stefan's studies of the history of opera in Vienna, covering the period from the seventeenth to the twentieth century. Benefits from the lack of inside interest in any one house on the part of Stefan at the time of writing. The third section, "Wiener Opernspiel in grossen Epochen," includes an essay "Mahler-Zeit," which is surely a late relative of Stefan's writings in *Gustav Mahlers Erbe*, *Das neue Haus*, and *Das Grab in Wien*, as well as the general conception in Stefan's editing of *Gustav Mahler: ein Bild seiner Persönlichkeit in Widmungen*.

468. Stein, Erwin. "Mahler and the Vienna Opera." *Opera* 4 (1953): 4-13, 145-52, 200-07, 281-85.
Extensive serialized four-part survey of Mahler's work at the Hofoper, an insider's observation of production standards and singers. Handsomely illustrated with photographs of singers in various roles, especially Gutheil-Schoder, Mildenburg and Slezak, and of some sets. The last section of the series was reprinted in *The Opera Bedside Book* (ed. by Harold Rosenthal), London: Victor Gollancz, 1965, pp. 314-17.

469. Stern, Julius. *Das Hofoperntheater 1848-1898*. 50 Jahre Hoftheater: Geschichte der beiden Wiener Hoftheater unter der Regierungszeit des Kaisers Franz Josef I, 2. Wien: Buch- und Kunstdruckerei "Steyrermühl," 1898. [128 pp.]
A survey of opera in Vienna over a fifty-year period ending shortly after Mahler became director of the Hofoper. Concentrates on the major singers rather than administration and conductor personnel. Bound with *Biographischer Index K.K. Hoftheater*, a 215-page listing of personnel with a chronological slant, and with an initial essay by Rudolf Lothar covering pp. 17-43. Pagination of the three volumes in one makes no sense, but this is still a useful source for those interested in singers in Vienna, especially background of house at the time Mahler took over.

470. Stiedry, Fritz. "Der Operndirektor Mahler." *Melos* 1 (1920): 134-40.
Eyewitness view of Mahler as director of the Hofoper, discussing his radical views, the controversy they caused among collaborators and outsiders. Particular attention to Wagner and Mozart productions and sharp criticism of shortsighted enemies whose maneuvers made

Mahler's life miserable but ultimately lost their effect in the face of longstanding reforms Mahler had begun.

471. Unterer, Verena. *Die Oper in Wien: ein Überblick.* Österreich-Reihe, 374/75. Wien: Bergland, 1970. 115 pp.
Survey of the history of opera in Vienna for the general reader.

472. Wallaschek, Richard. *Das k.k. Hofoperntheater. Die Theater Wiens,* 4. Wien: Gesellschaft für vervielfältigende Kunst, 1909. xiv, 195 pp.
Covers span of time primarily from the death of Mozart to the resignation of Jahn in 1897, thus antedating Mahler's accession as director of the Hofoper. Prose history of opera and ballet in Vienna during that period. Statistical table appendices included giving repertoire with composers, dates of Viennese premieres and number of performances in descending order. Lavishly illustrated with photographs of singers, dancers, conductors, theaters and sets. Mahler mentioned primarily in connection with production of *Die drei Pintos,* but data important as background for understanding of conditions at time of his arrival.

473. Wellesz, Egon. "Gustav Mahler und die Wiener Oper." *Neudeutsche Rundschau* 71 (1960): 255-61.
Based on lecture given by Wellesz at the Opera in Vienna on June 26, 1960 as celebration of the Mahler centennial. Oriented of course toward Mahler's work at the Hofoper, thereby slanted rather differently from other writings of Wellesz on Mahler; falls neither into category of general reminiscences nor of assessment of compositions, and is therefore unique from Wellesz.

474. Willnauer, Franz. *Gustav Mahler und die Wiener Oper.* Wien, München: Jugend und Volk, 1979. 315 pp. ISBN 3-7141-7104-5.
Exclusively devoted to Mahler's tenure at the Hofoper, prose account in chronological order; many references to reviews, documents and data; unfortunately sources of such materials not cited. Best used in combination with other sources on general history of the Opera, especially those published in Mahler's time.

475. Willnauer, Franz. "Kunst zwischen 'Präliminare' und

'Gebarungsabschluss': Gustav Mahlers Wiener Operndirektion unter dem Aspekt des künstlerischen Managements." *Art Management* 1, no. 3 (1983): 12-22. Surveys Mahler's tenure at the Hofoper from the point of view of the administrators with whom he worked on a daily basis, as well as his own administrative tasks. Different from the usual view of Mahler's time at the Hofoper, and not altogether attractive, but necessary for the sake of balanced view of day-to-day life in a major opera house.

476. Witeschnik, Alexander. "Von Gustav Mahler bis Richard Strauss." *Wiener Opernkunst von den Anfängen bis zu Karajan*. Wien: Kremayr und Scheriau, 1959, pp. 155-81.
An insider's view of operatic history in Vienna, chronological from the seventeenth century to the post-World War II reopening of the Staatsoper. The chapter on the period from Mahler to Strauss emphasizes the operatic reforms initiated by Mahler, many of which still stand.

Individual Productions

477. Blaukopf, Herta. "Max Kalbeck's 'Don Giovanni' Libretto of 1905." *NaMR*, no. 18 (October 1987): 13-16.
Chronicles the work of Kalbeck on the translation of da Ponte's *Don Giovanni* libretto into German, for the Mahler production of the opera at the Hofoper in 1905. Notes the close collaboration and cooperation between Kalbeck, Mahler and Roller in the preparation of the production. Worth comparing with discussion of the production by Werba (see no. 483 below).

478. Deutsch, Otto Erich. "*Hoffmann* in Wien." *OeMZ* 13 (1958): 16-20.
Chronicles the history of *Hoffmanns Erzählungen* in performance in Vienna from 1879 to 1958, showing special pride of place to Mahler's production in the Hofoper in 1901. Concentrates on chronology of productions with names of conductors and leading singers, with some attention to alterations in casting and production over time.

479. Kende, Götz Klaus. "Gustav Mahlers Wiener 'Figaro.'"

OeMz 26 (1971): 295-302.
A relatively early and well-documented account of Mahler's production of *Figaro* in Vienna in 1906. Relies on sources from the time of the production including accounts by Korngold and Kalbeck, the memoirs of Lilli Lehmann, and the early publication of Mahler's recitative additions to the score published by Peters. Compare with Robert Werba's account of the same work in *Wiener Figaro* (see no. 488 below).

480. Kügler, Ilka Maria. "Der Ring des Nibelungen: Studie zur Entwicklungsgeschichte seiner Wiedergabe auf der deutschsprachigen Bühne." Ph.D. diss., Universität Köln, 1967. 361 pp.
History of the first ninety years of productions of the *Ring* in the German-speaking countries, beginning with the original Bayreuth productions. See especially pp. 148-74, "Auf dem Wege zur Reform: Gustav Mahlers und Alfred Rollers Zusammenarbeit an der Wiener Hofoper 1903-1907." Well-balanced, giving the Vienna productions of Mahler and Roller pride of place as much as any of the "big" productions during the Nazi era.

481. Lederer, Josef-Horst. "Mahler und die beiden *Bohèmes*." *Festschrift Othmar Wessely zum 60. Geburtstag*. Hrsg. von Manfred Angerer, Eva Dietrich, Gerlinde Haus, Christa Harten, Gerald Florian Messner, Walter Pass und Herbert Seifert. Tutzing: Hans Schneider, 1982, pp. 399-406.
Covers the Viennese premieres of the two *Bohèmes* by Leoncavallo (which Mahler conducted) and Puccini (which he did not conduct).

482. Osthoff, Wolfgang. "Hans Pfitzner's 'Rose vom Liebesgarten': Gustav Mahler und die Wiener Schule." *Festschrift Martin Ruhnke zum 65. Geburtstag*. Neuhausen-Stuttgart: Institut für Musikwissenschaft der Universität Erlangen-Nürnberg, 1986, pp. 265-93.
The single most detailed study of *Die Rose vom Liebesgarten* as a work in its own right, giving the history of its premiere and discussing it in stylistic terms as a work of opera in turn-of-the-century context. From point of view of Pfitzner as author is the editor of ongoing series *Veröffentlichungen der Hans-Pfitzner-Gesellschaft* published by Hans Schneider of Tutzing (four volumes as of 1984).

483. Werba, Robert. "Mahlers Mozart-Bild: am Beispiel des 'Don Giovanni.'" *Wiener Figaro: Mitteilungsblatt der Wiener Mozartgemeinde* 42 (Mai 1975): 1-21.
 First in a series covering Mahler's Mozart performances at the Hofoper and with the Wiener Philharmoniker. Concentrates on Mahler's production of *Don Giovanni* in 1905, including specifications of casting and production and quoting extensively from the critical notices of the time with appendix including full reviews by Ludwig Hevesi and Berta Zuckerkandl. This section was translated into Italian by Sergio Sablich as "Il 'Don Giovanni' nella interpretazione di Gustav Mahler" in *N Riv Mus It* 9 (1975): 515-40.

484. Werba, Robert. "Mahlers Mozart-Bild: am Beispiel der 'Entführung aus dem Serail.'" *Wiener Figaro: Mitteilungsblatt der Wiener Mozartgemeinde* 43 (Januar 1976): 31-41.
 Second in a series of articles on Mahler's Mozart performances at the Hofoper and with the Wiener Philharmoniker. This section gives details of the production of *Abduction from the Seraglio* of 1906, including casting and production and quotations from critical notices of the time (from, among others, Graf, Wallaschek and Hirschfeld).

485. Werba, Robert. "Mahlers Mozart-Bild: am Beispiel der 'Zaide.'" *Wiener Figaro: Mitteilungsblatt der Wiener Mozartgemeinde* 43 (Mai 1976): 31-39.
 Third in a series documenting Mahler's Mozart performances at the Hofoper and with the Wiener Philharmoniker. This section surveys the casting and production values of *Zaide* with excerpts from the critical notices of 1902 (including reviews by Kalbeck, Graf, Korngold and Wallaschek) and a discussion on Mahler's relationship with the critic Robert Hirschfeld, who prepared the work for performance and is alleged to have turned against Mahler later when the work disappeared from the repertoire.

486. Werba, Robert. "Mahlers Mozart-Bild: 'Cosi fan Tutte.'" *Wiener Figaro: Mitteilungsblatt der Wiener Mozartgemeinde* 45 (Mai 1978): 11-17.
 Fifth in the series covering Mahler's Mozart performances at the Hofoper and with the Wiener Philharmoniker. This section includes production specifications, casting and critical notices from his production of

Così of 1905; among the critics represented are Graf, Korngold and Kalbeck.

487. Werba, Robert. "Mahlers Weg nach Wien." *OeMz* 34 (Oktober 1979): 486-98.
The story of the people and the events instrumental in Mahler's appointment to the directorship of the Hofoper, commencing with Mahler's previous engagement in Hamburg. Sources include the roles of Pollini, Mildenburg, Papier, Brahms, Karpath, Jahn and Rosé. Extensive reliance on contemporary accounts, especially in the Viennese newspapers, for almost day-by-day chronology.

488. Werba, Robert. "Mahlers Wiener Mozart-Taten: Die Hochzeit des Figaro." *Wiener Figaro: Mitteilungsblatt der Wiener Mozartgemeinde* 45 (Dezember 1978): 19-24.
Sixth in Werba's series of articles on Mahler's Mozart performances at the Hofoper and with the Wiener Philharmoniker (with a slight alteration in overall title of the series). This section covers the 1906 production of *Figaro* with production specifications, casting and excerpts from the critical notices of the time, including Julius Korngold among other reviewers. There is also considerable discussion of Mahler's previous work with *Figaro* in Budapest and Hamburg and the role of Kalbeck in the Vienna production. Compare discussions of same work by Kende (see no. 479 above) and Herta Blaukopf (see no. 477 above).

489. Werba, Robert. "Mahlers Wiener Mozart-Taten: Die Zauberflöte." *Wiener Figaro: Mitteilungsblatt der Wiener Mozartgemeinde* 46 (Mai 1979): 41-52.
Last in a series of articles on Mahler's Mozart performances at the Hofoper and with the Wiener Philharmoniker. This section concentrates on the production of *The Magic Flute* of 1897 including details of casting and production and excerpts from critical notices of the time. Among the reviewers are Josef Scheu and Elsa Bienenfeld.

490. Werba, Robert. "Mahlers Wiener Mozart-Taten: Zusammenfassung--Besetzungslisten--Namenverzeichnis." *Wiener Figaro: Mitteilungsblatt der Wiener Mozartgemeinde* 46 (Dezember 1979): 3-17.
Cumulation/index for the series of seven articles by

Werba documenting Mahler's Mozart performances at the Hofoper and with the Wiener Philharmoniker. Includes cast lists for each of the operatic productions. A fitting conclusion to a remarkable series of articles on an otherwise rather neglected subject.

New York

General

491. Deck, Marvin Lee von. "Gustav Mahler in New York: His Conducting Activities in New York City, 1908-1911." Ph.D. diss., New York University, 1973. 308 pp.
Surveys Mahler's tenure at the Metropolitan Opera and the New York Philharmonic Orchestra, with reference to documents in the archives of both organizations.

* Jokl, Ernst. "Gustav Mahler in Amerika." *Musikblätter des Anbruch* 2 (1920): 289-91.
Full citation under no. 16 above. Brief summary of Mahler's work in New York as conductor of opera and concerts including his own works.

Metropolitan Opera

492. Eaton, Quaintance. *The Miracle of the Met: an Informal History of the Metropolitan Opera, 1883-1967.* New York: Meredith Press, 1968. viii, 490 pp. Reprinted New York: Da Capo Press, 1984. xii, 490 pp. ISBN 0-306-76168-8.
Chatty, novelistic history of the Met. Not scholarly or well documented, but full of information and entertaining. Mostly in the form of inside descriptions of the house, singers and politics of production. Discussion of Mahler's tenure brief but accurate and positive.

493. Eaton, Quaintance. *Opera Caravan: Adventures of the Metropolitan on Tour (1883-1956).* Foreword by Rudolf Bing. New York, Toronto: Farrar, Straus and Cudahy, 1957. xv, 400 pp. Reprinted New York: Da Capo Press, 1978. 405 pp. ISBN 0-306-77596-4 (hard-

cover), 0-306-80089-6 (paper).
Less novelistic and more circumscribed than *Miracle of the Met* (see preceding entry). Divided into two sections: chronological prose account of the Metropolitan tours arranged by chapters under names of the company's general managers; and chronological lists of productions arranged by year and date, locations, cast members/conductors from 1883/84-1955/56 seasons. Mahler appears briefly in first section, more extensively in second under seasonal listings for 1907/08 and 1908/09. Real data from insider, easier source to consult than *Miracle of the Met*, if less entertaining.

494. Kolodin, Irving. *The Metropolitan Opera, 1883-1966: a Candid History.* 4th ed. New York: Alfred A. Knopf, 1966. xxi, 762, xlvii pp.
Supersedes previous editions (first edition Oxford University Press, 1936, second edition 1940, and third edition New York: Alfred A. Knopf, 1953). History of the house from its inception to 1966, heavily concentrating on house managers and artists as well as on repertoire. Information about Mahler's tenure (pp. 188-89, 200-05) is divided between the chapters "The Conreid Metropolitan Opera Company, 1903-1908" and "The Years of Toscanini, 1908-1915."

495. Krehbiel, Henry Edward. *Chapters of Opera: Being Historical and Critical Observations and Records Concerning the Lyrical Drama in New York from its Earliest Days down to the Present Time.* 2nd ed. New York: H. Holt, 1909. xvii, 435 pp. 3rd ed. New York: H. Holt, 1911. xvii, 460 pp. Reprinted New York: Da Capo Press, 1980. xvii, 435 pp. ISBN 0-306-76036-3.
Idiomatic history of opera in New York, especially the Metropolitan Opera from its inception to 1908, by a major New York critic who was a bitter enemy of Mahler. Da Capo Press edition apparently photographic reprint of second edition.

496. Krehbiel, Henry Edward. *More Chapters of Opera: Being Historical and Critical Observations and Records Concerning the Lyric Drama in New York from 1908-1918.* New York: Henry Holt, 1919. xvi, 474 pp.
Continuation of *Chapters of Opera* (see preceding entry) covering 1908-18 at the Metropolitan Opera, including Mahler's tenure which was briefly mentioned in the earlier volume. Author discusses Mahler briefly and

negatively in both books. Unreliable, especially when considered apropos of the account by Ossip Gabrilowitsch and cited by Clara Clemens (see no. 299 for that reference).

497. Mattfeld, Julius. *A Hundred Years of Grand Opera in New York, 1825-1925: a Record of Performances*. New York: New York Public Library, 1927; New York: AMS Press, 1976. 107 pp.
Cross-referenced alphabetical and chronological listings of operas performed in New York from 1825 to 1925; includes information on titles, librettists, composers, dates and places of performance. Useful background.

New York Philharmonic Orchestra

498. Aldrich, Richard. *Concert Life in New York 1902-1923*. New York: G.P. Putnam's Sons, 1941. xvii, 795 pp.
Collection of reviews by leading New York critic who covered concert life during Mahler's tenure with the New York Philharmonic Orchestra. See "New York Symphony Orchestra, Gustav Mahler" (pp. 238-40), "Philharmonic Orchestra, Gustav Mahler" (pp. 255-56) and "Philharmonic Orchestra, Gustav Mahler" (pp. 260-63) for discussion of concerts conducted by Mahler on November 30, 1908, April 1 and November 5, 1909; the repertoire in these concerts ranged from Beethoven and Schumann to Liszt and Wagner.

499. Huneker, James Gibbons. *The Philharmonic Society of New York and its 75th Anniversary: a Retrospect*. New York: Printed for the Society, 1917. 130 pp. Reprinted in *Early Histories of the New York Philharmonic*. New York: Da Capo Press, 1979. xxii, 495, x pp. ISBN 0-306-77537-9.
Seventy-fifth anniversary retrospective of the New York Philharmonic, concentrating on personnel and repertoire from the fiftieth to the seventy-fifth seasons (1892-1917). Not comprehensive or indexed, but valuable for chronological season-by-season lists of repertoire.

500. Shanet, Howard. "Reorganization (1909-11)." *Philharmonic: a History of New York's Orchestra*. Garden City, New York: Doubleday, 1975, pp. 207-20. ISBN

0-385-08861-2.
Exhaustive documentary history of the New York Philharmonic Orchestra relying on archival documents and other contemporary sources to illustrate the orchestra, its personnel, conductors, administration, programming and financial affairs. Written by an insider to the organization who shows a realistic attitude toward the often stormy history of the orchestra as well as an appreciation of its achievements. Assessment of Mahler's influence during his brief tenure is important in scope, considering the overweening nature of the history of the orchestra itself.

ALMA MAHLER-WERFEL

Biographical/Analytical

Primary

501. Colerus, Blanca. "Alma Mahler." *Die schöne Wienerin*. Hrsg. von Gyorgy Sebestyen. München: Kurt Desch, 1971, pp. 168-82.
Study of Alma Mahler-Werfel in context of Viennese society and history, especially as it relates to women in that society over a period in which women nurtured the men who formed the intellectual revolution (and did more, although barely acknowledged at the time in most cases).

502. Filler, Susan M. "Alma Mahler: *Der Erkennende*." *Historical Anthology of Music by Women*. Ed. by James R. Briscoe. Bloomington: Indiana Univ. Press, 1987, pp. 245-47. ISBN 0-253-21296-0.
Brief summary of Alma Mahler-Werfel's compositional *oeuvre* with particular emphasis on the song *Der Erkennende* originally published as no. 3 of *Fünf Gesänge* (Wien: Josef Weinberger, 1924), republished in this anthology of music by female composers. Includes complete translation of the poem by Franz Werfel (including portions not set by composer).

503. Filler, Susan M. "A Composer's Wife as Composer: the Songs of Alma Mahler." *Journal of Musicological Research* 4 (1983): 427-42.
A stylistic-literary study of the published songs of

Alma Mahler, citing her background education in composition and counterpoint and her familiarity with the poets and composers of her time. Notably includes discussion of the *Fünf Gesänge* published in 1924, which have generally been omitted in other studies by Warren Storey Smith and Karen Monson.

503a. Giroud, Françoise. *Alma Mahler, ou l'art d'être aimée*. Paris: Editions Robert Laffont, 1988. 260 pp. ISBN 2-221-05455-5.
Decent biography of Alma in French, straightforward, more accurate in detail than earlier biographies by Monson (see no. 507 below) and Wessling (see no. 514 below). For general readers, not musical specialists, as Alma's compositional work is virtually ignored in favor of her love life.

504. Mahler-Werfel, Alma. *And the Bridge is Love*. In collaboration with E.B. Ashton. New York: Harcourt, Brace and Co., 1958; London: Hutchinson and Co., 1959. 312 pp. (1958 ed.), 282 pp. (1959 ed.).
German version: *Mein Leben*. Vorwort von Willy Haas. Frankfurt am Main: S. Fischer, 1960. 376 pp.
Alma Mahler-Werfel's autobiography recapitulates some information given in *Gustav Mahler: Erinnerungen und Briefe* (see no. 339 above), then covers further events in her life. Told with wit, humor, courage, and more than a little self-deception, her life was definitely a fascinating story beyond the scope of her three marriages. Versions of the book in French (*Ma vie*, Paris: Julliard, 1961) and Spanish (*Mi vida amorosa*, Buenos Aires: Editorial Sudamericana, 1962) have also been published.

505. Mahler-Werfel, Alma. "Dem Genie die Steine aus dem Weg räumen (1902-1905)." *Frau und Musik*. Hrsg. von Eva Rieger. Die Frau in der Gesellschaft: frühe Texte. Hrsg. von Gisela Brinker-Gabler. Frankfurt am Main: Fischer Taschenbuch Verlag, 1980, pp. 117-26. ISBN 1280-ISBN-3-596-22257-5.
Selection from Alma's autobiography as part of collection of writings by women in music. Interesting comparison with other selections including entries by Cosima Wagner, Fanny Mendelssohn-Hensel and Clara Wieck-Schumann. Complemented by extensive bibliography covering nineteenth and twentieth century German women in music, and list of female German composers.

506. Mahony, Patrick. "Alma Mahler-Werfel." *Composer*, no. 45 (Autumn 1972): 13-17.
Brief study of Alma by a British friend. Not entirely accurate in certain details, but useful as a personal view by a friend outside the usual circles she gathered around herself.

507. Monson, Karen. *Alma Mahler: Muse to Genius--From Fin-de-Siècle Vienna to Hollywood's Heyday*. Boston: Houghton Mifflin, 1983. xviii, 348 pp. ISBN 0-395-32213-8.
Attempts to chronicle the life of Alma Mahler-Werfel in primarily biographical terms. Confused, often inaccurate and badly organized, aims at a lay audience over musical professionals but satisfies neither. An unfortunate failure in view of the fact that author had obtained access to unpublished sources which were not used to any advantage in solving problems that Mrs. Mahler-Werfel herself had created. German version, *Alma Mahler-Werfel: die unbezähmbare Muse* (München: Heyne, 1985) perpetuates errors and adds new problems through inexpert translation.

508. Perle, George. "Mein geliebtes Almschi. . . ." *OeMz* 35 (1980): 2-15.
Covers correspondence from Alban and Helene Berg to Alma Mahler-Werfel, comprising seventeen letters spanning the period from 1927 to 1937. Subjects range from personal (including the deaths of Manon Gropius and Alban Berg) to political, to musical (including *Lulu* and the dedication of the *Violinkonzert* to the memory of Manon). Careful and discreet editing by Perle.

509. Schollum, Robert. "Die Lieder von Alma Maria Schindler-Mahler." *OeMz* 34 (November 1979): 544-51.
Detailed discussion of the three published books of songs of 1910, 1915 and 1924, from historical and stylistic points of view, with musical examples from the first two books. With discussions by Warren Storey Smith (see next entry) and Filler (see no. 502 and no. 503 above), the only known discussion of Alma Mahler-Werfel as composer.

510. Smith, Warren Storey. "The Songs of Alma Mahler." *CD* 2 (1950): 74-78.
The first study of Alma Mahler-Werfel as composer, concentrating on the first two books of songs pub-

lished in 1910 (*Fünf Lieder*) and 1915 (*Vier Lieder*). Isolated in its time and for many years afterward, it serves an important purpose in making known the fact that Alma was a composer at all, but limited by (a) the complete lack of musical examples, and (b) omission of any mention of the *Fünf Gesange* of 1924, which were probably unknown to the author.

511. Sorell, Walter. "Alma Mahler-Werfel: Body and Mind." *Three Women: Lives of Sex and Genius*. London: Oswald Wolff; Indianapolis, New York: Bobbs-Merrill, 1975, pp. 3-69. ISBN 0-672-51750-7.
Long essay biography focusing on Alma Mahler-Werfel's struggle for self-identity despite the sexual standards of her time. Overweighted in her favor, often at the expense of the men in her life, but in many ways the most objective assessment of her life to date.

512. Werfel, Franz. "Manon." *Erzählungen aus zwei Welten*. 3. Band. Hrsg. von Adolf D. Klarmann. Frankfurt am Main: S. Fischer, 1954, pp. 392-99, 465.
Originally published in 1948 (Stockholm: Bermann-Fischer). A little-known essay by Franz Werfel written as a memorial to his stepdaughter, Manon, the daughter of Alma from her second marriage to Walter Gropius. Gives a personal view useful for comparison with Alma's description of Manon in *Mein Leben* (see no. 504 above).

513. Werfel, Franz. "A Personal Preface." *The Song of Bernadette*. Transl. by Ludwig Lewisohn. Garden City, New York: Sun Dial Press, 1944, pp. 5-7.
A brief but useful description of the circumstances under which the novel was written, including the story of the flight of Werfel and Alma from the Nazis which resulted in their emigration to the United States. Interesting for comparison with Alma's description in *Mein Leben* (see no. 504 above).

514. Wessling, Berndt W. *Alma: Gefährtin von Gustav Mahler, Oskar Kokoschka, Walter Gropius, Franz Werfel*. Düsseldorf: Claassen, 1983. 303 pp. ISBN 3-546-49593-4.
An uncritical, biased "biography" of Alma Mahler-Werfel as sex symbol, product of the times in which she had lived, seen through the quotations of Alma herself and those of the famous people she knew. Inadequately documented, making many statements open to question,

inconveniently arranged. No information about Alma as composer is offered. Not useful as critical source of information, apparently aimed at general German-speaking audience. Spanish version, *Alma: Companera de Gustav Mahler, Oskar Kokoschka, Walter Gropius, y Franz Werfel* (Barcelona: Ediciones de Nuevo Arte Thor, 1984) was translated by Karin Stadtlander.

515. Xenakis, Françoise. "Alma Schindler, 1880-1964." *Zut, on a encore oublié Madame Freud* . . . Paris: Jean-Claude Lattès, 1985, pp. 191-276.
One of a group of popular biographies on wives of important men. Primarily commentary on Alma's letters and diary, focusing on period 1901-11. Closer to reality than Monson or Wessling, best used in conjunction with earlier biographical studies by Mahony and Sorell.

Secondary

516. Ellert, Frederick. "Franz Werfel's Great Dilemma." *The Bridge: a Yearbook of Judaeo-Christian Studies*. Ed. by John M. Oesterreicher. New York: Pantheon Books, 1962, vol. 4, pp. 197-224.
Profiles the problem of Jewish conversion to Christianity (especially Catholicism) as a historical phenomenon and how it changed in the time between the Austrian Empire and the Third Reich. Pinpoints crisis of faith of Werfel, as expressed in his works including "Theologumena" (*Between Heaven and Earth*), *Paul Among the Jews, Barbara, The Song of Bernadette* and *Star of the Unborn*. Discusses Werfel's decision not to make formal conversion as a gesture of solidarity with victims of the Holocaust, although Werfel had adopted the Christian attitude to death. This is a strong contrast with the story of Mahler's conversion to Catholicism, but it is worth comparing with the accounts of Schoenberg's reconversion to Judaism as an example of the societal changes in Austria and Germany in the time in question. The editor's comment at the end of Ellert's article, suggesting that for Werfel "image and thought, poetry and theological speculation, seem to have had primacy over faith and commitment," are perhaps an unconscious comment on Werfel's Jewish orientation in intellectual if not formal terms.

517. Fry, Varian. *Surrender on Demand*. New York: Random

House, 1945. 243 pp.
Revised ed.: *Assignment Rescue*. New York: Four Winds Press, 1968. 187 pp.
Details the work of the committee which assumed the task of rescuing important refugees from the Nazis, including Franz Werfel and Alma Mahler-Werfel. Useful for comparison with Alma's account in *Mein Leben* (see no. 504 above) in which Mr. Fry himself plays a rather important role.

518. Goll, Claire. *Ich verzeihe keinem: eine literarische Chronique scandaleuse unserer Zeit*. Bern, München: Scherz, 1978. 333 pp.
Originally French (title, *La poursuite de vent*), translated into German by Ava Belcampo. Surveys the life and times of a close friend of Alma Mahler-Werfel early in the twentieth century.

519. Isaacs, Reginald. *Walter Gropius: der Mensch und sein Werk*. Transl. by Georg G. Meerwein. Berlin: Mann, 1983-84. 2 vols.
Authoritative study of the architect, including detailed citations from Gropius' personal papers and assessing his influence on twentieth century architectural style. Important to Mahler specialists as source of new information about his relationship with Alma, before, during and after their marriage, challenging and even disproving many assertions she made in her own writings.

520. Kandinsky, Nina. *Kandinsky und ich*. München: Kindler, 1976. 247 pp.
A biography of the artist Vasily Kandinsky, by his wife, a close friend of Alma Mahler. Alma appears prominently in the course of this account.

521. Klarmann, Adolf D. *Musikalität bei Werfel*. Ph.D. thesis, University of Pennsylvania, 1930. 82 pp.
"Printed in Germany" 1931, but without publisher's name. A discussion of the important role of music in the works of Franz Werfel, discussing many works from poetry to novels (especially *Verdi*). Shows that there is a parallel between Werfel's preferences in literature--others' as well as his own--and those of Mahler. No biographical connections, but very useful.

522. Kokoschka, Oskar. *Mein Leben*. Vorwort und dokumentarische Mitarbeit von Remigius Netzer. München:

Bruckmann, 1972. 339 pp.
English version: *My Life*. Transl. by David Britt.
New York: Macmillan, 1974. 240 pp.
Includes Kokoschka's own account of his affair with Alma, which compares fascinatingly with her account in *Mein Leben* and *And the Bridge is Love* (see no. 504 above). Offers perspective on Alma's views of the years following Mahler's death and her affair with Kokoschka, perhaps more candid and detailed than her account.

523. Mann, Thomas. "Franz Werfel." *Reden und Aufsätze*. Stockholmer Gesamtausgabe der Werke von Thomas Mann. [Oldenburg]: S. Fischer, 1965, vol. 1, pp. 271-73.
A memorial essay on Franz Werfel written shortly after Werfel's death in 1945, addressing the significance of Werfel's work rather than details of his life. Good counterpoint to Werfel's own views of his life and work.

524. Spielmann, Heinz. *Oskar Kokoschka: die Fächer für Alma Mahler*. Mit einer Umschlagzeichung des Künstlers und einem Vorwort von Lise Lotte Müller. Hamburg: H. Christians, 1969. 33 pp. [Revised ed. Bibliophilen Taschenbücher, 462] Dortmund: Harenberg, 1985. 113 pp.
A gem of a study focusing on the fans made especially for Alma by Kokoschka. Reproduces the originals and includes commentary offering artistic and biographical insight which makes interesting comparison of Alma's own account in her autobiography.

525. Vergo, Peter. *Art in Vienna 1898-1918: Klimt, Kokoschka, Schiele and Their Contemporaries*. London: Phaidon, 1975; Ithaca, New York: Praeger, 1975, 1981. 256 pp. ISBN 0-7148-1600-0.
Beautifully illustrated study of visual art and architecture in Vienna focusing on the Sezession and their followers. Valuable to Mahler scholars as connection to the work of Alfred Roller, including his collaboration with Mahler at the Opera; but especially important in coverage of work of Kokoschka at time he was living with Alma.

526. Zahn, Leopold. *Franz Werfel*. Köpfe des XX. Jahrhunderts, 42. Berlin: Colloquium, 1966. 95 pp.
A remarkably thorough introduction to the life and work of Werfel, involving considerable information on

Alma Mahler-Werfel as well. Ranks as the most objective and accurate biography available (surpassing Alma's *Mein Leben* in many ways). Profits from the passage of time in its studies of Werfel's work and its significance in both biographical and political terms.

LITERARY INFLUENCES

Alma Mahler-Werfel

527. Bierbaum, Otto Julius. *Gesammelte Werke*. Hrsg. von Michael Georg Conrad und Hans Brandenburg. München: G. Müller, 1912-22. 7 vols.
The first volume of the collected works of Bierbaum is devoted to his poetry, a major source of texts for Alma Mahler songs.

528. Dehmel, Richard. *Gesammelte Werke*. Berlin: S. Fischer, 1906-09. 10 vols.
New edition Berlin: S. Fischer, 1920. 3 vols.
Source of texts for several songs composed by Alma Mahler distributed between each of the three published books of her songs. In the edition of 1920, the following texts are found in volume I: *Waldseligkeit* (pp. 55-56), *Ansturm* (pp. 58-59), *Lobgesang* (pp. 71-72) and *Die stille Stadt* (pp. 158-59).

529. Falke, Gustav. *Gesammelte Dichtungen*. Hamburg: A. Janssen, 1912. 5 vols.
Allegedly the source of two texts set by Alma Mahler, *Erntelied* (*Vier Lieder*, 1915) and *Laue Sommernacht* (*Fünf Lieder*, 1910). However, Knud Martner has recently pointed out that the latter song is not a Falke setting but has been identified with *Gefunden* of Otto Julius Bierbaum.

530. Hartleben, Otto Erich. *Gedichte*. Ausgewählte Werke, 1. Auswahl und Einleitung von Franz Ferdinand Heitmüller. Berlin: S. Fischer, 1913. 231 pp.
Source of at least one text set by Alma Mahler, *In meines Vaters Garten* (no. 2 of *Fünf Lieder*, 1910).

531. Novalis [Friedrich von Hardenberg]. *Gesammelte Werke*. Hrsg. von Carl Seelig. Herrliberg-Zürich: Buhl-

Verlag, 1945. 5 vols.
Source of two texts set by Alma Mahler in *Fünf Gesänge* (1924): *Hymne* (no. 1) and *Hymne an die Nacht* (no. 5).

532. Rilke, Rainer Maria. *Sämtlichte Werke*. Hrsg. von Rilke-Archiv. Besorgt von E. Zinn. Wiesbaden: Insel-Verlag, 1955-1966. 6 vols.
Source of several texts set by Alma Mahler, including *Bei dir ist es traut* (*Fünf Lieder*, 1910) and at least one of the songs in the unpublished *Aus dem Zyklus "Mütter" von Rainer Maria Rilke*. Of many editions of the works of Rilke, this one is preferred because it is critical and apparently complete.

533. Werfel, Franz. *Das lyrische Werk*. Hrsg. von Adolf D. Klarmann. Gesammelte Werke. Frankfurt am Main: S. Fischer, 1967. 704 pp.
The most comprehensive and critical edition of the poetry of Franz Werfel, carefully edited from all available sources both printed and manuscript. Well documented historically and chronologically, therefore valuable as a source of information on the lives of Werfel and Alma as well as a window on Werfel's views of the world around him. Includes the full texts of poems that were published in earlier collections in abbreviated form, including *Der Erkennende*, which Alma set as no. 3 of *Fünf Gesänge* (1924)

Gustav Mahler: Symphonies

534. Goethe, Johann Wolfgang von. *Faust: der Tragödie erster und zweiter Teil. Urfaust*. Kommentiert von Erich Trunz. Neuaflage. Hamburg: C. Wegner, 1968. 659 pp.
Source of the text used by Mahler in Part II of the *Symphony no. 8*. Among many different editions of this famous work, this edition may be considered critically and carefully edited.

535. Jahnke, Sabine. "Materialen zu einer Unterreichtssequenz: Des Antonius von Padua Fischpredigt bei Orff--Mahler--Berio." *Musik und Bildung* 5 (1973): 615-22.
Traces *Des Antonius von Padua Fischpredigt* through works of Orff (*Schulwerk*), Mahler (*Des Knaben Wunderhorn* and the third movement of *Symphony no. 2*) and

Berio (*Sinfonia*). A traversal of musical thought and handling by means of a single textual idea.

536. Klopstock, Friedrich Gottlieb. *Klopstocks Oden und Elegien.* Darmstadt: Drukkerei von Wittig, 1771; facsimile reprint, Heidelberg: Carl Winter, 1924. 160 pp.
    See also Klopstock, Friedrich Gottlieb. *Ausgewählte Werke.* Hrsg. von Karl August Schleiden. Nachwort von Friedrich Georg Jünger (München: C. Hanser, 1962, 1378 pp.). These two editions are both applicable as sources for the *Auferstehungsode* which was set by Mahler (and amplified with his own text) in the last movement of the *Symphony no. 2*.

*   Matter, Jean. "Musique et littérature." *L'Arc* 67: 45-50.
    Full citation under no. 3 above. Discusses literary influences on Mahler with special reference to *Faust* and the *Symphony no. 8*.

537. Nietzsche, Friedrich. *Werke in drei Bänden.* Hrsg. von Karl Schlechta. München: Carl Hanser, 1954-56, 1960. 3 vols.
    Complete critically edited collection of the works of Nietzsche. Includes *Also sprach Zarathustra*, the source of the contralto solo in the fourth movement of the *Symphony no. 3*, in vol. II (pp. 275-561) and also other works of Nietzsche which evidently affected Mahler's philosophical thought, including *Die fröhliche Wissenschaft* in the same volume (pp. 7-274). See also dissertation by Nikkels (below, no. 538) for detailed discussion of Nietzsche and Mahler's personal philosophy.

*   Nikkels, Eveline. "'Licht, Leben, Lust'--trois des principaux concepts de Nietzsche dans l'oeuvre de Gustav Mahler." *Colloque 1985*: 52-56.
    Full citation under no. 5 above. Studies the effect of Nietzsche's concepts on Mahler's thinking during composition, especially with reference to the *Symphony no. 3*, the *Kindertotenlieder* and *Das Lied von der Erde*.

538. Nikkels, Eveline. "Mahler en Nietzsche: een vergelijkende studie." [Mahler and Nietzsche: a comparative study.] Diss., Rijksuniversiteit Utrecht, 1984. Published Amsterdam: Rodopi, 1984. 218 pp.

Comparison between Nietzsche and Mahler as men, their
similarities in life philosophy. Effect of Nietzsche's
work on Mahler's music considered in detail.

Gustav Mahler: Des Knaben Wunderhorn

539. Arnim, Ludwig Achim von und Clemens Brentano. *Des Knaben Wunderhorn: alte deutsche Lieder*. München: Winkler-Verlag, 1957, 1966. 935 pp.
    The most recent of several editions of Mahler's single most important source of poetic inspiration (texts for many songs, movements of three symphonies, literary touchstones and unclassifiables). Comparison of this edition with earlier ones shows that it is the most critically reliable since the original edition of 1805-08.

540. Filler, Susan M. "Mahler and the Anthology of *Des Knaben Wunderhorn*." *Journal of the Canadian Association of University Schools of Music* 8 (1978): 82-111.
    Discusses Mahler's use of the *Wunderhorn* anthology for sources of texts in his songs and symphonies, musical whetstones and lifestyle mottoes. Notes the types of changes Mahler was apt to make in the texts themselves before using them for various purposes. Notable for discussion of the texts of two songs which Mahler wrote using hybrid conceptions in different ways. Argues that the influence of the anthology did not disappear after the *Symphony no. 4*, thereby taking issue with others who allow virtually no influence of the anthology in the middle and late works.

541. Fischer, Kurt von. "Gustav Mahlers Umgang mit Wunderhorntexten." *Melos/NZfM* 4 (1978): 103-07.
    Surveys Mahler's long involvement with poems in the *Wunderhorn* anthology, noting his tendency to alter texts for musical purposes. Includes many textual examples and some musical ones. Refers back to earlier literature including Mitchell, Pamer and la Grange.

542. Gregory, Robin. "Mahler and 'Des Knaben Wunderhorn.'" *Monthly Musical Record* 83 (1953): 227-30, 265-70.
    A brief study of the anthology, the methods used by Arnim and Brentano in its compilation, its influence on Mahler's compositions and their place in the liter-

ary-musical trends of the nineteenth century.

* Matter, Jean. "Le 'Knaben Wunderhorn' dans l'oeuvre de Mahler." *Feuilles musicales* 1959: 122-24.
Full citation under no. 6 above. Discussion of the *Wunderhorn* anthology and its influence on Mahler's works in both vocal and symphonic forms. Too brief to be compared favorably with later studies.

543. Röllecke, Heinz. "Gustav Mahlers 'Wunderhorn'-Lieder: Textgrundlagen und Textauswahl." *Jahrbuch des Freien Deutschen Hochstifts 1981*. Tübingen: Max Niemeyer, 1981, pp. 370-78.
Nonmusical critico-literary and historical study of Mahler and the *Wunderhorn* anthology, especially notable for historical comparison of Mahler's use of texts with various editions of the anthology available at the time he was composing the settings. Unique.

544. Sams, Eric. "Notes on a Magic Horn." *MT* 115 (1974): 556-59.
Comments on the process by which Arnim and Brentano collected the texts for *Des Knaben Wunderhorn* anthology, and the nature of their editing; also considers Mahler and other composers who made use of the anthology in their works, and shows how they too made changes which suited their compositional purposes. Somewhat similar to preceding entry but rather more musically oriented.

545. Wadmann, Anne. "Gustav Mahler en 'Des Knaben Wunderhorn.'" *Levende talen* (1966): 681-99.
Originally published in *De tsjerne* (June-August 1960). An interesting early study of the influence of the *Des Knaben Wunderhorn* anthology on Mahler's early works. The 1960 version was written in Friesien and published in multisectional format; the 1966 version is in Dutch. Willem Smith (Alkmaar, Netherlands) translated the article into English in 1973, but this translation has never been published.

Gustav Mahler: Rückert Lieder/Kindertotenlieder

546. Gregory, Robin. "Mahler's Rückert Settings." *Monthly Musical Record* 84 (1954): 92-96.

Study of the *Kindertotenlieder* and the five *Rückert Lieder*, less about musical form than about literary background and Mahler's text-painting techniques in the spirit of history of German lied composition and events in Mahler's own life.

547. Roman, Zoltan. "Prelude and Finale: Musical Jugendstil in Selected Songs by Mahler and Webern." *Focus on Vienna 1900: Change and Continuity in Literature, Music, Art and Intellectual History*. Houston German Studies, 4. Ed. by Erika Nielsen. München: Wilhelm Fink, 1982, pp. 113-24. ISBN 3-7705-2092-0. Posits a definition of *Jugendstil* as applied to songs of both Mahler and Webern, showing how conscious divergence between a poem and its musical setting may be a major facet of the later Expressionist style. Examples chiefly *Ich atmet' einen Linden Duft* of Mahler and *Helle Nacht* of Webern.

548. Rückert, Friedrich. *Gesammelte Gedichte*. Frankfurt am Main: J.D. Sauerländer, 1843. 3 vols. Source of Mahler's texts for the *Kindertotenlieder* and the five texts of Rückert included in the *Sieben Lieder*. Editions of the works of Rückert are not easy to locate today, making this early edition (while long out of print) desirable when it can be located in libraries.

Gustav Mahler: Das Lied von der Erde

549. Bethge, Hans. *Die chinesische Flöte: Nachdichtungen chinesischer Lyrik*. Leipzig: Insel-Verlag, 1917. 118 pp. Originally published in 1907; this is the second edition. Mahler's source for the texts which comprise *Das Lied von der Erde*. Comparison with Mahler's score shows that he made adaptations and additions to the texts which have been exhaustively considered by Hu, Mitchell, Wenk and la Grange.

550. Hu Haiping. "Poetic Genesis and Musical Response in Gustav Mahler's 'Das Lied von der Erde.'" M.M. thesis, University of California-Los Angeles, 1985. 200 pp. Remarkable study of *Das Lied von der Erde* focusing es-

Literary Influences: Lied von der Erde/Early Works 159

pecially on the ancestry of the texts as incentive for the style of Mahler's settings. Should be read in conjunction with studies by la Grange and Mitchell because of its insight into the original Chinese sources as discussed by author who is, for once, a linguistic insider. Rare and little-known, but worth consulting.

551. Wenk, Arthur. "The Composer as Poet in *Das Lied von der Erde*." *19th C Mus* 1 (1977): 33-47.
Surveys the texts from *Die chinesische Flöte* selected by Mahler for use in *Das Lied von der Erde*, looking backward at the changes made by Bethge from the Chinese originals adapted in his book, but also looking forward at the modifications Mahler made in his turn. This study qualifies as the basis for the studies made by la Grange and Mitchell, although they--unlike Wenk --went so far as to consult the Chinese originals, while Wenk used literalistic English renditions. Important as a trend-setter in a difficult area of research because of the inaccessibility of the textual sources.

552. Zavadskaya, E. "Poeticheskii istochnik 'Pesn' o zemle.'" [The poetic sources of *Das Lied von der Erde*.] *Sovetskaya muzyka* 32 (July 1968): 117-20.
Early study of the history of Mahler's selections for the texts of *Das Lied von der Erde*, citing the Chinese poets individually, which is an improvement on the generalized discussions of Bethge's *Die chineseische Flöte* then current. Texts included in Russian prose versions. Limited, probably completely independent of later studies of Wenk, la Grange, Mitchell and Hu, but worth noting because it appears to be a first in point of view.

Gustav Mahler: Early Works

553. Bechstein, Ludwig. *Märchenbuch*. 4. illustrirte Ausgabe. Mit 187 Holzschnitten nach Originalzeichnungen von Ludwig Richter. Leipzig: G. Wigand, 1877. 296 pp.
Component source for Mahler's cantata *Das klagende Lied*. See next entry for second component source of same work.

554. Grimm, Jakob und Wilhelm Grimm. "Der singende Knochen." Kinder- und Hausmärchen. Hrsg. von Friedrich von der Leyen. Düsseldorf, Köln: Eugen Diederich, 1968, vol. I, pp. 13-15.
Joint source (with Das klagende Lied of Ludwig Bechstein cited in the previous entry) of Mahler's cantata Das klagende Lied. In contrast to the scarcity of editions of Bechstein's works, there is no shortage of editions of the stories of the Grimm brothers; however, many editions do not include this tale and are otherwise undesirable because they are not critically edited. This edition includes all known tales and is reliably edited, offering the story as Mahler used it without alteration for the benefit of juvenile readers.

555. Hefling, Stephen E. "The Road Not Taken: Mahler's Rübezahl." [Futurismo]: the Yale University Library Gazette 57 (1983): 145-70.
A study of Mahler's libretto for Rübezahl as a literary indicator of Mahler's youthful leanings. As Mahler did not set this libretto to music, the work is interesting primarily in comparison with other versions by Wolf and Weber.

556. Newlin, Dika. "Mahler's Opera." Opera News 36 (March 18, 1972): 6-7.
Surveys the libretto of Rübezahl, which Mahler drafted while a student at the Conservatory in Vienna and apparently never set to music (or set to music which is lost to posterity?).

557. Tirso de Molina [Gabriel Tellez]. Drei Dramen aus dem Spanischen de Tirso de Molina. Hrsg. von Karl Vossler. Deutsche Akademie der Wissenschaften zu Berlin Vorträge und Schriften, 45. Berlin: Akademie-Verlag, 1953. 332 pp.
Dramas of Tirso de Molina included Don Juan from which Mahler culled his texts for Serenade aus Don Juan and Phantasie aus Don Juan which he set as no. 4 and no. 5 of Lieder und Gesänge, vol. 1. Difficult writer to document, editions rare.

558. [Volkmann, Richard von.] Gedichte von Richard Leander. Leipzig: Breitkopf und Härtel, 1885. 3. Auflage. viii, 214 pp.
Source of the texts for Fruhlingsmorgen and Erinnerung, the first two songs of Lieder und Gesänge, vol. 1

(Mainz: B. Schotts Söhne, 1892). Both texts are found in the group called *Kleine Lieder* (originally published 1854-56).

General and Miscellaneous

559. Barker, Andrew W. "Gustav Mahler and German Literature." *Focus on Vienna 1900: Change and Continuity in Literature, Music, Art and Intellectual History.* Houston German Studies, 4. Ed. by Erika Nielsen. München: Wilhelm Fink, 1982, pp. 131-39. ISBN 3-7705-2092-0.
 Surveys Mahler as literarist in the German tradition, tracing his influential predecessors and considering his own methods with special emphasis on his revisions of pre-existing texts by others.

560. Fischer, Jens Malte. "Das klagende Lied von der Erde: zu Gustav Mahlers Liedern und ihren Texten." *Zeitschrift für Literaturwissenschaft und Linguistik: eine Zeitschrift der Gesamthochschule Siegen* 9, no. 34 (1979): 55-69.
 Surveys the texts of Mahler's vocal works in four sections: (1) *Das klagende Lied*, (2) Die *Wunderhorn*-Lieder, (3) Die Rückert-Lieder, and (4) *Das Lied von der Erde*. Short but cogent study of common threads running through Mahler's choice of literary sources.

561. Günther, Siegfried. "Texte und Textbehandlung in Gustav Mahlers Lyrik." *NZfM* 87 (1920): 268-70.
 Considers Mahler's handling of texts, pointing out his alterations in texts themselves and also his musical rebalancing techniques, especially from rhythmic standpoint. Many individual examples, mostly textual, some musical.

562. Hartmann, Ludwig. *Die drei Pintos: komische Oper in drei Aufzügen--Musik von Carl Maria von Weber.* Opernführer, 80. Leipzig: Hermann Seeman Nachf., 1901. 32 pp.
 Libretto of *Die drei Pintos* and introduction to the plot, for general opera-going audience. Not a critical discussion of the nature of Mahler's work on the performing version, less useful than later study by Rognoni (see no. 1044 below), but reasonable introduction.

563. Heine, Heinrich. *Gedichte*. Sämtliche Werke, 1. München: Winkler, 1972. 964 pp.
Source of song texts for both Mahler (an early unfinished song *Im wunderschönen Monat Mai*) and Alma (*Ich wandle unter Blumen*, the last of the *Fünf Lieder* of 1910).

564. Jung, Ute. *Die Musikphilosophie Thomas Manns*. Kölner Beiträge zur Musikforschung, 53. Hrsg. von Karl Gustav Fellerer. Regensburg: Gustav Bosse, 1969. iii, 160 pp. ISBN 3-7649-2544-2.
A study of Mann's work in the context of his musical contacts and background with special reference to Wagner and Mahler, Paul Bekker, Bruno Walter, as well as other German literarists including Adorno, Schopenhauer and Nietzsche. Shows how the characters and thought in his works reflect his philosophy of music, especially in *Der Tod in Venedig*, *Der Zauberberg* and *Doktor Faustus*.

565. Klusen, Ernst. "Die Liedertexte Gustav Mahlers." *Sudetendeutsche Zeitschrift für Volkskunde* 6 (1933): 178-84.
Early study of Mahler's songs from the point of view of his choice of texts rather than of musical style; complementary to Pamer (see no. 853 below), literary but not critically comparative in terms of published sources versus folk sources.

566. Mahler, Gustav. *Carl Maria von Weber: Die drei Pintos: komische Oper. Unter Zugrundelegung des gleichnamigen Textbuches von Th. Hell . . . der dramatische Theil von C. von Weber (Sohn), der musikalische von Gustav Mahler*. Leipzig: C.F. Kahnt, 1888. 53 pp.
Libretto of *Die drei Pintos* published at the time of the premiere with the constellation of scores, by the original publisher; antedates publication by Hartmann and may be basis for that study (see no. 562 above).

567. Mahler, Gustav und Alfred Roller. *Oberon: romantische Oper in drei Aufzügen von C.M. von Weber. Neue Bühneneinrichtung von Gustav Mahler*. Wien, Leipzig: Universal Edition, [1914]. 79 pp.
Complete text of the opera in revised version by Mahler and Roller, with an extensive introduction giving the place of this version in the history of the opera in performance.

Literary Influences: Miscellaneous 163

568. Mayer, Hans. "Gustav Mahler und die Literatur." *Ein Denkmal für Johannes Brahms*. Frankfurt: Suhrkamp, 1983, pp. 146-61.
    Transcribed from author's paper at the 1982 Gustav Mahler Weeks at Toblach. Considers Mahler's use of the literary tradition, both concretely in the vocal works and philosophically. Essentially disregards *Des Knaben Wunderhorn* and concentrates on the works of Rückert and Bethge.

*   Mayer, Hans. "Musik und Literatur." *Gustav Mahler* (1966): 142-56.
    Full citation under no. 7 above. Discusses literary influences on Mahler's musical work, in the context of such influences on his predecessors, contemporaries and some of his followers.

569. Rosenberg, Wolf. "Warum Mahler keine Oper schrieb: über Wortklang und Wortsemantik bei Gustav Mahler." *Forum* 14 (1967): 394-98.
    Not really about the reasons that Mahler never wrote an opera, rather an assessment of his place in the history of textual setting by Austro-German composers in non-operatic media (song, symphony, cantata). Special attention to *Das klagende Lied* and the *Symphony no. 8*.

570. Vill, Susanne. *Vermittlungsformer verbalisierter und musikalischer Inhalte in der Musik Gustav Mahlers*. Frankfurter Beiträge zur Musikwissenschaft, 6. Tutzing: Hans Schneider, 1979. 340 pp. ISBN 3-7952-0226-4.
    Originally the author's Ph.D. dissertation (Universität Frankfurt am Main, 1975). Remarkable study of the literary word function in Mahler's works, divided into two categories: literal use of words (including Mahler's alterations) in the songs and symphonies requiring voices; and use of the program conception in the first four symphonies, both instrumental and vocal. Emphasizes texts and literary concepts over musical structure, including few musical examples.

PUBLISHERS

General

571. Foreign Music Publications. New York: C.F. Peters, 1979. 16 pp.
See especially the sections "Editions Eulenberg" (p. 4), "Hinrichsen Edition" (p. 6) and "Kahnt" (pp. 7-8). Pamphlet for informational purposes, giving brief illustrated histories of the houses, which are represented by C. F. Peters in the United States.

572. Musikverlage in der Bundesrepublik Deutschland und in West-Berlin. Bonn: Musikhandel, 1965. 192 pp.
Profiles music publishers from West Germany and West Berlin, including the following houses which had published works of Mahler: Bote und Bock (Symphony no. 7), C.F. Peters (Symphony no. 5), C.F. Kahnt (Symphony no. 6, Kindertotenlieder, Sieben Lieder) and B. Schotts Söhne (Lieder und Gesänge).

573. Plesske, Hans-Martin, hrsg. "Leipzigs Musikverlage einst und jetzt." Jahrbuch der Deutschen Bücherei 1 (1965): 59-93.
A brief study of the history of music publishing in Leipzig, giving particular emphasis to Breitkopf und Härtel but also considerable information on C.F. Peters, C.F. Kahnt and Ernst Eulenberg, all of which published works of Mahler.

574. Plesske, Hans-Martin. "Wenn mich die Höhe der Honararforderung auch überrascht hat: Leipzigs Musikverlage und ihr Anteil an der Erstausgaben von Gustav Mahler, Richard Strauss und Hans Pfitzner." Jahrbuch der Deutschen Bücherei 14 (1978): 75-102.
Evaluates unpublished letters of Mahler, Strauss and Pfitzner in the Staatsarchiv Leipzig which document their dealings with Leipzig publishers including Peters and Kahnt. Intended as microcosm of development of Leipzig as music publishing center.

575. Revers, Peter. "Gustav Mahler's Copyists: F. Weidig." NaMR, no. 14 (October 1984): 3-6.
Surveys Mahler's working relationship with the copyist Weidig, who was involved with the preparation of publication sources for Mahler's work during his tenure in Hamburg (1891-97), which include portions of the Symphony no. 1, Symphony no. 2, several of the Lieder

und Gesänge, and the Lieder eines fahrenden Gesellen.

576. Revers, Peter. "Addenda to: Gustav Mahler's Copyists: F. Weidig." NaMR, no. 15 (October 1985): 14-16.
Corrects and supplements Revers's essay in the previous number of NaMR (see preceding entry) with respect to Weidig's participation in the preparation of certain works of Mahler for publication during Mahler's tenure in Hamburg.

Bote und Bock

577. Bock, Gustav. "Bote und Bock." MGG, vol. 2, cols. 152-54.
Detailed summary of the history of the house from its foundation to the post-World War II period. Written by a member of the controlling family, this article is the best source of information about the house except for the Festschriften marking the centenary and one hundred twenty-fifth anniversaries (see below, no. 581 and 580 respectively). Bibliography especially valuable.

578. Döll, Stefanie. "Das Berliner Musikverlagswesen in der Zeit von 1880 bis 1920." Ph.D. diss., Freie Universität Berlin, 1984. 216 pp.
Surveys the history of music publishing in Berlin during the period when Mahler contracted for publication of the Symphony no. 7 with Bote und Bock.

579. Elvers, Rudolf. "Bote und Bock." New Grove, vol. 3, pp. 87-88.
Briefly chronicles the history of the house which published Mahler's Symphony no. 7 and lists bibliography of sources giving detailed history.

580. Kunz, Harald. 125 Jahre Bote und Bock, 1838-1963. Berlin, Wiesbaden: Bote und Bock, 1963. 96 pp.
Documents the first hundred twenty-five years of the house, including the publication of Mahler's Symphony no. 7 (which the author correctly points out was acquired when the house took over Lauterbach und Kuhn, which had originally contracted for the work). Discusses the conservation of the house archive until World War II, followed by the destruction of the arch-

ive and its reconstitution after the war. An important in-house study emphasizing the people in the Bock family who managed the house from before Mahler's time to the present, and the roles they played in the procurement of entries to the house catalogue.

581. *Musikverlag Bote und Bock Berlin 1838-1938.* Berlin: Bote und Bock, 1938. 84 pp.
Details the history of the first century of the house which published the *Symphony no. 7*. Somewhat more reliable than such materials usually published in the Nazi period because this book was published by house personnel who had been involved for many years, before the Nazi purges had really affected the functioning of the house.

Ludwig Doblinger

582. *100 Jahre Musikverlag Doblinger: Ausstellung 9. Dezember 1976 bis 28. Jänner 1977.* Musiksammlung der Österreichische Nationalbibliothek, Institut für Österreichische Musikdokumentation. Wien: Österreichische Nationalbibliothek, 1976. 36 pp.
Documents the first hundred years of the publishing house responsible for the initial publication of the *Symphony no. 4*. An exhibition commemorating the centennial of the Doblinger house was mounted in the Austrian National Library and this book represents a guide to the exhibition, which included sources for the symphony.

583. *Ludwig Doblinger (Bernhard Herzmansky), Musikalienhandlung, Verlag, Antiquariat und Leihanstalt, Wien-Leipzig, 1876-1926.* Wien: H. Geitner, 1926. 20 pp.
Surveys the first fifty years' history of the Viennese house of Ludwig Doblinger, responsible for the initial publication of Mahler's *Symphony no. 4*.

584. Vogg, Herbert. *1876-1976: 100 Jahre Musikverlag Doblinger.* Wien, München: Ludwig Doblinger, 1976. [xiii], 216 pp. ISBN 3-900035-49-0.
A celebration of the centenary of the publishing house responsible for the first published prints of Mahler's *Symphony no. 4*. Differs from no. 582 above not only in being much longer but in different format, richly il-

lustrated series of essays focusing on the history of the house and treating Mahler and other composers as contributors to that history rather than as independent subjects in themselves; however, much more detail from in-house archive than in exhibition catalogue.

585. Weinmann, Alexander. "Doblinger." *New Grove*, vol. 5, p. 516.
Summarizes the history of the house originally responsible for publication of the *Symphony no. 4* until the work was taken over by Universal Edition. Bibliography basis of extended research with in-house publications cited above in preceding entries no. 582-84.

Ernst Eulenberg

586. Eulenberg, Kurt. "Ernst Eulenberg, Musikverlag." *MGG*, vol. 3, cols. 1615-16.
Summary of the history of the house, which published an early edition of the *Symphony no. 7* and later published four symphonies and two song cycles under the editorship of Hans Redlich. Valuable as written by a member of the controlling family. Covers the history of the house from foundation to the post-World War II period.

587. Plesske, Hans-Martin. "Ernst (Emil Alexander) Eulenberg." *New Grove*, vol. 6, pp. 291-92.
Summarizes the history of the house, which first published a work of Mahler in 1924 (the *Symphony no. 7*) and later worked with Hans Redlich on an "alternative" critical edition which included not only the *Symphony no. 7* (in a revised edition) but the *Symphony no. 1, Symphony no. 4, Symphony no. 6, Kindertotenlieder* and the *Lieder eines fahrenden Gesellen*.

C.F. Kahnt

588. Deaville, James. "The C.F. Kahnt Archive in Leipzig: a Preliminary Report." *MLA Notes* 42 (March 1986): 502-17.
Summarizes the history of the publishing house from its inception in 1851 to the present, with a descrip-

tion of the surviving archive in Leipzig after the house was moved to Wasserburg. Special attention to Mahler's version of *Die drei Pintos* of Weber and the *Symphony no. 6* as well as works of Liszt.

589. Plesske, Hans-Martin. "Christian Friedrich Kahnt." *New Grove*, vol. 9, pp. 770-71.
A rare source of information on the history of the house which published the *Symphony no. 6, Kindertotenlieder* and the *Sieben Lieder*. In the absence of anniversary *Festschriften* for the house's centenary and other important milestones, this article and the corresponding one in *MGG* (see next entry) are crucial to a basic knowledge of the history of this important house.

590. Vötterle, Karl. "C.F. Kahnt." *MGG*, vol. 7, col. 429.
Important summary of the history of the house, which was Mahler's most important publisher after Universal Edition. As noted in the previous entry, this article and the corresponding one in *New Grove* are very important to a basic knowledge of the long history of this important house, in the absence of anniversary commemorations.

C.F. Peters

591. *The C.F. Peters Music Publishing Tradition*. New York, London, Frankfurt: C.F. Peters, 1975. 13 pp.
Pamphlet for informational purposes, giving a brief illustrated history of the house from 1800-1975. Mahler figures prominently among the composers whose works were published by Peters, although the house published only a single work--the *Symphony no. 5*-- which is limited by comparison with other composers in the house catalogue. Emphasizes the far-reaching influence of the liberal standards of the house management in the adoption of a catalogue that has long been "modern" compared with those of other major publishers.

592. Lichtenwanger, William. "Walter Hinrichsen and the Establishment of C.F. Peters in America." *An Introduction to Music Publishing*. Ed. by Carolyn Sachs. New York: C.F. Peters, 1981, p. 17.

A brief informational essay surveying the establishment of the American branch of C.F. Peters which was brought about by the emigration of Walter Hinrichsen (second son of Henri Hinrichsen, who contracted with Mahler for the *Symphony no. 5*) from Germany at the time of the Nazi purges in the original Leipzig house.

593. Lindlar, Heinrich. *C.F. Peters Musikverlag: Zeittafeln zur Verlagsgeschichte (1800-1867-1967)*. Frankfurt, London, New York: C.F. Peters, 1967. 41 pp.
Documents chronologically the history of the C.F. Peters house from its inception to 1967. Summarizes the changes of personnel in the house and how they influenced the acquisition policies affecting the catalogue. Information concerning Henri Hinrichsen's negotiations with Mahler for the *Symphony no. 5* and the history of the house which affected the subsequent history of the work is found on pp. 24-36.

594. Lück, Rudolf. "Peters." *MGG*, vol. 10, cols. 1118-21.
Summarizes history of the house from its foundation in 1800 to the post-World War II period. Valuable for its bibliography which lists many of the house *Festschrift* publications issued for anniversaries, plus the *Peters Jahrbuch* and other periodicals documenting the history of the house and of German music in general.

595. Pachnicke, Bernd, hrsg. *Edition Peters, 1800/1975: Daten zur Geschichte des Musikverlages Peters*. Leipzig: [C.F. Peters], 1975. 70 pp.
Chronological survey of the publishing house, placing its publication of Mahler's *Symphony no. 5* in historical context. Comparable to the survey by Lindlar of 1967 (see no. 593 above), but different in emphasis in the post-World War II era due to political divisions between the offices of the house in East and West Germany.

596. Plesske, Hans-Martin. *Der Bestand Musikverlag C.F. Peters im Staatsarchiv Leipzig: Geschäftsbriefe . . . als Quellenmaterial für die Musikforschung und die Geschichte des Buchhandels*. Leipzig: [C.F. Peters], 1970. 26 pp.
Brief study of sources in the archives of the city of

Leipzig relating to the history of the publishing house, affecting Mahler's *Symphony no. 5*. Improves on the study of the house chronology by Lindlar published three years earlier (see no. 593 above) by virtue of the availability of sources in East Germany not accessible to the office of the house in West Germany, but too limited to be of major use. See later studies by Klemm (no. 379 above) and Pachnicke (see no. 595 above).

597. Plesske, Hans-Martin, with Mark Jacobs & W. Thomas Marrocco. "Peters." *New Grove*, vol. 14, pp. 576-77.
Summarizes the long history of the house which published the *Symphony no. 5*. Crucial for its bibliography which lists many house publications necessary for an understanding of the complicated history of this major firm.

B. Schotts Söhne

598. *Kurze Verlagsgeschichte Musikverlag B. Schott's Söhne, Mainz*. Mainz: B. Schott's Söhne, 1970. 31 pp.
Sketches the long history of the publishing house that brought out Mahler's *Lieder und Gesänge*, with many illustrations of lithographs, facsimiles, and photographs. In German with translations of main text in French (transl. by Jean Philippon) and English (transl. by Everett Helm). Too short to be detailed but good background history of the house personnel including those who dealt business with Beethoven, Wagner, Mahler and Hindemith among others.

599. Laaff, Ernst. "B. Schott's Söhne." *MGG*, vol. 12, cols. 50-52.
Summary of the history of the house, which published the *Lieder und Gesänge*, Books I-III, in 1892. Bibliography valuable as key to the publications released by the house itself which document its long history in detail.

600. *Musikverlag B. Schotts Söhne, Mainz: kleiner Abriss der Verlagsgeschichte*. Traduction française de Jacques Delalande. English translation by Everett Helm. Mainz: B. Schotts Söhne, [1961]. 24 pp.

Briefly surveys the history of the publishing house. For historical perspective rather than detail, since the scope of the book is not wide enough to include details of individual compositions published over a period of almost two centuries.

601. *200 [i. e. Zweihundert] Jahre Musikverlag Schott in der Rheingoldhalle zu Mainz Juni 1970: Ansprachen-Reden-Vorträge.* Mainz: [B. Schotts Söhne], 1970. 35 pp.
 Brief account of the first two hundred years of the history of this important house. This publisher released many sources documenting the history of the house, based on its archive which survived World War II intact (unlike those of other publishers mentioned in this book); but this is one of the most pertinent although limited in length.

Universal Edition

602. Hilmar, Ernst, hrsg. *75 Jahre Universal-Edition: Katalog zur Ausstellung der Wiener Stadt- und Landesbibliothek im historischen Museum der Stadt Wien--Dezember 1976/Jänner 1977.* Wien: Universal Edition, 1976. 103 pp. ISBN 3-7024-0121-0.
 Documents an exhibition in Vienna in 1976 celebrating the seventy-fifth anniversary of the founding of the house which became Mahler's most important publisher. Sources for Mahler's music are prominently mentioned, including manuscripts, early prints, proofs and letters.

603. Reimer, Lennard & Alexander Weinmann. "Universal Edition." *New Grove*, vol. 19, pp. 453-54.
 Summarizes the history of the firm which published the largest number of Mahler's compositions. Bibliography useful as basis for extended research; with comparable article in *MGG* (see no. 605), most useful as basis for comprehensive analysis.

604. "Die Universal Edition 1901-1951." *1901 bis 1951 Universal Edition Wien.* Wien: Universal Edition, 1951, pp. 5-13.
 Gives a year-by-year history of notable events affecting the house, including publications of major works

by Mahler and others in his circle. Also includes information on the political events of the 1930s and 1940s which affected the policies of the house at that time and after World War II. Rare and difficult to obtain compared to the corresponding house publications commemmorating the twenty-fifth and seventy-fifth anniversaries (see no. 602 above for latter).

605. Weinmann, Alexander. "Universal-Edition A.G." *MGG*, vol. 13, cols. 1091-93.
Summary of the history of the publishing house from its inception in 1901 to the post-World War II period. Bibliography is an important key to house publications documenting the history of the firm in detail.

Josef Weinberger

606. Weinmann, Alexander. "Josef Weinberger." *New Grove*, vol. 20, pp. 313-14.
Summarizes the history of the house which published the early editions of the first three symphonies, the *Lieder aus "Des Knaben Wunderhorn"*, *Das klagende Lied* and the *Lieder eines fahrenden Gesellen*. While the three symphonies, the cantata and the *Wunderhorn* songs were later taken over by Universal Edition, the *Gesellen* cycle continues to be published by this house to the present day. In the absence of house *Festschrift* publications, this account is crucial to understanding of the house so important to Mahler.

MAHLER'S PLACE IN MUSICAL HISTORY

607. Abraham, Gerald. *A Hundred Years of Music*. Chicago: Aldine Publishing Co.; London: Gerald Duckworth, 1964. 3rd ed. 325 pp.
See especially the chapter "The Music of Yesterday and Today," in which the music of Mahler is discussed on pp. 261-64. This is highly opinionated and individual but is worth noting for the sake of considering a decidedly dated British view of Mahler's music.

608. Adler, Guido. "Musik in Österreich." *Studien zur Musikwissenschaft*. Beihefte der *Denkmäler der Ton-*

kunst in Österreich, 16. Wien: Universal Edition, 1929, pp. 3-31.
Brief history of music in Austria from the tenth century to the time of writing. Organized chronologically by types of musical activity and major musical forms with names and dates of composers active in each period and type. Discussion of music in the late nineteenth and early twentieth centuries (pp. 25-31) is rather more personal than the preceding materials, since Adler had known many of the subjects well; his assessment of Mahler as composer and conductor is heartwarming without being sentimental, giving Mahler due importance which other musicological commentators of that time might not have afforded.

609. Antcliffe, Herbert. "Mahler and Modern Dutch Music." Monthly Musical Record 84 (1954): 234-37.
Rather rare study of the influence of Mahler's work on Dutch composers since his time, traced through the collaboration of Mengelberg in establishing Mahler's popularity in the Netherlands, through Diepenbrock, Pijper, Monnikendam and Landré.

610. Beaufils, Marcel. "De Gustav Mahler à Schoenberg." Le Lied romantique allemand. Pour la musique, 2. Paris: Gallimard, 1956, pp. 265-94.
History of the German lied from Mozart to Schoenberg. Series of essays in French, of which this one surveys Mahler's songs from the early ones for voice and piano to Das Lied von der Erde. Relates nature of the songs to biographical influences. Not presented or documented in a scholarly manner but intelligent and well conceived.

611. Bekker, Paul. Die Sinfonie von Beethoven bis Mahler. Berlin: Schuster und Loeffler, 1918. 61 pp. Reprinted in Neue Musik. Gesammelte Schriften, 3. Stuttgart, Berlin: Deutsche Verlags-Anstalt, 1923, pp. 1-40.
A short but trenchant study of the romantic and postromantic symphony in the German-speaking countries, with special attention to Beethoven at the beginning of the line and Mahler at the end. A Russian version, Simfoniya ot Betkhovena do Malera (transl. by R. Grubeva and ed. by I. Glebova) was published in Leningrad in 1926, testifying to the importance of this study.

612. Berny-Negrey, Wiesława. "Architektonika symfonii Gustava Mahlera." [Architectonics of Gustav Mahler's Symphonies.] *Muzyka* 22, no. 4 (1977): 38-59.
Polish study of Mahler as "Januskopf" in terms of musical language in the symphonies, the predominant influence being his forebears but considerable evidence in the later works of experimentation foreshadowing the Second Viennese School. Also summary in English.

* Chamouard, Philippe. "Gustav Mahler, précurseur du XXe siècle." *Colloque 1985*: 9-15.
Full citation under no. 5 above. The directions of musical innovation in the twentieth century and the methods used by Mahler which set the example followed by other composers later are sketched.

613. Clapp, Philip Greeley. "All in the Family." *CD* 2 (1950): 33-41.
Traces a psychological line from Beethoven through Wagner and Bruckner to Mahler and finally to Delius, which curiously foreshadows the musical leanings of Deryck Cooke.

614. Colles, Henry Cope. "Elgar and Mahler." *Essays and Lectures*. London, New York: Oxford University Press, Humphrey Milford, 1945, 1947, pp. 83-85.
A curious and brief essay comparing Mahler and Elgar, shortsighted, comparison distinctly favoring Elgar over Mahler. Dating from 1930, typical of English reception of Mahler's music at that time.

615. Cooke, Deryck. *The Language of Music*. London, Oxford, New York: Oxford University Press, 1959. xiv, 289 pp.
Sensitive discussion of what music is, with illustrations from plainchant to Stravinsky. Widely based, liberal, choosing examples for their musical value rather than their fashionability. Discussion of the musical style of Mahler widely disseminated, covering many different works in both song and symphony forms. Places Mahler in historical context with other composers in a remarkable way; should be required reading for musicians and nonmusicians alike.

* Danuser, Hermann. "Karl Horwitz' *Vom Tode*--ein Dokument der Mahler-Verehrung aus der Schönberg-Schule." *Mahler-Interpretation 1985*: 177-90.

Full citation under no. 24 above. Considers the life and work of Horwitz, a lesser-known student of Schoenberg who died in 1925, and shows his orchestral song *Vom Tode* (1922) as inspired by Mahler's life and work.

616. Davies, Laurence. "Mahler and the Beethoven Succession." *Paths to Modern Music: Aspects of Music from Wagner to the Present Day.* New York: Charles Scribner's Sons, 1971, pp. 51-70. ISBN 0-684-12440-8 (hardbound), 0-684-12790-3 ([paper]).
Strange assessment of Mahler's role in the history of music, concentrating almost entirely on the symphonies at the expense of the vocal works. Occasionally factually inaccurate, often unsympathetic and obtuse.

617. Demuth, Norman. "The Austrian Debacle--Mahler, Schreker, Hauer, Wellesz." *Musical Trends in the Twentieth Century.* London: Rockliff, 1952, pp. 202-08.
Surprisingly positive view of Mahler's place in the musical history of the twentieth century, by a British commentator who favored Mahler at a time when his views were in the minority. Brief but clear, less concerned with biographical or analytical detail than with musical history and its political affiliations.

618. Deutsch, Max. "Tschaikowski--Mahler." *Mercure de France* 324 (ler août 1955): 619-31, et 325 (ler septembre 1955): 58-75.
Explores the question of Mahler's familiarity with Tchaikovsky's work and how it may have affected his own compositions. Documented by references to contemporary sources addressing the lives and works of both composers. Little attempt to make examples of musical connections and no musical illustrations.

619. Diether, Jack. "Mahler and Atonality." *Music Review* 17 (1956): 130-33.
Raises the question of whether the early movement in "atonality" was so logical and progressive in straight line as proposed by Newlin and others. Suggests that, while Mahler undoubtedly influenced Schoenberg and his followers, Schoenberg may have reciprocally influenced Mahler, i.e., that new movements in music may be a two-way street or more.

620. Diether, Jack. "Mahler's Place in Musical History." *CD* 2 (1963): 165-79.

Discusses Mahler's style with reference to the musical and literary trends of his time and after, referring especially to the literary thought of Kafka and the musical trends influenced by the Second Viennese School as direct heirs of Mahler. Worth comparing discussion of Mahler's influence on Schoenberg and his students with same author's earlier discussion of such influences as a two-way street (see preceding entry).

621. Eggebrecht, Hans Heinrich. "Symphonische Dichtung." AfMw 39 (1982): 223-33.
Sketches the history of the symphonic poem and its influence on program music in the traditional symphony, from Liszt and Berlioz through Mahler. Discusses the semantic distinctions between the forms with particular reference to Mahler's *Symphony no. 3* and *Symphony no. 4*.

* Faltin, Peter. "Semiotische Dimensionen des Instrumentalen und Vokalen im Wandel der Sinfonie (Beethoven--Mahler--Shostakowitsch)." *Sinfonie und Wirklichkeit*: 157-71.
Full citation under no. 10 above. History of the use of the human voice in the symphony over time, citing examples of Beethoven, Mahler and Shostakovich. More concerned with the differing approaches of the composers, as influenced by changing historical-literary background, than with individual examples.

* Flothuis, Marius. "Kapellmeistermusik." *Mahler-Interpretation 1985*: 9-16.
Full citation under no. 24 above. Considers the old question of whether Mahler's music was written by a conductor for a conductor (i.e., is it good or not, by implication of its compositional circumstances?) and concludes that it is music of a composer in his own right, not dependent on works of other composers whose works Mahler had conducted or otherwise known.

* Flotzinger, Rudolf. "Gustav Mahler--ein Romantiker?" *Sinfonie und Wirklichkeit*: 40-51.
Full citation under no. 10 above. Addresses the question of Mahler as composer in the romantic tradition, especially in terms of the forms he used in his work and the literary background.

622. Flotzinger, Rudolf und Gernot Gruber, hrsg. *Vom Barock*

zur Gegenwart. Musikgeschichte Österreichs, 2. Im Auftrag der Österreichischen Gesellschaft für Musikwissenschaft. Graz, Wien, Köln: Styria, 1977. 608 pp. ISBN 3-222-10976-1.
History of music in Austria comprised of various essays by different authors arranged in quasi-chronological order. See especially Chapter 17, "Die Auseinandersetzung mit der Tradition," by Friedrich Heller, pp. 385-432, in which Mahler and his contemporaries are discussed.

* Forchert, Arno. "Mahler und Schumann." *Mahler-Interpretation 1985*: 45-61.
Full citation under no. 24 above. Considers Mahler's long involvement with music of Schumann as executant (both pianist and conductor), editor, and spiritual heir. Particular attention to Schumann's *Symphony no. 3*. More extended and broader in scope than essay by Hilmar in same book.

623. Geissmar, Berta. *Two Worlds of Music*. New York: Creative Age Press, 1946. 327 pp.
Originally issued as *The Baton and the Jackpot: Recollections of Musical Life* (London: H. Hamilton, 1944) and also translated into German as *Musik im Schatten der Politik* (Freiburg im Breisgau, Zürich: Atlantis, 1945). A study of musical trends and their ebb and flow as influenced by political pressures from the time of Mahler to the Nazi period. The author was a friend of Alma Mahler-Werfel and personal assistant to Wilhelm Furtwängler and Sir Thomas Beecham in turn. A Dutch version of her book, *Politiek en Dirigeerstok* (Amsterdam: Holdert), was issued in 1947.

624. Graf, Max. *Geschichte und Geist der modernen Musik*. Die Universität, 40. Stuttgart, Wien: Humboldt, 1953. 216 pp.
In the chapter "Das Vordringen der Naturalismus" there is a discussion of Mahler as composer-mystic on pp. 116-18. This discussion forms part of a general view of the spirit of romantic crisis from the nineteenth century to Stravinsky.

625. Graf, Max. *Modern Music: Composers and Music of Our Time*. Transl. by Beatrice R. Maier. New York: Philosophical Library, 1946. Reprinted Westport, Connecticut: Greenwood Press, 1977. vi, 320 pp. ISBN 0-313-20185-4.

Amid extended discussion of Mahler, the essay "Gustav Mahler, the Mystic," on pp. 89-101, is of a piece with Graf's discussion in *Geschichte und Geist der modernen Musik* (see preceding entry), but is much more extended. Following the chapter "Richard Strauss, the Realist," this chapter contrasts Mahler's spiritual view of life with Strauss's earthbound realism. Surprisingly, concludes that Strauss the "realist" was naive compared to Mahler's subtlety, with citation of individual works to support the contrast. This article on Mahler was also published in *CD* 2 (1946): 51-60.

626. Hoffman, Eva. "Mahler for Moderns." *Commentary* 59 (June 1975): 52-59.

Visualizes Mahler the man in the context of cultural, musical and general history, accounting for the changing historical attitudes which have resulted in the popularity of Mahler's music where it was unpopular in the composer's own lifetime.

* Jameux, Dominique. "Gustav Mahler et Pierre Boulez: parallélisme/divergences." *Colloque 1985*: 73-82. Full citation under no. 5 above. Compares and contrasts Mahler and Pierre Boulez in terms of attitudes to life and music, and shows instances of Mahler's influence on Boulez, in the results of such attitudes.

627. *Jugendstil-Musik? Münchner Musikleben 1890-1918: Ausstellung 19. Mai-31. Juli 1987.* Wiesbaden: Dr. Ludwig Reichert Verlag, 1987. 336 pp. ISBN 3-88226-380-6.

Devoted to a series of essays concerning various musicians who affected the musical life of Munich from the turn of the century to the end of World War I, followed by listings covering objects on exhibition from May to July 1987 sponsored by the Bayerische Staatsbibliothek. Mahler is widely discussed, especially in the essay "Gustav Mahlers Münchener Apotheose: die Ausstellung 'München 1910' und die Musik" by Kurt Dorfmüller (pp. 49-68) and in many entries describing items in the exhibition (especially nos. 97, 98.1-6 and 99, which cover the premiere of the *Symphony no. 8*). Handsomely illustrated reference with useful information, if somewhat circumscribed in subject.

628. Kapp, Reinhard. "Schumann Reminiszenzen bei Mahler." *OeMZ* 37 (1982): 241-48.

Traces connections from Schumann to Mahler with thematic comparisons focusing on Schumann's *Symphony no. 2* and *Symphony no. 3* and Mahler's first two symphonies, the *Symphony no. 7* and *Symphony no. 8*.

* Kauder, Hugo. "Mahlers Instrumentation." *Musikblätter des Anbruch* 2 (1920): 277-78.
Full citation under no. 16 above. Brief examination of Mahler's revolutionary style in scoring and its impact in view of past composers from Beethoven to Berlioz.

629. Langevin, Paul-Gilbert. "De Mahler à l'école serielle: rupture ou continuité?" *Révue musicale*, no. 298-299 (1975): 109-80.
Comprises the last section of a three-part study *Le siècle de Bruckner: essais pour une nouvelle perspective sur les maîtres viennois du second âge d'or*, with participation by Eric-Paul Stekel and Gustave Kars besides Langevin. Explores the traditions of musical form and literary background among the Viennese composers from Bruckner to the serialists, Franz Schmidt and Franz Schreker. The essay "Gustav Mahler et sa posterité" (pp. 111-25) is concerned with Mahler's position among Austrian composers, his musical relations with the Schoenberg circle, and the continuation of musical progress between them as opposed to their differences.

630. Lichtenfeld, Monika. "Zemlinsky und Mahler." *Alexander Zemlinsky: Tradition im Umkreis der Wiener Schule*. Studien zur Wertungsforschung, 7. Hrsg. von Otto Kolleritsch. Wien, Graz: Universal Edition für Institut für Wertungsforschung, 1976, pp. 101-10.
Comparison of Zemlinsky's *Lyrische Symphonie* with *Das Lied von der Erde*, based on an analogy raised by Zemlinsky himself in a letter to his publisher.

* Lichtenfeld, Monika. "Zur Klangflächentechnik bei Mahler." *Mahler: eine Herausforderung*: 120-34.
Full citation under no. 20 above. Mahler as compositional "Januskopf" from the point of view of scoring quality to the author's view of "lack" of developmental movement. One-sided, misses the mark due to myopic view of Mahler's use of form.

631. Ligeti, Gyorgy und Clytus Gottwald. "Gustav Mahler und die musikalische Utopie." NZfM 135 (1974): 7-11, 288-91, 292-95.
Three-part study: "Musik und Raum" (one composer considering influence of a predecessor--Mahler--with reference to particular Mahler works including Symphonies 2-5); "Collage" (the collage technique from Mahler and Ives to Cage and Ligeti); and "Die Achte" (the Symphony no. 8 as product of its time, a musically and philosophically cyclic work in the eyes of others in Mahler's circle including Pfitzner and Berg). The first two parts of this article document a conversation between Ligeti and Gottwald; the third part (which was reprinted in Mahler: eine Herausforderung, cited above as no. 20) is entirely by Gottwald. Includes documentation from previously unknown letter of Stravinsky in which he acknowledges that the conclusion of his Symphony of Psalms was inspired by material from the Symphony no. 8.

632. McGuinness, Rosamund. "Mahler und Brahms: Gedanken zu 'Reminiszenzen' in Mahlers Sinfonien." Melos/ NZfM 3 (1977): 215-24.
Traces musical "reminiscences" of Brahms works in the works Mahler wrote in the 1890s, drawing attention to the cooperative relations between the two composers at the time discussed as a causative factor.

* Mengelberg, Curt Rudolf. "Gustav Mahler und sein Werk." Mahler-Fest Amsterdam: 4-16.
Considers Mahler's works less on their individual merits than as a collective sociological characterization in the line of Bach and Beethoven. Compares Mahler to Beethoven as populist because of the politics of the class structure in his time, and to Bach in the contrast between religious and secular in musical expression.

633. Mersmann, Hans. Musik der Gegenwart. Berlin: Julius Bard, 1924. 84 pp.
Curious study of twentieth century music, focusing on composers as diverse as Mahler, Scriabin and Milhaud, with artistic illustrations presumably intended to draw connections between art and musical styles. References to Mahler (pp. 13-14, 18-20, 26-27 and 31-32) focus on Das Lied von der Erde.

* Meyer, Krzystof. "Mahler und Schostakowitsch." *Sinfonie und Wirklichkeit*: 118-32. Full citation under no. 10 above. Draws connections between Mahler and Shostakovich with reference to shared formal-melodic usages in many individual works, also comparing their similarities in *Weltanschauung* based on political conditions in their respective eras.

634. Mnatsakova, E. "Gustav Maler: nachalo puti." [Gustav Mahler: beginning of the journey.] *Ot Lyulli do nashikh dney*. [From Lully to our day.] Ed. by I. Slepnev and compiled by V. Konen. Moskva: Muzyka, 1967, pp. 177-92.
An introduction to Mahler in the context of a series of essays on music from Lully to Prokofiev. Assembled as a sixtieth birthday celebration for F. Lev Abramovich Masel. Among the essays this is one of four on non-Russian subjects.

635. Morgan, Robert. "Ives and Mahler: Mutual Responses at the End of an Era." *19th C Mus* (1978): 72-81.
Draws parallels between Ives and Mahler (outwardly two composers without anything in common) in terms of their reactions to historical stimuli, their conceptions of form and melody, their use of borrowing techniques from other musical material. Revolutionary in its concept of the likenesses between the two composers, and worth exploring at length, this article offers a challenge that has not yet been picked up as of this writing.

636. Moser, Hans Joachim. *Das deutsche Lied seit Mozart*. Berlin, Zürich: Atlantis, 1937. 2 vols. 2., wesentlich umgearbeitete und erg. Ausgabe mit einem Geleitwort von Dietrich Fischer-Dieskau und einem Prosa-Prolog von Hermann Hesse. Tutzing: Hans Schneider, 1968. 2 Bande in einem. 440 pp.
Brief, unsatisfactory attempt to summarize Mahler's works for voice and piano/voice and orchestra, in Chapter 12 (pp. 208-11). Negative, marred by factual error even in the 1965 revision, which is not surprising if one compares this with Moser's other writings (for example no. 172 above).

637. Neill, E.D. "Bruckner e Mahler." *Rassegna musicale curci* 23 (Marzo 1970): 11-16.
Compares Mahler and Bruckner as symphonists and--uniquely in the literature--as conductors, with the latter premise illustrated by silouettes of both by Böhler.

638. Niemann, Walter. *Die Musik der Gegenwart und der letzten Vergangenheit bis zu der Romantikern, Klassizisten und Neudeutschen*. 5. bis 8., reich vermehrte und sorgfältig durchgesehene Auflage. Berlin: Schuster und Loeffler, 1913. xvi, 303 pp. 18.-20. Auflage, 1922.
Original title in the first four editions: *Die Musik seit Richard Wagner* published by Schuster und Loeffler in 1913 (xvi, 296 pp.). Concentrates primarily on music by composers from German-speaking countries from Wagner to the early twentieth century. Essentially conservative, favoring the earlier composers over Mahler, Strauss and the Second Viennese School.

639. Pinzauti, Leonardo. "Mahler e Puccini." *N Riv Mus It* 16 (1982): 330-39.
Interesting comparison of Mahler and Puccini as men and composers, noting the strong contrasts in their personal backgrounds and musical orientation (both forms and styles) with discussion of Mahler's work with Italian opera generally. Based on author's lecture "Das Verhältnis Mahler--Puccini" at the 1982 Musikwoche in Toblach on July 21, 1982.

640. Ploderer, Rudolf. "Marx und Mahler." *23*, nr. 11/12 (30. Juni 1933): 13-17.
Primarily a comparison of the work of the two composers, whose personal contact had been minimal (Mahler did not conduct any of Josef Marx's works or mention him in his correspondence as far as is known). Cites Marx's writings on Mahler in *Betrachtungen eines romantisches Realisten* (hrsg. von Oswald Ortner, Wien: Gerlach und Wiedling, 1947) in which Marx discussed Mahler's works with special reference to the *Symphonies 1, 3* and *9* and *Das Lied von der Erde*. More background on Marx can be found in the correspondence between Berg and Schoenberg (see no. 333 above).

641. Redlich, Hans Ferdinand. *Alban Berg: Versuch einer Würdigung*. Wien, Zürich, London: Universal Edition, 1957. 393 pp.
Primarily on the life and work of Berg, heavily documented, but merits inclusion here because discussion of Mahler's work and its influence on Berg's is extremely widespread. Alma is also cited for biographical connections with Berg and his wife.

642. Redlich, Hans Ferdinand. *Gustav Mahler: eine Erkenntnis*. Nürnberg: Hans Carl, 1919. 33 pp.
Briefly surveys Mahler's work in the context of his musical predecessors and the literary and social influences of his time. Not a biography, this book was one of the earliest to discuss Mahler as a legatee of his environment and his history. Redlich's first known publication on Mahler's music, beginning of a long line which culminated in the 1960s with his work as editor of Mahler's works in the Eulenberg Edition.

* Redlich, Hans. "Mahlers Wirkung in Zeit und Raum." *Anbruch* 12 (1930): 92-96.
Comparatively early contribution to the Mahler literature by Redlich (but see also his contribution to same journal ten years earlier and his book of 1919 cited in the previous entry), contrasting oddly with earlier essay by Adorno in same book in its view of Mahler's ties to the musical past as well as the future. Full citation under no. 1 above.

* Salten, Felix. "Wien und die Musik." *Mahler-Fest Amsterdam*: 29-33.
Closely related to Salten's chapter on Mahler in *Gestalten und Erscheinungen* (see no. 696 below), but slightly more contextually generalized. A clear literary eye on the nature of musical life in Vienna in the Golden Age and how those who succeeded in making music their life were divided in standards from their audiences. Full citation under no. 11 above.

643. Sargeant, Winthrop. "Mahler, Last of the Romantics." *CD* 2 (1940): 35-38.
Mahler as man and creator in the Romantic tradition, while simultaneously Schoenberg, Stravinsky and others were making explosions heard in the future. One-sided, looking back, not accounting for Mahler's true position as *Januskopf*.

644. Schmoll-Eisenwerth, Regina, hrsg. *Die Münchner Philharmoniker von der Gründung bis heute*. München: C. Wolf, 1985. 447 pp. ISBN 3-922979-21-1.
This history of the Münchner Philharmoniker covers the years from the establishment of the Kaim Orchestra in 1893 until the time of writing. The essay "Gustav Mahler und die Münchner Philharmoniker" by Dietmar Holland (pp. 183-206) discusses Mahler's guest engagements

in the city from 1897 to 1910, as well as the premieres of his works under direction of other conductors, including Bruno Walter's premiere of *Das Lied von der Erde* after Mahler's death. Also discusses the critical reaction to the performances including the famous exchange between Ehlers and Holtzmann at the premiere of the *Symphony no. 8* (worth comparing with treatment by Namenwirth cited under no. 690 below). Carefully chosen illustrations include photographs, score facsimiles, programs and posters. A second useful source in this book is "Dirigenten, Ur- und Erstaufführungen der Münchner Philharmoniker, 1893-1973" by Gabriele Meyer (pp. 431-46), which includes listings of first performances of Mahler works in Munich under his own and other conductors' direction.

645. Schollum, Robert. "Gustav Mahler." *Das Österreichische Lied des 20. Jahrhunderts*. Publikationen des Instituts für Österreichischen Musikdokumentation, 3. Tutzing: Hans Schneider, 1977, pp. 33-39.
Discusses Mahler as composer of songs (and how his lyric outlook affected the symphonies as well) and assesses his place in the song tradition from Schubert to Cerha, especially from Brahms onwards. While limited by a total lack of musical examples, covers the entire tradition including lesser composers influenced by Mahler; also considers fashion in texts as well as musical styles.

* Schorske, Carl E. "Mahler et Ives: archaisme populiste et innovation musicale." *Colloque 1985*: 87-97. Full citation under no. 5 above. Compares and contrasts the lives and works of these contemporaries. See also discussion by Robert Morgan (no. 635 above) which seems more sophisticated than this concrete discussion.

646. Smith, Warren Storey. "Bruckner and Mahler and Tonality." *CD* 2 (1948): 27-29.
Brief discussion of Bruckner and Mahler's uses of the expanding tonal horizons of the nineteenth century, comparing and contrasting their styles. Concludes that they spoke their own language but were not "tonal anarchists" even compared with Wagner.

647. Smith, Warren Storey. "Bruckner vs. Brahms and Mahler vs. Strauss: a Study in Contrasts." *CD* 2 (1958): 33-48.
Speaks for itself--personal and musico-stylistic con-

trasts between the two pairs, allowing each one his space and noting that Mahler and Strauss were friends and colleagues by contrast with Bruckner and Brahms who were made into enemies by politics.

648. Sollertinskiy, Ivan Ivanovich. "Die Sinfonien Gustav Mahlers." *Von Mozart bis Schostakowitsch.* Übersetzt von Christoph Rüber. Hrsg. von Michael Druskin. Leipzig: Philipp Reclam, 1979, pp. 166-86.
Originally written in Russian, probably the same as essay "Gustav Maler i problema evropeyskovo simfonizma" [Gustav Mahler and the problems of the European symphony] in *Muzykal'noy al'manakh.* Discusses Mahler in the context of the history of the symphony, recognizing his importance in that history, not as the end of a tradition but as innovator who set examples affecting other composers who followed him to present date.

649. Sopeña Ibáñez, Federico. *Introducción a Mahler: maestro y procursor de la música actual.* Libros de bolsillo. Madrid: Rialp, 1960. 86 pp.
First Spanish book exclusively devoted to Mahler, mostly essays on aesthetic questions à la Adorno. Author views Mahler's music as the beginning of the revolution in twentieth century music, ignoring the nineteenth century romantic influences which would have been a balancing factor. One-tracked in theory but a breakthrough especially for the time in which it was published.

* Specht, Richard. "Mahler." *Merker* 3: 161-65.

Full citation under no. 12 above. Assesses Mahler as composer for contemporary and future considering his effect in both symphonic and lyric forms; also recognizes particularly his innovations in scoring and dismissing charges of banality.

650. Stahmer, Klaus Hinrich. "Drei Klavier Quartette aus den Jahren 1875/76--Brahms, Mahler und Dvořák im Vergleich." *Brahms und seine Zeit: Symposion Hamburg 1983.* Hrsg. von Constantin Floros, Hans Joachim Marx und P. Peterson. Hamburger Jahrbuch für Musikwissenschaft, 7. Hamburg: Wagner, 1984, pp. 113-23.
Discusses Mahler's piano quartet vis-à-vis history of chamber music in the late nineteenth century, specifically comparing the work with those in the same form

by Brahms and Dvořák. Considering that Mahler wrote his quartet at the age of sixteen, comes off rather well in the comparison.

651. Stefan, Paul. "Gustave Mahler et la jeune génération." *Revue musicale* 12 (1931): 195-200.
A French study of Mahler in his time and after, in terms of his compositional impact among his peers; the "young generation" mentioned refers to Mahler's composer-successors and also to listeners in his audience.

652. Stefan, Paul. *Neue Musik und Wien.* Leipzig: E.P. Tal, 1921. 76 pp.
Less a study of Mahler (although he is frequently cited) than a study of his milieu and circle, current to his time, by an insider. Covers Wagner-Bruckner-Brahms to Schoenberg and Korngold. A complementary piece, "Österreichische Musik seit Mahler," appeared in *Musikblätter des Anbruch* 5 (Mai 1923): 131-33, focusing on Austrian music from Mahler to Schoenberg with discussion also of Marx, Zemlinsky and Bittner; these two sources together show Stefan as a historian of the Austrian musical milieu with Mahler as a focus ("Mahler was never a teacher, but always and for many an example") rather than a one-shot biographer.

653. Stein, Erwin. "Mahler, Reger, Strauss und Schönberg: kompositionstechnische Betrachtungen." *25 Jahre neue Musik: Jahrbuch 1926 der Universal-Edition.* Hrsg. von Hans Heinsheimer und Paul Stefan. Wien, Leipzig, New York: Universal Edition, 1926, pp. 63-78.
English version: "Mahler, Reger, Strauss and Schoenberg: Some Observations on the Technique of Composition." *Orpheus in New Guises*: 36-46.
English version cited in full under no. 23 above. Discusses similarities and differences in compositional outlook of the composers cited, especially with reference to tonality and counterpoint. English version translated by Hans Keller.

* Stephan, Rudolf. "Gedanken zu Mahler." *OeMz* 34 (1979): 257-66.
Full citation under no. 19 above. Far-ranging discussion of Mahler as composer and his place in the history of music, especially his influence in the long term as well as his background.

* Stephan, Rudolf. "Zum Thema 'Bruckner und Mahler.'" *Gustav Mahler Kolloquium 1979*: 76-83. Full citation under no. 8 above. Compares styles of Bruckner and Mahler in melodic construction and forms rather than outmoded concept seeking similarities in scoring.

654. Tischler, Hans. "Mahler's Impact on the Crisis of Tonality." *Music Review* 12 (1951): 113-21. Discusses Mahler's harmonic language in the context of history and its influences on his successors (including not only Schoenberg and his followers but Busoni, Bartók and Stravinsky). Useful especially in tandem with author's Ph.D. dissertation on same subject (see no. 731 below).

655. Tsitsiklis, Michalis. *Between Symphony and Opera (The Symphonies of Mahler)*. Thessaloniki: privately pub. by author, [1970]. 32 pp. In Greek. Aesthetic analysis of Mahler's works, in terms of his antecedents in both absolute symphonic forms and opera/music drama.

656. Vestdijk, Simon. *Keurtroepen van Euterpe: 8 Essays over Componisten*. Den Haag: Daamen, 1957. 234 pp. Individual essays on composers in the late nineteenth and early twentieth centuries. Discussion of Mahler on pp. 99-141.

657. Voit-Hilmar, Renate. "Anton Webern's Cultivation of Mahler's Works." *NaMR*, no. 13 (March 1984): 11-16. Shows Webern's work as conductor and collector with Mahler's symphonies and songs, referring to documentation from the period Mahler and Webern both lived and worked in Vienna until the 1930s.

658. Waldstein, Wilhelm. "Gustav Mahler." *OeMz* 3 (1948): 97-100. An early postwar assessment of Mahler as composer in the context of his predecessors from Beethoven onward; somewhat in the style of Kahan's essay in *La emoción de la música* (see no. 120 above), arguing Mahler's stature as reaction against the depredations wrought by the Nazis not long before.

659. Wallis, Alfons. "Gustav Mahler." *Österreichs grosse Musiker*. Bücher der Heimat, 8. Wien: Steyrermühl, 1935, pp. 77-82.

Essay on Mahler among others on great composers from Gluck to Johann Strauss. Represents a middle ground in Austrian scholarship on Mahler in the generations immediately following Mahler's death, avoiding the partisan controversy about Mahler characteristic of the time and simply discussing his life and work, especially as conductor; conversely, makes different strong contrast with the poison of the Nazis already prevalent in German musicology which reached Austria only a few years later.

660. Walter, Bruno. *Von der Musik und vom Musizieren.* Frankfurt am Main, Tübingen: S. Fischer, 1957, 1975. 254 pp.
English version: *Of Music and Music-Making.* Transl. by Paul Hamburger. New York: W.W. Norton; London: Faber and Faber, 1961. 222 pp.
Bruno Walter's treatise on the art of making music, illustrated with examples that he himself conducted during his long career, including works of Mahler, Mozart and Bach. Mahler figures in this book as both composer and conductor.

661. Warrack, John. "Mahler and Weber." *MT* 108 (1967): 120-23.
Shows the influence of Weber on the work of Mahler, not only with reference to Mahler's work with *Die drei Pintos* and *Oberon* but in Mahler's own works, notably the *Symphony no. 1.*

662. Weingartner, Felix [von]. *Die Symphonie nach Beethoven.* Leipzig: Breitkopf und Härtel, 1901, 1909, 1926. 109 pp. (2nd ed.).
English versions: (a) *The Symphony Since Beethoven.* Transl. by Maude Barrows Dutton. Boston, New York: Oliver Ditson/C.M. Dutson, 1904. 98 pp. (b) *The Symphony Writers Since Beethoven.* Transl. by Arthur Bles. London: Reeves, 1925. Reprinted Westport, Connecticut: Greenwood Press, 1977. vii, 168 pp. ISBN 0-8371-4396-1.
In this account of the symphonic tradition in the nineteenth century, Weingartner advocates Mahler as a composer in the German-Austrian tradition, presumably having gotten over the bitterness expressed in his autobiography (see no. 327 above).

663. Wessem, Constant von. "Mahler." *Uren met musici.*

Baarn: Hollandia-Drukkerij, 1922, pp. 145-75.
Dutch essay on Mahler among eight such essays on composers from Couperin to Debussy. General, for the lay Dutch reader, but remarkable in its time when any literature on Mahler for general readers was rare.

* Wildgans, Friedrich. "Gustav Mahler und Anton von Webern." *OeMZ* 15 (1960): 301-05.
Full citation under no. 18 above. Discusses the significance of Mahler's influence in Viennese musical life, as seen through the eyes of Anton von Webern and documented by his diaries and letters.

664. Worbs, Hans Christoph. *Gustav Mahler*. Hesses kleine Bücherei, 6. Berlin-Halensee-Wunsiedel/Ofr: Max Hesse, 1960. 98 pp.
A short early study of Mahler focusing more on his influence as a composer than on biographical detail. A Dutch version (Den Haag: Dieben, 1960) was published shortly after the German original.

RECEPTION/HISTORIOGRAPHY

* Bachmann, Claus-Henning. "Mahlers Musik--Schauplatz grosser Zeitkonflikte Internationales Symposion in Graz." *Musik und Bildung* 5 (1973): 629-31.
Full citation under no. 17 above. Reports on the Graz symposium on Mahler of 1973.

665. Banks, Paul. "Mahler Manuscripts Come to Light." *NaMR*, no. 18 (October 1987): 3-6.
Lists manuscripts auctioned at Sotheby's in London and Stargardt in Marburg, as well as individual sources from Hans Schneider of Tutzing, the Bibliothèque Musicale Gustav Mahler in Paris, and the Pierpont Morgan Library in New York which have recently surfaced. Prices and some names of owners cited, also historical implications of many sources, which include songs, symphonic movements or portions thereof, and Mahler's arrangements of works by other composers, in his hand or in those of copyists.

666. Barford, Philip. "Mahler Today." *Music Review* 18 (1957): 177-82.
Discusses Mahler as an expression of his time and,

posthumously, of ours. Compare assessment by la Grange (see no. 674 below).

* Blaukopf, Herta. "Als Mahlers Zeit noch nicht gekommen war." *OeMz* 34 (1979): 294-97.
Full citation under no. 19 above. Factual account of the early work of the IGMG which assisted in the process of "making Mahler's time come."

667. Blaukopf, Kurt. "Auf neuen Spuren zu Gustav Mahler." *Hi Fi Stereophonie* 5 (1971): 356-66.
Two main emphases in this essay: first, select discography of works of Mahler contemporary with discography of Weber (see no. 61 above), and second, discussion of trends in Mahler research with individual references primarily devoted to the German-speaking countries. Factual, preceding the *NaMR* in spirit and subject material.

* Blaukopf, Kurt. "Hintergrunde der Mahler-Renaissance." *Sinfonie und Wirklichkeit*: 16-23.
Full citation under no. 10 above. Traces the changing status of Mahler's reputation among the concertgoing public and professional musicians in terms of musical style and its changing historical context.

* Bonnet, Jacques. "Mahleriana." *L'Arc* 67: 1-2.
Full citation under no. 3 above. Introductory musing about Mahler's standing from his time to present. Sets stage for articles following in this symposium volume.

* Buenzod, Emmanuel. "Solitude de Mahler." *Feuilles musicales* 1959: 113-15.
Full citation under no. 6 above. "The loneliness of the long-distance runner" as applied to Mahler in his time and for a long while after because his innovations in composition were not widely understood or accepted.

* Dahlhaus, Carl. "Die rätselhafte Popularität Gustav Mahlers." *Musik und Bildung* 5 (1973): 590-92./ Kühn, Hellmut. "Mahlers 'rätselhafte Popularität.'" *Musik und Bildung* 5 (1973): 592-93.
Companion and contrasting views of Mahler's comparatively newfound "popularity"--in historical perspective (Dahlhaus) and in the present-day performing media

(Kühn). Curious pairing, not for every taste. Both cited in full under no. 17 above; the Dahlhaus essay only is reprinted in *Mahler: eine Herausforderung* (see no. 20 above for full citation).

668. Dorfmüller, Kurt. "Gustav-Mahler-Dokumente in München." *Fontes Artis Musicae* 13 (1966): 33-39.
    Surveys Mahler source materials in Munich including autographs in the Bayerische Staatsbibliothek (both musical holographs and letters) and cites published literature spotlighting the original materials, from Schiedermair in 1900 to the 1960 centennial exhibition catalogue from Vienna.

669. Finlay, Ian F. "Gustav Mahler in England." *Chesterian* 34 (Summer 1959): 1-8.
    Surveys the history of performance of Mahler's works in England and research by British musicologists, noting the comparative lack of either in the early period after Mahler's death and the steady growth after World War II and the approach of the centennial.

670. Flothuis, Marius. "Mahler Plays Mahler." *NaMR*, no. 9 (September 1981): 6-7.
    Documents the Welte piano rolls still in existence on which Mahler himself is heard at the piano playing movements from the *Symphony no. 4* and *Symphony no. 5* and one or two songs. Brief, but valuable because the subject is not explored in any other Mahler literature.

671. Fürnberg, Louis. *Gustav Mahlers Heimkehr*. [Wien]: W. Verkauf, [1946]. 17 pp.
    Also in: *Musik und Gesellschaft* 11 (1961): 264-68.
    Also in: *Österreichisches Tagebuch*, no. 2 (12. April 1946): 9-10.
    Also in: *Gesammelte Werke*. Hrsg. von der Akademie der Künste der DDR. Berlin: Aufbau, 1965-77. 6 vols. (vol. 5, pp. 143-50)
    In the form of a letter to an unnamed friend, considers the society in which Mahler made his career and how his time is "coming" as of the end of the Nazi regime with the changes in Austrian society.

* "Gespräch mit einem Mahler-Interpreten." *Sinfonie und Wirklichkeit*: 93-102.
    Full citation under no. 10 above. Sort of musical press conference cum panel discussion in which differ-

ent musicologists question the conductor Ernst Märzendorfer about Mahler through the eyes of a conductor.

672. Grant, [William] Parks. "Mahler Eighteen Years Afterward." CD 2 (1950): 66-73.
Essay on the hard-won and growing interest in Mahler's music in the public sector and among musical professionals, noting where Mahler may be a role model for young composers of the postwar generation.

* Gutmann, Hanns. "Der banale Mahler." Anbruch 12 (1930): 102-05.
Full citation under no. 1 above. Considers then prevailing view of Mahler's "banal" style, the factors that might have influenced it, and why it is more apparent than real. Notable because author is one of a few who does not make Mahler's Jewish background a factor in this sensitive subject!

* Kolleritsch, Otto. "Historischer Versuch über Gustav Mahlers Aktualität." Sinfonie und Wirklichkeit: 24-39.
Full citation under no. 10 above. Traces changing historiography in the Mahler literature, favoring the German literature, over the period from the Nazis to the time of writing. Rather neglected area of Mahler research carefully summarized here.

* Lachenmann, Helmut. "Antworten auf fünf Fragen des Herausgebers." Mahler: eine Herausforderung: 51-65.
Full citation under no. 20 above. Author considers Mahler's "sudden" acceptance by the public as a phenomenon of commercialization and subjective aesthetic analysis promulgated by Adorno, but points out that the public may still misinterpret Mahler's work as symphonic potpourri. Personal view of author, not entirely convincing. Newly written as rebuttal to earlier essay of Ruzicka which was reprinted from Musik und Bildung (see no. 17 above).

* la Grange, Henry-Louis de. "Mahler heute." Musik und Bildung 5 (1973): 594-96.
Full citation under no. 17 above. Considers Mahler's musical reputation today, especially among musical professionals, and how he came to the position from late romanticism.

673. la Grange, Henri L. de. "Mahler prigionero della leg-

genda." *N Riv Mus It* 3 (1969): 246-62.
English version: "Mistakes about Mahler." *Music and Musicians* 21 (October 1972): 16-22.
Discusses current assessment of Mahler's life and work and shows how certain aspects of these assessments are based on misrepresentation or misinterpretation of existing sources including the writings of Alma Mahler-Werfel. Not documented exhaustively, but raises good questions and gives intelligent answers which have led to documentation by other researchers. The Italian version was translated from the original French by Laura Padellaro. The English version first appeared in shortened form in *Saturday Review* but was later expanded for *Music & Musicians*.

674. la Grange, Henry-Louis de. "Mahler Today/Actualité de Mahler/Mahler heute." *World of Music* 11 (March 1969): 7-17.
Considers the changing public attitude to Mahler's music and the effect of Mahler scholarship on the change, from the time of Mahler's own introduction of his works to the major surge in interest at the time of the centenniel. In three languages, parallel, essentially the same text in each.

675. Lipman, Samuel. "The Mahler Everyone Loves." *Commentary* 61 (November 1977): 55-60.
Analyzes the public attitude to Mahler the composer and conductor, considering the reception by his fellow musical professionals from his lifetime to the present.

676. Mellers, Wilfrid. "Mahler as Key-Figure." *Scrutiny: a Quarterly Review* 9 (1941): 343-51. Reprinted in *Studies in Contemporary Music*. London: Dennis Dobson, 1947, pp. 109-19.
Discusses Mahler as subject of controversy, giving both sides of the view of Mahler as remarkable or awful, and generally concluding in his favor. May be considered precursor to Cooke and Mitchell in terms of pro-Mahler movement in England (see nos. 615 and 677 for examples).

* Mengelberg, C[urt] Rudolf. "Über den Stand der Mahler-Pflege." *Moderne Welt* 3 (1921): 30-31.
Full citation under no. 13 above. Briefly assesses Mahler's reputation as composer in various countries, concluding that little had changed since Mahler's death despite alterations in social circumstances af-

ter World War I. Concludes that only Holland really shows evidence of supporting Mahler in the long term, as evidenced by Amsterdam Mahler festival a year earlier.

677. Mitchell, Donald. "Gustav Mahler: Prospect and Retrospect." *RMA Proceedings* 87 (1960-61): 83-97. Reprinted in *CD* 2 (1963): 138-48.
Surveys the changing reputation of Mahler's music from the composer's lifetime to the "Mahler boom" at the time of the centennial. Based on an address to the Royal Musical Association, the emphasis of this article is on the prospect of the scholarly aspects of Mahler research, especially textual analysis and critical editing.

678. Nest'ev, I[zrael Vladimirovich]. "Zametzki o Malere." [Notes on Mahler.] *Sovetskaya muzyka* 24 (July 1960): 72-82.
Discusses Mahler's life and work with references to literature current at time of centennial. Portrait illustrations but no facsimiles or musical examples; general summary rather than blow-by-blow account of individual works.

679. Oswald, Peter. "Perspektiven der Neuen: Studien zum Spätwerk von Gustav Mahler." Ph.D. diss., Universität Wien, 1982. 262 pp.
Study of *Das Lied von der Erde* and the *Symphony no. 9*, nonmusical in emphasis, considering the historiographical literature on the two works and the documentation in the scores themselves, as well as the emotional impact of Mahler's style.

680. Percy, Gosta. "Gustav Mahler--det universellas tondikters." *Musikrevy* 15 (1960): 145-54.
Swedish study of Mahler's musical style. Pure analysis in context of musical history before and after Mahler's time.

681. Redlich, Hans. "Gustav Mahler: Probleme einer Kritische Gesamtausgabe." *Mf* 19 (1966): 378-401.
Written about the time of Redlich's work on selected symphonies and songs of Mahler in the Eulenberg Edition, this essay is a trenchant comment on the need for a critical edition and the conditions affecting the work of the editor: historical, textual and lit-

erary. A rare source detailing the problems of the editor much more closely than the introductions in the volumes of the Critical Edition then being released by the IGMG in Vienna (but see no. 796 below for views of Grant on same subject).

* Reeser, Eduard. "Die Mahler-Rezeption in Holland 1903-1911." *Mahler-Interpretation 1985*: 81-103.
Full citation under no. 24 above. Extended discussion of Mahler's relations with his Dutch colleagues until his death, performances of his works in the Netherlands from the beginning (the *Symphony no. 3* in 1903) to March 1911. Focuses on work of Mahler himself, Mengelberg and Diepenbrock especially. Invaluable with same author's edition of Mahler's correspondence with his Dutch colleagues (see no. 391 above). Documents critical reception of the repertoire during same period. A shorter version of this article in French, "La réception des oeuvres de Mahler en Hollande entre 1903 et 1911," appeared on pp. 83-86 of *Colloque 1985* (see no. 5 above).

* Revers, Peter. "Gustav Mahler und die Formanalyse: Reflexionen über ein gestörtes Verhaltnis." *Gustav Mahler Kolloquium 1979*: 96-101.
Full citation under no. 8 above. History of formal analysis of Mahler works embracing Specht, Nodnagel and Schiedermair among others. Historiographical, not historical, therefore rather unusual in outlook.

* Revers, Peter. "Zum Stand der Mahler-Forschung." *OeMz* 34 (1979): 289-93.
Full citation under no. 19 above. Summarizes recent scholarship concerning Mahler and his work from the mid-1950s to the late 1970s, with classification of research types and discussion of possible future trends. Favors German-language references over ones in other languages, therefore somewhat limited in outlook.

682. Rozenshil'd, K[onstantin Konstantinovic]. *Gustav Maler*. Seriya "Iz istorii zarubezhnoy muzyki XX veka." [Series "From history of foreign music of the twentieth century."] Moskva: Muzyka, 1975. 208 pp.
Analyzes the symphonies against background of Austrian culture during Mahler's time and explores Mahler's own

ideas about music, in a series of disconnected essays focusing on individual elements of his musical style. Considerably enhanced by large number of musical examples distinctive among coverage in Russian sources.

683. Samaroff-Stokowski, Olga. "The Peace Conference of Amsterdam: Holland Honours Mahler and Mengelberg." *An American Musician's Story*. New York: W.W. Norton, 1939, pp. 157-69.
Also reprinted in *CD* 2 (1940): 27-34. Eyewitness account of the 1920 Mahler festival in Amsterdam as seen by an educated American pianist observing without restraints; fascinating because of author's purely personal interest combined with intelligent knowledge of the world of musical performance.

684. Schmid, Leopold. "Gustav Mahler." *Erlebnisse und Betrachtungen: aus dem Musikleben der Gegenwart--Beiträge zur zeitgenössischen Kunstkritik*. Mit einem Geleitwort von Richard Strauss. Berlin: A. Hoffman, 1909, 1913, pp. 281-86.
Mixed assessment of Mahler as composer, based mostly on the *Symphony no. 2* and *Symphony no. 3*, labelling Mahler a "phenomenon" and a composer of monstrosities virtually simultaneously. Correctly assesses his unpopularity in his time and shortly after, and makes no attempt to consider his long-term influence.

685. Smith, Warren Storey. "Some Mahlerian Misconceptions." *CD* 2 (1946): 61-64.
Surveys the literature on Mahler to that time and shows how many differing opinions of Mahler's life and work contribute to a confused impression of Mahler's relative importance and result in serious factual misconceptions.

* Specht, Richard. "Gustav Mahlers Gegenwart." *Moderne Welt* 3 (1921): 1-3.
Full citation under no. 13 above. Rare in this group of essays, an assessment of Mahler as composer rather than conductor, ten years after Mahler's death by author who was a long-time observer of Mahler as man and composer.

* Specht, Richard. "Gustav Mahlers Sieg." *Mahler-Fest Amsterdam*: 34-40.
Full citation under no. 11 above. Considers the history

of Mahler's works in performance by various conductors (including Mahler himself). Suggests that Mahler was not the best interpreter of his own music and that another conductor would be able to approach that task with less personal involvement than the composer himself, a radical view in its time. Chooses Mengelberg over other conductors as best interpreter. Curious and personal.

* Stefan, Paul. "Gustav Mahler in der Literatur." *Moderne Welt* 3 (1921): 8-9.
Full citation under no. 13 above. Surveys major historiographical coverage of Mahler's life and work to that date. Not a bibliography but rather a discussion of individual coverage in books by Nodnagel, Specht, Stefan, Neisser, Bekker, Ritter and Curt Rudolf Mengelberg.

* Tibbe, Monika. "Anmerkungen zur Mahler-Rezeption." *Mahler: eine Herausforderung*: 85-100.
Full citation under no. 20 above. Considers the history of public reaction to Mahler's work.

* Ullrich, Hermann. "Gustav Mahler und Wien im Wandel der Zeiten." *OeMz* 15 (1960): 297-301.
Full citation under no. 18 above. History of Mahler's professional reputation in Vienna from his own time through the Third Reich and to the centennial.

686. "The William Malloch Tapes." *NaMR*, no. 9 (September 1981): 8-9.
Surveys the content of several tapes made by the American Mahler specialist William Malloch, which recorded interviews with orchestral musicians who played in the New York Philharmonic during Mahler's tenure 1908-10, as well as with the film composer Max Steiner and with Anna Mahler. A copy of these tapes is now located in the archive of the IGMG.

MEDIA AND CRITICISM

687. Langford, Samuel. "Gustav Mahler Amsterdam, 1920." *Music Criticisms*. Ed. by Neville Cardus. London: Oxford University Press, Humphrey Milford, 1929, pp. 2-13.

Three-part discussion of Mahler as composer, based on performances at the 1920 Amsterdam festival but much more than current criticism. Somewhat guarded but essentially more positive than the assessments usually seen among British commentators at that time.

688. Lockspeiser, Edward. "Mahler in France." *Monthly Musical Record* 90 (March/April 1960): 52-57.
Interesting study of Mahler vis-à-vis the French, leading in two directions: Mahler's own involvement with music of French composers including Berlioz, Charpentier and Bizet, and, conversely, the French reaction to Mahler's own works, including the critical coverage of Ritter and Casella and the personal reactions of Debussy, Pierné etc. Questions existing impressions left by Alma Mahler-Werfel and boldly raises questions of political antisemitism among the French in the wake of the Dreyfus case as a factor in reception of Mahler's music.

689. Martner, Knud. "Dansk Mahler reception 1904-79." *DMT* 54 (Marts 1979): 209-12.
In Danish. Surveys seventy-five years of performances of Mahler's works in Denmark and the press reception of the works. Rare for Danish sources on subject.

690. Namenwirth, S[imon] Misha. "Polemics Galore: the Critical Reception of Mahler's Eighth Symphony." *Sacra-Profana: Studies in Sacred and Secular Music for Johannes Riedel.* Ed. by Audrey Ekdahl Davidson and Clifford Davidson. Minneapolis: Friends of Minnesota Music, 1985, pp. 3-19.
Example of the wide variety in critical reception of Mahler's works in the form of an exchange between Paul Ehlers and Robert Holtzmann at the premiere of the *Symphony no. 8.* Straightforward with relatively little perspective by Namenwirth, who chooses to base essay on extensive quotations from Ehlers' and Holtzmann's articles in the *Allgemeine Musikzeitung* and the *Neue Musikzeitung* in his own translations, then throws forth questions about Mahler's appeal or lack thereof according to listeners' orientation to Mahler's Jewish identity. Makes an interesting attempt to trace history of Mahler criticism in light of ideological controversy between Jews and antisemites, but ultimately adds nothing to subject because of superficial treatment in short space. Further weakened by less than

optimum use of English language. Critical controversy better exemplified in treatment by Manfred Wagner (see no. 700 below).

691. Raynor, Henry. "Gustav Mahler: Without Prejudice." *Monthly Musical Record* 83 (January 1953): 4-13.
Takes on British critics of Mahler's work by citing facts that have been overlooked or distorted, e.g. deployment of heavy scoring used by Mahler, constructional organization vis-à-vis emotional balance, and so-called isolation of style instead of mainstream connection with contemporaries and followers. Refreshingly "without prejudice" as in cases of Cardus (see no. 788), Mellers (see no. 676) and Sorabji (see no. 823).

* Ritter, William. "Deux symphonies de Mahler." *Feuilles musicales* 1959: 116-21.
Full citation under no. 6 above. Brief discussions of the *Symphony no. 7* and the *Symphony no. 9*. Qualifies more as historical criticism than as formal analysis by virtue of Ritter's long involvement with Mahler's works as critic from Mahler's own time almost to centenniel.

692. Ritter, William. "Gustave Mahler." *La semaine littéraire* 15 (1907): 111-13, 131-32.
A two-part article attempting to "make sense" of Mahler's message in his works up to the *Symphony no. 6*. Not particularly positive in tone, critical, showing lack of understanding by attempting to compare Mahler with other composers as one would compare apples with oranges.

693. Ritter, William. "Pèlerinage à la neuvième symphonie et à la tombe de Gustav Mahler." *Revue française de musique* 10 (1912): 369-84, 415-38.
Extensive study in French by major critic shortly after Mahler's death, covering the newly premiered *Symphony no. 9* and linking it with the idea of death by a personal visit to Mahler's grave. Rather more than ordinary review of a new work, but somewhat limited in value by author's personal prejudices and immediacy of situation after Mahler's death.

694. Ritter, William. "Un symphoniste viennois: M. Gustave Mahler." *Études d'art étranger*. Paris: Société du Mercure de France, 1906, pp. 244-88.

First known essay on Mahler by the critic who continued to write from that time on several occasions from personal acquaintance and hearing of performances of Mahler's works. This piece is somewhat more generalized introduction to Mahler's work than the later essays which deal with specific subjects and individual works.

695. Salten, Felix. "Mahler." *Geister der Zeit: Erlebnisse.* Berlin, Wien, Leipzig: Paul Zsolnay, 1924, pp. 59-75.
    Comprises two essays dating from 1904 and 1911, the first concerned with Mahler's character as a manifestation of the society in which he lived (and how he in turn influenced people and events in that society), the second throwing a retrospective look back at the tenure of Mahler at the Hofoper in Vienna and the effect of his personality on the events and people contributing to the "Golden Era" there.

696. Salten, Felix. "Mahler." *Gestalten und Erscheinungen.* Berlin: S. Fischer, 1913, pp. 121-40.
    Reprints two newspaper articles by the *Jung Wien* literatus, the first originally in *Die Zeit* (Vienna) on December 18, 1904 (surveying Mahler's accomplishment at the Hofoper to that point), the second originally entitled "Die Mahler-Zeit" in *Berliner Tagblatt* a few days after Mahler's death (an obituary recognizing Mahler's influence at the Hofoper in Vienna, overall but after the fact). More than an ordinary critic, Salten--like Hermann Bahr--was a keen observer of European intelligentsia from an inside vantage point, making his essays and books, like Bahr's, enduringly valuable.

697. Schlüter, Wolfgang. "Studien zur Rezeptionsgeschichte der Symphonik Gustav Mahlers." Ph.D. diss., Fachbereich Geschichte- und Kommunikationswissenschaften der Technischen Universität Berlin, 1981. 228 pp.
    History of Mahler's music as represented in the media (printed word, recording and film). Notable for willingness to consider Nazi writings about Mahler in historical context, which is rare among historians of the present day.

698. Schuschitz, Elisabeth Desirée. "Die Wiener Musikkritik in Der Ära Gustav Mahlers 1897 bis 1907: eine his-

torisch-kritische Standortbestimmung." Ph.D. diss.,
Universität Wien, 1978. 360 pp.
History of music criticism in Viennese press at the
time of Mahler's tenure at the Hofoper, focusing heavily on documentation from the major newspapers dealing
with Mahler as conductor and composer.

699. Tessmer, Hans. "Gustav Mahler in Berlin." *Merker* 9
(1918): 439-41.
This critic-cum-musicologist (who contributed historical articles on Mahler to the *Neue Musik-Zeitung, Rheinische Musik- und Theater-Zeitung, Neues Wiener Journal, Deutsche Tonkünstlerzeitung* and the *Tägliche Rundschau*)
here mounts a rather misguided or even prejudiced
attack on Berlin for its lack of Mahler tradition.
His praise of Vienna at the expense of Berlin in terms
of reception of Mahler's music is off the mark. In
the same journal, the physician and musicologist Kurt
Singer wrote a response, "Gustav Mahler in Berlin"
(*Merker* 9: 567-68) in which he rebutted Tessmer's
arguments, calling down Vienna as being in no position to pride itself on its reception of Mahler's
music, having denied Mahler any real success during
his lifetime; Singer also pointed out that shortages
during World War I affected performances in Vienna as
much as in Berlin. It is incidentally useful to consider data cited by Martner documenting Mahler performances in Berlin (with the composer as both piano
accompanist and conductor) from 1895-1907, which included the first four symphonies and many songs. This
data supports Singer's arguments against Tessmer's.

700. Wagner, Manfred, [hrsg.]. *Geschichte der Österreichischen Musikkritik in Beispielen.* Mit einem einleitenden Essay von Norbert Schulik. Tutzing: Hans
Schneider, 1979. vii, 672 pp. ISBN 3-7952-0255-8.
Unusual premise, tracing history of music criticism in
Austrian newspapers from Mozart to von Einem. Organized chronologically by individual works of thirty composers, reproducing reviews from different newspapers
under each heading. Example by Mahler is the premiere
of the *Symphony no. 9* in 1912 under Bruno Walter, including reviews from seventeen newspapers, notably *Neue
Freie Presse, Wiener Allgemeine Zeitung* and *Österreichische Volkszeitung*. Editor deliberately chose reviews
expressing widely divergent opinions, ranging from
excoriations in the antisemitic press to sympathetic

memorials from Mahler's colleagues including Korngold and Specht.

* Wagner, Manfred. "Mahler und die österreichischer Musikkritik seiner Zeit." *Gustav Mahler Kolloquium 1979*: 89-95.
Full citation under no. 8 above. Brief study of Mahler as subject of professional criticism in his time. Precursor of Wagner's monumental compendium embracing not only Mahler but whole history of such criticism in documents (see preceding entry).

701. Wandruszka, Adam. *Geschichte einer Zeitung: das Schicksal der "Presse" unter der "Neuen Freien Presse" von 1848 bis zur zweiten Republik*. Wien: Neue Wiener Presse, 1958. 170 pp.
Detailed study of the influential Viennese newspaper which offers valuable contextual information on life in Vienna including music, politics, art and literature among many other subjects. Includes indispensable information on the paper's contributors including Korngold and Herzl.

PHILOSOPHICAL VIEWS

702. Adorno, Theodor Wiesengrund. *Mahler: eine musikalische Physiognomik*. Die musikalische Monographien. Hrsg. von Gretel Adorno und Rolf Tiedemann. Frankfurt-am-Main: Suhrkamp, 1986, pp. 149-319.
French version: *Mahler: une physionomie musicale*. Transl. by Jean-Louis Leleu et Theo Leydenbach. Paris: Minuit, 1976. 266 pp.
Adorno's book was originally published in 1960 (Bibliothek Suhrkamp, 62) and reprinted in 1971 (*Gesammelte Schriften*, 13). Considers Mahler's style in his time and since, a philosophical and theoretical discussion sharing many points raised in Adorno's essays (see following entry no. 703 for summary). The section "Variante et forme" was reproduced from the French version in *L'Arc* 67, pp. 32-40 (cited in full above as no. 3). An Italian version, *Wagner-Mahler: due studi* (transl. by G. Manzoni), was published in Torino in 1966; a Spanish version (*Mahler: una fisionómica musical*), with prologue by J. Soler, was published in 1987.

703. Adorno, Theodor Wiesengrund. *Musikalische Schriften.* Gesammelte Schriften, 16-18. Frankfurt-am-Main: Suhrkamp, 1978-84. 5 vols. in 3. ISBN 3-518-07477-6, 3-518-07476-8 (vol. 16), 3-518-57610-0, 3-518-57609-7 (vol. 17), 3-518-57696-8, 3-518-57695-X (vol. 18).
Edited by Rolf Tiedemann and others. Includes essays on a wide variety of subjects, some reprinted from books, newspapers, magazines and journals, others transcribed from lectures and radio broadcasts. Vol. 16 (three volumes in one) includes "Mahler: Wiener Gedenkrede 1960" (originally a lecture given in June 1960 for the Mahler centennial, published in *Neue Zürcher Zeitung* in July 1960 and in *Neue Deutsche Hefte* in 1961, later in *Musikalische Schriften*, vol. 2, Frankfurt-am-Main: Suhrkamp, 1963, pp. 115-37, and in *Gustav Mahler* in 1966, pp. 189-215, cited above as no. 7); "Epilegomena" (originally companion lecture to the preceding, published in the same periodicals as its companion, as well as in *Forum* in September 1961, and in *Musikalische Schriften* 2, pp. 138-54, and *Gustav Mahler* in 1966, pp. 215-34). These two essays are concerned with Mahler's musical style in the symphonies and songs; they are rather more concrete than some of Adorno's esoteric philosophical discussions. They comprise sections of *Quasi una fantasia*. In vol. 17 is *Impromptus*, which includes "Zu einer imaginären Auswahl von Liedern Gustav Mahlers" on pp. 189-97; this essay was originally published Frankfurt-am-Main: Suhrkamp, 1968, pp. 30-38, and reprinted in 1969 and 1973. It is a short study of Mahler as composer of songs, concerned with compositional formalism of the songs in the lied tradition (uses of march rhythms, strophic form etc.), giving special attention to the early songs for voice and piano, *Des Knaben Wunderhorn* and *Sieben Lieder*. Unfortunately this discussion is weakened by absence of musical examples.
Vol. 18 includes the following essays: "Mahler heute," on pp. 226-34 (originally published in *Anbruch* 12 in 1930, pp. 86-92, which is concerned with facets of Mahler's style making him a law unto himself and how his originality affects other musicians after his time); "Marginalien zu Mahler" on pp. 235-40 (original title "Marginalien zu Mahler: bei Gelegenheit des 25en Todes Tages: 18. Mai 1936" in *23*, 8. Juni 1936, pp. 13-19--in this instance Adorno used the name of Hektor Rottweiler, but later published the essay under

his own name in Vienna by Otto Kerry in 1971): "Mahlers Aktualität" on pp. 241-43 (originally in *Dichten und Trachten* 16, Berlin, Frankfurt-am-Main: Suhrkamp, 1960, pp. 52-55); "Zu einem Streitgespräch über Mahler" on pp. 244-50 (originally published in *Musik und Verlag: Karl Vötterle zum 65. Geburtstag*, hrsg. von Richard Baum und Wolfgang Rehm, Kassel: Bärenreiter, 1968, pp. 123-27); "Fragment als Graphik: zur Neuausgabe von Mahler's Zehnter Symphonie" on pp. 251-53 (originally in *Süddeutsche Zeitung*, 8./9. März 1969); and three essays transcribed from radio broadcasts of September and November 1960 on pp. 584-87, 588-603 and 604-22 respectively (the first of the three, "Aus dem ersten Mahler-Vortrag," is identified as "der in der Gedenkrede fehlende Teil zum Abdruck, der sich auf die Aufführung der Neunten Symphonie bezieht," i.e. that this is a missing portion of "Wiener Gedenkrede 1960," which Adorno used in the 1960 lecture but did not reproduce in published form). The time span of these selections ranges from 1930 to 1969, especially the period 1960 forward. The subjects fall into two general categories: philosophical speculation about Mahler's background and *modus operandi* as composer and the changing status of his musical reputation over time; and concrete discussions of individual songs and symphonies. Adorno's book *Mahler: eine musikalische Physiognomik* (see preceding entry no. 702) is closely related to these essays.

704. Dettelbach, Hans von. "Kosmische Einsamkeit." *Breviarium Musicae: Probleme, Werke, Gestalten*. Darmstadt: Wissenschaftliche Buchgesellschaft (H. Gentner), 1958, pp. 273-79.
Study of Mahler as world-viewer, considering him as man and creator, in the context of a group of essays devoted to individual composers from Bach to Blacher (mostly covering the late nineteenth century to the present). Generally positive view recognizing Mahler's importance, a little ahead of its time in that respect.

* Floros, Constantin. "Weltanschauung und Symphonik bei Mahler." *Gustav Mahler Kolloquium 1979*: 29-39.
Full citation under no. 8 above. This is a philosophical/aesthetic study of Mahler's attitudes to life and the world and their effect on his symphonic work akin to same author's multivolume study (see no. 208 above).

705. Franklin, Peter R. "Mahler and the Crisis of Awareness." Ph.D. diss., University of York, 1973. 471 pp.
Considers Mahler as a product of his time musically, historically and culturally, making him representative example of the emotional "Renaissance Man" of the late nineteenth century. Somewhat along the same lines as Holbrook and Greene (see following two entries), but more successful than either in provoking thought about the continuity of the human spirit.

706. Greene, David B. *Mahler, Consciousness and Temporality*. New York, London, Paris, Montreux, Tokyo: Gordon and Breach, 1984. x, 314 pp. ISBN 0-677-06160-9.
Philosophical discussion of musical logic in four symphonies of Mahler (the *Symphonies 3, 5, 8* and *9*). Utilizes concepts advanced by Heidegger, Sartre and other twentieth-century philosophers. Interesting experiment in a type of analysis seldom found in the musicological literature, but not successful in usual type of musical analysis from harmonic-formal terms. Best viewed as an opening step in a style which may well bear extension by other writers in the future.

707. Holbrook, David. *Gustav Mahler and the Courage to Be*. Studies in the Psychology of Culture. London: Vision Press, 1975. Reprinted New York: Da Capo Press, 1981. 270 pp. ISBN 0-306-76095-9.
Strange psychological/philosophical study of Mahler as man and creator, early predecessor of Greene et al., written by fantasist who has no credentials in either medicine or philosophy. Too dependent on Alma Mahler-Werfel's accounts concerning the sexual angle of Mahler's life. Concludes with detailed thematic analysis of *Symphony no. 9* which seems to have been author's touchstone for the entire book. Controversial and noticed by many, but ultimately does not satisfy.

708. James, Burnett. *The Music of Gustav Mahler*. Rutherford, Madison and Teaneck, New Jersey: Fairleigh Dickinson University Press; London: Associated University Presses, 1985. 230 pp. ISBN 0-8386-3167-3.
Interesting semi-musical, semi-philosophical discussion, often opinionated, occasionally inaccurate.

* Kauder, Hugo. "Vom Geiste der Mahlerschen Musik." *Musikblätter des Anbruch* 2 (1920): 262-65. Full citation under no. 16 above. Two-part study of Mahler as musical metaphysician with particular reference to works of first period.

* Knepler, Georg. "Gustav Mahlers Musik--Versuch einer Wertung." *Sinfonie und Wirklichkeit*: 9-15. Full citation under no. 10 above. Speculates on the long-term identity and value of Mahler's music in terms of form, musical language and philosophical background.

709. Kulenkampff, Hans-Wilhelm. "Widerbild der Welt: Totalität und Einspruch bei Gustav Mahler." *Neue Rundschau* 85 (1974): 622-41. Mahler as rebel building his symphonic "world" backward by means of his personal language in music. Reprinted in *Mahler: eine Herausforderung* (see full citation under no. 20 above).

710. Lea, Henry. "Gustav Mahler und der Expressionismus." *Aspekte des Expressionismus: Periodisierung--Stil --Gedankenwelt.* Hrsg. von Wolfgang Paulsen. Heidelberg: Lothar Stiehm, 1969, pp. 85-102. Discusses a generic definition for "expressionism" and where Mahler's musical style fits into that definition. Early seeds of Lea's later arguments of Mahler as "man on the margin" already traceable in late pages of this essay in remarks concerning Mahler's supranational alienation.

711. McGrath, William J. "The Metamusical Cosmos of Gustav Mahler." *Dionysian Art and Populist Politics in Austria.* New Haven, London: Yale University Press, 1974, pp. 120-62. ISBN 0-300-01656-5. A remarkable discussion of the aesthetic-philosophical background which influenced Mahler's musical work, with particular emphasis on the influence of Wagner, Schopenhauer and Nietzsche as embodied in the *Symphony no. 3*.

712. Nowak, Adolf. "Der religiöse Sinn der 'Wunderhorn-Sinfonien' Gustav Mahlers: zur Deutung der Dritten und Vierten Sinfonie Gustav Mahlers." *Religiöse Musik in nicht-liturgischen Werken von Beethoven bis Reger.* Studien zur Musikgeschichte des 19. Jahr-

hunderts, 51. Gemeinsam mit Günther Massenkeil und Klaus Wolfgang Niemöller hrsg. von Walter Wiora. Regensburg: Gustav Bosse, 1978, pp. 185-94. ISBN 3-7649-2135-8.
A study of religious meaning in the *Symphony no. 3* and *Symphony no. 4*. Interesting, but curious that the *Symphony no. 2* was not included as well.

713. Ringel, Erwin. "Das Problem der Todesbewältigung am Beispiel Gustav Mahlers." *Die österreichische Seele: Zehn Reden über Medizin, Politik, Kunst und Religion.* Dokumente zu Alltag, Politik und Zeitgeschichte, 5. Hrsg. von Franz Richard Reiter.. Wien, Köln, Graz: Hermann Bohlau, 1984, pp. 271-320.
Idiosyncratic essay on the subject of death as manifested in Austrian creativity and its effect on the life and work of Mahler. Actually explores medical questions concerning Mahler's death preoccupation more than most psychiatrists have done in writing on the same subject.

714. Rognoni, Luigi. *Fenomenologia della musica radicale.* Biblioteca di cultura moderna, 624. Bari: Laterza, 1966. 175 pp.
Comprises eight essays on various musicophilosophical subjects centered primarily on music and musicians of the late nineteenth and early twentieth centuries. The essay "Riscatto e attualità di Gustav Mahler" (pp. 77-102) is especially devoted to Mahler; it was reprinted from *L'Approdo musicale*, no. 16/17 (pp. 59-84), cited above under no. 2, discussing Mahler as man and creator in his time, heir to established musicoliterary traditions and innovator as seminal to later musical developments. Rognoni also discusses Mahler in other essays. These include "Musica sperimentale e musica radicale," "Alienazione e intenzionalità musicale," "Dalla tonalità alla atonalità: introduzione alla *Harmonielehre* di Schönberg" and especially "Il significato dell'espressionismo come fenomenologia del linguaggio musicale."

715. Rubin, Marcel. "Humanista Gustav Mahler." *Hudební rozhledy* 13 (1960): 515-18.
This writer, who contributed to the *Volksstimme* of Vienna and to Czech and Russian periodicals almost simultaneously in the 1950s and 1960s, is primarily concerned with Mahler's music as expression of his

humanistic views. Other essays which show this facet of Mahler's work besides the present one are "Gustav Mahler--kompozitor--humanist" in *Sovetskaya muzyka* (1958): 69-78, and "Gustav Mahlers musikalische Bedeutung" in *Volksstimme* (9. Juli 1950).

* Ruzicka, Peter. "Befragung des Materials: Gustav Mahler aus der Sicht aktueller Kompositionsästhetik." *Musik und Bildung* 5 (1973): 598-603.
Full citation under no. 17 above. Considers Mahler in the aesthetic tradition of music. Reprinted in *Mahler: eine Herausforderung* in which it is opposed with essay by Lachenmann newly written for that book (see full citation under no. 20 above).

716. Schreiber, Ulrich. "Gustav Mahler: une musique des contradictions sociales." *Critique* 31 (août/septembre 1975): 919-39.
Originally written in German, translated by Hans Hildebrand and Claude Mouchard. Attempts to describe the contradictions in content of Mahler's works as manifestations of the contradictions of the society in which he lived.

717. Subotnick, Rose Rosengard. "The Historical Structure: Adorno's 'French' Model for the Criticism of Nineteenth Century Music." *19th C Mus* 2 (1978): 36-60.
Places the work of Theodor Adorno in historical context, including the models for his writing on Mahler's music cited above under no. 702 and 703. Shows his musical philosophy with reference to the time span from Beethoven through Brahms and Wagner to Mahler and Schoenberg.

718. Tenschert, Roland. "Der faustische Zug in Gustav Mahlers Wesen und Werk." *Die Musik* 19 (1927): 651-56.
Surveys the influence of Goethe's *Faust* in Mahler's life philosophy and his work, most notably of course in the second part of the *Symphony no. 8*, but also in textual and musical echoes in other works.

STYLE

Form/Harmony/Melody

719. Agasaryan, Loretta S. "Osobennosti sonatnoy formy v simfoniyakh Gustava Malera." [Peculiarities of the sonata form in the symphonies of Gustav Mahler.] Ph.D. diss., Erevan, 1974/1975. 197 pp.
Historical consideration of sonata form and Mahler's modifications in the form, their structural and dramatic functions.

720. Barford, Philip. "Mahler: a Thematic Archetype." *Music Review* 21 (1960): 297-316.
Focuses on one particular "fingerprint" of Mahler's melodic style, i. e. the three-steps-jump-and-return (especially up then down) and speculates on the meaning behind Mahler's frequent use of the gesture (psychological, structural or both).

721. Barsova, Inna. "Problemy formy v rannikh simfoniyakh Gustava Malera." [Problems of form in early symphonies of Gustav Mahler.] *Voprosy muzykal'noy formy* [Questions of musical form] 2 (1972): 202-60.
Detailed examination of forms prominently used in Mahler's first period, their historical derivation and his own effect on them.

* Berio, Luciano. "Une mélodie de Gustav Mahler." *Colloque 1985*: 108-15.
Full citation under no. 5 above. Surveys characteristic Mahlerian melody, especially with reference to the third movement of the *Symphony no. 6*. One composer's assessment of another, differing from the essay on Mahler and Boulez by Dominique Jameux in same book because this one is offered by the composer himself.

* Burch, Noël. "Une jeune femme intimidante." *L'Arc* 67: 41-44.
Full citation under no. 3 above. Thoughts on the question of whether Mahler "develops" his thematic material, occasioned by a remark from "an intimidating young woman" who categorically dismissed Mahler's music because she believed he could not develop and integrate his material.

* Caetani, Oleg. "Le point de vue d'un chef d'orchestre sur la Première Symphonie." *Colloque 1985*: 98-100. Full citation under no. 5 above. This is a conductor's assessment of the *Symphony no. 1*. Not a technical map of the territory and how to order it, but a brief discussion of forms in the classical tradition, literary influences.

722. Durney, Daniel. "Aspects du problème de la forme dans la musique instrumentale au tournant du siècle: Mahler-Schönberg, Berg, Webern-Debussy, 1980-1910." Thèse Doctorat, 3e Cycle, Université de Paris, Sorbonne, Paris IV, 1981. 562 pp. Study of the use of musical form in instrumental works by the five composers above about the turn of the century. Works of Mahler analyzed include individual movements in the *Symphonies 2-6* and *9*. Also includes historical background from works of Brahms and Wagner.

723. Forchert, Arno. "Zur Auflösung traditioneller Formkatagorien in der Musik um 1900: Probleme formaler Organisation bei Mahler und Strauss." *AfMw* 32 (1975): 85-98. Shows innovations in formal organization made by Mahler (with examples from the symphonies) and Strauss (in the tone poems and the *Sinfonia Domestica*). More weighted toward Mahler than Strauss. Author wisely avoids any comparison between the two composers.

724. Hopkins, Robert George. "Secondary Parameters and Closure in the Symphonies of Gustav Mahler." Ph.D. diss., University of Pennsylvania, 1983. Not available for examination. Cited by Adkins and Dickinson in *Doctoral Dissertations in Musicology* (1984) and by Agawu (see no. 997 below).

* Komma, Karl Michael. "Vom Ursprung und Wesen des Trivialen im Werk Gustav Mahlers." *Musik und Bildung* 5 (1973): 573-78. Full citation under no. 17 above. Discusses Mahler's various uses of "trivial" material in nontrivial ways, with comparisons of particularly characteristic melodies of Mahler with similar melodies by other composers of his time including Bruckner and Tchaikovsky.

725. Litzenburg, Deborah Ann. "The Sonata-Allegro Form in the Late Romantic Period as Exemplified in Selected

Style: Form/Harmony/Melody

Symphonies of Brahms, Bruckner and Mahler." Ph.D. diss., University of Pennsylvania, 1961. Not available for examination. Cited by Vondenhoff (see no. 60) and Namenwirth (see no. 49).

* "Mahler et la subjectivité actuelle." *L'Arc* 67: 26-30.
Full citation under no. 3 above. Dialogue between George Aperghis, Noël Burch and Catherine Clement. Appears to be about constructional form in Mahler's works and why it is so subtle as to allow subjectivism in the content of the works as the primary factor. Odd discussion at end about why Mahler did not write opera, with Catherine Clement suggesting that an opera composer required bisexual viewpoint but that Mahler was too female-oriented.

726. Rivier, David. "A Note on Form in Mahler's Symphonies." *CD* 2 (1954): 29-33.
Discusses Mahler as heir to the classical tradition in symphonic forms, especially the sonata-allegro form. Particular emphasis on the first movement of the *Symphony no. 9* as example. Worth comparing with views expressed by Ratz on the same movement a year later (see no. 992 below).

727. Schmidt, Heinrich. "Formprobleme und Entwicklungslinien in Gustav Mahlers Symphonien: ein Beitrag zur Formenlehre der musikalischen Romantik." Ph.D. diss., Universität Wien, 1929. 209 pp.
One of the earliest dissertations on Mahler's music, focusing on formal construction and melodic balancing in the symphonies. Author's views later compromised by cooperation with the new criticism under the Nazi regime (see no. 177 above).

728. Schoenberg, Arnold. *Harmonielehre*. Wien, Leipzig: Universal Edition, 1911, 1922. 3. ed. (1911), xii, 516 pp.; 4. ed. (1949), xii, 524 pp.
Monumental treatise on the use of harmony (and, by extension, form and rhythm) in composition, written by Schoenberg with his students in mind. Dedicated to the memory of Mahler, who is cited frequently in the text. Together with later *Die neue Instrumentation* of Wellesz (see no. 749 below), this book offers a wonderful overview of the basis of the new styles developed by Mahler, his contemporaries and his followers.

729. Smith, Warren Storey. "The Cyclic Principle in Musical Design and Use of it by Bruckner and Mahler." *CD* 2 (1960): 3-32.
History of the cyclic technique in the nineteenth century symphony and especially the development of its use by Bruckner and Mahler. Discussion of the principle in Mahler covers the first eight symphonies.

* Stahmer, Klaus Hinrich. "Mahlers Frühwerk--eine Stiluntersuchung." *Form und Idee*: 9-28.
Full citation under no. 21 above. Discusses major facets of style in Mahler's early period. Important especially in tandem with subsequent essays on *Symphony no. 1* by Hoyer and Sponheuer (see section on that work below).

* Stein, Erwin. "Mahlers Sachlichkeit." *Anbruch* 12 (1930): 99-101.
Full citation under no. 1 above. Strictly concerned with Mahler as formal-orchestral technician and how his innovations in those respects affected others. Remarkably objective considering tendency at that time to write of Mahler as wild Romantic rebel rather than classical strategist. English translation by Hans Keller "Mahler the Factual" in *Orpheus in New Guises*: 15-18, cited above under no. 23; it is so placed in that book as to follow general essay "Mahler" as a logical continuation.

730. Storjohann, Helmut. "Die formalen Eigenartigen in den Sinfonien Gustav Mahlers." Ph.D. diss., Universität Hamburg, 1954. 279 pp.
First German dissertation on Mahler after World War II, taking up where Heinrich Schmidt left off in his dissertation in 1929 (see no. 727 above) in study of form in the symphonies. Complements work of Schaefers in area of instrumentation (see no. 745 below) and of Tischler in harmony (see next entry). Rather general but appropriate for scholarship of its time and still a solid foundation for more specialized studies since.

731. Tischler, Hans. "Die Harmonik in den Werken Gustav Mahlers." Ph.D. diss., Universität Wien, 1937. 164 pp.
One of the earliest of all dissertations on Mahler's music, reviewing then current literature documenting Mahler's life and harmonic style in his works, then

Style: Form/Harmony/Melody 213

   analyzing periodic-formal structure in many of his
   works. Organized by subject of analysis rather than
   by work.

732. Tischler, Hans. "Key Symbolism versus 'Progressive
   Tonality'." *Musicology* 2 (1949): 383-88.
   Critical debate with Dika Newlin's thesis of "progressive tonality" as proposed in *Bruckner-Mahler-Schoenberg* (see no. 233 above), not as an idea in itself but
   as a misapplied term which Tischler would replace with
   "dramatic key symbolism." Discusses Mahler's use of
   form as a dramatic structure with the interactions of
   key balances, with particular reference to the *Symphony
   no. 5*.

733. Tischler, Hans. "Musical Form in Gustav Mahler's
   Works." *Musicology* 2 (1949): 231-42.
   A pioneering study of the use Mahler makes of the
   "classical" forms in his symphonies, including sonata-
   allegro, rondo, theme-and-variations. Unusual in its
   emphasis on Mahler's connections with his predecessors,
   thereby showing him as heir to the classical tradition
   rather than adopting the prevailing view of him as a
   "hysterical" romantic. This article was also abstracted in *JAMS* 2 (1949): 199.

734. Tischler, Hans. "The Symphonic Problem in Mahler's
   Work." *CD* 2 (1941): 15-21.
   Analyzes Mahler's position in the history of the symphony, grounded in forms established by his predecessors yet using revolutionary tonal/harmonic methods to
   formulate his own style.

*   Velten, Klaus. "Über das Verhältnis von Ausdruck und
   Form im Werk Gustav Mahlers und Anton von Weberns."
   Musik und Bildung 10 (1978): 159-64.
   Full citation under no. 17 above. Compares and contrasts the work of Mahler and Webern in terms of form
   and melodic rhythm, and discusses Mahler's influence
   on Webern; unfortunately lacks musical examples of
   either composer's works, but does support arguments
   with verbal citations.

Orchestration

735. Bostley, Edward John. "The Horn in the Music of Gustav Mahler." Ph.D. diss., University of Missouri-Kansas City, 1980. xxix, 182 pp.
Circumscribed, but well-defined study of a single instrument that developed as a major figure in all of Mahler's symphonies and works for voice and orchestra. Considers the instrument as soloist and participant in group.

736. Chamouard, Philippe. "Caractère et evolution de l'orchestre dans l'oeuvre symphonique de Gustav Mahler." Thèse Doctorat, 3e Cycle, Université de Paris, Sorbonne, Paris IV, 1978. 419 pp.
Study of Mahler as orchestrator in the context of the history of orchestration in general and his own evolution according to time and circumstances in particular.

737. Danuser, Hermann. "Versuch über Mahlers Tón." *Jahrbuch des Staatlichen Instituts für Musikforschung Preussischer Kulturbesitz 1975*. Berlin: Merseburger, 1976, pp. 46-79. ISBN 3-87537-142-9.
Discusses Mahler's musical language (especially harmonic and orchestral) with special reference to the second movement of the *Symphony no. 4*, with secondary reference to the finale of the *Symphony no. 6* and the second movement of the *Symphony no. 7*.

738. Erpf, Hermann Robert. *Studien zur Harmonie- und Klangtechnik der neueren Musik*. Leipzig: Breitkopf und Härtel, 1927. v, 235 pp.
Thoughtful appraisal of melodic/harmonic and orchestral styles in music, particularly from Wagner to the Second Viennese School. Compare with *Die neue Instrumentation* of Wellesz (see no. 749 below) for understanding contemporary focus on the revolution in musical style during the crucial period when Mahler was experimenting with his own revolution.

739. Grant, [William] Parks. "Bruckner and Mahler--the Fundamental Dissimilarity of Their Styles." *Music Review* 32 (1971): 36-55.
A revolutionary study taking the opposite of the usual point of view which pairs Mahler with Bruckner, show-

Style: Orchestration

ing that Mahler was only superficially Bruckner's imitator and that the few resemblances between their styles consist in the use of certain harmonic idioms rather than their orchestration. Remarkable in its time and borne out in the long run by other studies.

740. Grant, [William] Parks. "Mahler's Use of the Orchestra." *CD* 1 (1939): 15-24.
A study of Mahler's characteristic use of orchestral instruments, individually and in combination, as a part of his melodic-harmonic-contrapuntal style. Concrete and pointed, and more concise than most studies written by other commentators later.

741. Hanson, Wesley Luther. "The Treatment of Brass Instruments in the Symphonies of Gustav Mahler." D.M.A. diss., University of Rochester (Eastman School of Music), 1976. ix, 360 pp.
Discusses Mahler's style in the use of brass instruments, in the context of nineteenth century orchestral techniques. Considers solo and obbligato brass as well as multiple groupings. Concludes with overview of uses in individual works and Mahler's alterations from version to version.

742. Holen, Jacques van. "Gustav Mahler als orkestrator: niewe perspectieven." *Adem* 18 (1982): 226-31.
Shows Mahler as a *Januskopf* in his concepts of orchestration, looking back to the romantic period in the size of his orchestra but presaging the new century in the use of orchestral polyphony in chamber-sized *Klangfarbenmelodie* for timbre and volume. In Dutch, with summaries in French and English.

743. Mikorey, Stefan. "Klangfarbe und Komposition: Besetzung und musikalische Faktur in Werken für grosses Orchester und Kammerorchester von Berlioz, Strauss, Mahler, Debussy, Schönberg und Berg." Ph.D. diss., Universität München, 1980. Published München: Minerva-Publikation, 1982. 263 pp. ISBN 3-597-10373-1.
Comparative study of orchestration from late Romantic period to the Second Viennese School. Focuses on the sounds rather than the changing circumstances behind the works of each of the six composers.

744. Schäfer, Wolf-Dieter. *Entwurf einer quantitativen Instrumentationsanalyse: ein Beitrag zur Methodik von*

Instrumentationsuntersuchung; dargestellt an Beispielen aus der Wiener Klassik und der Spätromantik. Europäische Hochschulschriften, Reihe 36, Musikwissenschaft, 4. Frankfurt-am-Main, Bern: Lang, 1982. 422, lxxxix pp. ISBN 3-8204-7203-7. Originally author's Ph.D. dissertation (Universität Bochum, 1981). Comparative study of orchestration with examples from the contrasting periods of the classic and postromantic periods (Haydn and Mozart compared with Mahler, Bruckner and Strauss).

745. Schaefers, Anton. "Gustav Mahlers Instrumentation." Ph.D. diss., Rheinischen Friedrich-Wilhelms-Universität zu Bonn, 1935. Later published Düsseldorf: Dissertations-Verlag G.H. Nolte, 1935. iii, 66 pp. An early dissertation on Mahler's use of the orchestra at a time when few dissertations on Mahler were being written at all. Refers to both symphonies and vocal works, and points out Mahler's unique methods of orchestration as distinct from those of other composers of his time. Rare positive assessment of Mahler's work from German-speaking countries during the Third Reich.

746. Taylor, Virginia Sue. "The Harp and Mahler's *Klangfarbengruppe*." Ph.D. diss., Washington University, St. Louis, 1988. 350 pp. This is a pioneering study of a neglected area in the context of Mahler's orchestration. Mahler's style in writing for the harp is explored with reference to the soloistic and ensemble roles of the instrument, and the author shows how this style influenced the work of the Second Viennese School and, by extension, that of many other composers of the twentieth century. The body of the study is devoted to the songs and symphonies of Mahler's middle and late periods. Important foundation for further study not only in the area of orchestration but for cultural connection with the *Jugendstil* movement.

747. Volbach, Fritz. *Das moderne Orchester in seiner Entwicklung.* Leipzig: B.G. Teubner, 1910. 118 pp. Surveys the innovations in orchestration from various composers of the nineteenth and the beginning of the twentieth centuries. Orchestration in Mahler's works is prominently featured. From author's own experience in coverage of the concert life for periodicals includ-

ing *Die Musik*.

* Wellesz, Egon. "Mahlers Instrumentation." *Anbruch* 12 (1930): 106-10.
  Full citation under no. 1 above. Second study of the works of Mahler as examples of revolutionary orchestration in 1930, the other being "Mahler's Orchestration" (see next entry). Both are concise summaries of theories presented in detail in *Die neue Instrumentation* (see no. 749 below), which had been published in the two preceding years; both articles simultaneously show Mahler's ties to the past and note his individuality with respect to his contemporaries.

748. Wellesz, Egon. "Mahler's Orchestration." *Monthly Musical Record* 60 (1930): 321-23.
   Summation of the author's survey of Mahler's style of orchestration in *Die neue Instrumentation* (see following entry). Considers Mahler in the context of orchestral style and practice in the late nineteenth and early twentieth centuries. Comparable to "Mahlers Instrumentation" published in same year (see preceding entry).

749. Wellesz, Egon. *Die neue Instrumentation*. Max Hesses Handbücher, 90-91. Berlin: Max Hesse, 1928-29. 2 vols.
   Fantastic discussion of instrumental style in the late nineteenth and early twentieth centuries. Works of Mahler are more widely used as examples of orchestration than those of any other composer cited in this book, with examples from the first nine symphonies, the *Kindertotenlieder* and *Das Lied von der Erde* scattered over both volumes. Illuminating about Mahler as a composer with influence on other composers (including Wellesz himself). A major plug for Mahler which should be reprinted today.

Program, Nature and Folk

750. Bălan, George. *Gustav Mahler sau cum exprima muzica idei*. [Gustav Mahler or the musical presentation of the idea.] București: Editura Musicală a Uniunii Compozitorilor, 1964. 196 pp.
   Only known Romanian study in the Mahler literature.

Chronological study of Mahler's works, concerned with his musical style and the nonmusical background of his compositions. Brief chronology of Mahler's life, discography and bibliography at end of book. Musical examples numerous but cited continuously by number toward end of book, somewhat weakening impact by necessitating frequent jumping back and forth by reader.

751. Berges, Ruth. "Mahler and the Great God Pan." *Musical Courier*, vol. 161 no. 1 (January 1960): 10-11, 37.
Considers Mahler's attitude to nature, the seasons and Earth in connection with such works as the *Symphony no. 3* and *Das Lied von der Erde*.

752. Bergfeld, Dennis. "The Symphonies of Gustav Mahler: a Study of Musical Process and Symphonic Structure as Related to the Composer's Programmatic Intentions and Literary Expositions." Ph.D. diss., University of Texas.
Unavailable for examination. Listed by Cecil Adkins in *Doctoral Dissertations in Musicology* (Fifth Edition, 1971) as "in progress" as of that date.

* Borris, Siegfried. "Mahlers holzschnitthafter Liedstil." *Musik und Bildung* 5 (1973): 578-87.
Full citation under no. 17 above. Wonderful discussion of "folklike" characteristics in Mahler's lyric lines, focusing on the early symphonies, the *Wunderhorn* and Rückert settings. Copiously illustrated with musical examples.

753. Danuser, Hermann. "Konstruktion des Romans bei Gustav Mahler." *Musikalische Prosa*. Studien zur Musikgeschichte des 19. Jahrhunderts, 46. Regensburg: Gustav Bosse, 1975, pp. 87-117. ISBN 3-7649-2113-7.
Considers Mahler as "musical novelist" in the programmatic tradition with special attention to the *Symphony no. 3*. Notes particularly literary forebears from the nineteenth century German tradition.

* Duse, Ugo. "Origini popolari di canto Mahleriano." *L'Approdo musicale*, no. 16/17: 85-120.
Full citation under no. 2 above. Discusses Mahler as lyricist and draws connections between his melodies and folk tunes. Risky premise but still interesting.

754. Eggebrecht, Hans Heinrich. *Die Musik Gustav Mahlers*. München: R. Piper, 1982, 1986. 304 pp. ISBN 3-492-10637-4.
 Less a study of individual works of Mahler than a study of concepts of nature and people living illustrated by works of Mahler. Refers to the historical context of the concepts and the music Mahler used, with comparisons to works of other composers. Slightly favors the works from the "early period" (especially the *Symphony no. 3*) over works from the middle and late periods. Favors the musico-literary context over the philosophical.

755. Hansen, Mathias. "Dialektik von Werk und Ideologie bei Gustav Mahler." Ph.D. diss., Institut für Musikwissenschaft, Berlin, 1966.
 Not available for examination. Cited by Vondenhoff (1983) and Namenwirth.

756. Hansen, Mathias. "Zur Funktion von Volksmusikelementen in Kompositionen Gustav Mahlers." *BzMw* 23 (1981): 31-35.
 A specialized consideration of the role of folk music in Mahler's works, not concerned with the literary influences but rather with the role of folk melody as a component of rhythm, form and lyric line.

757. Karbusicky, Vladimir. *Gustav Mahler und seine Umwelt*. Impulse der Forschung, 28. Darmstadt: Wissenschaftliche Buchgesellschaft, 1978. viii, 158 pp. ISBN 3-534-07952-3.
 Trenchant study of the effect of the "social lament" of the Iglau region where Mahler lived as a child on his melodic style. Special attention to the songlike episode in the third movement of the *Symphony no. 5*. Refutes influence of Moravian folk song proposed by earlier writers and leaves untouched questions of folklore influence.

758. Klusen, Ernst. "Gustav Mahler und das Volkslied seiner Heimat." *Journal of the International Folk Music Council* 15 (1963): 29-37.
 Demonstrates the influence of Moravian, Bohemian and other folk music idioms (including melodic and rhythmic figures, formulaic repetition and textural scoring) on Mahler's works. Argues for strong influence from Mahler's youth in Kališté and Iglau.

* la Grange, Henry-Louis de. "'Ma musique est vécue'--la biographie comme outil d'analyse." *Colloque 1985*: 31-39.
  Full citation under no. 5 above. Shows how biographical conditions may be used to understand Mahler's works, especially those with programs behind them. Age-old question given topical answer useful for guideline in subsequent discussions.

759. Ledeč, Jan. "Gustav Mahler and Czech Musical Culture." *Music News from Prague*, no. 2-3 (1986): 1-3.
   One of a series of articles by this author sketching the history of musical life in Bohemia/Czechoslovakia and the particular contributions of individuals including Mahler and other composers. Emphasizes Mahler's birth in Bohemia, his stints as conductor in Olomouč and Prague. Notes the two-way influences between the composer and Bohemian culture--its effect on his compositions, and his effect in turn on the later musical life of Bohemia/Czechoslovakia even when he was working outside the country. Modest in length but important in scope, written by insider to history of Czech music.

* Lemery, Denys. "Le sentiment populaire." *L'Arc* 67: 18-25.
  Full citation under no. 3 above. Surveys "popular" bases of Mahler's works (earlier composers, Mahler's childhood, folk elements in life and literature). Opinionated and not always factually accurate.

760. Nebolyubova, Larisa S. "Specificeskiye zakonomernosti dramaturgii simfonii Gustava Malera." [Specific regularities of dramaturgy in Gustav Mahler's symphonies.] Ph.D. diss., University of Kiev, 1978. 182 pp.
   Associates Mahler's creative genius with the Expressionist movement in Austria, especially with literary as well as musical expressionism.

761. O'Brien, Sally. "The 'Programme' Paradox in Romantic Music as Epitomized in the Works of Gustav Mahler." *Studies in Music* [University of Western Australia Press], no. 5 (1971): 54-65.
   Amazing little-known study of Mahler and the programmatic tradition in romantic music, summarizing the conflict between "hidden" and "open" programs.

Style: Program, Nature & Folk

762. Quoika, Rudolf. "Über die Musiklandschaft Gustav Mahlers." *Böhmen, Mähren, Schlesien* 2 (1960): 100-06.
  Considers musical influences on Mahler from his Bohemian/Moravian background. Outgrowth of same author's book *Die Musik des Deutschen in Böhmen und Mähren* (Berlin: Merseburger, 1956, 161 pp.).

763. Rychetský, Jiří. "'Eits a Binkel Kasi (Hrasi)'." *NaMR*, no. 17 (April 1987): 7-8.
  Identifies song reported by Natalie Bauer-Lechner and later Henry-Louis de la Grange to have been sung by Mahler in childhood as a Czech song of journeymen and popular at large among Bohemian people. Disproves earlier claims that song is Yiddish (and implicitly raises question about Mahler's musical orientation in the mixed environment of his youth).

* Storjohann, Helmut. "Gustav Mahlers Verhältnis zur Volksmusik." *Musica* 1960: 357-59.
  Full citation under no. 14 above. Briefly discusses the question of folk influence on Mahler's music, drawing on the writings of Adler and Stefan but not demonstrating examples in music.

764. Tancibudek, S. "The Interaction between Gustav Mahler and the Bohemian-Moravian Musical Tradition." Thesis, University of Adelaide, 1983.
  Not available for examination. Cited in *Acta Musicologica* 56 (1984), p. 132 by Kartomi and in *Studies in Music* 17 (1983) in the annual list of theses at universities in Australia; however, it is not clear if this thesis was for the master's or doctoral degree.

765. Vetter, Walther. "Gustav Mahlers sinfonischer Stil: eine Skizze." *Deutsches Jahrbuch der Musikwissenschaft für 1961*. Hrsg. von Walther Vetter. Leipzig: Edition Peters, 1962, pp. 7-18.
  Considers the literary influences on Mahler's symphonic style with particular reference to the *Symphony no. 1* and *Symphony no. 8*.

766. Wanninger, Forrest I. "Dies irae: its Use in Non-Liturgical Music from the Beginning of the Nineteenth Century." Ph.D. diss., Northwestern University, 1962. ii, 188 pp.
  Studies the "death motive" in music of the Romantic per-

iod, using examples by selected composers from Berlioz and Liszt to Dallapiccola. Mahler's *Symphony no. 2* is discussed on pp. 96-108.

767. Zenck, Martin. "Die Aktualität Gustav Mahlers als Problem der Rezeptionsästhetik: Perspektiven von Mahlers Naturerfahrung und Formen ihrer Rezeption." *Melos/NZfM* 3 (1977): 225-32.
Discusses "Mahler and Nature," objectively considered as a factor in the progressive reaction to his music from 1912 to present.

COLLECTIVE ANALYSES

Symphonies and Songs, etc.

768. Abendroth, Walter. "Phantastik zwischen der Zeiten: Gustav Mahler." *Vier Meister der Musik: Bruckner, Mahler, Reger, Pfitzner.* München: Prestel, 1952, pp. 38-73, 142.
A limited study of the first nine symphonies and the vocal works, made in the context of Mahler's position among his predecessor Bruckner, his contemporary Reger, and his younger successor Pfitzner.

769. Abraham, Gerald. "An Outline of Mahler." *ML* 13 (1932): 391-400.
Ambivalent overview of Mahler's compositional career, advocating performances of many of his works as aids to understanding, yet following the familiar negative lines of banality, patchy borrowing and vulgarity. Not as bad as the literature the Nazis published at that period, but unsatisfying and narrow.

770. Barford, Philip. *Mahler Symphonies and Songs.* BBC Music Guides. Seattle: University of Washington Press, 1970. 64 pp.
A brief study of Mahler's *oeuvre* best used for introduction to laymen. The songs are sacrificed for space in comparison to the symphonies; *Das klagende Lied* is not even mentioned, and the *Symphony no. 10* is shortchanged because the discussion is limited to its first movement. Author seems to have virtually ignored the literature in general and lists no other sources which

might improve on this inadequate discussion. Greek translation by Giorges Leotsakos (Athens: Leskhē, 1978, 161 pp., in the series "Mousikoi Odēgoi tēs Deskhēs") actually improves on the English original with capsule descriptions of important people from Mahler's associates to Donald Mitchell and Deryck Cooke, list of works and discography.

771. Cooke, Deryck. *Gustav Mahler 1860-1911: a Companion to the BBC's Celebration of the Centenary of his Birth*. Foreword by Bruno Walter. London: British Broadcasting Corp., 1960. 47 pp.
Revised edition: *Gustav Mahler: an Introduction to his Music*. Cambridge: Cambridge University Press, 1980. vii, 127 pp. ISBN 0-521-23175-2 (hardcover), 0-521-29847-4 (paper).
An important study of Mahler's *oeuvre* giving equal weight to the symphonies and the vocal works (including *Das klagende Lied*, which was neglected by Barford later in his volume). Cites texts and translations in all vocal works, and considers Mahler's own background in connection with his conception of his works. Shows extensive familiarity not only with Mahler's life and literary sources but with existing literature on Mahler's life and work, and becomes a source of historical importance because it was the immediate impetus for Deryck Cooke's work on the performing version of the last symphony. An Italian version, *La musica di Mahler* (edited by Colin and David Matthews) was published in 1983 by Mondadori of Milan (203 pp.).

772. Diether, Jack. "Notes on Some Mahler Juvenilia." *CD* 3 (1969): 3-100.
A far-reaching discussion of Mahler's earliest works in the repertoire, covering the complete three-part version of *Das klagende Lied*, the five-movement version of the *Symphony no. 1*, the *Poisl Lieder* and the two Heine settings. Refers additionally to the literary sources for these works, including Heine, Jean Paul Richter, Ludwig Bechstein and the brothers Grimm.

773. Forchert, Arno. "Techniken motivisch-thematischer Arbeit in Werken von Strauss und Mahler." *Zur Musikgeschichte des 19. Jahrhunderts*. Hamburger Jahrbuch für Musikwissenschaft, 2. Hamburg: Karl Dieter Wagner, 1977, pp. 187-200. ISBN 3-921029-53-8.
Study of thematic integration and organization in

works of Strauss and Mahler, comparing and contrasting, with particular attention to Mahler's *Symphony no. 6* and Strauss's *Heldenleben.*

* Lustgarten, Egon. "Mahlers lyrisches Schaffen." *Musikblätter des Anbruch* 2 (1920): 269-72. Full citation under no. 16 above. Discusses Mahler's works for human voice (both songs and symphonic movements) with particular reference to the *Des Knaben Wunderhorn* settings, but, inexplicably, nothing on *Das klagende Lied* or *Das Lied von der Erde.*

774. Marliave, Joseph de. "Gustave Mahler." *Études musicales.* Paris: Librairie Félix Alcan, 1917, pp. 174-83.
Originally written in 1910, one of several essays on the works of various composers of the late nineteenth and early twentieth centuries, grouped by nationalities. No attempt to compare Mahler with other composers including Fauré, Elgar, Albeniz, the Russian nationalists, Heller, Bruckner and Strauss. Series of individual studies written over period of time, but does recognize Mahler's importance despite limited scope.

775. Mitchell, Donald. *Gustav Mahler: Songs and Symphonies of Life and Death.* Berkeley, Los Angeles: University of California Press, 1985. 659 pp. ISBN 0-520-05578-8.
Studies exhaustively the ten Rückert songs, *Das Lied von der Erde* and the *Symphony no. 8*, with considerably less emphasis on the "middle" *Symphonies 5-7*. Considers the texts as well as the musical substance, especially in the case of *Das Lied*, which includes a study of the Chinese originals and the alterations made by Mahler and the translators. Extremely detailed in areas of vocal emphasis, but curiously biased against nonvocal works. Difficult to use because of problems of organization.

776. Mitchell, Donald. *Gustav Mahler: the Early Years.* London: Rockliff, 1958. xviii, 275 pp. Revised edition ed. by Paul Banks and David Matthews, Berkeley, Los Angeles: University of California Press, 1980. xxii, 338 pp. ISBN 0-520-04141-0.
A major pioneering study of Mahler's early works including his student compositions. Focuses on the

works themselves rather than on biographical detail. First published at a time when information on the early years was almost totally lacking, the book has been extensively revised and updated in the second edition. Full of important information, but difficult to use because of idiosyncratic organization, not for all tastes.

777. Mitchell, Donald. *Gustav Mahler: the Wunderhorn Years --Chronicles and Commentaries*. London: Faber and Faber, 1975; Boulder, Colorado: Westview Press, 1976; Berkeley: University of California Press, 1980. 461 pp. ISBN 0-571-10674-9 (1975 ed.), 0-89158-509-5 (1976 ed.), 0-520-04220-4 (1980 ed.). Takes up where *Gustav Mahler: the Early Years* (see preceding entry) left off, with the conventional "early period" covering the first four symphonies and the *Wunderhorn* influences. A major source of information, but, as in other books by this author, difficult to use because of idiosyncratic organization.

778. Ratz, Erwin. "Gustav Mahler." *NZfM* 116 (1955): 127-30.
Briefly surveys Mahler's life and works chronologically and stylistically.

* Redlich, Hans Ferdinand. "Gustav Mahler e la sua opera." *L'Approdo Musicale*, no. 16/17: 5-58.
Full citation under no. 2 above. Chronological discussion of Mahler's works without musical examples other than a single reproduction of the last page of the fourth movement of the *Symphony no. 10.*

779. Roman, Zoltan. "Connotative Irony in Mahler's 'Todtenmarsch in "Callots Manier."'" *MQ* 59 (1973): 207-22.
Important contribution to the debate about the musicohistorical context of the *Symphony no. 1*, with considerable sidelight on *Lieder eines fahrenden Gesellen* and the *Symphony no. 2*. Special concern with the penultimate movement of the *Symphony no. 1* and the method by which Mahler achieved the disturbing effect of mockery with *Bruder Martin* and the other main motives.

* Schnebel, Dieter. "Das Spätwerk als Neue Musik." *Gustav Mahler* (1966): 157-88.
Full citation under no. 7 above. Considers *Das Lied von der Erde* and the *Symphony no. 9* in the context of

Mahler's style as it developed over his compositional career, showing stylistically how these point to Schoenberg and his followers, in contrast to the classically oriented earlier works. A Czech version of this article, "Mahlerovo pozdní dílo jako nová hudba," appeared in Hudební rozhledy 24 (1971): 127-33.

780. Schumann, Karl. Das kleine Gustav Mahler Buch. Salzburg: Residenz, 1972. 123 pp. ISBN 3-7017-0036-2. Surveys Mahler's works by genre, placing them in the context of the history of the symphony and the solo song, rather than concerning itself with Mahler's life as such.

781. Smith, Warren Storey. "Mahler Quotes Mahler." CD 2 (1954): 7-13. Surveys the process of cross-fertilization in Mahler's works, showing how the continuity moves between song and symphony, and between symphony and symphony.

782. Tibbe, Monika. Über die Verwendung von Liedern und Liedelementen in instrumentalen Symphoniesätzen Gustav Mahlers. Berliner Musikwissenschaftliche Arbeiten, 1. Hrsg. von Carl Dahlhaus und Rudolf Stephan. München, Salzburg: Emil Katzbichler, 1971, 1977. 134 pp. Published version of author's Ph.D. dissertation (Freie Universität Berlin, 1970). Study of Mahler's use of songs as structural factors in instrumental movements in the symphonies. Differentiates between examples of (a) whole songs transmuted into movements, (b) portions of songs lifted bodily into movements, and (c) fleeting citations, whether developed beyond a single line or not. Circumscribed, but very well defined and a major illumination of a subject usually treated incidentally rather than specifically.

* Vignal, Marc. "Matériau musical et dialectique historique." L'Arc 67: 12-17. Full citation under no. 3 above. Surveys the first nine symphonies and some of the songs, but far too briefly; should never have been attempted in essay of this length. Point of view seems to stress literary influences in the early symphonies, formal architectonics in the middle ones, and the path to the future in the late symphonies and Das Lied von der Erde, but contributes little that is original.

783. Williamson, John C. "The Development of Mahler's Symphonic Technique with Special Reference to the Compositions of the Period 1899-1905." Ph.D. diss., Oxford University, 1975. 355 pp., plus 209 pp. examples unpaginated.
Monumental study of the last two songs from *Des Knaben Wunderhorn*, the Rückert settings and the *Symphonies 5-7*, vis-à-vis form, thematic structure, harmony, counterpoint and textural scoring.

Symphonies

784. Barsova, Inna. *Sinfonii Gustava Malera*. Moskva: Sovetskiy Kompozitor, 1975. 495 pp.
Major study of the symphonies in Russian, showing familiarity with earlier German sources, less with references in other languages.

784a. Boschot, Adolphe. *Chez les musiciens (du XVIIIe siècle à nos jours)*. Paris: Plon-Nourrit, 1922. 285 pp.
Includes brief discussions of the *Symphony no. 5* (pp. 116-18) and the *Symphony no. 4* (pp. 118-20) which are anything but positive; worth comparing and contrasting with discussions by Ritter at same period.

785. Bekker, Paul. *Gustav Mahlers Sinfonien*. Berlin: Schuster und Loeffler, 1921. Reprinted Tutzing: Hans Schneider, 1969. 360 pp.
Wonderful comprehensive discussion of the symphonies (excluding the *Symphony no. 10*, which was unknown at the time Bekker wrote the book), and *Das Lied von der Erde*. Thorough, painstaking and unusually sympathetic to Mahler in its time considering the neglect of the music in the generation following Mahler's death. Its reprint in 1969 is a valid index to its stature over time and changing views of Mahler's music.

786. Cardus, Neville. "Gustav Mahler." *Ten Composers*. London: Jonathan Cape, 1945, 1946, 1948, 1952; Sydney: Collins, 1947, pp. 63-78.
Reprinted in *A Composers Eleven*. London: Jonathan Cape, 1958; New York: G. Braziller, 1959, pp. 105-26.
Same essay in both versions. Early British study of

Mahler obviously precursor to extended work by Cardus on all the symphonies for which he completed only the first volume (*Gustav Mahler: His Mind and His Music*, cited below under no. 788). Sharp analysis, positive, considers Mahler the man as creator of works which mirror his life and thought.

787. Cardus, Neville. "Gustav Mahler." *Sechs deutsche Romantiker*. München: Albert Langen/Georg Müller, 1961, pp. 133-63.
German essay on Mahler's life and work equivalent to the English essay in preceding entry.

788. Cardus, Neville. *Gustav Mahler: His Mind and His Music*. Vol. 1: The First Five Symphonies. With musical examples copied, written and edited by Rudolf Schwartz. New York: St. Martin's Press; London: V[ictor] Gollancz, 1965. 192 pp.
A sensitive study in depth of the first five symphonies by a major British commentator. Volume 2, which would presumably have covered the remaining symphonies and possibly *Das Lied von der Erde*, was never published, which must be considered a major loss.

789. Combé, Edouard. "Les symphonies de Mahler." *Revue musicale* 3 (Juillet 1922): 42-56.
Early French discussion of Mahler as symphonist, less a work-by-work traversal than a general assessment of Mahler's concepts and how he applied them in the first nine symphonies and *Das Lied von der Erde*. Overall assessment of Mahler's works positive but not forceful.

790. Cooke, Deryck. "Mahler's Melodic Thinking." *Vindications: Essays on Romantic Music*. Cambridge, London, New York, New Rochelle, Melbourne, Sydney: Cambridge University Press, 1982, pp. 95-107. ISBN 0-521-24765-9 (hardcover), 0-521-28947-5 (paper).
Shows how Mahler uses melody as a functional component of harmonic-contrapuntal texture, with special reference to the second movement of *Symphony no. 2*, the third movement of *Symphony no. 5* and the last movement of *Symphony no. 9*.

791. De Kock, J.P. "Mahlerboek: hoe te luisteren naar de sinfonische werken von Gustav Mahler." [How to listen to the symphonic works of Gustav Mahler.] In manu-

script. iii, 143 pp.
In Dutch, dating from 1968. Unusual historiographical discussion of the symphonies and *Das Lied von der Erde*, rare and difficult to locate.

792. Diepenbrock, Alphons. *Verzamelde Geschriften.* Bijeengebracht en toegelicht door Eduard Reeser in Samenwerking met Thea Diepenbrock. Utrecht: Het Spectrum, 1950. 432 pp.
Major collection of essays by Mahler's Dutch colleague including "Mahler's Vierde Symphonie" (pp. 246-50), "Mahler's Achtste Symphonie" (pp. 347-55), obituary and brief discussion of other Mahler works. Language varies, usually Dutch but some French and German.

793. DuPree, R.D. "Recurring Thematic and Motivic Material in Gustav Mahler's Symphonies I-IX." Ph.D. diss., North Texas State University, [1970]. 190 pp.
Good premise which unfortunately does not quite succeed. Although this study is intended to concentrate on certain special techniques common to more than one work rather than exhaustive individual analyses of each, it fails because (a) such technical analysis requires more extended treatment than it is given here, (b) the idea is not original, having been treated previously in German and English by others including Specht, Nodnagel, Ratz, Schiedermair, Sorabji, Cardus and Grant, and (c) the artificial exclusion of the *Symphony no. 10* from this discussion as late as 1970 shows partisanship against the work which contravenes the whole argument.

794. Filler, Susan Melanie. "Editorial Problems in Symphonies of Gustav Mahler: a Study of the Sources of the Third and Tenth Symphonies." Ph.D. diss., Northwestern University, 1977. xi, 630 pp.
A critical study and comparison of the manuscript and early published sources of the two symphonies, showing the many changes Mahler tended to make at various stages of the compositional process. Points out that the composer deviated consciously from his usual *modus operandi* when writing the *Symphony no. 10*, with the result that the manuscript, while unfinished, had progressed far beyond the stage generally found in the conventionally "finished" works. Argues that, since Mahler was a compulsive "reviser," the major facet of his revisional process is not the quantity

but rather the quality of the changes he made, no matter when. Also argues for conservative handling by the editor of any Mahler score, finished or unfinished, in view of the long history of editorial abuse beginning even in Mahler's lifetime.

795. Flothuis, Marius. *Notes on Notes: Selected Essays by Marius Flothuis*. Transl. by Sylvia Broere-Moore. [Amsterdam]: Frits Knuf, 1974. 178 pp.
Two essays in this collection are of special interest: "From Quotation to Plagiarism" (pp. 139-57), in which author makes the proper distinction between quotation of music between one composer and another, and outright appropriation, urging differentiation on the basis of causative factors in the process; and "Reflections on Mahler's Ninth Symphony" (pp. 159-71), in which Flothuis discusses the thematic connection between that work and Beethoven's *Leb' wohl* motif, and the formal and integrative use of such material which gives the symphony its emotional impact. Special and sensitive, unlike many other discussions of Mahler's compositional *modus operandi*.

796. Grant, [William] Parks. "Mahler Research and Editing in Vienna." *CD* 3 (1969): 101-15.
A personal view of the experience of editing the Critical Edition which has been in progress under the auspices of the IGMG for the past thirty-odd years. Discusses the process of editing from the available source materials for four works, positing questions concerning the limitations of the sources and how problems were individually solved. Concentrates especially on the *Symphonies 2, 3, 8* and *9*, which have since appeared.

797. Kaplan, Nathan. *Simfoni Muzik: kurtse Derklerungen iber dem Inhalt fun di vikhtigste Simfonis; mit biografishe Notitsn un Bilder fun di velt barimte Kompozitores un a Verterbukh fun muzikalishe Terminen*. New York: Gems of Art, 1925. 210 pp.
Short analyses of works by fifty-two composers from Bach to Schoenberg and Stravinsky, arranged alphabetically by composer, with biographical sketches of each composer. There is a brief biographical sketch of Mahler on page 93, followed by analyses of the *Symphony no. 1* (pp. 93-94) and the *Symphony no. 2* (pp. 94-95), which is incorrectly labelled "A Zomer Morgen

Collective Analyses: Symphonies

Troym," a subtitle which actually applies to the *Symphony no. 3* (which is not discussed here)! Author obviously more familiar with Yiddish than English as evidenced by errors of spelling as well as information in English transliteration, but this is still an interesting attempt to introduce Mahler as composer of stature to potential audience in the United States at a time when little had been published in this country about Mahler in any case. List of musical terms pp. 183-210. Each composer including Mahler also represented by unusual small line drawing evidently made by publishers of book, as the drawing of Mahler does not resemble illustrations seen in other sources.

798. Koenig, Arthur William, Jr. "The Orchestral Techniques of the Mahler Symphonies, with Emphasis on Symphonies II and IX and Their Influences on Twentieth-Century Music." Ph.D. diss., Michigan State University, 1971. 225 pp.
Somewhat circumscribed study of Mahler's orchestration with discussions of contrasting *Symphony no. 2* and *Symphony no. 9* representing early and late periods. Might have benefitted from similar discussion of a work from the "middle" period which influenced composers of twentieth century as much as the late works and perhaps more than the earlier works. Best when considered as discussion of scoring on its own merits, weaker in context of historical continuity.

799. Kralik, Heinrich von. *Gustav Mahler: eine Studie.* Hrsg. und eingeleitet von Friedrich Heller. Österreichische Komponisten des XX. Jahrhunderts, 14. Wien: Elisabeth Lafite/Österreichische Bundesverlag, 1968. 70 pp.
Short but pointed study of Mahler primarily concerned with analysis of his individual works but briefly sketching the course of his life and his place in the Austria of his time. Suffers from heavy verbal description with serious lack of musical illustration.

800. Kühn, Hellmut und Georg Quander, hrsg. *Gustav Mahler: ein Lesebuch mit Bildern. Ein Buch der Berliner Festwochen.* Zürich: Orell Fussli, 1982. 192 pp.
Published in connection with the almost-complete cycle of Mahler's works in the 1982 Berlin Festival. Amounts to an educated layman's coverage of Mahler's life and works, heavily illustrated, beyond the usual scope of program notes.

801. Mahlers Symphonien. Meisterführer, 10. Einleitung von Edgar Istel. Berlin: Schlesinger'sche Buch- und Musikhandlung (Rob. Lienau); Wien: Carl Haslinger qdm. Tobias, n.d. 183 pp.
Covers the first nine symphonies and Das Lied von der Erde. Essays by Edgar Istel, Ludwig Schiedermair, Hermann Teibler, Karl Weigl and Georg Gräner. The analysis of the Symphony no. 9 is unsigned. Several of these essays are reprinted from previous publications. Vondenhoff cites a date of publication of 1910, but this cannot be true in view of the inclusion of essays on the Symphony no. 9 and Das Lied von der Erde. An educated guess would place this compendium between 1912 and 1924 in view of the inclusion of those two works and the omission of the Symphony no. 10.

802. Matthews, Colin. "Mahler at Work: Aspects of the Creative Process." Ph.D. diss., University of Sussex, 1977. 209 pp.
Study of Mahler's compositional modus operandi as exemplified in the symphonies and Das Lied von der Erde, through study of the manuscript sources. Ambitious and not quite successful, aiming at comprehensive coverage of too many sources in one limited work; not without value but less than other theses which concentrate on particular works or aspects of general style.

803. Matthews, Colin. "Mahler at Work: Some Observations on the Ninth and Tenth Symphony Sketches." Soundings [University College, Cardiff], no. 4 (1974): 76-86.
Surveys Mahler's compositional process in the manuscript sources of the last two symphonies. Related to the same author's Ph.D. dissertation (see preceding entry), which was in progress when this article was published.

804. Mengelberg, Curt Rudolf. Mahler feestboek (6-21 Mei 1920): t.g. v[an] het 25jarig jubileum v[an] W[illem] Mengelberg als dirigent v[an] h[et] Concertgebouw te Amsterdam. Amsterdam: [Concertgebouw], 1920. 232 pp
Incorporates discussions of the first nine symphonies, Lieder eines fahrenden Gesellen, Kindertotenlieder, Rückert Lieder, Das Lied von der Erde and Das klagende Lied, all of which were performed in the Mahler cycle

conducted by Willem Mengelberg in 1920. More than an ordinary book of program notes, this is a major discussion of the majority of Mahler's works, and apparently the first in the Dutch language. Also includes exhaustive chronologies of all performances of Mahler works conducted by Mengelberg up to the time of this cycle, and profiles of Mengelberg himself and the soloists in the vocal works. Written by Mengelberg's nephew, who was deeply involved with the planning of the cycle and also edited a German symposium compiled at the same time as the program book (cited above as no. 11).

805. Monnikendam, Marius. *50 meesterwerken der muziek*. Den Haag: H.G. Dieben, 1956-61. 3 vols. Includes the following essays analyzing individual works: in vol. 1, "Mahler's 3e Symphonie" (pp. 80-82), "Mahler's 4e Symphonie" (pp. 82-84), and "Mahler's *Das Lied von der Erde*" (pp. 84-86); in vol. 2, "Mahler's *Des Knaben Wunderhorn*" (pp. 45-46), and "Mahler's 9e Symphonie" (pp. 47-48); in vol. 3, "Mahler's 3e Symphonie" (pp. 36-39), and "Mahler's 4e Symphonie" (pp. 39-41). All in Dutch, brief as individual components, but collectively a major achievement. No explanation for two analyses of the *Symphony no. 4*.

806. Murphy, Edward W. "Sonata-Rondo Form in the Symphonies of Gustav Mahler." *Music Review* 36 (1975): 54-62. Survey of the first nine symphonies, the *Adagio* and *Purgatorio* of the *Symphony no. 10*, and *Das Lied von der Erde* for Mahler's use of the classical "sonata-rondo" hybrid form, especially in the opening movements.

807. Nodnagel, Ernst Otto. *Jenseits von Wagner und Liszt: Profile und Perspektiven*. Königsberg in Pr.: Ostpreussischen Druckerei und Verlagsanstalt, 1902. x, 192 pp. Comprises ten essays on musical/literary subjects focusing on composers of the late nineteenth and early twentieth centuries. The essay "Gustav Mahler" (pp. 3-19) outlines Mahler's work as conductor and composer to the turn of the century and surveys the first three symphonies, the *Lieder und Gesänge* and the *Lieder eines fahrenden Gesellen*. "Gustav Mahler's 'Vierte'" (pp. 185-92) is an addendum at the end of the book, a delightful analysis of the *Symphony no. 4* with a brief

reference at the end to *Des Knaben Wunderhorn* and *Das klagende Lied*. Focus of both essays is to place Mahler among his contemporaries, especially Richard Strauss, and Mahler comes off the better of the two in Nodnagel's opinion. This book is the forerunner of Nodnagel's individual analyses of *Symphonies 1-3* and *5-6*, which were published in the years immediately following. Even in this early book he shows appreciation for Mahler's works as *Gesamtkunstwerke* in their special ways.

808. Ratz, Erwin. "Gustav Mahler." *Musikrevy* 16 (1961): 254-57.
    Brief study in Swedish (presumably translated from German original) summarizing Mahler's works in chronological order and commenting briefly on each. Limited by author's prejudice against *Symphony no. 10* which is mentioned virtually without comment.

809. Ratz, Erwin. *Gustav Mahler: Vortrag gehalten anlässlich einer Schallplattenaufführung der V. Symphonie in der Akademie fur Musik und darstellende Kunst, Wien, am 15. November 1954*. Wien: Internationale Gesellschaft für Neue Musik, [1955]. 20 pp.
    This is a typewritten transcript of a lecture given by Professor Ratz in the year before the IGMG was established. The first part of the lecture deals with Mahler's life and his place in the music of his era. Author then turns to discussion of Mahler's works through the *Symphony no. 4*, with their personal and literary associations and their effect on the work of composers who followed. As the lecture was a prelude to the performance of the *Symphony no. 5* in the class setting, author then presents an overview of that work with examples of the previous four symphonies and some of the vocal works, then concludes with a broad introduction to the *Symphony no. 5* in terms of form and melody. The Dutch literature refers to *Gustav Mahler: ein Vortrag* (Wien: Drucksache der IGMG, Sektion Holland, 1956) which may be a later version of this lecture "gehalten im Holland Festival Club."

810. *Ravinia Festival '79 Mahler Cycle*. Highland Park, Illinois: Ravinia Festival, 1979. 53 pp.
    Program notes by Arrand Parsons, Susan M. Filler and Richard Green. Introduction by James Levine. Translations by Lola Rand, Friedel Becker, Peggie Cochrane

and Susan M. Filler. This program book includes analyses of the ten symphonies (including the performing version of the Symphony no. 10 by Deryck Cooke) and Das Lied von der Erde, all of which were performed in the cycle.

811. Redlich, Hans F. "Gustav Mahler's Last Symphonic Trilogy." Hans Albrecht in Memoriam: Gedenkschrift mit Beiträgen von Freunden und Schülern. Hrsg. von Wilfried Brennecke und Hans Hasse. Kassel, New York: Bärenreiter, 1962, pp. 246-50.
Brief study of Das Lied von der Erde, Symphony no. 9 and the first and third movements of the Symphony no. 10. Suffers from cavalier treatment of the internal movements of the Symphony no. 9 and really does not do justice to the Symphony no. 10; although discussion benefits from knowledge of the facsimile of the manuscript published in 1924, there is no consideration of the work as a five-movement conception, despite the fact that this essay dates from a time when Redlich should have known of the work of Deryck Cooke, even if he had not seen or heard it.

812. Redlich, Hans Ferdinand. "La 'trilogia della morte' di Mahler." Rassegna musicale 28 (1958): 177-86.
Surveys the "death trilogy" of Das Lied von der Erde and the last two symphonies. Slightly better than the author's discussion in "Gustav Mahler's Last Symphonic Trilogy" (see preceding entry) in that the works are treated somewhat more as a group with common characteristics of style than as one work and another which hardly helped arguments in favor of the Symphony no. 10.

* Redlich, Hans Ferdinand. "Die Welt der V., VI. & VII. Symphonie." Musikblätter des Anbruch 2 (1920): 265-68.
Full citation under no. 16 above. Considers the three middle symphonies as a trilogy in terms of conceptual basis, philosophy and formal construction. One of the author's earliest essays in Mahler literature, following closely on Gustav Mahler: eine Erkenntnis (see no. 642 above) in time span and viewpoint, and showing already his penchant for controversial subjects, since the works discussed in this article were probably the least understood of all at the time of writing.

813. Revers, Peter. *Gustav Mahler: Untersuchungen zu den späten Sinfonien.* Salzburger Beiträge zur Musikwissenschaft, 18. Hamburg: Karl Dieter Wagner, 1985. 193 pp.
Originally the author's Ph.D. dissertation, "Die Liquidation der musikalischen Struktur in den späten Symphonien Gustav Mahler" (Universität Salzburg, 1980, 270 pp.). Considers the formal concepts of Mahler and his predecessors and shows how they apply in the cases of *Das Lied von der Erde, Symphony no. 9* and the first movement of the *Symphony no. 10.*

814. Richolson-Sollitt, Edna. "Over Mahler." *Mengelberg spreekt.* De Muziek, Deel 5. Den Haag ('s-Gravenhage): J. Philip Kruseman, [1936], pp. 30-54.
This Dutch essay on Mahler is based on two articles in *Musical Courier*, vol. 108 (Part I, January 6, 1934, p. 6, and Part II, January 13, 1934, p. 6, both entitled "Annotations on the Symphonies of Mahler"). The first section includes sections on "The Picturesque First," "Mengelberg Translates the Second," "Becoming a Perfect Mahlerite," "The Interpretations by the Composer," "Cullings from 'Knaben Wunderhorn'," "Absolute v. Pictorial Interpretation" and "Third a Relative Rarity." The second section comprises "Parody or Idyll?" "A Romantic Adagietto," "Problems of Heavenly Length," "The Sixth and Seventh Symphonies," "The Monumental Eighth," "Titanic Task of Rehearsal" and "Mahler's 'Birth Pangs' of Composition." The two-part discussion offers a rather uneven traversal of the first nine symphonies in chronological order, giving special weight to the first three and the *Symphony no. 8* and less to the others, especially *Symphonies 6-7* and *9*. The last symphony is barely discussed at all. While not uniformly positive in its critical assessments or wholly accurate in factual detail in light of later discoveries and changing critical orientation, this discussion performs an important service in the Netherlands and the United States: it gives information to the general public about repertoire seldom heard at that time and represents the prevailing historiographical view of Mahler through the eyes of his colleague Mengelberg as reported by the author.

815. Rusk, J. Wayne, III. "Thematic Structure and Contrapuntal Technique in the Symphonies V-X of Gustav Mahler." Ph.D. diss., Indiana University.

Not available for examination. Cited by Adkins in *Doctoral Dissertations in Musicology* (Fifth Edition, 1971) as "in progress" as of that date.

816. Schibler, Armin. *Zum Werk Gustav Mahlers.* Lindau: C.F. Kahnt, 1955. 16 pp.
Brief but concentrated introduction to Mahler's *oeuvre* in both vocal and symphonic forms, for professionals, not laymen; musicological rather than biographical. A single section, "Das Liedelement in der Sinfonik Mahlers" (pp. 6-7) was translated into French as "L'element mélodique dans les symphonies de Mahler" and published in *Feuilles Musicales* 1959 (full citation above as no. 6) on pp. 125-26.

817. Schiedermair, Ludwig. "Gustav Mahler." [Tonsetzer der Gegenwart, 8.] *NZfM* 101 (1905): 421-25.
Differs from Schiedermair's other writings in being entirely devoted to a survey of Mahler's works as of the date of the article, with special attention to the first five symphonies. Considers Mahler as composer in the context of nineteenth century composition in general. Essentially the first attempt to place Mahler in the symphonic tradition of his time. Reprinted in *Monographien moderner Musiker: kleine Essays über Leben und Schaffen zeitgenössischer Tonsetzer*, vol. 1 (Leipzig: C.F. Kahnt, 1906, pp. 82-94). Based though it is on the first half only of Mahler's works, it is far-reaching on the basis of an ongoing assessment of Mahler's works still valuable today.

818. Schiedermair, Ludwig. "Gustav Mahler als Symphoniker." *Die Musik* 1 (1901-02): 506-10, 603-08, 696-99.
Farsighted serialized study of Mahler's first three symphonies in his own time by a critic who bucked public pressure, declaring that these unpopular works should be heard as the beginning of the musical wave of the future. First assessment later developed in 1905-06 (see preceding entry).

819. Schmitt, Theodor. *Der langsame Symphoniesatz Gustav Mahlers: historisch-vergleichende Studien zu Mahlers Kompositionstechnik.* Studien zur Musik, 3. Hrsg. von Rudolf Bockholdt. München: Wilhelm Fink, 1983. 205 pp. ISBN 3-7705-2078-5.
Originally author's Ph.D. dissertation, "Der langsame

Satz in der spätromantischen Wiener Symphonik besonders bei Mahler und Bruckner" (Musikwissenschaftliches Seminar der Ludwig-Maximilian-Universität München, 1981). Study of the theme and variation form in Mahler's slow movements with special attention to *Symphonies 2-4, 6, 9* and *10*.

820. Seidl, Arthur. "Gustav Mahler: Zweite und vierte Symphonie." *Neuzeitliche Tondichter und zeitgenössische Tonkünstler: Gesammelte Aufsätze, Studien und Skizzen*. Deutsche Musikbücherei, 18/19. Regensburg: Gustav Bosse, 1926, vol. I, pp. 287-99. Early analyses of the *Symphony no. 2* and *Symphony no. 4* by a musicologist and critic who had been a friend of Mahler and had written a short biography of him concentrating on both the composer and the conductor (see no. 403 above). Difficult to locate this item today as the publisher's later pro-Nazi policy resulted in political destruction and war damage.

821. Sharp, Geoffrey. "Gustav Mahler." *The Symphony*. Ed. by Ralph Hill. Harmondsworth, Middlesex: Penguin Books, 1956, pp. 297-312. Originally published by Pelican Books in 1949. Concentrates primarily on the *Symphony no. 4* and *Symphony no. 9* as representative Mahler works in the repertoire most likely to be heard by the average concertgoer.

822. Shlifshtein, Natalva. "O nektor'iy osobennost'iyakh 'simfoniy finalov' Malera." [On some peculiarities of the symphonic finales of Mahler.] *Sovetskaya muzyka* 37 (September 1973): 94-99. Discussion focuses on the first two symphonies, the *Symphony no. 6* and *Das Lied von der Erde* with special reference to the roles of the final movements in the concept of thematic unity in the works as whole entities.

822a. Sine, Nadine. "The Evolution of Symphonic Worlds: Tonality in the Symphonies of Gustav Mahler with Emphasis on the First, Third and Fifth." Ph.D. thesis, New York University, 1983. xii, 294 pp. Not available for examination as of the present date of this book.

823. Sorabji, Kaikhosru [Leon Dudley]. "Notes on the Symphonies of Mahler." *Around Music*. London: Unicorn

Press, 1932, pp. 178-93.
An unusually sympathetic study of the first nine symphonies and *Das Lied von der Erde* by a British critic and composer, written at a time when British critics in general did not understand or appreciate Mahler's music. Inaccurate in some small details but otherwise excellent.

824. Sponheuer, Bernd. *Logik des Zerfalls: Untersuchungen zum Finalproblem in der Symphonien Gustav Mahlers.* Tutzing: Hans Schneider, 1978. 500 pp. ISBN 3-7952-0218-3.
Originally author's Ph.D. dissertation (Universität Kiel) according to listing in Adkins/Dickinson (*Acta Musicologica* 1981). Study of the problems of form in Mahler's final movements, especially the first seven symphonies and the *Symphony no. 9*.

825. Stefan, Paul. *Mahler für Jedermann.* Die Wiedergabe, 2. Reihe, Bd. 7. Wien, Leipzig: Wila, 1923. 54 pp.
Shorter and less widely known than Stefan's other writings on Mahler, but remarkably detailed introduction to Mahler's works for length. General introduction by a sympathetic friend attempting to reach the potential public audience.

826. Swarowsky, Hans. *Wahrung der Gestalt.* Wien: Universal Edition, 1979. 303 pp.
Includes two essays: "Mahler: *Das Lied von der Erde*" (pp. 121-34) and "Mahler: *VII. Symphonie*" (pp. 135-59). This is a conductor's view of the two works, a discussion of balancing and phrase as components of a whole seen through overview.

827. Swift, Richard. "Mahler's Ninth and Cooke's Tenth." *19th C Mus* 2 (1978): 165-72.
Compares the "completed" *Symphony no. 9* with the "unfinished" *Symphony no. 10*, critical of the concept of a performing version of the latter; disguised as a review of the facsimile of the first three movements of the *Symphony no. 9* (see no. 991 below) and the score of Deryck Cooke's performing version of the *Symphony no. 10* (see no. 1017 below). Simplistic, often misinterpreting the concepts adopted by Cooke. Biased against the concept of a performing version, but gives little information on the actual quality of the scores which should have been present in a real review.

828. Timoshenkova, Galina Andreevna. "Pozdneye tvorchestvo Gustava Malera." [Late works of Gustav Mahler.] Ph.D. diss., Leningrad Institute of Theater, Music and Cinematography, 1977. 186 pp.
Study of *Das Lied von der Erde, Symphony no. 9* and the first movement only of the *Symphony no. 10*, musically and philosophically, drawing connections between the styles of Mahler and Shostakovich.

829. Timoshenkova, G[alina Andreevna]. "Stroficheskaya variantnaya forma u Malera." [Stanzaic variation form of Mahler.] *Sovetskaya muzyka* 36 (June 1972): 86-89.
Shows Mahler's modifications in strophic form with special reference to *Das Lied von der Erde*, particularly its first movement. Secondary discussion of the first movements in the last two symphonies. Illustrated with diagrammatic and musical examples. Considers the works themselves on own merit rather than in historical context.

830. Truscott, Harold. "Gustav Mahler (1860-1911)." *The Symphony*. Ed. by Robert Simpson. Baltimore: Penguin Books, 1967, vol. 2, pp. 29-51.
An introductory study of Mahler the composer in terms of his significance as a symphonist. Primarily valuable for its study of the *Symphony no. 6* as selected example for analysis in depth illustrating author's theories.

831. Truscott, Harold. "Some Aspects of Mahler's Tonality." *Monthly Musical Record* 87 (1957): 203-08.
Considers Mahler as tonal innovator in the symphonies. Interesting comparison with same author's chapter on Mahler in *The Symphony* (see preceding entry), taken in tandem with discussion of the *Symphony no. 6*.

832. Vestdijk, Simon. *Gustav Mahler: over de structuur van zijn symfonisch oeuvre*. Den Haag: Bert Bakker /Damen, 1960. 160 pp.
Major Dutch study of the first nine symphonies and *Das Lied von der Erde*. Surveys each work individually from historical, literary-programmatic and psychological viewpoints, considering overall movement balances more than key and thematic structure. No musical examples, which somewhat limits overall effect of book.

833. Wellesz, Egon. "The Symphonies of Gustav Mahler." *Music Review* 1 (1940): 2-23.
An early study of the first nine symphonies, considering form, orchestration and melodic-contrapuntal textures. Qualifies as a sympathetic appraisal by an insider, as Wellesz by that time was already experienced in writing about Mahler's style (see nos. 1, 748 and 749 above for examples) and was an insider to the Schoenberg circle, having known Mahler personally also.

834. Wessem, Constant von. *Gustav Mahler en zijn kunst: over de 8ste symphonie en "Das Lied von der Erde."* Amsterdam: Voorh. Harms Tiepen, 1913. 28 pp.
Earliest known Dutch book exclusively devoted to Mahler, emphasizing analyses of the *Symphony no. 8* and *Das Lied von der Erde*, an unusual pairing. Wessem went on to write of Mahler in three other books and one article in *Caecilia*; in one way or another, the other writings all stemmed from this brief book.

835. Williamson, John. "Liszt, Mahler and the Chorale." *RMA Proceedings* 108 (1981/82): 115-25.
Compares and contrasts Liszt and Mahler through their conceptions of the function of the chorale in concert music. Special attention to Liszt's oratorio *Die Legende von der heiligen Elisabeth* and Mahler's *Symphonies 1, 2, 5* and *8*.

836. Wörner, Karl Heinrich. *Das Zeitalter der thematischen Prozesse in der Geschichte der Musik.* Studien zur Musikgeschichte des 19. Jahrhunderts, 18. Regensburg: Gustav Bosse, 1969. xxix, 291 pp. ISBN 3-7649-2032-7.
This book includes two essays, "Mahlers Auferstehungssinfonie" (pp. 42-50) and "Mahlers Neunte" (pp. 53-57). The two thematic analyses are made against a context of the history of music from the Baroque period to Stravinsky and the Second Viennese School. Besides these essays, Mahler's name is frequently cited in essays on other composers, showing the organized way author views historical stylistic development. Frequent citations of other sources allow for extended study of subject.

Songs

837. Abendroth, Walter. "Das Geheimnis der Gesangmelodie bei Mahler." *Allgemeine Musikzeitung* 55 (1928): 163-65.
Author's personal journey through the land of Mahler song stylistics, referring particularly to the inspiration of text in the *Kindertotenlieder* and *Das Lied von der Erde* and, to a lesser extent, *Des Knaben Wunderhorn* and the *Lieder eines fahrenden Gesellen*. Melodic facet especially emphasized in the length of line ("unendliche Fortsetzung").

838. Agawu, V[ictor] Kofi. "Mahler's Tonal Strategies: a Study of the Song Cycles." *Journal of Musicological Research* 6 (1986): 1-47.
Study of Mahler's compositional techniques in *Lieder eines fahrenden Gesellen, Kindertotenlieder* and *Das Lied von der Erde* in terms of key structure, harmony and form, as they evolved over the course of his compositional career. Special reference to the first movement of *Das Lied von der Erde* in terms of form. Schenkerian analyses, especially with reference to key balances, harmony and voice leading.

839. Bie, Oskar. "Mahler." *Das deutsche Lied*. Berlin: S. Fischer, 1926, pp. 251-56.
Considers Mahler as lyricist in context of history of the German song from the eighteenth century to the Second Viennese School. Views Mahler's vocal works as dramatic entities joining poetry with symphonic vision of medium, almost like *scenas*.

840. Bruner, Ellen Carole. "The Relationship of Text and Music in the Lieder of Hugo Wolf and Gustav Mahler." Ph.D. diss., Syracuse University, 1974. 389 pp.
Considers the two composers separately and comparatively in their status in the history of the German song, especially with reference to poetical sources, harmony, tonality and form.

841. Danuser, Hermann. "Der Orchestergesang des Fin de siècle: eine historische und ästhetische Skizze." *Mf* 30 (1977): 425-51.
Surveys the solo song with orchestra from Berlioz, Mahler, Strauss, Schoenberg and Delius, with side-

Collective Analyses: Songs

lights on Sibelius, Wolf, Pfitzner and Zemlinsky.

842. Dargie, Elisabeth Mary. *Music and Poetry in the Songs of Gustav Mahler.* European University Studies, Series I (German Language and Literature, 401). Berne: Peter Lang, 1981. 349 pp.
Originally the author's Ph.D. dissertation, University of Aberdeen, 1979 (547 pp.). Study of the relationship of music and text in Mahler's songs with particular emphasis on *Lieder eines fahrenden Gesellen, Des Knaben Wunderhorn* and the Rückert settings. Traces the "folk-song heritage" and classifies the songs according to mood and subject in the tradition of the nineteenth century German song.

843. Duse, Ugo. "Studio sulla poetica liederistica di Gustav Mahler." *Classe di scienze morali e lettere* 119 (1960-61): 75-124.
Published in Venice by the Istituto Veneto di Scienze, Lettere ed Arte. Early Italian study of the literary influences on Mahler's vocal work, surprisingly detailed and extensive, probably influenced by earlier German studies.

844. Fischer, Kurt von. "Bemerkungen zu Gustav Mahlers Liedern." *Musikoloski zbornik* 13 (1977): 57-66.
Originally published as "Zu Gustav Mahlers Liedern" in *Neue Zürcher Zeitung*, 5./6. Juli 1975, and reprinted in *Musik und Bildung* 9 (1977): 400-02. In its original form this article discusses Mahler as lyricist in the context of the history of the German song, particularly comparing and contrasting his work with that of Schubert in musicological and literary terms. The extended version in *Musikoloski zbornik* raises a radical idea: not only does it consider Mahler's small-scale lyrical works (especially *Des Knaben Wunderhorn* settings) as the germ-seeds for the symphonies, but suggests that the songs are also the "goal" (summation?) of the symphonies. This is partially an extension of the idea of synthesis of song and symphony proposed by Engel, but it is new in its idea of song as capsule symphonic form in its own right.

* Göhler, Georg. "Gustav Mahler Lieder." *Die Musik* 10 (1911): 357-63.
Full citation under no. 15 above. Surveys Mahler's songs, complementary in some ways to the analyses of

the symphonies published primarily by Specht.

845. Günther, Siegfried. "Der Lyriker Gustav Mahler." *Die Laute* 5 (1. Januar 1922): 35-38.
This article, together with the subsequent three-part article "Zur Tonsprache der Mahler'schen Lyrik" in the same journal (vols. 5-6) comprises a serialized study of Mahler's songs. While not as comprehensive as the contemporary study by Pamer (see no. 853 below), it is wide-ranging and deserving of study. The three-part article includes "Melodik und Kontrapuntik" (1. April 1922, pp. 55-59), "Orchesterbesetzung und Instrumentation" (1. April 1923, pp. 52-56) and a middle section which has not been located by this author or described in the Mahler literature.

846. Günther, Siegfried. "Form und Wesen des Mahlerschen Liedes: Orchester- und Kammerlied." *NZfM* 88 (1921): 2-5.
An early assessment of Mahler as composer of songs, in the context of the history of solo song in the nineteenth century. Few specific citations of individual works, general overview instead; presumably forerunner study of the same author's multipartite treatment in *Die Laute* (see preceding entry).

847. Hoffmann, Rudolf Stefan. "Mahlers Lied." *Musikwelt* 1 (1921): 164-66.
Early study of Mahler's songs, antedating Fritz Egon Pamer's dissertation on the same subject and treatment by Siegfried Günther. Author, a physician who had studied composition with Zemlinsky and was involved from 1904 with the Vereinigung Schaffender Tonkünstler in Wien, followed this article shortly after with "Unbekannte Jugendlieder Mahlers" (*Musikwelt* 2, 1921/1922), which was also published in *Neues Wiener Journal* (21. Dezember 1921): 3-4. The two articles together comprise an introduction to Mahler's songs followed by a rare glimpse (for that time) of Mahler's three songs dedicated to Josephine Poisl.

848. Kravitt, Edward F. "The Orchestral Lied: an Inquiry into its Style and Unexpected Flowering Around 1900." *Music Review* 37 (1976): 209-26.
Surveys the growth of the solo song with orchestra and its manifold facets in the works of Wolf, Mahler, Strauss, Pfitzner and Reger. Contrasts the attitudes

and mechanisms of each of the composers with those of the others, vis-à-vis the composition of songs with orchestra versus songs with piano, and shows the changes in societal attitudes to the role of solo song influenced by these men and their works.

849. Kravitt, Edward F. "Tempo as an Expressive Element in the Late Romantic Lied." *MQ* 59 (1973): 497-518. Discusses the methods by which late Romantic composers used tempo modification as a dramatic element in their songs, with particular reference to Brahms, Liszt, Wolf and Mahler. Discussion of Mahler focuses especially on *Urlicht*.

850. Kravitt, Edward F. "The Trend Toward the Folklike, Nationalism and Their Expression by Mahler and His Contemporaries in the Lied." *CD* 2 (1963): 40-56. Discusses the movement in German nationalism in the nineteenth century as expressed in the anthology of *Des Knaben Wunderhorn*, and the effect of the anthology on many composers, of whom Mahler was only one, in terms of their musical styles as a simplifying "folklike" element. Points out that Mahler was not entirely unique in his extensive use of the anthology and that his great reliance on it was criticized by some contemporaries who suggested that his compositional style was not "German" enough to suit the style of the texts.

851. Mylemans, P. *De Orkestliederen van Gustav Mahler*. Antwerpen: De Nederlandsche Bockhandel, 1964. 38 pp.
Brief study in Dutch of Mahler's songs with orchestra.

852. Oehlmann, Werner. "Gustav Mahler." *Reclams Liedführer*. Universal-Bibliothek, 19215. Stuttgart: Philipp Reclam Jun., 1973, pp. 626-44. ISBN 3-15-010215-4.
Brief individual discussions of Mahler's songs from *Lieder und Gesänge* to the Rückert settings. Emphasizes the contrast between the fantastical world of the earlier songs based on Romantic ideals and sources including *Des Knaben Wunderhorn* and the realism of the poems by Rückert. Briefly considers formal-melodic-rhythmic character of many individual songs.

853. Pamer, Fritz Egon. "Gustav Mahlers Lieder." *Studien zur Musikwissenschaft* 16 (1929): 116-38, and 17 (1930): 105-27.

Originally the author's Ph.D. dissertation, "Gustav Mahlers Lieder: eine stilkritische Studie" (Universität Wien, 1922, 225 pp.). A valuable early source discussing Mahler's individual songs, song cycles and vocal movements in the *Symphonies 2-4*. Probing and comprehensive, this dissertation considers the songs in terms of melody, form, orchestration and poetic derivation. This reference, while since superseded in certain details of chronology in Mahler's life, has been influential in many subsequent studies of Mahler's songs and remains a model of its genre even today.

854. Roman, Zoltan. "Mahler's Songs and Their Influence on His Symphonic Thought." Ph.D. diss., University of Toronto, 1970. 2 vols.
Major far-reaching study of the songs, on their own merits and as germ cells for organization of the symphonies. Concerned not only with usual questions of thematic cross-fertilization from song to symphony but with large-scale organizational methods. Indispensible.

855. Roman, Zoltan. "Structure as a Factor in the Genesis of Mahler's Songs." *Music Review* 35 (1974): 157-66.
Surveys Mahler's songs from the point of view of form (strophic, bar-form, arch form, rondo, theme-and-variations, through-composed), showing that Mahler leaned heavily toward the theme-and-variations form as an almost ideal method of pairing music and text as equal partners. Refreshing compared to the usual discussions of the songs as literary subjects, and essentially unique in the literature about the songs; unorthodox viewpoint which works very well indeed.

856. Schering, Arnold. "Gustav Mahler als Liederkomponist." *NZfM* 72 (1905): 672-73, 691-93, 753-55.
Rare assessment of Mahler's songs at the time they were quite new, by a musicologist not generally known for concentration on works of Mahler in particular. This series of three articles gives special attention to the Rückert settings which had just been published; however, Schering discusses the songs in the context of the history of the orchestral song as a manifestation of influence from Wagner's theory of poetic interpretation by orchestral setting. Curious theory of Schering that these Mahler settings be considered as arias controversial at best, but his support of the

quality of the songs themselves is very unusual from German musical historians of that time.

* Werba, Erik. "Ein 'Mahler'-Brief." *OeMz* 15 (1960): 292-94.
  Full citation under no. 18 above. Discusses Mahler's songs and their originality in the context of the German song repertoire, from the point of view of an important pianist specializing in the accompaniment of such repertoire. Addressed to a mezzo-soprano not named.

Lieder eines fahrenden Gesellen

857. Blaukopf, Herta. "When did Mahler Write the 'Wayfarer's' Songs? Contribution to a Discussion." *NaMR*, no. 12 (October 1983): 3-6.
   Picks up discussion of the chronology of the piano and the orchestral versions of the cycle where Zoltan Roman and Donald Mitchell left off, and strongly suggests that Mahler composed the piano version in 1884-85 but did not orchestrate the cycle until early 1892. Date of orchestral version based on consideration of a letter Mahler wrote to Laura Hilgermann in 1982.

858. Mahler, Gustav. *Lieder eines fahrenden Gesellen*. Ed. by Hans Redlich. London, New York: Ernst Eulenberg, 1959. Introduction by Hans Redlich, pp. iii-ix.
   History and analysis of the cycle, explaining in detail the conflicts between the orchestral and piano versions.

859. Mahler, Gustav. *Lieder eines fahrenden Gesellen*. London: Josef Weinberger, Ltd., 1977. Introduction by Donald Mitchell and editorial note by Colin Matthews, both translated by Stefan de Haan, pp. iii-x.
   Primarily a justification of the piano version of the cycle as a work in its own right rather than a preliminary to the orchestral version. Traces the editors' theory of the chronology of the cycle between 1883 and 1896, independently of theories proposed by other scholars.

860. Mahler, Gustav. *Lieder eines fahrenden Gesellen.*
Kritische Gesamtausgabe, 13 (Teilband 1), 14 (Teilband 1). Wien, Frankfurt am Main, London: Josef Weinberger, 1982. Revisionsbericht und Anmerkung des Herausgebers von Zoltan Roman, pp. v-xxi. Exhaustively surveys the source materials, chronology and content of the texts and music. Accounts for discrepancies between the piano and orchestral versions of the work, and considers critical ambiguities in both versions on a bar-by-bar basis.

861. Riehn, Rainer. "Über Mahlers *Lieder eines fahrenden Gesellen* und *Das Lied von der Erde* in Arnold Schönbergs Kammerfassungen." *Schönbergs Verein für musikalische Privataufführungen.* Musik-Konzepte 36 (März 1984): 8-30.
An important study on an obscure subject, i.e. Schoenberg's chamber versions of *Lieder eines fahrenden Gesellen* and *Das Lied von der Erde*, giving the history behind Schoenberg's decision to make the arrangements and comparing Schoenberg's reduced scoring with the originals by Mahler himself. Quotes extensively from documentation in the Schoenberg archive in Los Angeles.

* Ringger, Rolf Urs. "Mahlers 'Lieder eines fahrenden Gesellen.'" *Musica* 1960: 362-63.
Full citation under no. 14 above. Briefly surveys the formal structure of the cycle, somewhat weakened because the discussion includes no musical examples.

862. Wältner, Ernst Ludwig. "Lieder-Zyklus und Volkslied-Metamorphose: zu den Texten der Mahler'schen Gesellenlieder." *Jahrbuch des Staatlichen Instituts für Musikforschung Preussischer Kulturbesitz 1977.* Berlin: Merseburger, 1978, pp. 61-95. ISBN 3-87537-165-8.
Exhaustive textual-thematic study of Mahler's *modus operandi* in setting of the lied with special emphasis on *Lieder eines fahrenden Gesellen*, particularly the first two songs. Musical discussion includes study of melodic, harmonic and orchestral features of Mahler's style.

Des Knaben Wunderhorn

863. Mikheeva, Lyudmila. "Chudesn'iy rog mal'chiska." [*Des Knaben Wunderhorn*.] *Sovetskaya muzyka* 24 (July 1960): 83-87.
Early Russian study of Mahler's Wunderhorn settings.

864. Rexroth, Dieter. "Zu Gustav Mahlers 'Wunderhorn'-Lieder." *Heinrich Sievers zum 70. Geburtstag.* Hrsg. von Günter Katzenberger in Verbindung mit Richard Jakoby. Tutzing: Hans Schneider, 1978, pp. 139-54.
Primarily concerned with Mahler's place in the history of the German song as a musico-literary art form, as exemplified in his *Wunderhorn* settings, this essay had been presaged by more general ones including "Über einige Text-Musik-Strukturen in Mahlers Liedern" (*Tagung Frankfurt/Main* 9./10. Juli 1971), as well as a lecture on Hessische Rundfunk, "Das Kunstlied in Romantik und Gegenwart: zum Liedschaffen Gustav Mahlers" which Rexroth gave on December 3, 1975. While the present essay is more specialized than Rexroth's previous contributions in subject matter, it continues the premise of the thread of the song as art form in the Romantic tradition.

Rückert settings

865. Gerlach, Reinhard. "Mahler, Rückert und das Ende des Liedes: Essay über lyrisch-musikalische Form." *Jahrbuch des Staatlichen Instituts für Musikforschung Preussischer Kulturbesitz 1975*. Berlin: Merseburger, 1976, pp. 7-45. ISBN 3-87537-142-9.
Considers Rückert as poetic influence on nineteenth century composers and explores Mahler's settings of Rückert's poetry. Shows importance of Mahler's songs in context of the history of nineteenth century textual setting and in Mahler's own career as lyricist and symphonist. This essay is the germ seed for same author's full-length book cited in next entry.

866. Gerlach, Reinhard. *Strophen von Leben, Traum und Tod: ein Essay über Rückert-Lieder von Gustav Mahler.* Taschenbücher zur Musikwissenschaft, 83. Wilhelmshaven: Heinrichshofen, 1983. 129 pp. ISBN 3-7959-0356-4.

Full-fledged book expanded from same author's essay of 1975 (see preceding entry). Study of the Rückert settings of Mahler as philosophical, formal and emotional entities. Emphasizes text somewhat over music in source documentation.

867. Grant, [William] Parks. "Mahler: Kindertotenlieder." *CD* 2 (1960): 62-72.
Detailed analytical study of the history, music and text of the cycle placing it in the perspective of Mahler's middle period stylistically.

868. Hansen-Appel, Gabriele. "Gustav Mahlers Kindertotenlieder: Quellenstudien und Interpretationen." Ph.D. diss., Universität Saarbrucken, 1973.
Not available for examination. Cited by Vondenhoff (1978 and 1983), Namenwirth, and Adkins and Dickinson in *Acta Musicologica* (1978).

869. Mahler, Gustav. *Kindertotenlieder*. Ed. by Hans Redlich. Zürich, London, Mainz: Ernst Eulenberg, 1961. Introduction by Hans Redlich, pp. iii-v.
Brief history and analysis of the cycle, concentrating on the orchestral version.

870. Mahler, Gustav. *Kindertotenlieder*. Kritische Gesamtausgabe, 13 (Teilband 3), 14 (Teilband 3). [Lindau]: C.F. Kahnt, 1979. Vorwort, Revisionsbericht und Anmerkung des Herausgebers von Zoltan Roman, pp. iv-xix.
Critically surveys the text of the cycle, considering the date of composition, the evolution of the manuscript and published sources during Mahler's lifetime, and the problems posed to the editor of the Critical Edition.

INDIVIDUAL ANALYSES

Das klagende Lied

871. Diether, Jack. "Mahler's *Klagende Lied*--Genesis and Evolution." *Music Review* 29 (1968): 268-87.
Traces the composition of the work from the time Mahler wrote the text (with reference to other texts and music

Individual Analyses: Das klagende Lied 251

he was writing at the same period) to the deletion of Part I (*Waldmärchen*) and the final revisions of the orchestration in the remaining two sections.

872. Fiske, Richard Allen. "Mahler's *Das klagende Lied*: A Conductor's Analysis of the Original Tripartite Manuscript and Its Bipartite Revisions." D.M.A. Project, Conducting, Indiana University, 1983. xiv, 265 pp.
    Study of scoring, tempi and dynamic contrasts in the various versions of *Das klagende Lied*, including the original unpublished version containing the *Waldmärchen*. Less historical than comparative and technical.

873. Holländer, Hans. "Ein unbekannter Teil von Mahlers 'Klagendem Lied.'" *Auftakt* 14 (1934): 200-02.
    Very early piece pointing out the existence of the *Waldmärchen* which was, however, left essentially unnoticed for another thirty-odd years. Shows that Holländer was insider with rare information but he apparently did not have the means to bring that information to an audience wide enough to have forced the issue of publication of the *Waldmärchen* at the time of the premiere in that year.

874. Mahler, Gustav. *Waldmärchen/A Forest Legend (Das klagende Lied: I)*. Melville, New York: Belwin-Mills, 1973. Foreword by Jack Diether, pp. iv-vii.
    Summarizes the story of the composition of the original 1880 version of *Das klagende Lied*, the deletion of the *Waldmärchen* section, and the rediscovery and restoration. Argues for inclusion of the section as a necessary component of Mahler's full conception. Not a critical textual survey, but a consideration of the reasons for restoration of the section in the light of the nature of the full work as a "torso" in the form generally known until twenty years ago.

875. Mahler, Gustav. *Das klagende Lied*. Kritische Gesamtausgabe, 12. Wien: Universal Edition, 1978. Vorwort und Revisionsbericht [including "Übersicht über die Quellen zur letzten Fassung," "Mahlers letzte Revision," and "Das Gedicht"] von Rudolf Stephan, 11 pp.
    Critical survey of the musical and poetical text of *Das klagende Lied* in the two-part version omitting the *Waldmärchen*, in which it is most often heard. Consid-

ers the various manuscript and published sources without engaging in the question of the relative merits of a two-part vs. a three-part version.

876. Mitchell, Donald. "Mahler's Waldmärchen: the Unpublished First Part of 'Das klagende Lied.'" *MT* 111 (1970): 375-79.
Surveys the long missing *Waldmärchen* section historically and in musical context as an integral part of the cantata.

877. Nolthenius, Helene. "Gustav Mahlers 'Klagende Lied.'" *Mens en melodie* 7 (1952): 311-14.
Comparatively early study of the revised version of *Das klagende Lied* in Dutch, considering Parts II and III only and making no mention of the *Waldmärchen*. Sparse musical substance, concentrating particularly on literary derivations and place of the work in the early compositional career of Mahler, including also the *Gesellen* cycle for perspective; also concerned with the lineage of the work in the Wagnerian influences of the time in which it was written.

* Rosenberg, Wolf. "Die Moritat vom singenden Knochen: Das klagende Lied." *Mahler: eine Herausforderung*: 135-49.
Full citation under no. 20 above. Surveys *Das klagende Lied* as quasi-opera through text and dramatic action.

878. Zenck, Martin. "Mahlers Streichung des 'Waldmärchen' aus dem 'Klagenden Lied': zum Verhältnis von philosophischer Erkenntnis und Interpretation." *AfMw* 38 (1981): 179-93.
Based on author's lecture at the 1979 Mahler Colloquium in Vienna. Critical study of the history of the composition of *Das klagende Lied*, using all available resources including manuscripts and secondary documents, among them Mahler's letters. Demonstrates the importance of the *Waldmärchen* section to the cohesive organization of the whole work and advocates full performance of original version rather than hybridized with latter versions of Parts 2-3.

Das Lied von der Erde

879. Broeckx, Jan L. *Gustav Mahler's Das Lied von der Erde.*
 Musico-literaire verhoudingen. Antwerpen: Uitgeverij Metropolis, 1975. 157 pp.
 Very thorough Dutch study of *Das Lied von der Erde* considering literary background of the texts (with comparison of Bethge with Mahler's changes), musical structure, Mahler's personal and musical background to the work, and limited discography.

880. Brusatti, Otto. "Mahler interpretiert Mahler: zur Interpretation des Lieds von der Erde." *Protokolle: Wiener Halbjahresschrift für Literatur, bildende Kunst und Musik* 77 (1977): 205-18.
 Primarily devoted to one little-known source for *Das Lied von der Erde* (Wiener Stadtbibliothek MH 14260), i.e. Universal Edition proofs of the orchestral score with handwritten annotations by Mahler and Julius Weis-Ostborn, who conducted the Austrian premiere of the work on March 19, 1912 in Graz. Source not used in Critical Edition of the work (see no. 887 below), therefore of special interest to musicologists as a missing link between the *Stichvorlag* and the first edition of 1912.

881. Danuser, Hermann. *Gustav Mahler: Das Lied von der Erde.* Meisterwerke der Musik, 25. München: Wilhelm Fink, 1986. 139 pp.
 Detailed study of *Das Lied von der Erde* surveying literary background, musical and verbal sources (comparing Bethge and Mahler's changes) and musical structure. Extensive bibliography and quotations from sources by Mahler's associates including Bruno Walter who had conducted the premiere.

882. Danuser, Hermann. "Gustav Mahlers Symphonie 'Das Lied von der Erde' als Problem der Gattungsgeschichte." *AfMw* 40 (1983): 276-86.
 Considers *Das Lied von der Erde* as a hybrid in the historical context of alteration of traditional forms during the romantic period, tracing the lines from Berlioz and Liszt through Mahler himself (as symphonist and lyricist) to Schoenberg's *Gurrelieder*.

883. Danuser, Hermann. "Mahlers Lied 'Von der Jugend', ein musikalisches Bild." *Art Nouveau--Jugendstil und*

Musik. Hrsg. aus Anlass des 80. Geburtstages von Willi Schuh von Jürg Stenzl. Freiburg im Breisgau, Zürich: Atlantis, 1980, pp. 151-69.
A detailed study of the third movement of *Das Lied von der Erde* with particular emphasis on Mahler's use of "chinoiserie" in his setting of the text and its connection with the artistic influences of the *Jugendstil* movement in Vienna in the first decade of the century. See also two preceding entries for same author's related publications on this work, especially full book cited under no. 881.

884. Hefling, Stephen E. "Mahler Autograph Re-Discovered: Das Lied von der Erde--A Version for Voice and Piano." *NaMR*, no. 13 (March 1984): 3-4.
Summarizes a paper presented by the author at the 1983 meeting of the American Musicological Society. Notes that the version of *Das Lied von der Erde* stands on its own in many ways, besides providing an important comparative source for the orchestral materials used in the Critical Edition earlier.

885. Kenkel, Konrad O. "Gustav Mahler's *Song of the Earth*: Farewell or Escape?" *Focus on Vienna 1900: Change and Continuity in Literature, Music, Art and Intellectual History.* Houston German Studies, 4. Ed. by Erika Nielsen. München: Wilhelm Fink, 1982, pp. 125-30. ISBN 3-7705-2092-0.
Considers *Das Lied von der Erde* less in terms of the composer's own personal struggle with death than with his view of the decadent society in which he lived, i.e. the personal future vs. the general present. Unusual and fascinating theory.

886. Kralik, Heinrich von. *Gustav Mahler: Das Lied von der Erde. Ein Führer durch das Werk mit Gesangtexten und zahlreichen Notenbeispielen.* Leipzig, Wien, Berlin: Steyrermühl, [1933]. 31 pp.
Early analysis of the text and music of *Das Lied von der Erde* by a writer who, more recently, became known as an authority of the history of the Vienna Philharmonic Orchestra and the Hofoper/Staatsoper. Rare entry in the Mahler literature from its time, when most literature on Mahler was Nazi junk defaming the composer and his works.

887. Mahler, Gustav. *Das Lied von der Erde.* Kritische Ge-

samtausgabe, 9. Wien: Universal Edition, 1964. Revisionsbericht von Erwin Ratz, 3 pp.
A brief survey of the extant sources of *Das Lied von der Erde*, with representative examples of the critical decisions made by the editor. Not sufficiently detailed, useful only as a guide to those who wish to pursue critical studies of the source materials in depth and document their findings in detail.

888. Mitchell, Donald. "Mahler's 'Abschied': a Wrong Note Righted." *MQ* 71 (1985): 200-04.
Development of a point briefly mentioned in *Gustav Mahler: Songs and Symphonies of Life and Death* (see no. 775 above), suggesting that evidence in the manuscript sources of the work points to an error in one pitch in the passage "Ich werde niemals" in the last movement. Urges emendation in performance and future publication.

* Mitchell, Donald. "New light on 'Das Lied von der Erde.'" *Colloque 1985*: 20-30.
Full citation under no. 5 above. Discusses the reasons for re-evaluation of the "Chinese dimension" of *Das Lied von der Erde*, in text and music, and suggests reassessment of certain elements of the music based on study of the manuscript sources.

889. Mulder, Ernest Willem. *Gustav Mahler "Das Lied von der Erde": een critisch-analytische studie*. Amsterdam: Holland Uitgevers Maatschappij, 1951. 78 pp.
Extended Dutch-language analysis of the text and music of *Das Lied von der Erde*.

890. Reeser, Eduard. "Mahler's tekst- en vormbehandeling in 'Das Lied von der Erde.'" *Caecilia en de muziek* 93 (1936): 322-33.
Companion piece with two others by Reeser in the same periodical of that year, although issued in a subsequent month (the commemmorative piece on Mahler's death-anniversary and the analysis of the *Symphony no. 9* cited as no. 240 and no. 993 in this bibliography were in May, while this essay was in June). More extended than either of the others as this analysis is textual as well as thematic, giving the German text of Bethge along with the altered text in the same language by Mahler. Main body of essay except for the textual comparison is in Dutch.

891. Reuter, Evelyn. "Gustav Mahler et 'Le Chant de la Terre.'" *Revue musicale*, no. 212 (Avril 1952): 99-109.
Discusses *Das Lied von der Erde* as a phenomenon in the history of music in the twentieth century, but also looks back to works by Mahler's forebears and his own earlier vocal works. Not entirely accurate in factual material and sorely lacking in musical examples, but does place Mahler in the context of a group of essays covering work of his peers from many countries. (The entire number of this journal is entitled *L'oeuvre du XXe siècle*.)

* Riehn, Rainer. "Über Mahlers *Lieder eines fahrenden Gesellen* und *Das Lied von der Erde* in Arnold Schönbergs Kammerfassungen." *Schönbergs Verein für musikalische Privataufführungen*. Musik-Konzepte 36 (März 1984): 8-30.
Cited above as no. 861.

892. Roman, Zoltan. "Aesthetic Symbiosis and Structural Metaphor in Mahler's *Das Lied von der Erde*." *Festschrift Kurt Blaukopf*. Hrsg. von Irmgard Bontinck und Otto Brusatti. Wien: Universal Edition für Internationales Institut für Musik, Tanz und Theater in der audiovisuellen Medien und Institut für Musiksoziologie, 1975, pp. 110-19. ISBN 3-7024-0113-X.
Considers *Das Lied von der Erde* as an entry in Mahler's evolving concepts of the structuralization of the symphony, with particular emphasis on the concept as compared to the *Symphony no. 3* which author views as the philosophical precursor of *Das Lied von der Erde*. Unusual and even revolutionary pairing of these two works.

893. Rozenshil'd, K[onstantin Konstantinovich]. "'Pesn' o zemle.'" *Sovetskaya muzyka* 37 (March 1973): 77-82.
Russian study of *Das Lied von der Erde*, concentrating on biographical conditions surrounding Mahler's composition of the work and the nature of the work itself. Musical analysis limited, no examples of musical substance or nature of musical organization. See no. 552 above for very different treatment by Zavadskaya five years earlier in same journal.

894. Slonimskiy, Sergey Mikhaylovich. "'Pesn' o zemle': Gustava Malera i voprosy orkestrovoy polifonii."

Individual Analyses: Das Lied von der Erde

[*Das Lied von der Erde*: Gustav Mahler and questions of orchestral polyphony.] *Voprosy sovremennoy muzyki.* [Questions of contemporary music.] Ed. by Mikhail Semenovich Druskin. Leningrad: Gosudarstvennoye Muzikal'noye Izdatel'stvo, 1963, pp. 179-202.
Russian study of *Das Lied von der Erde* as example of Mahler's late style in orchestration contrasting with the "strict" polyphony of the works in the middle period.

895. Specht, Richard. "*Das Lied von der Erde.*" *Merker* 2 (1911): 1169-74.
Written shortly after the world premiere of the work in Munich, this is more than an ordinary review but not as concrete in analytical style as the analysis by Wöss published in 1912 by Universal Edition (see no. 898 below).

896. Tischler, Hans. "Mahler's 'Das Lied von der Erde'." *Music Review* 10 (1949): 111-14.
Brief analysis of *Das Lied von der Erde* concentrating on scoring, formal organization and tonality, thus akin to author's doctoral dissertation (see no. 731 above).

897. Vartanyan, Z. "Pesn' o zemle." *Sovetskaya muzyka* 19 (April 1955): 98-109.
Early Russian study of *Das Lied von der Erde*, more extended than later studies by Rozenshil'd (see no. 893 above) and Zavadskaya (see no. 552 above) but evidently less specialized than either, although in same journal.

898. Wöss, Josef V[enatius] von. *Gustav Mahler: Das Lied von der Erde (thematische Analyse).* Wien, Leipzig: Universal Edition, 1912. 38 pp.
Thematic analysis by Mahler's oft-time arranger/collaborator Wöss, issued as part of the set of materials for the work including scores, shortly after Mahler's death. Includes a short essay on Mahler's style and complete citation of texts. More concrete than essay by Specht several months earlier (see no. 895 above).

Symphony no. 1

899. Ablang, Willy d'. "De symphonieën van Gustav Mahler: Eerste Symphonie (D-dur)." *Symphonia* 13 (1930): 215-17, 239-42.
Analysis of the Symphony no. 1 in Dutch, arguing for the work as a concrete symphonic form while acknowledging its programmatic content. Apparently intended as the beginning of a collection of essays on all of the symphonies.

900. Dahlhaus, Carl. "Geschichte eines Themas: zu Mahlers Erster Symphonie." *Jahrbuch des Staatlichen Instituts für Musikforschung Preussische Kulturbesitz 1977*. Hrsg. von Dagmar Droysen. Berlin: Merseburger, 1978, pp. 45-60. ISBN 3-87537-165-8.
Traces Mahler's varied yet similar use of a single theme as a component of formal organization with reference to the last movement of the symphony. Concerned with thematic transformation rather than with scoring.

901. Engel, Gabriel. "Mahler's First." *CD* 2 (1941): 47-54.
Analysis of the symphony by movements, concentrating on music as the voice of emotion and nature rather than on technicalities.

* Hoyer, Michael. "Die multiperspektivische Totalität von Mahlers erster Sinfonie." *Form und Idee*: 29-116.
Full citation under no. 21 above. Considers the derivational background of the symphony in terms of nature and daily life of Mahler and ordinary people; less concerned with literary background than other commentators on this work. Would have benefitted from musical examples, especially in so extended an essay.

902. Jones, Robert Frederick. "Thematic Development and Form in the First and Fourth Movements of Mahler's First Symphony." Ph.D. diss., Brandeis University, 1980. 123 pp.
Considers the two movements as examples of sonata form with Mahler's special modifications including long static introduction of the first movement. Places discussion in context of romantic alterations in sonata form including the changing roles of the recapitula-

Individual Analyses: Symphony no. 1   259

tion, the function of cyclic use, and the effect of
dramatic-literary ideas on the continuity of the music.

903. Mahler, Gustav. *Symphony no. 1. Introduction in English and Spanish by Fritz Stiedry.* London: Boosey and Hawkes, 1943. 171, 6 pp.
Primarily an introductory study of the form of each movement, with major themes in single-line format.

904. Mahler, Gustav. *Symphony no. 1 D major.* London, Zürich, Mainz, New York: Ernst Eulenberg, Ltd., 1964. Introduction by Hans Redlich, pp. iii-xxii.
Rivals the Critical Edition (see following entry) in its introduction to the sources and critical problems of the musical text, and surveys the chronology of the composition of the work.

905. Mahler, Gustav. *Symphonie Nr. 1. Kritische Gesamtausgabe,* 1. Wien: Universal Edition, 1967. Revisionsbericht von Erwin Ratz, 2 pp.
Briefly lists the manuscript and early printed sources of the symphony and gives examples of the textual problems affecting the work of the editor.

906. Nodnagel, Ernst Otto. "Gustav Mahlers erste Symphonie in D dur. [Technische Analyse.]" *Neue Musik-Zeitung* 26 (1905): 353-57, 376-79.
Detailed thematic analysis of the symphony dating from Mahler's lifetime, by an early critic who supported Mahler's work and wrote many analyses of individual works.

907. Specht, Richard. *Gustav Mahler: Symphonie I D-dur (thematische Analyse).* Wien, Leipzig: Universal Edition, n.d. 14 pp.
Thematic analysis of the symphony issued as part of the full line of materials taken over by Universal Edition from Josef Weinberger. Author was insider in Mahler circle but demonstrates no knowledge of the missing *Blumine* andante.

*   Sponheuer, Bernd. "Der Durchbruch als primäre Formkategorie Gustav Mahlers: eine Untersuchung zum Finalproblem der ersten Symphonie." *Form und Idee*: 117-64.
Exhaustive study of the form of the last movement of the symphony, especially the function of the climax

fanfare and the subtle planning which makes it inevitable when it occurs. Full citation under no. 21 above.

* Weyer, Reinhold. "Ansätze zur unterrichtlichen Behandlung der 1. Sinfonie von Gustav Mahler." *Musik und Bildung* '5 (1973): 622-29. Full citation under no. 17 above. Shows how to analyze and conduct the work from formalist point of view. Realistic, technical.

908. Zenck, Martin. "Exkurs: Anmerkung zur ersten Sinfonie Gustav Mahlers." *Kunst als begrifflose Erkenntnis: zum Kunstbegriff der ästhetischen Theorie Theodor W. Adornos*. Theorie und Geschichte der Literatur und der schönen Kunst, 29. München: Wilhelm Fink, 1977, pp. 41-44. ISBN 3-7705-1365-7. Commentary on Adorno's theory concerning Mahler's music and the "sounds of nature" in the *Symphony no. 1*.

Symphony no. 2

909. Ablang, Willy d'. "De symphonieën van Gustav Mahler: de Tweede Symphonie (c-moll), voltooid in 1895." *Symphonia* 14 (1931): 177-79, 196-98, 217-20. Analysis of the symphony in Dutch, following by one year the analysis of the *Symphony no. 1* by the same author in this periodical (see no. 899 above). Apparently intended as a factual study of the work as an absolute symphonic form, a rare kind of treatment in its time. The series of projected articles on all of the symphonies of Mahler begun with the first analysis ended with this second one; no more was published after this installment.

910. Casella, Alfredo. "Gustav Mahler et sa deuxième symphonie." *Revue Société Internationale de Musique* 6 (1910): 238-50. One of the first French analyses of a work of Mahler, in this case written by the Italian composer who was residing in Paris at the time of the performance of the *Symphony no. 2* for the first time in that city. Thoughtful and positive, written at the time Mahler assisted in Casella's search for a publisher, and while Casella was working on his transcription of the *Symphony no. 7* for Bote und Bock.

Individual Analyses: Symphony no. 2 261

911. Danzinger, Gustav. "Die zweite Symphonie von Gustav Mahler." Ph.D. diss., Universität Wien, 1976. 266 pp.
Exhaustive source study of the symphony including manuscript musical and biographical sources, especially the score of *Todtenfeier*, critical/historical reception, and formal/stylistic study of musical and verbal texts in the context of Mahler's other symphonies from the early period.

912. Franklin, Peter. "'Funeral Rites'--Mahler and Mickiewicz." *ML* 55 (1974): 203-08.
Major discussion of the *Todtenfeier* of Adam Mickiewicz (1798-1855) and its effect on the first movement of Mahler's *Symphony no. 2* in its first "tone poem" version independent of the symphony. Worth comparing with later discussion by Hefling (see no. 915 below).

913. Fürnberg, Louis.. "Das jüngste Gericht: Gustav Mahler, Symphonie Nr. 2 in c-moll." *Das Fest des Lebens*. Zürich, New York: Oprecht, 1939, pp. 19-32.
See also: *Gesammelte Werke*. Hrsg. von der Akademie der Kunste der DDR. Berlin: Aufbau, 1965-77. 6 vols.
Semipoetical musing on Mahler, God and the meaning of life and death as occasioned by an experience of the *Symphony no. 2*. More thought-provoking than most conventional musical analyses of the work. The reprint of this essay in *Gesammelte Werke* is in vol. 3 (pp. 12-20), published in 1976.

914. Grant, [William] Parks. "Mahler's Second Symphony." *CD* 2 (1958): 76-85.
Structural analysis of the symphony, discussing both music and texts.

915. Hefling, Stephen E. "The Making of Mahler's 'Todtenfeier': a Documentary and Analytical Study." Ph.D. diss., Yale University, 1985. 3 vols.
Exhaustive study of the "tone poem" which later became the first movement of the *Symphony no. 2*; documents history of its composition through contemporary accounts, analyzes form, quality of the manuscript itself, significance in the history of the full symphony. Same author later published "Mahler's 'Todtenfeier' and the Problem of Program Music," *19th C Mus* 12 (Summer 1988): 27-53, which addresses specifically the

question of the structure of the movement with reference to its literary forebear by Adam Mickiewicz.

916. Mahler, Gustav. *Symphony no. 2.* Introduction in English and Spanish by Fritz Stiedry. London: Boosey and Hawkes, 1939, 1942, 1943. 209, 6 pp.
Primarily an introductory study of the form of each individual movement, with major themes in single-line format.

917. Mahler, Gustav. *Symphonie Nr. 2.* Kritische Gesamtausgabe, 2. Wien: Universal Edition, 1970. Vorwort und Revisionsbericht von Erwin Ratz, 3 pp.
Briefly introduces the manuscript and early published sources of the symphony and gives examples of the textual problems affecting the work of the editors of the Critical Edition.

918. Mahler, Gustav. *Symphony no. 2 in c minor "Resurrection."* New York: Kaplan Foundation; London: Faber Music Ltd., 1986. 364 pp. ISBN 0-571-100643.
Facsimile of the fair copy full score of the symphony with extensive introductory documentation of great value in its own right. The quality of the facsimile is unique. The documentation includes a discussion of the history of the composition of the work, a survey of the extramusical programs, a collection of ninety-two letters from Mahler relating to the work, a brief survey of the critical reaction to the symphony in Mahler's lifetime, a discussion of all known manuscript sources by Edward Reilly, and a carefully chosen bibliography.

919. Nodnagel, Ernst Otto. "Gustav Mahlers zweite Sinfonie: technische Analyse mit 25 Notenbeispielen." *Die Musik* 2 (1903): 337-53.
Detailed thematic-textual analysis of the symphony by an early critic who published many individual analyses of Mahler's works and supported Mahler in his own lifetime.

* Reilly, Edward. "Die Skizzen zu Mahlers zweiter Symphonie." *OeMZ* 34 (1979): 266-85.
Full citation under no. 19 above. Exhaustive discussion of the manuscript sources for the symphony, chronological development with comparative context from Mahler's letters, reminiscences of Bauer-Lechner and dates in the manuscript material. Originally in

English, translated by Rudolf Klein.

920. Specht, Richard. *Gustav Mahler: Symphonie II c-moll (thematische Analyse)*. Wien: Universal Edition, 1916. 30 pp.
Thematic analysis of the symphony published as part of complete set of materials including scores, although this item apparently dates from after Mahler's death while the score materials were published during his lifetime.

921. Stephan, Rudolf. *Mahler II. Symphonie c-moll*. Meisterwerke der Musik: Werkmonographien zur Musikgeschichten, 21. München: Wilhelm Fink, 1979. 96 pp.
Thorough thematic analysis with references not only to the structure of the symphony but citation of manuscript sources, historical background with long quotations from documents dating from time of composition and performances during Mahler's lifetime and after. Extensive citation of existing literature and many musical examples. Refers to Natalie Bauer-Lechner and Mahler's letters, as well as analyses by Weingartner, Kretzschmar and Graf.

Symphony no. 3

922. Franklin, Peter. "The Gestation of Mahler's Third Symphony." *ML* 58 (1977): 439-46.
Surveys the sketches for the symphony in the Österreichische Nationalbibliothek and at Stanford University Library for paper types, continuity and musical content. Discussion of both groups of sketches at Stanford uneven; concentration is primarily on the first movement of the symphony. Compare with discussions by Williamson (see no. 930) and Filler (see no. 794).

923. Mahler, Gustav. *Symphony no. 3*. Introduction in English and Spanish by Fritz Stiedry. London: Boosey and Hawkes, 1943. 231, 6 pp.
Primarily an introductory study of the form of each individual movement, with major themes in single-line format.

924. Mahler, Gustav. *Symphonie Nr. 3*. Kritische Gesamt-

ausgabe, 3. Wien: Universal Edition, 1974. Vorwort und Revisionsbericht von Erwin Ratz, 2 pp. Briefly introduces the manuscript and early published sources for the symphony and gives examples of the textual problems affecting the work of the editors of the Critical Edition.

925. Nodnagel, Ernst Otto. *Gustav Mahlers III. Symphonie: Analyse*. Darmstadt: Ed. Roether, 1904. 31 pp.
Detailed thematic-textual analysis of the symphony, third individual analysis by author who published such guides to Mahler's individual works in Mahler's lifetime in important attempt to support Mahler in his work.

926. Redlich, Hans Ferdinand. "Mahler's Third Symphony." *Chesterian* 35 (Winter 1961): 77-80.
Brief history of the composition of the symphony and survey of the movements. Some discrepancies in factual background since corrected, but good introduction to the work. Somewhat weakened by complete lack of musical examples.

* Reilly, Edward. "A re-examination of the manuscripts of Mahler's Third Symphony." *Colloque 1985*: 62-72.
Full citation under no. 5 above. Considers all available manuscript sources for the symphony, based on research by Filler, with reassessment by virtue of the recent location of three manuscripts not available at the time of Filler dissertation (see no. 794 above).

* Schnebel, Dieter. "Sinfonie und Wirklichkeit am Beispiel von Mahlers Dritter." *Sinfonie und Wirklichkeit*: 103-17.
Full citation under no. 10 above. Considers the symphony as a "world," musically, in literary terms, historically and sociologically.

927. Schnebel, Dieter. "Über Mahlers Dritte." *NZfM* 135 (1974): 283-88.
Summarizes the history of the composition of the symphony, surveys the forms and textual balance, and documents literary influences behind the work. Contrasts with later analysis of the work by Filler (see no. 794 above) as Schnebel regards work as a suite, Filler as tripartite symphony. Reprinted in *Mahler: eine Herausforderung* (cited above in full as no. 20).

Individual Analyses: Symphony no. 3

927a. Sheratsky, Rodney. "Mahler's Third--Beyond Beethoven's Ninth." *Dika Caecilia: Essays for Dika Newlin, November 22, 1988.* Ed. by Theodore Albrecht. Parkville, Missouri: Park College, 1988, pp. 142-51.
Interesting discussion of the symphony as manifestation of Mahler's debt to Beethoven, linking this work with Beethoven's *Symphony no. 9* in musical style and philosophical basis with reference to the texts chosen by the two composers for their vocal movements. Extensive reference to Mahler's letters at the time of composition of the work documenting the process of his work. Marred by factual error in places but still original in conception of the connection between the two works beyond the usual attempts to draw definitive thematic links.

928. Specht, Richard. *Gustav Mahler: Symphonie III d-moll (thematische Analyse).* Wien: Universal Edition, [1916]. 27 pp.
Detailed thematic analysis of the symphony, concentrating solely on the musical organization, not on the historical background or chronology. More comprehensive in its musical examples than most other such analyses. Released with the Universal Edition scores of the work or perhaps later.

929. Werck, Isabelle. *La symphonie de la terre et du ciel: 7 variations sur la troisième symphonie de Gustav Mahler.* Lyon: Éditions a Coeur Joie, 1985. 51 pp.
A movement-by-movement study of the symphony, primarily a discussion of "nature" concepts and how Mahler represented them in the music. Unusual alternative to the normal type of survey concentrating on musical mechanics of individual Mahler works, and for that reason refreshing and good reading for both musical professionals and general readers.

930. Williamson, John. "Mahler's Compositional Process: Reflections on an Early Sketch for the Third Symphony's First Movement." *ML* 61 (1980): 338-45.
Examines the sketches for the first movement of the symphony in the Österreichische Nationalbibliothek for paper types, continuity and musical content. Compare with discussions by Franklin (see no. 922 above) and Filler (see no. 794 above).

931. Zender, Hans. "Eine Probenwoche mit Mahlers 'Drit-

ter.'" *Melos/NZfM* 3 (1977): 233-35.
Conductor's jottings during preparation for performance of the symphony; informal, concerned with the conductor as re-creator of the composer's vision, the problems appertaining thereto. Encompasses concrete problems of particular passages, interpretation of emotional content, concerns of those who have written about composer as read by the conductor. Special and unique. Reprinted in *Orchester* 25 (1977): 334-36, and in *Mahler: eine Herausforderung* (full citation above under no. 20).

Symphony no. 4

* Hefling, Stephen E. "'Variations *in nuce*': a Study of Mahler Sketches, and a Comment on Sketch Studies." *Gustav Mahler Kolloquium 1979*: 102-26.
Full citation under no. 8 above. Study of sketches for the third movement of the *Symphony no. 4*, in the context of the composition of the whole work.

* Kropfinger, Kraus. "Gerettete Herausforderung: Mahlers 4. Symphonie--Mengelbergs Interpretation." *Mahler-Interpretation 1985*: 111-75.
Full citation under no. 24 above. Exhaustive study of the copy of the symphony in the Mengelberg archive now in the Haags Gemeentemuseum, which contains handwritten annotations and emendations, as well as other sigla, by Mahler and Mengelberg. Given perspective by citations from Mahler's correspondence and Mengelberg's *Gedenkboek*.

932. Mahler, Gustav. *Symphony no. 4*. Introduction in English and Spanish by Fritz Stiedry. London: Boosey and Hawkes, 1943. 125, 7 pp.
Primarily an introductory study of the form of each individual movement, with major themes in single-line format.

933. Mahler, Gustav. *Symphonie Nr. 4*. Kritische Gesamtausgabe, 4. Wien: Universal Edition, 1963. Revisionsbericht von Erwin Ratz, 3 pp.
Briefly introduces the manuscript and early printed sources of the symphony and gives examples of the textual problems affecting the work of the editor.

Individual Analyses: Symphony no. 4

934. Mahler, Gustav. *Symphony no. 4.* London, Zürich, Mainz, New York: Ernst Eulenberg, Ltd., 1966. Introduction by Hans Redlich, pp. iii-xxxv.
An exhaustive introduction to the history, sources and critical problems of the text of the symphony. Occasionally inaccurate in its assessments of the meaning of sources from the chronological viewpoint, but valuable as an introduction to the problems of establishing priorities among the manifold sources.

* Neuwirth, Gösta. "Zur Geschichte der 4. Symphonie." *Mahler-Interpretation 1985*: 105-10.
Full citation under no. 24 above. Sharply focused study of the early performances and publication history of the symphony, concerned especially with the print containing Mahler's emendations now in the library of the Grazer Landeskonservatoriums.

935. Specht, Richard. *Gustav Mahler: Symphonie IV in G-dur (thematische Analyse).* Wien: Universal Edition, 1920. 15 pp.
Published in connection with the complete corpus of sources and arrangements of the symphony, released by Universal Edition some time after Mahler's death and the takeover of the score materials from Ludwig Doblinger.

936. Stein, Erwin. "Eine unbekannte Ausgabe letzter Hand von Mahlers IV. Symphonie." *Pult und Taktstock* 6 (1929): 31-32.
English version: "The Unknown Last Version of Mahler's Fourth Symphony." *Orpheus in New Guises*: 31-33.
Discusses Mahler's last revisions to the scoring of the symphony, unknown at the time these articles were published, since incorporated into the Critical Edition. English version cited in full above under no. 23, translated by Hans Keller.

937. Stephan, Rudolf. "Betrachtungen zu Form und Thematik in Mahlers Vierter Symphonie." *Neue Wege der musikalischen Analyse.* Veröffentlichungen des Instituts für Neue Musik und Musikerziehung Darmstadt, 6. Kassel: Merseburger, 1966, pp. 23-42. ISBN 3-87537-074-0.
Thematic analysis of the symphony, rather more condensed and specialized than author's monograph on the same work published in the same year (see next entry).

For analysis only, not for historical background.

938. Stephan, Rudolf. *Mahler IV. Symphonie G-dur*. Meisterwerke der Musik, 5. München: Wilhelm Fink, 1966. 40 pp.
A comprehensive thematic analysis of the symphony with background on the historical context in which it was written, thus distinguishing it from same author's article on same work (see preceding entry).

939. Tovey, Donald Francis. "Mahler: Symphony in G Major, No. 4." *Essays in Musical Analysis*. London: Oxford University Press/Humphrey Milford, 1939, 1940, vol. 6, pp. 73-83.
The famous early British analysis by a musicologist who was the "Establishment," which advocated Mahler (in a detached way) when little else was being written about Mahler by anyone in England. Surprisingly cogent analysis of the symphony as representative of Mahler's style in general.

940. Zychowicz, James. "Sketches and Drafts of Gustav Mahler 1892-1901: the Sources of the Fourth Symphony." Ph.D. diss., University of Cincinnati, 1988. 683 pp.
Critical and historical study of the symphony from the sketches to the fair copy with brief discussion also of the compositional revisions after publication. Includes correlated study of the early history of *Das himmlische Leben* with reference to the *Symphony no. 3*, as well as the *Scherzo in c minor* and *Presto in F major* based on earlier study by Filler (see no. 1038 below). Familiar with previous related literature by Filler, Reilly, Williamson, Franklin, Mitchell and Martner.

Symphony no. 5

941. Baxendale, Carolyn. "The Finale of Mahler's Fifth Symphony: Long-Range Musical Thought." *RMA Journal* 112 (1987): 257-79.
Discusses the last movement of the symphony in the context of function in terms of the symphony as a whole (especially with reference to the chorale), concept of movement form in nineteenth century tradition, and har-

Individual Analyses: Symphony no. 5 269

monic/thematic evolution in the movement itself, with its effect on sonata and rondo components of form. Heaviest emphasis on the latter area, owing much to Williamson; would have benefitted from equal emphasis on the first two subjects.

942. Brincker, Jens. "Et liedcitat i Gustav Mahlers V. symfoni." [Lyric elements in Gustav Mahler's Fifth symphony.] *Musikvidenskabelige essays uidgivet af Musikvidenskabeligt Institut ved Københavns Universitet.* København: [Akademisk Forlag], 1974, pp. 9-15.
  Discusses effect of Mahler's lyrical style on the composition of the symphony, referring to the songs he wrote at that period. In Danish.

943. Forte, Allen. "Middleground Motives in the Adagietto of Mahler's Fifth Symphony." *19th C Mus* 8 (1984): 153-63.
  Analyzes the fourth movement of the symphony using the methods of Heinrich Schenker, with a comparative discussion of the second song in the *Kindertotenlieder* as a close relative of the *Adagietto* in melodic style and content.

944. Grant, [William] Parks. "Mahler's Fifth Symphony." *CD* 2 (1963): 125-37.
  A formal analysis of the symphony emphasizing the cyclic features and contrapuntal style which make the work a unified entity.

945. Mahler, Gustav. *Symphonie Nr. 5. Kritische Gesamtausgabe,* 5. Frankfurt, London, New York: C.F. Peters, 1964. Revisionsbericht von Erwin Ratz, 2 pp.
  Briefly introduces the manuscript and early published sources of the symphony and gives examples of the textual problems affecting the work of the editors of the Critical Edition. Offers fascinating insights into the disposition of sources during the generations after Mahler's death, especially during the 1930s and 1940s, which are extremely rare in the conservative introductions to the volumes of the Critical Edition dating from the 1960s.

946. Nodnagel, Ernst Otto. *Gustav Mahlers fünfte Symphonie (technische Analyse).* Leipzig: Peters, 1905. 39 pp.

Thematic analysis of the symphony by a critic who supported Mahler in his time and wrote many individual analyses of Mahler's works. Preceded by an analysis in *Die Musik* 4 (1904): 243-55, 314-23. The 1905 monograph was published by Peters as part of its constellation of materials including orchestral scores and piano transcriptions.

947. Stresemann, Wolfgang. "Mahler's Fifth Symphony." *CD* 2 (1948): 30-33.
Movement-by-movement discussion of the symphony, emphasizing form and to some extent emotional content.

948. Wilkens, Sander. "Mahler's Trieste Conduction Score: an Unknown Source in the History of the Fifth Symphony." *NaMR*, no. 19 (March 1988): 11-14.
Critically surveys a conductor's score of the symphony with handwritten alterations by Mahler and a copyist, now in the library of the Tartini Conservatory in Trieste. Compares source with similar ones in collections of Bruno Walter and Willem Mengelberg and concludes that it is a compilation used for performance in Trieste on December 1, 1905 rather than a wholly independent source. Surveys briefly the nature of the changes in the score. Essential source with the Critical Edition and the study of the correspondence by Klemm (see no. 379 above).

Symphony no. 6

* Andraschke, Peter. "Gustav Mahlers Retuschen im Finale seiner 6. Symphonie." *Mahler-Interpretation 1985*: 63-80.
Full citation under no. 24 above. Detailed study of the sources for the symphony and Mahler's instrumental retouches in the last movement. With Redlich's analysis in the Eulenberg Edition of the work (see no. 955 below), best such analysis available, much more detailed than Ratz's introduction to the Critical Edition of the work (see no. 956 below); however, draws on Ratz's earlier essay analysis of the work (see no. 958 below).

949. Andraschke, Peter. "Struktur und Gehalt im ersten Satz von Gustav Mahlers sechster Symphonie." *AfMw* 35 (1978): 275-96.
Exhaustive thematic-rhythmic analysis of the first move-

Individual Analyses: Symphony no. 6

ment of the symphony, with secondary essays on (a) Mahler's short score of the movement, (b) the use of scoring in the "Nature" episode, and (c) retouches in the scoring of the complete work and the problem of the order of the two inner movements.

950. Del Mar, Norman René. *Mahler's Sixth Symphony: a Study*. With an Introduction by Colin Matthews. London: Eulenberg Books, 1980. Reprinted New York: Da Capo Press, 1982. 153 pp. ISBN 0-903873-29-X.
Thorough study of the symphony including history of its composition, formal analysis, critical commentary referring to all major editions (except, apparently, the Critical Edition). Problem of the order of the inner movements is handled by retaining *Andante* as second movement and *Scherzo* as third movement, thus foreswearing both Critical Edition edited by Ratz and Eulenberg's own edition edited by Redlich, a controversial decision.

951. Engel, Gabriel. "With Hammer and Cowbells: Mahler's Sixth Comes to America." *CD* 2 (1948): 1-12.
Ostensibly a review of the American premiere of the symphony, but in reality the first known discussion of the work in English outside the few brief references in general studies of Mahler's life and works in that language.

952. Hansen, Mathias. "Marsch und Formidee: analytische Bemerkungen zu sinfonische Sätzen Schuberts und Mahlers--Anmerkungen." *BzMw* 22 (1980): 3-23.
Analyzes the march as influence in nineteenth century symphonic music, contrasting and comparing its use in works of Schubert and Mahler. Examples in the discussion of Mahler include the first and last movements of the *Symphony no. 6* (melody, rhythm and scoring).

953. Jülg, Hans-Peter. *Gustav Mahlers sechste Symphonie*. Freiburger Schriften zur Musikwissenschaft, 17. Hrsg. von Hans Heinrich Eggebrecht. München, Salzburg: Emil Katzbichler, 1986. 163 pp. ISBN 3-87397-087-2.
Originally author's Ph.D. dissertation (Universität Freiburg im Breisgau). Critical study of the forms, manuscript and published sources and history of the reception of the symphony, updating accounts by Redlich and Ratz.

954. Klemm, Eberhardt. "Notizen zu Mahler." *Festschrift Heinrich Besseler zum 60. Geburtstag.* Hrsg. vom Institut für Musikwissenschaft der Karl-Marx-Universität. Leipzig: VEB Deutscher Verlag für Musik, 1961, pp. 447-55.
Various aphorisms about Mahler's melodic/rhythmic style, focusing particularly on the last movement of the *Symphony no. 6*. Reprinted in *Mahler: eine Herausforderung* (cited in full above as no. 20).

955. Mahler, Gustav. *Symphony no. 6.* Zürich, London, Mainz, New York: Edition Eulenberg, 1968. Introduction by Hans Redlich, pp. iii-xxxi.
A definitive introduction to the three different versions of the symphony published in 1906, necessitated by the fact that this score reproduces the original version rather than the final version adopted in the Critical Edition. Exhaustively covers the chronology of the various alterations Mahler made between versions distinguishing between revisions in the order of the movements and revisions in the scoring at various stages; demonstrates critical knowledge of the various prints and their plates.

956. Mahler, Gustav. *Symphonie Nr. 6.* Kritische Gesamtausgabe, 6. Lindau: C.F. Kahnt, 1963. Revisionsbericht von Erwin Ratz, 2 pp.
Briefly introduces the manuscript and early printed sources of the symphony and gives examples of the textual problems affecting the work of the editor. Unfortunately brief in comparison with the exhaustive survey of the various sources in the score of the first version published by Eulenberg (see preceding entry); makes little attempt to justify the work of the editor necessitated by the important differences between the first two versions and the third reproduced here.

957. Nodnagel, Ernst Otto. "Sechste Symphonie in A-moll von Gustav Mahler." *Die Musik* 5 (1906): 233-46.
Thematic analysis of the symphony by early critic who published individual analyses of most of the symphonies in his effort to support Mahler during the composer's lifetime.

958. Ratz, Erwin. "Zum Formproblem bei Gustav Mahler: eine Analyse des Finales der VI. Symphonie." *Mf* 9 (1956): 156-71. Reprinted in "Zum Formproblem" in *Gustav*

Mahler (1966): 90-122. Reprinted again in Ratz, Erwin. *Gesammelte Aufsätze*. Hrsg. von E.C. Heller. Wien: Universal Edition, 1975, pp. 131-46. English version: "Musical Form in Gustav Mahler: Analysis of the Finale of the Sixth Symphony." Transl. by Paul Hamburger. *Music Review* 29 (1968): 34-48. Formal-thematic analysis of the last movement of the symphony by the general editor of the Critical Edition, perhaps preparatory to the edition of the complete work (see no. 956 above), but actually surpassing it in detail. Reprint of 1966 followed by author's similar analysis of the first movement of *Symphony no. 9* (see no. 992 below); full citation for both in the 1966 reprint cited above under no. 7.

959. Redlich, Hans Ferdinand. "Mahler's Enigmatic Sixth." *Festschrift Otto Erich Deutsch zum 80. Geburtstag*. Hrsg. von Walter Gerstenberg, Jan LaRue und Wolfgang Rehm. Kassel: Bärenreiter, 1963, pp. 250-56. Probably a precursor of Redlich's extensive introduction to his edition of the symphony (see no. 955 above). Thematic study with some discussion also of the emotional overtones in this work which was at that time still neglected in the literature.

960. Specht, Richard. *Gustav Mahler: sechste Symphonie (thematische Führer)*. Kahnts Musikführer. Leipzig: C.F. Kahnt, 1906. 48 pp.
Thematic analysis of the symphony published simultaneously with the corpus of scores and arrangements by C.F. Kahnt. Evidently illustrates the third version in which Mahler had reversed the inner movements so that the slow movement is discussed before the scherzo.

Symphony no. 7

961. Davison, Peter S. "The *Nachtmusiken* from Mahler's Seventh Symphony: Analysis and Reappraisal." M. Phil. diss., Jesus College, Cambridge, 1985. 95 pp.
An unusual analysis of the second and fourth movements of the symphony concentrating less on conventional formal structure than on literary/programmatic narrative in the context of variable passage flow. Wide ranging and challenging, especially when compared with

previous analyses by Williamson, Specht, Mitchell and others who wrote along more conventional lines than this author did.

962. Gross, Allen Robert. "Mahler's Seventh Symphony: Analysis and Performance." D.M.A. final project, Stanford University, 1978. 64 pp.
Movement-by-movement analysis of the symphony from melodic-formal-instrumental point of view, meant as outline for would-be conductors.

* Jungheinrich, Hans-Klaus. "Nach der Katastrophe: Anmerkungen zu einer aktuellen Rezeption der 7. Symphonie." *Mahler: eine Herausforderung*: 181-98.
Full citation under no. 20 above. Considers the question of why this symphony is still least understood of all, why audiences react to it more often with puzzlement than support.

963. Kneif, Tibor. "Collage oder Naturalismus? Anmerkungen zu Mahlers 'Nachtmusik I'." *NZfM* 134 (1973): 623-28.
Considers the second movement of the symphony as either a "collage" of external influences (from the cowbells especially) or a mirror of naturalism, depending on how Mahler's instructions in the score are realized. Considers this contrast in the context of Mahler's use of unusual instrumentation in other works, especially the *Symphony no. 6*.

964. Mahler, Gustav. *Symphony no. 7*. London, Zürich, Mainz, New York: Ernst Eulenburg, 1924. Introduction by Adolf Aber, 7 pp.
Revised edition: *Symphony no. 7*. London, Zürich, Mainz, New York: Ernst Eulenburg, 1965. Introduction by Hans Redlich, pp. iii-xii.
Comparison of the two introductions to these scores shows the change in the general attitude to the symphony over the lapse of forty years. The introduction to the 1924 score is a basic-level study of the form of the symphony; the introduction to the 1965 score, like the other essays written by Redlich in the Eulenberg Editions, advances to the history of the sources and the critical job of the editor.

965. Mahler, Gustav. *Symphonie Nr. 7. Kritische Gesamtausgabe*, 7. Berlin: Bote und Bock, 1960. Revis-

Individual Analyses: Symphony no. 7

ionsbericht von Erwin Ratz, 6 pp.
Unusually thorough and extensive introduction to the chronology of the sources for this problematic work, with an especially long listing of problems in the course of the text of the symphony.

* Revers, Peter. "'Return to the Idyll'--the Night Pieces in Gustav Mahler's Seventh Symphony." *Colloque 1985*: 40-51.
Full citation under no. 5 above. Discusses the role of real-life experience as a background to the two *Nachtmusiken*, especially considering the result in scoring and harmony.

966. Specht, Richard. "Thematische Novitäten-Analysen: Mahlers siebente Symphonie." *Der Merker* 1 (1909): 88ff. (9 pages).
Thematic analysis of the symphony, published at the time the score itself was printed but not in the corpus of materials issued by the publisher. Differs from the majority of Specht's analyses in being published in a periodical rather than in monograph form, raising questions about why Specht was not contracted by the publisher in the usual manner with other works.

967. Stephan, Rudolf. "Überlegungen zur Taktgruppenanalyse: zur Interpretation der 7. Symphonie von Gustav Mahler." *Logos Musicae: Festschrift für Albert Palm*. Hrsg. von Rüdiger Görner. Wiesbaden: Franz Steiner, 1982, pp. 202-10.
Analyzes the symphony by phrased measure groupings with reference to *Wahrung der Gestalt* of Swarowsky (see no. 826 above). Particular attention to first movement with analysis by Hermann Scherchen as well as Swarowsky.

968. Williamson, John. "Deceptive Cadences in the Last Movement of Mahler's Seventh Symphony." *Soundings* 9 (1982): 87-96.
Analyzes the final movement of the symphony in terms of unexpected modulatory passages and surprise cadences, which have the effect of making a mockery of the apparent C-major basis of the tonality (and implicitly alter the nature of the final impression of the symphony as a whole).

969. Williamson, John. "The Structural Premises of Mahler's

Introductions: Prolegomena to an Analysis of the First Movement of the Seventh Symphony." *Music Analysis* 5 (1986): 29-57.
Very thorough for a "prolegomena," focusing on the thematic structure of the introductory section of the first movement of the symphony and its importance to the whole movement through use of the "upbeat" tetrachord in both large and small scale. While major emphasis is given to the *Symphony no. 7*, there is quite a lot of valuable secondary discussion of the *Symphony no. 1* and other works as well. Author's discussion of the *Symphony no. 7* in this article and his previous one in *Soundings* (see preceding entry) as well as his dissertation show long-term involvement with the work which arouses eager anticipation for more in the future.

Symphony no. 8

970. Breig, Werner, hrsg. *Schütz-Jahrbuch*. Bd. 4/5. In Verbindung mit Hans Michael Beuerle, Friedheim Krummacher und Stefan Kunze. Im Auftrage der Internationale Heinrich-Schütz-Gesellschaft. Kassel, Basel, London: Bärenreiter, 1983. 113 pp. ISBN 3-7618-0709-0.
A series of four essays is included in this volume, all covering various aspects of the *Symphony no. 8*: "Fragen zu Mahlers VIII. Symphonie" by Friedheim Krummacher (pp. 71-72), "Mahlers Hymnus" by Adolf Nowak (pp. 92-96), "Zu Mahlers Komposition der Schluss-szene von Goethes Faust" by Rudolf Stephan (pp. 97-102) and "Die Idee der absoluten Musik aus ihr (ausgesprochenes) Programm: zum unterlegten Text des Mahlerschen Achten" by Stefan Strohm (pp. 73-91). These essays treat the symphony as a quasi-dramatic work in the tradition of the semi-dramatic liturgical works written by German composers from the baroque period onward.

971. Cooke, Deryck. "The Word and the Deed: Mahler and his Eighth Symphony." *Vindications: Essays on Romantic Music*. Cambridge, London, New York, New Rochelle, Melbourne, Sydney: Cambridge University Press, 1982, pp. 108-15. ISBN 0-521-24765-9 (hardcover), 0-521-28947-5 (paper).

Originally published in *The Listener*, July 2, 1964, pp. 22-23. Studies the humanistic-religious traditions behind Mahler's "assimilated Jewish" status and explores the way in which they affected Mahler's selection of texts and composition of music in the *Symphony no. 8*.

972. Engel, Gabriel. "Mahler's Eighth: the Hymn to Eros." *CD* 2 (1950): 12-32.
Analysis of the text set by Mahler in the symphony, differing from many other analyses by virtue of its emphasis on nature as opposed to the usual Christian-oriented interpretation. Major quotations from the correspondence of Mahler at the time are included as documentary support.

973. Gray, Cecil and Kaikhosru Sorabji [Leon Dudley]. "Mahler's Eighth Symphony." *Monthly Musical Record* 60 (1930): 168-70.
Early study of the symphony at a time when the work was rarely performed, by two English-speaking writers who were among the earliest to write in that language. Gray was involved early with the Bruckner Society of America, while Sorabji--a composer in his own right and also a critic--continued to champion Mahler's music in England against almost complete indifference. In this case, the two writers offer point-counter-point opinions, Gray concentrating on his negative reaction to Mahler's grandiose effects in the symphony as a result of a single hearing of the work, while Sorabji not only offers a positive response but adds a note of perspective in the history of Mahler performance which was sorely lacking in quality until much later.

974. Lazarov, Stefan. "Chopin--Wagner--Mahler." *Rocnik Chopinowski* [Annales Chopin] 7 (1965-68): 100-08.
In Polish. Traces melodic parallels between Chopin, Wagner and Mahler with reference to several of Chopin's piano pieces, *Die Walküre* and Mahler's *Symphony no. 8*.

975. Mahler, Gustav. *Symphony no. 8*. Introduction in English and Spanish by Fritz Stiedry. London: Boosey and Hawkes, 1939. 218, [6] pp.
Primarily an introductory study of the form and text of the symphony, with major themes in single-line format. Draws connection between the nature of the verbal texts and Mahler's musical conception.

976. Mahler, Gustav. *Symphonie Nr. 8. Kritische Gesamtausgabe*, 8. Wien: Universal Edition, 1977. Vorwort und Revisionsbericht von Karl Heinz Füssl, 9 pp.
Briefly introduces the manuscript and early printed sources of the symphony and gives examples of the textual problems affecting the work of the editor. Gives the musical substance priority almost to the exclusion of the verbal texts and their significance to the conception of the whole work.

977. Ponnelle, Lazare. "Apres la VIIIe Symphonie de Gustave Mahler." *À Munich: Gustav Mahler, Richard Strauss, Ferruccio Busoni*. Paris: Fischbacher, 1913, pp. 3-17.
Reprinted from *Journal des débats* (1er Octobre 1910), written on the occasion of the premiere of the symphony in Munich. More than a review of the performance, this is a study of the personal reaction of a major writer of the era.

978. Sondheimer, Robert. "Gustav Mahler und Carl Loewe." *Die Musik* 22 (1930): 356-61.
Draws a causal line from Loewe's oratorio *Die Zerstörung von Jerusalem* (1830) to Mahler's *Symphony no. 8* in terms of both music and textual meaning. Makes no attempt to place the resemblances in historical context, merely pointing out specific examples.

979. Specht, Richard. *Gustav Mahler: Symphonie VIII B^b-dur (thematische Analyse): mit einer Einleitung, biographischen Date und dem Porträt Mahlers*. Wien, Leipzig: Universal Edition, 1912. 48 pp.
English version: *Gustav Mahler's Eighth Symphony: Thematic Analysis*. Transl. by Philip H. Goepp. Philadelphia: Philadelphia Orchestra Assn., 1916. 48 pp.
Full citation of texts and thematic analysis of the symphony, Specht's original being issued as part of the full run of materials by Universal Edition. Unique English version issued at time of American premiere conducted by Stokowski.

980. Teweles, Heinrich. "Mahler in Prag." *Moderne Welt* 3 (1921): 32.
Less useful than other contemporary accounts of the work of Mahler in Prague. Concentrates on a brief as-

sessment of certain Mahler works in performance there, especially the Prague premiere of the *Symphony no. 8* in 1912 under the direction of Teweles. Essentially a remote second to Foerster.

981. Werck, Isabelle. *Le huit et l'infini: variations sur la huitième symphonie de Gustav Mahler*. Lyon: Éditions a Coeur Joie, 1987. 39 pp.
Brief philosophical study of the symphony with poetic discussion of the "infinite" as concepts in the text and Mahler's music and how they interrelate.

982. Werker, Gerard. "De achstete symphonie van Gustav Mahler." *Mens en melodie* 9 (1954): 164-68.
Concise Dutch thematic analysis of the symphony with brief historical background. More concerned with thematic-harmonic organization than with scoring.

983. Williamson, John. "Mahler and Veni Creator Spiritus." *Music Review* 44 (1983): 25-35.
Fantastic discussion of Mahler's craft in the first movement of the *Symphony no. 8*, in the context of the composer's other works during the late period. Treats the movement as a combination of sonata-allegro and Baroque fugue, a thoroughly well-founded judgement, however revolutionary it sounds.

Symphony no. 9

984. Andraschke, Peter. *Gustav Mahlers IX. Symphonie: Kompositionsprozess und Analyse*. Beihefte zum *AfMw*, 14. Hrsg. von Heinrich Besseler in Verbindung mit Kurt von Fischer, W[alter] Gerstenberg und A. Schmitz. Wiesbaden: Franz Steiner, 1976. 94 pp. ISBN 3-515-02114-0.
Originally the author's Ph.D. dissertation (Universität Freiburg im Breisgau, 1973). Study of the compositional process and thematic structure in the symphony as exemplified in (a) the Partiturentwurf of the first three movements, and (b) the published score in the Mengelberg Stichting with handwritten annotations of Mengelberg. Includes a brief selection of Mahler's letters to Mengelberg at the end.

985. Dahlhaus, Carl. "Form und Motiv in Mahlers neunter

Symphonie." *NZfM* 135 (1974): 296-99.
Motivic analysis of the symphony, referring to earlier analyses by Adorno and Ratz.

986. Diether, Jack. "The Expressive Content of Mahler's Ninth: an Interpretation." *CD* 2 (1963): 69-107.
A dual-polar discussion of the symphony concentrating on the novel means Mahler used in harmonic melody to produce the emotional process from despair at his confrontation with death to catharsis and acceptance.

987. Fischer, Kurt von. "Die Doppelschlagfigur in den zwei letzten Sätzen von Gustav Mahlers 9. Symphonie: Versuch einer Interpretation." *AfMw* 32 (1975): 99-105.
Demonstrates the thematic ties between the last two movements of the symphony with particular attention to the "turn" figure characteristic of Mahler's melodic phrasing in general.

* la Motte, Diether de. "Das komplizierte Einfache: Anmerkungen zum 1. Satz der 9. Sinfonie von Gustav Mahler." *Sinfonie und Wirklichkeit*: 52-67.
Full citation under no. 10 above. Considers the formal, melodic, harmonic and orchestral construction of the first movement of the symphony.

988. Lewis, Christopher Orlo. *Tonal Coherence in Mahler's Ninth Symphony*. Studies in Musicology, 79. Ann Arbor, Michigan: UMI Research Press, 1983, 1984. xvii, 130 pp. ISBN 0-8357-1585-X.
Originally the author's Ph.D. dissertation, "Tonality and Structure in the Ninth Symphony of Gustav Mahler," Eastman School of Music, University of Rochester, 1983 (237 pp.). Cogent analysis of the "progressive" tonality of the symphony.

989. Mahler, Gustav. *Symphony no. 9*. Introduction in English and Spanish by Fritz Stiedry. London: Boosey and Hawkes, 1939, 1940, 1941, 1944. 182, 11 pp.
Primarily an introductory study of the form of each individual movement, with major themes in single-line format.

990. Mahler, Gustav. *Symphonie Nr. 9*. Kritische Gesamtausgabe, 10. Wien: Universal Edition, 1969. Vorwort und Revisionsbericht von Erwin Ratz, 6 pp.
Briefly introduces the manuscript and early printed

sources of the symphony and gives examples of the textual problems affecting the work of the editor.

991. Mahler, Gustav. *IX. Symphonie.* Faksimile nach der Handschrift. Hrsg. von Erwin Ratz. Wien: Universal Edition, 1971. 54, 48 and 46 pp., plus 6 pp. unpaginated introduction.
Facsimile of the *Partiturentwurf* of the first three movements, with brief introductory background complementing same editor's introduction in the Critical Edition (see preceding entry).

992. Ratz, Erwin. "Zum Formproblem bei Gustav Mahler: eine Analyse des ersten Satzes der IX. Symphonie." *Mf* 8 (1955): 169-77. Reprinted in *Gustav Mahler* (1966): 123-41. Reprinted again in Ratz, Erwin. *Gesammelte Aufsätze.* Hrsg. von E.C. Heller. Wien: Universal Edition, 1975, pp. 156-64.
Formal-thematic analysis of the first movement of the symphony by the general editor of the Critical Edition, perhaps preparatory to the edition of the complete work (see no. 990 above) but surpassing it in detail. Reprint of 1966 preceded by author's similar analysis of the last movement of the *Symphony no. 6* (see no. 958 above); the full citation of the paired essays in the 1966 reprint is cited in full under no. 7 above.

993. Reeser, Eduard. "Wie ein schwerer Kondukt." *Caecilia en de muziek* 93 (1936): 278-81.
Follows immediately Reeser's general article about Mahler on the twenty-fifth anniversary of Mahler's death (see no. 240 above). Although the title is in German (owing of course to the direct quotation of Mahler's instructions from the score), the article itself is in Dutch. This is an early analysis of *Symphony no. 9*, colored by the comparative lack of any information on the state of the *Symphony no. 10* at the time of writing. Thematic analysis, brief, but sorely needed as its only known predecessor--the analysis in the 1920 *Feestboek* of Curt Rudolf Mengelberg cited as no. 804 above--was not widely distributed.

994. Revers, Peter. "Liquidation als Formprinzip: die formprägende Bedeutung des Rhythmus für das Adagio der 9. Symphonie von Gustav Mahler." *OeMz* 33 (1978): 527-33.
Traces transformation principle in the motivic rhythm

of the last movement of the symphony, showing how one or two motives are used in many different ways to unify the movement and also proceed with its final calculated disintegration.

* Rosenberg, Wolf. "Mahler und die Avantgarde: Kompositionstechnisches Vorbild oder geistige Sympathie?" *Sinfonie und Wirklichkeit*: 81-92. Full citation under no. 10 above. Considers the first movement of the *Symphony no. 9* as precursor to the stylistic innovations of the Second Viennese School and the more recent avant-garde composers; then concerns itself with Mahler's poetic inclinations, especially in the *Symphony no. 2*.

* Schenck, Rüdiger. "Zur Neunten Symphonie Gustav Mahlers." *Form und Idee*: 165-221. Full citation under no. 21 above. A series of fifty-eight aphorisms on the symphony, ranging in subject from the symphonic history written by Mahler and his predecessors which culminates in this work, to the formal organization of the symphony itself, to a critical disputation on the score issued in the Critical Edition. The last two sections, in contrast to the first fifty-six, are extensive in scope. Unusual and thought-provoking, rare in content and format among literature in essay references.

995. Specht, Richard. *Gustav Mahler IX. Symphonie: thematische Analyse mit Thementafel*. Wien: Archiv-Exemplar der Universal-Edition, n.d. 6 pp. Different from usual thematic analyses of the symphonies published in connection with the scores, this is a concentrated study of the thematic materials in the symphony with much music and very little prose explanation.

* Spinnler, Burkhard. "Zur Angemessenheit traditioneller Formbegriffe in der Analyse Mahlerscher Symphonik: ein Untersuchung des ersten Satzes der neunten Symphonie." *Form und Idee*: 223-76. Full citation under no. 21 above. Bar-by-bar formal analysis of the first movement of the symphony, making extensive use of diagrams and bar numbers but hampered to a certain extent by complete lack of musical examples.

996. Stein, Erwin. "Die Tempogestaltung in Mahlers neunter Sinfonie." *Pult und Taktstock* 1 (1924): 97-99, 111-14.
English version: "Organizing the Tempi of Mahler's Ninth Symphony." *Orpheus in New Guises*: 19-24.
A view of the symphony for those who conduct it and might not understand its overall structure in terms of tempo gradations. Brief but valuable. English version cited in full under no. 23 above translated by Hans Keller.

Symphony no. 10

997. Agawu, V[ictor] Kofi. "Tonal Strategy in the First Movement of Mahler's Tenth Symphony." *19th C Mus* 9 (Spring 1986): 222-33.
Analyzes the formal-harmonic structure of the *Adagio* in the context of Mahler's style and the style of his predecessors in the nineteenth century. Speaks more closely to the point adopted than Bergquist managed to do in his article in 1980 (see following entry).

998. Bergquist, Peter. "The First Movement of Mahler's Tenth Symphony: an Analysis and an Examination of the Sketches." *Music Forum* 5 (1980): 335-94.
An exhaustive Schenkerian analysis of the *Adagio* which sometimes strays into discussion of the other four movements. Very effective in terms of analysis of the first movement, but suffers from ill-defined conception of the symphony as a whole.

999. Block, Frederick. "Mahler's Tenth." *CD* 2 (1941): 43-45.
An early discussion of the symphony in English, and one of the first to take account of all five movements. Far-reaching in its influence because Block dared to voice his conception of a five-movement symphony during the period when only the first and third movements were being performed. The only available resource on the version by Block himself of the second, fourth and fifth movements which has never been published.

1000. Bouwman, Frans. "Kán en mág Mahlers 'unvollendete' worden voltooid? De aanstaande Mahler-manifestatie in Utrecht." *Mens en melodie* 41 (October 1986):

408-28.
Dutch article weighing the question of the morality vs. reality of the performing versions of the symphony, as a prelude to the symposium in Utrecht (November 1986) focusing on the work. Heavy reference to all known performing versions and discussions by musicologists from Krenek to Cooke to Filler.

1001. Brandt, Maarten. "Discussies over die tiende van Mahler." *Mens en melodie* 42 (1987): 26-37.
Report on the symposium on the *Symphony no. 10* in Utrecht, held in November 1986 in conjunction with the Vredenburg Mahler exhibition and concert cycle featuring various versions of the work. Includes individual coverage of many participant speakers at the symposium. Useful summary especially when used in connection with the exhibition catalogue (see no. 47 above).

1002. Carpenter, Clinton. "My Work on the Mahler Tenth." Unpublished manuscript, Mt. Prospect, Illinois, n.d. 17 pp.
This essay, written for the Gustav Mahler Stichting Nederland, comprises seven sections: "My Work on the Mahler Tenth," "The Tenth Symphony--A Continuing Story," "The Tenth Symphony--First Movement: Is the Critical Edition Best?" "The Tenth Symphony: That Problematical Second Movement," "The Tenth Symphony--The Third Movement, a Throw-Back to an Earlier Period," "The Tenth Symphony--Fourth Movement," and "The Tenth Symphony--The Fifth Movement: Problem and Final 'Abschied'." The essay offers an illuminating look at the problems of working with an unfinished manuscript and is interesting by virtue of its bold point of view with respect to Carpenter's solutions for the problems of the editor in such a situation. Not all readers may agree with his theories, especially as they influence his orchestration of the work; but this is still a valuable document for anyone interested in the problems of the symphony.

1003. Cooke, Deryck. "The Facts Concerning Mahler's Tenth Symphony." *CD* 2 (1963): 3-27. Reprinted in *Vindications: Essays on Romantic Music*. Cambridge, London, New York, New Rochelle, Melbourne, Sydney: Cambridge University Press, 1982, pp. 72-94. ISBN 0-521-24765-9 (hardcover), 0-521-28947-5 (paper).
An early study of the symphony concentrating on the

state of the manuscript and arguing for the conception of a performing version of all five movements for orchestra, by the man whose version is considered by many to be the definitive one. Written while his version was banned from performance and publication by Alma Mahler-Werfel, therefore valuable as a historical document of propaganda.

1004. Cooke, Deryck. "Mahler's Tenth Symphony: Artistic Morality and Musical Reality." *MT* 102 (1961): 351-54.

    A sharp analysis of the problem confronting anyone who would make a performing version of any unfinished work, especially this one. Based upon an understanding of the state of the manuscript versus the conception of the person who works to make it performable, and how the two "halves" of the problem may be balanced with each other. Magnificent.

1005. Cooke, Deryck. "Mahler's Tenth Symphony: Sonority, Texture and Substance." *Composer*, no. 16 (July 1965): 2-8.

    A study of the symphony in terms of overall balance considering harmony, counterpoint and intramovement form. Complementary to two previous essays by same author (see two preceding entries) in terms of hard analytical facts as arguments for the work in itself, essentially apart from the moral arguments concerning the performing version.

1006. Cooke, Deryck. "Mahler's Unfinished Symphony." *Essays on Music: an Anthology from "The Listener."* Ed. by Felix Aprahamian. London: Cassell, 1967, pp. 146-50.

    A brief analysis of the *Symphony no. 10* comparable to Cooke's article "Mahler's Tenth Symphony: Artistic Morality and Musical Reality" (see no. 1004 above) but somewhat more popular in nature than that article. Originally published at the time when Cooke's version was banned but reprinted in this form after release and first performances.

1007. Cooper, Martin du Pré. "Mahler's Sketches for a Tenth Symphony." *MT* 73 (1932): 1083-85.

    An early thematic analysis of the *Adagio*, marred by inaccuracies apparently from misreading of the 1924 facsimile, but not without value considering that literature on the subject in any language was notable by its absence at the time of publication.

1008. Dömling, Wolfgang. "Zu Deryck Cookes Ausgabe der X. Symphonie Gustav Mahlers." *Mf* 32 (1979): 159-62.
Summarizes the history of the symphony from 1910-59, then traces Cooke's work on his performing version from 1960 to the publication of the final version in 1976. Considers the textual problems causing differences of opinion between Cooke and Ratz (the *Adagio* movement necessarily being the major subject of discussion in that respect).

1009. Filler, Susan M. "The Case for a Performing Version of Mahler's Tenth Symphony." *Journal of Musicological Research* 3 (1981): 275-93.
Argues in favor of the principle of the performing versions of the symphony, considering the condition of the manuscript as Mahler left it rather than judging the merits of the various versions. Takes cue from the arguments advanced by Cooke in his articles of the early 1960s (see nos. 1003-1006 above).

1010. Jongbloed, Jan. "Structurele en semantische analyse van Gustav Mahlers tiende symfonie." [Structural and semantic analysis of Gustav Mahler's Tenth Symphony.] Unpublished manuscript, Stedelijk Conservatorium te Groningen, 1981. 98 pp.
Thoughtful study of the formal, melodic and harmonic organization of the symphony, owing something to Maurer-Zenck (see no. 1029 below) and Filler (see preceding entry, also no. 794 above), but adding new dimensions to subject. Unfortunately difficult to obtain.

1011. Kaplan, Richard. "Interpreting Surface Harmonic Connections in the Adagio of Mahler's Tenth Symphony." *In Theory Only* 4 (May-June 1978): 32-44.
Sequel article: "The Interactions of Diatonic Collections in the Adagio of Mahler's Tenth Symphony." *In Theory Only* 6 (November 1981): 29-39.
Two interrelated papers addressing questions of harmonic balance in the *Adagio*, progressing from small-scale in the earlier article to medium-scale in the later. Schenkerian analysis important especially in the second paper. Would have benefitted from analysis in the context of all five movements, but still useful in ways similar to discussion by Bergquist (see no. 998).

Individual Analyses: Symphony no. 10

1012. Klemm, Eberhardt. "Gustav Mahlers X. Sinfonie: zur Geschichte einer Konzertfassung." *Musik und Gesellschaft* 28 (1978): 549-53.
    Factual history of the symphony in performance and publication from the facsimile of 1924 (see no. 1014 below) to the final version by Cooke published in 1976 (see no. 1017 below). Straightforward summary with fewer details than in article by Claudia Maurer-Zenck (see no. 1029 below), suitable for intelligent nonspecialists.

1013. Klemm, Eberhardt. "Über ein Spätwerk Gustav Mahlers." *Deutsches Jahrbuch der Musikwissenschaft für 1961*. Hrsg. von Walther Vetter. Leipzig: Edition Peters, 1962, pp. 19-32.
    Primarily a thematic study of the *Adagio* only, with some comparative remarks about the two preceding symphonies and *Das Lied von der Erde*.

* la Motte, Diether de. "Liebes-Erklärung an die 10. Symphonie von Gustav Mahler." *Mahler-Interpretation 1985*: 17-28.
    Full citation under no. 24 above. Thematic study of the *Adagio* only, based on principles of thematic transformation and integration. Considers the movement self-sufficient, but would have benefitted from references to the other movements in the work.

1014. Mahler, Gustav. *Zehnte Symphonie*. Berlin, Wien, Leipzig: Paul Zsolnay, 1924. Vorwort by Alma Maria Mahler, 1 page.
    Appended pamphlet by Richard Specht: *Gustav Mahlers nachgelassene Zehnte Symphonie: einführende Bemerkungen*. Berlin, Wien, Leipzig: Paul Zsolnay, 1924. 17 pp.
    Amazingly detailed introduction to the manuscript and form of the unfinished work from Specht, showing important themes in single-line format and discussing the total conception of the five-movement structure. Quite revolutionary for its time insofar as its conception of a full five-movement work is concerned. The brief foreword by Alma Mahler-Werfel is a personal view of Mahler's thoughts and her own experiences following his death rather than a critical introduction to the work itself.

1015. Mahler, Gustav. *Zehnte Symphonie: Faksimile nach der*

Handschrift. Hrsg. von Erwin Ratz. München: Walter Ricke; Meran: Laurin, 1967. Vorwort von Erwin Ratz und Nachwort von Arnold Schoenberg, 3 pp.
Primarily a continuation of the argument against performing versions of the symphony begun by editor in the Critical Edition (see next entry). The statement of Schoenberg on the subject of the symphony was borrowed from his collected writings in *Style and Idea* (see no. 370 above) and its use many years after his death is suspect, although the publication of this facsimile (which is considerably more extensive than its predecessor cited in the previous entry) is in itself a notable achievement.

1016. Mahler, Gustav. *Adagio aus der Symphonie Nr. 10*. Kritische Gesamtausgabe, 11a. Wien: Universal Edition, 1964, revised ed. 1969. Vorwort/Preface und Revisionsbericht von Erwin Ratz, 5 pp. (1964 edition), 7 pp. (1969 edition). Translator of English version of preface unnamed.
Primarily an argument against the performing versions of the symphony, viewing the *Adagio* as the only movement worthy of preservation in critical score and performance. The extension of the listing of critical problems in the second edition of 1969 shows the influence of the editor's study of the manuscript which resulted in the publication of the facsimile of 1967 (see preceding entry).

1017. Mahler, Gustav. *A Performing Version of the Draft for the Tenth Symphony Prepared by Deryck Cooke*. New York: Associated Music Publishers; London: Faber Music Ltd., 1976. Introduction and notes by Deryck Cooke, German translation by Berthold Goldschmidt, pp. ix-xxii, xxviii-xliii, 165-93.
A critical argument in favor of the symphony as a full five-movement work, directly contrary to the theories advanced in the Critical Edition of the first movement and the facsimile of the manuscript published in 1967 (see two preceding entries). Exhaustive survey of the history of the symphony in various incarnations, and thorough listing of critical problems of the texts of the five movements.

1018. Malloch, William. "Deryck Cooke's Mahler Tenth: an Interim Report." *Music Review* 23 (1962): 292-304.
Surveys the nature of Deryck Cooke's first version of

Individual Analyses: Symphony no. 10 289

the symphony as broadcast on the BBC in 1960, and concludes that Cooke had not gone far enough in his efforts and should make a complete concert version so as to close gaps in the work. This was published at the time Cooke's version had been banned from performance or publication by Mahler's widow, but--after she changed her mind and allowed him freedom to have the work performed and published--Cooke did indeed fill in the gaps. See following entry for sequel to this article in *High Fidelity*.

1019. Malloch, William. "Gustav Mahler: the Unfinished Tenth Quickened to Vibrant Life." *High Fidelity* 16 (1966): 65-66.
Compare this article with earlier article by same author in preceding entry, and the story of the removal of Alma Mahler-Werfel's ban on Cooke's performing version and of the premiere of the first "complete" version of the *Symphony no. 10* is filled in. Malloch's amazing earlier criticism of the "incompleteness" of the version broadcast by the BBC (as opposed to the "presumption" that would have been more rationally expected) is here reversed completely; this brief article praises Cooke for having the courage to continue his work under the difficult circumstances of Alma Mahler-Werfel's ban, and fully supports the principle of the performing version of the work.

1020. Martner, Knud. "Gustav Mahlers 10. Symfoni." *DMT* 54 (Marts 1979): 196-201.
In Danish. An introduction to the history of the symphony, in composition and performance; also surveys the state of the manuscript as Mahler left it, with a description of the work done by Deryck Cooke in his performing version.

* Meylan, Claude. "La *Dixième Symphonie*, oeuvre ouverte: autour de quelques réalisations." *Colloque 1985*: 16-19.
Full citation under no. 5 above. Compares and contrasts the performing versions of the symphony by Carpenter, Cooke, Mazzetti and Wheeler, and alludes to the version by Hans Wollschläger.

1021. Meylan, Claude. "La dixième Symphonie reconstitutée de Gustav Mahler." *Schweizerische Musikzeitung* 104 (1964): 357-64.

Supports the concept of the performing versions of the symphony, based on a hearing of the concert premiere in London in August 1964 and on a consideration of the state of the manuscript. Takes issue with the polemics offered by Ratz in the introduction to the score of the *Adagio* in the Critical Edition (see no. 1016 above).

1022. Mitchell, Donald. "Some Notes on Mahler's Tenth Symphony." *MT* 96 (1955): 656-57.
Briefly surveys the history of the symphony to the mid-1950s, primarily restricting itself to discussion of the first and third movements, but advocating the principle of a performing version of all five movements and citing Frederick Block (see no. 999 above) and Joseph Wheeler in connection with the theory.

1023. Newlin, Dika. "Conversation Piece: Mahler and Beyond." *CD* 2 (1960): 117-19.
A discussion of the *Adagio* reprinted from *New York Philharmonic Program Notes* (January 14-17, 1960). Expressionistic view of the movement, seen as the threshold of the Second Viennese School. Personal and fascinating considering author's status as former student of Schoenberg and composer of the next generation.

1024. Paap, Wouter. "De tiende Symfonie van Gustav Mahler bij zijn oeuvre ingelijfd." [Gustav Mahler's Tenth Symphony incorporated with his oeuvre.] *Mens en melodie* 30 (1975): 236-40.
Summary of the history of the symphony from its composition in 1910 to the work of Deryck Cooke. Essentially advocates the principle of the performing versions but does not cite versions besides those of Cooke and the 1924 version of the first and third movements.

1025. Reid, Charles. "Mahler's 'Tenth.'" *Music Review* 26 (1965): 318-25.
Sympathetically surveys the symphony in its full five-movement conception, influenced by the performing version of Deryck Cooke.

* Rohland, Tyll. "Zum Adagio aus der X. Symphonie von Gustav Mahler." *Musik und Bildung* 5 (1973): 605-15.
Full citation under no. 17 above. Analyzes the *Adagio*

Individual Analyses: Symphony no. 10 291

only, historically, thematically, formally, melodically, harmonically, metrically and orchestrally.

1026. Rosack, Henry Peter. "'Symphony No. 10' by Gustav Mahler: the Fundamental Performance Problems of the Adagio." D.M.A. thesis, Stanford University, 1979. iv, 132 pp.
A conductor's view of the first movement only in the various performing versions. Suffers from neglect of the rest of the symphony, as discussion of tempo balancings, scoring and dynamics would have benefitted from appraisal of these facets in the cyclic manner between movements, as well as comparisons between the versions. Curious that a writer who apparently espouses the idea of a truncated symphony consisting of a single movement would go to the trouble of comparing different performing versions of that movement.

1027. Roy, Klaus George. "The Creative Process and Mahler's Tenth Symphony." *CD* 2 (1958): 17-32.
Semi-musical, semi-psychological study of the compositional process and how it affected Mahler's *modus operandi* when he wrote this symphony. Highly individual but shows some points in common with arguments of this kind of Reik (see no. 275) and Greene (see no. 706).

1028. Selden-Goth, Gisella. "La 'decima' di Mahler." *La scala*, no. 127 (Guigno 1960): 18-21.
An early Italian study of the symphony focusing on the materials Mahler himself left behind--manuscript study with some history for perspective. Before the controversy about performing versions had begun, essentially important for perspective in the context of events since the centennial.

1029. Zenck, Claudia Maurer. "Zur Vorgeschichte der Uraufführung von Mahlers zehnter Symphonie." *AfMw* 39 (1982): 245-70.
Exhaustive coverage of the early history of the symphony, showing documentation of the involvement of Specht, Krenek, Schalk, Zemlinsky and Berg in performance and publication of the first and third movements. Cites all available sources from Universal Edition and Associated Music Publishers. Essential reading, with dissertation by Filler (see no. 794 above) for anyone involved with the work. Based on author's lecture at 1979 Mahler Colloquium in Vienna.

1030. Zenck, Martin. "Ausdruck und Konstruktion im Adagio der 10. Sinfonie Gustav Mahlers." *Kunst als begriff-lose Erkenntnis: zum Kunstbegriff der ästhetischen Theorie Theodor W. Adornos*. Theorie und Geschichte der Literatur und der schönen Kunst, 29. München: Wilhelm Fink, 1977, pp. 188-211. ISBN 3-7705-1365-7.
A trio of essays referencing Adorno's philosophical/aesthetic theories as applied to the first movement of the symphony in melodic/formal/emotional construction.

OTHER WORKS

Klavierquartett

1031. Mahler, Gustav. *Klavierquartett*. Hamburg: Edition Sikorski, 1973. Editorial Remarks in German and English and Editionsbericht in German by Peter Ruzicka, pp. 3-5, 31.
Traces the historical background of the piano quartet in the context of Mahler's compositional career while a student at the Conservatory in Vienna. Surveys the rest of the quartet itself, and briefly considers the work in the historical perspective of chamber music during the nineteenth century.

1032. Newlin, Dika. "Gustav Mahler's Piano Quartet in a minor." *CD* 2 (1963): 180-83.
A very early study of the piano quartet Mahler wrote as a student at the Conservatory in Vienna. Shows some indication of musical substance of the work, unique at that time since the quartet was unpublished and was not published until ten years after this essay was released (see preceding entry). Newlin had actually transcribed the work from the manuscript into fair copy and based this article on her knowledge gained during the editing process.

Symphonic Prelude [spurious]

1033. Banks, Paul. "An Early Symphonic Prelude by Mahler?" *19th C Mus* 3 (1979): 141-49.
Speculates that a manuscript in the Austrian National

Library of a *Symphonic Prelude in c minor* is an early work of Mahler, although there is no documentary evidence to support this theory and the manuscript is not in Mahler's hand. Theory dubious at best.

1034. Hiltl, Wolfgang. "Symphonisches Präludium: ein vergessenes, unerkanntes Werk Anton Bruckners?" *Studien zur Musikwissenschaft* 36 (1985): 52-85.
 Argues for Bruckner as true composer of *Symphonic Prelude* believed by Mitchell, Banks and Gürsching to be a youthful work of Mahler. Tantamount to refutation of arguments advanced by Banks (see preceding entry) and therefore of interest to Mahler as well as Bruckner specialists.

1035. Stephan, Rudolf. "The 'Symphonic Prelude': Not a Composition by Mahler." *NaMR*, no. 17 (April 1987): 3-4.
 Essentially the end of the controversy about the *Symphonic Prelude* believed by Mitchell, Banks and Gürsching to be a youthful composition of Mahler, at least insofar as Mahler specialists are concerned. Traces the history of the manuscript materials to date and weighs contesting views of authorship for Bruckner and Rudolf Krzyzanowski, rejecting Mahler as composer for lack of convincing evidence.

Four Early Symphonies

1036. Becqué, Robert. "Mahler's Four 'Early Symphonies'." *NaMR*, no. 3 (July 1978): 7-8.
 Continues discussion of unknown early Mahler symphonies mentioned by Paul Stefan in 1938 after visiting widow of the grandson of Carl Maria von Weber (see following entry). Considers developments in the forty-year interval including possible fate of the sources during World War II.

1037. Stefan, Paul. "Four Unknown Early Mahler Symphonies Found in Dresden: Mengelberg Tells of Coming Upon the Manuscript-Scores in Possession of the Widow of Weber's Grandson." *Musical America* 58 (April 10, 1938): 20.
 Reports discovery of manuscripts of symphonies Mahler apparently wrote while a student at the Conservatory

in Vienna. Becqué, in *NaMR*, no. 3 (see preceding entry), cites an article in the Dutch periodical *De Telegraaf* (March 7, 1938), which may be analogous to this one. Difficult to substantiate the subject matter today as the widow of Weber's grandson is deceased and the manuscripts apparently disappeared during the Second World War.

Scherzo in c minor and Presto in F major

1038. Filler, Susan M. "Mahler's Sketches for a Scherzo in c minor and a Presto in F major." *College Music Symposium* 24 (Fall 1984): 69-80.
Discusses two symphonic movements Mahler sketched but did not complete, placing them chronologically about the time of the *Symphony no. 4* and *Symphony no. 5* but pointing out that they do not correspond to any movements in the ten symphonies in the repertoire. Argues that the two drafts were left in a state which allows work on a performing version comparable to the work on the *Symphony no. 10*, and offers insights into the process by which such a version may best be made, notably has been made by the author. Suggests that the movements are linked with each other and would have been nucleus of a completely different symphony from the ten in the repertoire. Introduces the author's own version of the two movements which, as of present date, is unperformed and unpublished. Based on author's paper at the 1983 meeting of the American Musicological Society.

Editions of Works by Other Composers

Weber, Die drei Pintos

1039. Blaukopf, Herta. "Eine Oper 'Aus Weber.'" *OeMz* 33 (1978): 204-08.
History of *Die drei Pintos* from its composition by Weber through Meyerbeer in 1846 to Mahler's work on the score in 1888. Summarizes Mahler's work on the performing version and cumulates the sources Mahler culled from other works of Weber. Brief quotation

Editions of Works by Other Composers: Die drei Pintos

from letters between Strauss and Bülow at the end of the article, illustrating their opposing opinions of Mahler's work on the score.

1040. Hanslick, Eduard. "Die drei Pintos." *Musikalisches und Litterarisches*. Die moderne Oper, 5. Berlin: Allgemeiner Verein für deutsche Litteratur, 1889, pp. 87-95.
Excellent introduction to Mahler's version of the Weber opera, giving history of the work since Weber's death, plot of the opera, description of Mahler's role in the preparation of the work for performance. Current to the 1888 premiere, by a leading critic of his time, and generally positive view of Mahler's accomplishment.

1041. Hartmann, Ludwig. "Die drei Pintos von C. M. von Weber." *Die Musik* 5 (1. Juniheft 1906): 303-10.
Discusses the history of the opera from its composition by Weber, later through Meyerbeer to Mahler's performing version of 1888, summarizing the plot and illustrating with musical examples.

1042. Heusgen, Birgit. *Studien zu Gustav Mahlers Bearbeitung und Ergänzung von Carl Maria von Webers Opernfragment "Die drei Pintos."* Kölner Beiträge zur Musikforschung, 133. Hrsg. von Heinrich Hüschen. Regensburg: Gustav Bosse, 1983. 152 pp. ISBN 3-7649-2273-7.
Originally the author's Ph.D. dissertation, Musikwissenschaftlichen Institut der Universität Köln. Surveys the sources for the opera and the methods and materials Mahler used to make his performing version. Much more detailed and well documented than any other discussion of the work.

1043. Holländer, Hans. "Gustav Mahler vollendet eine Oper von Carl Maria von Weber: vier unbekannte Briefe Mahlers an seine Eltern." *NZfM* 116 (1955): 130-32.
A study of Mahler's work on Weber's opera as documented in several letters Mahler wrote in 1888; however, cited here rather than in above section devoted to Mahler's letters as they address one particular subject and are cited in other sources.

1043a. Laux, Karl. "In Erinnerung gebracht *Die drei Pintos*: zum 150. Todestag Carl Maria von Webers." *Musik-*

bühne 76 (1976): 89-111.
Detailed essay on the opera valuable for coverage of
the history of the work prior to Mahler's involvement
with it (with special emphasis on involvement of Meyerbeer). Comparatively brief discussion of Mahler's
performing version and its critical reception and table
of sources for all numbers in the opera with details
of their original forms when not from the work as
Weber left it. Good introduction but nowhere near so
comprehensive as coverage by Heusgen (see no. 1042
above).

1044. Rognoni, Luigi, ed. *Carl Maria von Weber: Die drei Pintos, komische Oper in drei Aufzügen von Theodor Hell/I Tre Pinto, opera comica in tre atti.* Opera collana di guide musicali (Serie prima, 8). Dir. da Alberto Basso. Torino: Unione Tipografico-Editrice Torinese, 1975. viii, 197 pp.
Complete libretto of the opera, in original German followed by Italian translation, including illustrations of the sets and costumes for the production at the Teatro Regio of Torino, for which this book was published. Also includes commentary in Italian by Rognoni detailing the history of the work from the lives of Weber and Mahler, the structure of the opera itself (with many musical examples) and a review of the literature on the subject.

1045. Sittard, Joseph. "Die drei Pintos: komische Oper von Karl Maria von Weber (April 1888)." *Alte und neue Opern--musikalische Gedenktage--Aphorismen.* Studien und Charakteristiken, 3. Hamburg, Leipzig: Leopold Voss, 1889, pp. 87-94.
Covers the history of the opera from Weber's unfinished sketch to the world premiere of Mahler's version in 1888. Gives synopsis of action and musical format, and discusses Mahler's role in the final disposition of the work. Not entirely uncritical but generally positive. Original source of 1888 review from which this is reprinted in book form is not cited.

1046. Weber, Carl von. "Carl Maria von Weber's unvollendet hinterlassene komische Oper 'Die drei Pintos'." *NZfM* 55 (1888): 5-6, 20, 32-33, 44-45, 65-66.
A detailed introduction to the history of the opera by Weber's grandson, written at the time he had commissioned Mahler to prepare a performing version of

Editions of Works by Other Composers: Retouches

the work for premiere in Leipzig and publication. As librettist of the Mahler version of the work and possessor of the manuscript of the unfinished opera, Captain von Weber is an important source of information on the work; while this multisectional study is not of the technical nature that would have been written by a musical professional, it is the only known contemporary source by an insider.

Retouches: General

1047. Roman, Zoltan. "Gustav Mahler: Conductor and Composer as Music Historian." *Alte Musik als ästhetische Gegenwart/Bach--Händel--Schütz: Bericht über den Internationalen Musikwissenschaftlichen Kongress Stuttgart 1985.* Hrsg. von Dietrich Berke und Dorothee Hanemann. Kassel, Basel, London, New York: Bärenreiter, 1987, vol. 2, pp. 330-36.
Published under the auspices of the Gesellschaft für Musikforschung. A thoughtful discussion of Mahler's opinions concerning the performance of works by older masters, especially Bach, and how they compared with the opinions of performers and musicologists of his time. Refers to comparative views of Guido Adler and Hermann Kretzschmar. Documented with quotations from Adler, Natalie Bauer-Lechner, Mahler's letters, and the famous interview in *Etude* (1911). A very important contribution to a neglected subject spotlighted previously only by Paul Nettl.

1048. Stein, Erwin. "Mahlers Instrumentations-Retuschen." *Pult und Taktstock* 4 (1927): 117-22. Reprinted in *Anbruch* 2 (Februar 1928): 42-46.
English version: "Mahler's Re-scorings." *Orpheus in New Guises*: 25-30.
Discusses Mahler's retouches to Beethoven's *Symphony no. 7, Symphony no. 9, Leonore 2* and *3 Overtures*, the overtures to *Egmont, Coriolan* and *Consecration of the House*, Schubert's *Symphony no. 9*, Schumann's symphonies and *Manfred*, with special attention to the works by Schumann. English version cited in full above as no. 23 translated by Hans Keller.

Retouches: Bach

1049. Naegele, Philipp Otto. *Gustav Mahler and Johann Sebastian Bach*. Northampton, Massachusetts: Smith College, 1983. 43 pp.
Based on the 1981 Katherine Asher Engel Lecture given by Naegele at Smith College. Raises the idea of Mahler and Bach as musical and personal complements, observed through Mahler's professional involvement with Bach's music, his personal compositional standards influenced by Bach's (especially in the vocal works) and the parallels between the two composers' lives. Unusual and thought-provoking.

1050. Scherliess, Volker. "'Ganz nach Art der Alten': Gustav Mahler als Interpret Bachs. Ein Beitrag zur Rezeptionsgeschichte." *NZfM* 86 (Mai 1986): 4-8.
Mahler as editor of works by other composers, with particular reference to his involvement with music of Bach. Detailed consideration of his edition of four selected movements from the Bach suites (published by G. Schirmer in 1910) and its evidence as example of "Romantic" arrangement of Baroque music.

Retouches: Beethoven

* Hilmar, Ernst. "Mahlers Beethoven-Interpretation." *Mahler-Interpretation 1985*: 29-44.
Full citation under no. 24 above. Considers Mahler as conductor and editor of the works of Beethoven, focusing concretely on Mahler's alterations in the orchestration rather than the historical circumstances behind Mahler's actions. Particularly heavy coverage of the *Symphony no. 7* of Beethoven, enumerating many details with illustrations; narrow in its vision but not without its uses.

1051. Kalisch, Volker. "Zu Mahlers Instrumentationsretuschen in den Sinfonien Beethovens." *Schweizerische Musikzeitung* 121 (1981): 17-22.
Discusses Mahler's emendations in the scores of the Beethoven symphonies with special reference to the last movement of the *Symphony no. 7*. More a classification of technical details than a discussion of historical background for such practices.

Editions of Works by Other Composers: Retouches

1052. McCaldin, Denis. "Mahler and Beethoven's Ninth Symphony." RMA Proceedings 107 (1980-81): 101-10. Fascinating study of Mahler's work with Beethoven's Symphony no. 9, considering the traditions of re-editing suggested in Wagner's essay on the work dating from 1873, the categories of changes in melody and scoring considered appropriate, and a point-by-point comparison of Wagner, Mahler and Weingartner on the work. Shows Mahler to have been the most daring of the three in light of historical views about editing and performance of Beethoven's works. Based directly on study of Mahler's annotated copy of the work at the University of Southampton.

1053. McKinney, William Bruce. "Gustav Mahler's Score of Beethoven's Ninth Symphony--a Document of Orchestral Performance Practice in the Nineteenth Century." D.M.A. diss., University of Cincinnati, 1973. v, 166 pp. Critically surveys the alterations Mahler made in the score of the symphony, incorporating a detailed Revisionsbericht, and considering the history behind the decision Mahler made to modify Beethoven's score.

Retouches: Bruckner

1054. Blaukopf, Kurt. "Gustav Mahler und Bruckners dritte Symphonie." Hi Fi Stereophonie 13 (1974): 1140-42. Briefly surveys Mahler's arrangement of Bruckner's Symphony no. 3 for piano four hands, which was published in 1878 by Theodor Rättig in Vienna. Rare treatment of subject for its own sake rather than as brief component of Mahler's life, comparable to treatment by Mitchell.

1055. Hilmar, Ernst. "'Schade, aber es muss(te) sein': zu Gustav Mahlers Strichen und Retuschen insbesondere am Beispiel der V. Symphonie Anton Bruckners." Bruckner-Studien: Festgabe der Österreichischen Akademie der Wissenschaften zum 150. Geburtstag von Anton Bruckner. Hrsg. von Othmar Wessely. Veröffentlichungen der Komission für Musikforschung, hrsg. von Franz Grasberger, 16. Österreichische Akademie der Wissenschaften Philosophisch-Historische Klasse Sitzungsberichte, 300. Wien: Verlag

der Österreichischen Akademie der Wissenschaften, 1975, pp. 187-201.
Critical study of Mahler as editor of others' works through the example of his alterations to the score of Bruckner's *Symphony no. 5*. Considers the technical changes in the score as priority over the historical significance of such practices in general. Narrow and limited in overall scope, but useful as concrete example of Mahler's *modus operandi* in such functions.

Retouches: Schubert

1056. Andraschke, Peter. "Die Retuschen Gustav Mahlers an der 7. Symphonie von Franz Schubert." *AfMw* 32 (1975): 106-16.
Examines closely the nature of Mahler's retouches to Schubert's "Great C Major" *Symphony*, classifying them as (a) alterations in dynamics, (b) elimination or, conversely, strengthening in doublings in the scoring, and (c) cuts in form sections. Studies subject on its own merits without historical perspective of such practices in Mahler's time.

* Gülke, Peter. "Eine verborgene Station auf dem Weg von Schubert zu Mahler: das Andante aus dem Symphonischen Fragment D. 936A." *Gustav Mahler Kolloquium 1979*: 84-88.
Full citation under no. 8 above. Considers the fragment by Schubert as basis for possible reworking in Mahler's own works. Not convincing.

1057. Whaples, Miriam K. "Mahler and Schubert's a minor Sonata D. 784." *ML* 65 (1984): 255-63.
Surveys the role of music by Schubert in Mahler's education and follows with argument for the function of Schubert's sonata D. 784 as a seminal influence in Mahler's borrowing techniques. Special attention to the *Symphony no. 1* and *Symphony no. 7*.

Retouches: Schumann

1058. Bing, Albert. "Zu Mahlers Retuschen an Schumann's Symphonien." *Pult und Taktstock* 5 (Mai/Juni 1928): 53.

Brief, technical article concerned with Mahler's instrumental retouches in Schumann's *Symphony no. 2*, especially in the woodwinds and brass. Author, who had studied with Pfitzner, had been in turn Kapellmeister in Hamburg, the Komische Oper Berlin and the Friedrichs-Theater in Dessau before becoming Generalmusikdirektor at the Coburg Landestheater. This article was published a year after Erwin Stein's article in the same journal (see no. 1048 above), which profiled Mahler's work on all of Schumann's symphonies, and it may therefore be considered a perspective comment on Stein's report.

MISCELLANEOUS

1059. Balanchine, George. *Balanchine's New Complete Stories of the Great Ballets*. Ed. by Francis Mason. Drawings by Marta Becket. Garden City, New York: Doubleday, 1954, 1968. xxi, 626 pp.
An important source of information on productions of two ballets based on Mahler's music: "Dark Elegies" (pp. 111-12) and "The Song of the Earth" (pp. 384-89). Describes in detail the conceptions of the two ballets and how they were planned in relation to Mahler's music with unusual sensitivity (the first ballet is based on *Kindertotenlieder*).

1060. Gleede, E., and Alfred Oberzaucher. "Ballets to Music by Gustav Mahler." *NaMR*, no. 4 (February 1979): 11-13.
Supplement, "Ballets Set to Mahler's Music," by Jack Diether, in *NaMR*, no. 6 (January 1980): 16.
Documents the use of Mahler's music in ballets since 1937, concentrating primarily on the period from the 1960s to 1980. Classifies the ballets by title, use of Mahler works, choreographer and date and place of premiere.

* "Ein Jugendgedicht Gustav Mahlers." *Merker* 3: 183.

Full citation under no. 12 above. First publication of *Die Nacht blickt mild* written by Mahler in Kassel in December 1884.

1061. Soublette, Luis Gaston. "Oda a Gustav Mahler." Re-

vista musicale chilena 14 (Julio-Agosto 1960): 30-33.
Dedicated to Mahler on the centennial of his birth.

* Stockhausen, Karlheinz. "MAHLERs Biographie." Musik und Bildung 5 (1973): 596-97.
Full citation under no. 17 above. "MAHLER is" . . . a prose "ode" to Mahler from a twentieth century composer who recognizes Mahler's influence on compositional styles of this century, including Stockhausen's own style.

1062. Williams, Jonathan. Mahler. New York: Cape Goliard Press in Association with Grossman Publishers, 1969. [Unpaginated, 54 pp.] ISBN 206-61675-9 (hardcover), 206-61676-7 (paper).
A survey of the ten known symphonies and Das Lied von der Erde by a poet who dedicates one poem to each movement in each symphony (except the Blumine movement of Symphony no. 1, which was relatively new to the repertoire at the time of publication and may not have been known to the poet). This is an offbeat study of the symphonies in the spirit of Disney's Fantasia: a depiction of the thoughts of a nonprofessional who experiences music intelligently as a catalyst to his own creative genius.

* Zweig, Stefan. "Der Dirigent: für Gustav Mahler."
Gustav Mahler: ein Bild seiner Persönlichkeit in Widmungen: 58-61.
Full citation under no. 22 above. A congratulatory poem for Mahler's fiftieth birthday by a major Viennese literatus who had observed Mahler's work as a critic covering Mahler's performances at the Hofoper.

Indexes

INDEX OF COMPOSERS, AUTHORS, EDITORS, COMPILERS, TRANSLATORS, CONTRIBUTORS, ARRANGERS, LIBRETTISTS AND POETS

[All numbers are item numbers in the bibliography]

Abendroth, Walter, 341, 768, 837
Aber, Adolf, 964
Ablang, Willy d', 899, 909
Abraham, Gerald, 607, 769
Adler, Guido, 11, 14, 16, 22, 293, 608
Adorno, Gretel, 3, 702
Adorno, Theodor Wiesengrund, 1, 3, 7, 20, 702, 703
Agasaryan, Loretta, 719
Agawu, Victor Kofi, 838, 997
Albrecht, Theodore, 109a, 927a
Aldrich, Richard, 498
Allemandou, André, 255
Altmann, Wilhelm, 393
Andraschke, Peter, 24, 949, 984, 1056
Angerer, Manfred, 481
Antcliffe, Herbert, 609
Aperghis, George, 3
Aprahamian, Felix, 1006
Arnim, Ludwig Achim von, 539
Asfeld, M. d', 380
Asfeld, R. d', 380
Ashton, E.B., 504
Auer, Max, 334, 382

Babin, Pierre, 5
Bachmann, Klaus-Henning, 17
Bälan, George, 750
Bahr, Hermann, 16, 22, 294-96, 354-55
Bahr-Mildenburg, Anna, 13, 22, 297
Baker, Paul, 189
Baker, Theodore, 118
Balanchine, George, 1059
Banks, Paul, 29, 278-79, 665, 776, 1033
Barea, Ilsa, 62
Barford, Philip, 666, 720, 770
Barker, Andrew, 559
Barsova, Inna, 8, 25, 35, 380, 721, 784
Bartos, Vydal Frantisek, 380
Basso, Alberto, 31, 1044
Bata, András, 377
Batka, Richard, 12, 100, 356-57
Bauer, Anton, 444
Bauer-Lechner, Natalie, 12, 16, 192, 298, 304
Baum, Richard, 7, 703
Baxendale, Carolyn, 941
Beach, Amy Marcy Cheney, 9
Beaufils, Marcel, 610
Bechstein, Ludwig, 553
Becker, Friedel, 810
Becket, Marta, 1059
Becqué, Robert, 386, 1036
Beetz, Wilhelm, 445
Behn, Hermann, 358
Bekker, Paul, 13, 611, 785
Belcampo, Ava, 518
Berg, Alban, 332-33
Berg, Helene, 332
Bergauer, Josef, 198
Berges, Ruth, 751

Bergfeld, Dennis, 752
Bergquist, Peter, 998
Berke, Dietrich, 1047
Berl, Heinrich, 101-02
Bernet-Kempers, Karel Philippus, 280
Berny-Negrey, Wiesława, 612
Besseler, Heinrich, 984
Bethge, Hans, 549
Betti, Adolfo, 425
Beuerle, Hans Michael, 970
Biba, Otto, 394
Bie, Oskar, 839
Bienenfeld, Elsa, 13
Bierbaum, Otto Julius, 527
Bing, Albert, 1058
Bing, Rudolf, 493
Bittner, Julius, 37
Black, Leo, 370
Blaukopf, Kurt, 8, 10, 17, 19, 189, 203, 381, 667, 1054
Blaukopf, Herta, see: Singer-Blaukopf, Herta
Bles, Arthur, 662
Blessinger, Karl, 149-50
Bloch, Ernst, 103
Block, Friedrich (Frederick), 999
Blume, Friedrich, 151-52, 577, 586, 590, 594, 599, 605
Bock, Gustav, 577
Bockholdt, Rudolf, 819
Böhler, Otto, 13
Boese, Helmut, 428
Bohle, Bruce, 27
Bonnet, Jacques, 3
Bontinck, Irmgard, 892
Borris, Siegfried, 17
Boschot, Adolphe, 784a
Bostley, Edward John, 735
Bottenheim, Sam, 281
Boulez, Pierre, 195
Bouwman, Frans, 1000
Braakenburg, Johannes, 78
Brand, Juliane, 33
Brandenburg, Hans, 527

Brandt, Maarten, 1001
Braunwarth, Peter Michael, 344
Breig, Werner, 970
Brennecke, Wilfried, 411, 811
Brentano, Clemens, 539
Brincker, Jens, 942
Brinker-Gabler, Gisela, 505
Briscoe, James, 502
Britt, David, 522
Brod, Max, 104-07, 111
Broeckx, Jan, 26, 879
Broere-Moore, Sylvia, 795
Bronsen, David, 126
Brosche, Günter, 60, 346
Brownjohn, J. Maxwell, 310
Bruckner, Anton, 334
Brückner, Hans, 175
Bruner, Ellen Carole, 840
Brusatti, Otto, 880, 892
Bücken, Ernst, 153-54
Bülow, Hans von, 335, 347
Bülow, Marie von, 335
Buenzod, Emmanuel, 6
Burch, Noël, 3
Burckhard, Max, 22
Busoni, Ferruccio Benvenuto, 336

Caetani, Oleg, 5
Cardus, Neville, 687, 786-88
Carner, Mosco, 4
Carpenter, Clinton, 1002
Carsten, Francis Ludwig, 81
Casals, Pablo, 8
Casella, Alfredo, 11, 910
Chadwick, George Whitefield, 9
Chamouard, Philippe, 5, 736
Chevalley, Heinrich, 423
Christy, Beverly, 256
Christy, Nicholas, 256
Clapp, Philip Greeley, 613
Clark, T.E., 323
Clemenceau, Paul, 359
Clemens, Clara, 9, 299
Clement, Catherine, 3
Cochrane, Peggie, 810

Index of Composers, Authors etc.

Cohen, Judith, 136
Cohen, Maxwell Tillman, 108
Cohen, Yehuda Walter, 106
Colerus, Blanca, 501
Colles, Henry Cope, 614
Collins, Dean, 257
Combé, Edouard, 789
Conrad, Michael Georg, 527
Cooke, Deryck, 615, 771, 790, 971, 1003-06, 1017
Cooper, Martin du Pré, 1007
Crandall, John, 258-59
Crankshaw, Edward, 63
Creighton, Basil, 339
Crichton, Ronald, 319
Cronheim, Paul, 289
Cvetko, Dragotin, 407

Dahlhaus, Carl, 17, 782, 900, 985
Dallapiccola, Laura, 339
Damisch, Heinrich, 155
Damon, Lindsay Todd, 82
Damrosch, Walter, 300
Danuser, Hermann, 24, 737, 753, 841, 881-83
Danzinger, Gustav, 911
Dargie, Elizabeth Mary, 842
Davidson, Clifford, 690
Davidson, Audrey Ekdahl, see: Ekdahl-Davidson, Audrey
Davies, Laurence, 616
Davison, Peter, 961
Dawson, W.H., 70
Deaville, James, 588
Deck, Marvin Lee van, 491
Decsey, Ernst, 15
de Haan, Stefan, 859
Dehmel, Richard, 337, 528
De Kock, J.P., 791
Delalande, Jacques, 600
Deliège, Celestin, 3
Del Mar, Norman René, 950
Demuth, Norman, 617
Dent, Edward J., 44
Dernoncourt, Sylvie, 204

Dettelbach, Hans von, 704
Deutsch, Max, 618
Deutsch, Otto Erich, 446, 478
Diepenbrock, Alphons (Alfons), 338, 360, 792
Diepenbrock, Thea, 792
Diether, Jack, 207, 260-61, 619-20, 772, 871, 874, 986, 1060
Dietrich, Eva, 481
Dobers, Ernst, 167
Döll, Stefanie, 578
Dömling, Wolfgang, 1008
Dorfmüller, Kurt, 627, 668
Drage, Geoffrey, 64
Draper, Paul, 9
Dreyer, Ernst Adolf, 147
Droysen, Dagmar, 900
Druskin, Mikhail [Michael] Semenovich, 648, 894
Dühring, Eugen, 148
DuPree, R.D., 793
Durney, Daniel, 722
Duse, Ugo, 2, 193, 205-06, 843
Dutch, O.O., 111
Dutton, Maude Barrows, 662

Eaton, Quaintance, 492-93
Ebbers, Ursula, 306
Effenberger, Rudolf, 429
Eggebrecht, Hans Heinrich, 621, 754, 953
Ehlers, Paul, 156
Eichenauer, Richard, 157
Eisenburger, Sylvia, 86
Ekdahl-Davidson, Audrey, 690
Ellenberger, Hugo, 198
Ellert, Frederick, 516
Elvers, Rudolf, 579
Endler, Franz, 328
Engel, Gabriel, 27, 207, 901, 951, 972
Engelbrecht, Christiane, 411
Engel de Janosi, Joseph [pseud., J.E. de Sinoja], 109
Epstein, Julius, 12
Erpf, Hermann Robert, 738

Eulenberg, Kurt, 586

Fähnrich, Hermann, 14
Falke, Gustav, 529
Faltin, Peter, 10
Faltis, Viktor, 190
Farga, Franz, 447
Farrar, Geraldine, 301
Feder, Stuart, 262-64
Federmann, Reinhard, 331
Feldmann, Fritz, 407
Fellerer, Karl Gustav, 564
Filler, Susan M., 35, 109a, 502-03, 540, 794, 810, 1009, 1038
Finlay, Ian, 669
Fischer, Jens Malte, 560
Fischer, Kurt von, 541, 844, 984, 987
Fischer, Theodor, 110
Fischer-Dieskau, Dietrich, 636
Fiske, Richard Allen, 872
Flatauer, Suzanne, 189
Floros, Constantin, 8, 208, 650
Flothuis, Marius, 24, 282, 381, 670, 795
Flotzinger, Rudolf, 10, 622
Foerster, Josef Bohuslav, 16, 302, 361
Forchert, Arno, 24, 723, 773
Ford, P.R.J., 189
Forte, Allen, 943
Fraenkel, Josef [author], 111
Franklin, Peter, 298, 705, 912, 922
Freigedank, Karl [pseud. of Richard Wagner], 185
see also: Wagner, Richard
Freyenfels, Jodok, 430
Frieburger-Brunner, M. Vera, 37
Friedrich, Julius, 158
Fritsch, Theodor, 159
Fritz, Otto, 457

Fröhlich, Heinrich, 448
Frotscher, Gotthold, 160
Fry, Varian, 517
Fuchs, Anton, 191
Fülop, Peter, 38
Fürnberg, Louis, 671, 913
Füssl, Karl Heinz, 976
Furtwängler, Wilhelm, 432

Gabrilowitsch, Ossip, 9, 16, 299
Gador, Agnes, 377
Gal, Hans, 345
Gallarati, Paolo, 11
Galston, James, 325
Ganz, Rudolf, 9
Ganzer, Karl Richard, 161
Gartenberg, Egon, 209
Gedeon, Tibor, 210
Geissmar, Berta, 623
Gerigk, Herbert, 162, 181
Gerlach, Reinhard, 865-66
Gerstenberg, Walter, 460, 959, 984
Giroud, Françoise, 503a
Girschner, Otto, 163
Gishford, Anthony, 347
Glebova, I., 611
Gleede, E., 1060
Glockemeier, Georg, 83
Godard, Natalie, 339
Göhler, Georg, 15
Goepp, Philip, 979
Görner, Rüdiger, 967
Goethe, Johann Wolfgang von, 534
Goldblatt, David, 112
Goldhammer-Sahawi, Leo, 93
Goldschmidt, Berthold, 1017
Goll, Claire, 518
Goodwin, Inge, 203
Gottwald, Clytus, 20, 631
Gradenwitz, Peter, 111, 113-15
Gräner, Georg, 164, 801
Graf, Max, 37, 265, 283, 426, 431, 449, 624-25

Index of Composers, Authors etc.

Grainger, Percy, 9
Grant, [William] Parks, 672, 739-40, 796, 867, 914, 944
Grasberger, Franz, 39, 59, 351, 1055
Gray, Cecil, 973
Green, Richard, 810
Greene, David, 706
Gregory, Robin, 542, 546
Grimm, Jakob, 554
Grimm, Wilhelm, 554
Grohma, Otto, 67
Gross, Allen Robert, 962
Gruber, Gernot, 622
Grubeva, R., 611
Grünfeld, Heinrich, 303
Grünwald, Max, 94
Grun, Bernard, 332
Grunberger, Richard, 95, 111
Grunfeld, Frederic, 65
Grunsky, Karl, 165
Gülke, Peter, 8
Günther, Siegfried, 561, 845-46
Gutheil-Schoder, Marie, 12-13, 305
Gutmann, Albert, 427
Gutmann, Danielle, 40
Gutmann, Emil, 15
Gutmann, Hanns, 1

Haas, Gerlinde, 481
Haas, Robert Maria, 450
Haas, Willy, 504
Hadamowsky, Franz, 41, 451
Hailey, Christopher, 333
Hajdu, Andre, 5
Halban, Desi, 306
Hamburger, Paul, 7, 660, 958
Hanemann, Dorothee, 1047
Hansen, Mathias, 380, 755-56, 952
Hansen-Appel, Gabriele, 868
Hanslick, Eduard, 1040
Hanson, Wesley Luther, 741
Hantsch, Hugo, 84
Harcourt, Eugène d', 396

Harris, Donald, 284, 333
Harten, Christa, 481
Hartleben, Otto Erich, 530
Hartmann, Ludwig, 562, 1041
Hasse, Hans, 811
Hauptmann, Gerhard, 432
Hefling, Stephen, 8, 555, 884, 915
Heine, Heinrich, 563
Heinisch, Eduard Christoph, 196
Heinsheimer, Hans, 23, 653
Heitmüller, Franz Ferdinand, 530
Hell, Theodor, 566, 1044
Heller, E.C., 7, 958, 992
Heller, Friedrich, 195, 622, 799
Hellmer, Edmund, 353
Helm, Everett, 598, 600
Hempel, Gunter, 418
Herttrich, Ernst, 392
Herzfeld, Friedrich, 397
Heskes, Irene, 116
Hesse, Hermann, 636
Heuberger, Richard, 362
Heusgen, Birgit, 1042
Higelke, Kurt, 167
Hildebrand, Hans, 716
Hill, Ralph, 821
Hilmar, Ernst, 24, 42, 602, 1055
Hiltl, Wolfgang, 1034
Hinrichsen, Henri, 379
Hirschfeld, Ludwig, 13
Hirschfeld, Robert, 452
Hoffman, Eva, 626
Hoffmann, Rudolf Stefan, 847
Holbrook, David, 707
Holde, Artur, 117
Holen, Jacques van, 742
Holländer, Hans, 118, 211-13, 378, 873, 1043
Holland, Dietmar, 644
Hopkins, Bill, 380
Hopkins, Robert George, 724
Hoyer, Michael, 21

Hüschen, Heinrich, 1042
Hu Haiping, 550
Huneker, James Gibbons, 499
Hutschenruijter, Wouter, 214
Hyman, Paul E., 98

Irkowsky, Rudolf, 166
Isaacs, Reginald, 519
Isenghi, Th., 42a
Istel, Edgar, 801

Jacobs, Mark, 597
Jahnke, Sabine, 535
Jakoby, Richard, 864
James, Burnett, 708
Jameux, Dominique, 5
Janik, Allen, 66
Jemnitz, Alfred, 420
Jenks, William Alexander, 85
Jephcott, Edmund, 385
Jerger, Wilhelm, 432-33
Johnston, William, 67
Jokl, Ernst, 16
Jones, Ernest, 307
Jones, J. Sydney, 86
Jones, Robert Frederick, 902
Jongbloed, Jan, 1010
Josewsky, Erwin, 167
Jülg, Hans-Peter, 953
Jünger, Friedrich Georg, 536
Jung, Ute, 564
Jungheinrich, Hans-Klaus, 20
Junk, Victor, 343

Kadar, Jolantha, 421-22
Kahan, Salomon, 120
Kaiser, Ernst, 345, 380
Kaiser, Joachim, 121
Kalbeck, Max, 37
Kalisch, Volker, 1051
Kandinsky, Nina, 520
Kann, Robert, 87-88
Kaplan, Nathan, 797
Kaplan, Richard, 1011

Kapp, Reinhard, 628
Karas, Joža, 122
Karbusicky, Vladimir, 757
Karpath, Ludwig, 13, 308-09
Kars, Gustave, 629
Kartomi, Marguerite, 764
Katzenberger, Günter, 864
Kauder, Hugo, 16
Kaznelson, Siegmund, 96
Keener, Andrew, 398
Keller, Hans, 1, 23, 653, 936, 996, 1048
Keller, Otto, 15
Kende, Götz Klaus, 479
Kenkel, Konrad, 885
Kennedy, Michael, 215
Kerner, Dieter, 266-67
Kernkamp, H.F., 216
Kesten, Hermann, 312
Kestenberg-Gladstein, Ruth, 119
Killian, H.J., 298
Kitzwegerer, Liselotte, 453
Klarmann, Adolf, 512, 521, 533
Klein, Rudolf, 19, 446, 454
Klemm, Eberhardt, 20, 379, 954, 1012-13
Klemperer, Otto, 7, 310
Kletzl, Otto, 415
Kligerman, Charles, 274
Klopstock, Friedrich Gottlieb, 536
Klusen, Ernst, 565, 758
Kneif, Tibor, 963
Knepler, Georg, 10
Koch, Thilo, 121
Koenig, Arthur William, Jr., 798
Kokoschka, Oskar, 522
Kolbenheyer, E.G., 432
Kolleritsch, Otto, 10, 630
Kolodin, Irving, 494
Komma, Karl Michael, 17
Konen, V., 634
Korngold, Julius, 434
Kralik, Heinrich [von], 435, 455-56, 799, 886

Index of Composers, Authors etc. 311

Kraus, Hedwig, 436
Kraus, Karl, 78
Kravitt, Edward, 268, 848-50
Krebs, Carl, 399
Krehbiel, Henry Edward, 495-96
Krenek, Ernst, 325
Kroher, Ekkehard, 325
Kroll, Erwin, 188
Kropfinger, Kraus, 24
Krummacher, Friedhelm, 970
Kučerová, Dagmar, 408
Kügler, Ilka Maria, 480
Kühn, Hellmut, 17, 800
Kuehn, John L., 269
Kulenkampff, Hans-Wilhelm, 20, 709
Kunz, Harald, 580
Kunze, Stefan, 970
Kuret, Primož, 285
Kurz-Halban, Selma, 13

Laaff, Ernst, 599
Lachenmann, Helmut, 17, 20
la Grange, Henry-Louis de, 5, 17, 28, 40, 195, 217-18, 339, 673-74
la Motte, Diether de, 10, 24
Landau, Anneliese, 123
Landau, Ludwig, 168
Landman, Isaac, 33
Lang, Anne-Marie, 103
Lang, Paul Henry, 124
Langevin, Paul-Gilbert, 629
Langford, Samuel, 687
La Rue, Jan, 460, 959
Latraverse, François, 3
Laux, Karl, 1043a
Lawrence, L.J., 324
Lazarov, Stefan, 974
Lea, Henry A., 125-27, 710
Lébl, Vladimir, 412
Lebrecht, Norman, 311
Ledeč, Jan, 759
Lederer, Josef-Horst, 481
Lederer, Zdenek, 119
Leleu, Jean-Louis, 3, 702

Lelieveld, K., 43, 47
Lemery, Denys, 3
Leotsakos, Giorges, 770
Lert, Ernst J.M., 400
Levine, James, 810
Levy, David, 270
Levy, Simon, 128
Lewis, Christopher Orlo, 988
Lewisohn, Ludwig, 513
Ley, Rosamond, 336
Leydenbach, Theo, 3, 702
Leyen, Friedrich von der, 554
Libermann, Arnoldo, 219
Lichtenfeld, Monika, 20, 630
Lichtenwanger, William, 592
Ligeti, György, 20, 631
Lillieroth, Emanuel, 339
Lindlar, Heinrich, 593
Lipman, Samuel, 675
List, Kurt, 129
Litterscheid, Richard, 169
Litzenburg, Deborah Ann, 725
Lockspeiser, Edward, 688
Loeser, Norbert, 220
Löhr, Friedrich, 12, 16
Loewenberg, Alfred, 44
Loman, Daisy, 189
Loschnigg, Franz, 221
Lothar, Rudolf, 469
Louis, Rudolf, 170
Ludvová, Jitka, 413-14
Lück, Rudolf, 594
Lustgarten, Egon, 16

Märzendorfer, Ernst, 10
Mahler, Arnošt, 286, 409
Mahler, Gustav, 12, 46, 304, 363, 377-92, 566-67, 858-60, 869-70, 874-75, 887, 903-05, 916-18, 923-24, 932-34, 945, 955-56, 964-65, 975-76, 989-91, 1014-17, 1031
Mahler-Werfel, Alma Maria, 311, 339, 504-05
Mahony, Patrick, 506
Maier, Beatrice, 625
Malloch, William, 686, 1018-19

Mann, Erika, 340
Mann, Thomas, 312, 340, 523
Manzoni, G., 3, 702
Marcus, Steven, 307
Marliave, Joseph de, 774
Marrocco, W. Thomas, 597
Martinez Aragon, J., 385
Martner, Knud, 48, 222, 298, 314, 339, 380, 386, 689, 1020
Marx, Hans Joachim, 650
Marx, Joseph, 432, 640
Mason, Daniel Gregory, 9
Mason, Francis, 1059
Massenkeil, Günther, 712
Mathe, Miklós, 210
Mathis, Alfred, 223
Matter, Jean, 3, 6, 224-25
Mattfeld, Julius, 497
Matthews, Colin, 771, 802-03, 859, 950
Matthews, David, 771, 776
Maurer-Zenck, Claudia, 1029
Mayer, Hans, 7, 568
Mayer, Sigmund, 97
McCaldin, Denis, 226, 1052
McGrath, William J., 8, 711
McGuinness, Rosamund, 632
McKinney, William Bruce, 1053
Meerwein, Georg G., 519
Mell, M., 432
Mellers, Wilfrid, 676
Mengelberg, [Curt] Rudolf, 11, 13, 227, 387, 804
Mengelberg, Willem, 313, 814
Mersmann, Hans, 171, 633
Messchaert, Johannes, 392
Messner, Gerald Florian, 481
Meyer, Gabriele, 644
Meyer, Krzystof, 10
Meylan, Claude, 5, 1021
Mikheeva, Lyudmila, 228, 863
Miklin, Richard, 344
Mikorey, Franz, 401
Mikorey, Stefan, 743
Mitchell, Donald, 5, 29, 229, 271, 287, 339, 677, 775-77, 859, 876, 888, 1022
Mittag, Erwin, 18, 437
Mnatsakova, E., 634
Moldenhauer, Hans, 364, 388
Moldenhauer, Rosaleen, 364
Monnikendam, Marius, 805
Monson, Karen, 507
Mooney, William E., 272
Moore, Deborah Dash, 98
Morgan, Robert, 635
Morice, G., 437
Morton, Frederic, 68
Moser, Hans Joachim, 172, 636
Mouchard, Claude, 716
Müller, Lise Lotte, 524
Mueller von Asow, Erich H., 389
Mulder, Ernst Willem, 889
Murphy, Edward W., 806
Myers, Rollo, 342
Mylemans, P., 851

Nadel, Arno, 130
Naegele, Philipp Otto, 1049
Namenwirth, Simon Michael [Misha], 49, 690
Nebehay, Christian Michael, 69, 198
Nebolyubova, Larisa S., 760
Nectoux, Jean-Michel, 40
Neill, E.D., 637
Neisser, Arthur, 13, 230
Neitzel, Otto, 16
Nejedly, Zdenek, 231
Nemeth, Amade, 232
Nemeth, Carl, 233
Nest'ev, Izrael Vladimirovich, 678
Nettl, Paul, 119, 390, 415
Netzer, Remigius, 522
Neumann, Angelo, 22
Neuwirth, Gösta, 24
Newlin, Dika, 131, 233, 273, 288, 298, 370, 556, 1023, 1032
Newman, Ernest, 319

Nickl, Therese, 344
Nielsen, Erika, 547, 559, 885
Niemann, Walter, 638
Niemöller, Klaus Wolfgang, 712
Nietzsche, Friedrich, 537
Nikkels, Eveline, 5, 538
Nodnagel, Ernst Otto, 807, 906, 919, 925, 946, 957
Nolthenius, Helene, 877
Nonveiller, Heinz, 350
Novalis [pseud. of Friedrich von Hardenberg], 531
Novelletto, A., 307
Novelletto, M., 307
Nowak, Adolf, 712, 970

Oberzaucher, Alfred, 1060
O'Brien, Sally, 761
Ocadlik, Mirko, 132
Oehlmann, Werner, 852
Oesterreicher, John, 516
Orange, J.R.L., 437
Orel, Alfred, 37
Ortner, Oswald, 640
Osherova, S., 380
Osthoff, Wolfgang, 482
Oswald, Peter, 679

Paap, Wouter, 289, 1024
Pachnicke, Bernd, 595
Padellaro, Laura, 673
Pala, F., 302
Palmer, Francis H.E., 70
Pamer, Fritz Egon, 853
Parsons, Arrand, 810
Pass, Walter, 481
Paulsen, Wolfgang, 710
Pekelska, Frantiska, 325
Peltz, Mary Ellis, 53
Percy, Gösta, 680
Perez de Arteaga, Jose L., 234
Perger, Richard von, 438
Perle, George, 508
Pertlik, Susanne, 344
Petermann, Reinhard E., 71

Peterson, P., 650
Pfitzner, Hans Erich, 341, 365
Pfohl, Ferdinand, 314
Philippon, Jean, 598
Piers, Maria, 274
Pinzauti, Leonardo, 639
Pirchan, Emil, 457
Piron-Audard, Catherine, 103
Plesske, Hans-Martin, 573-74, 587, 589, 596-97
Ploderer, Rudolf, 640
Pollak, Michael, 72
Pollock, George, 274
Ponnelle, Lazare, 977
Powell, Nicolas, 199
Prawy, Marcel, 195, 458
Prieberg, Fred K., 173
Principe, Quirino, 235
Pringsheim, Klaus, 366
Przistaupinsky, Alois, 392, 459
Pugliese, Giuseppe, 236
Pulzer, Peter G.J., 89, 111

Quander, Georg, 800
Quoika, Rudolf, 762

Raabe, Peter, 174
Raaben, Lev Nikolaevich, 228
Rachmaninoff, Sergei, 315
Rand, Lola, 810
Ratz, Erwin, 7, 18, 237, 778, 808-09, 887, 905, 917, 924, 933, 945, 956, 958, 965, 990-92, 1015-16
Ravina, Menashe [Manasseh Rabinowitz], 133
Raynor, Henry, 238, 691
Redl, Renate, 73
Redlich, Hans Ferdinand, 1, 2, 16, 30, 239, 641-42, 681, 811-12, 858, 869, 904, 926, 934, 955, 959, 964
Reeser, Eduard, 24, 240, 338, 381, 391, 890, 993
Rehm, Wolfgang, 3, 460, 703, 959

Reich, Willi, 134, 460
Reid, Charles, 1025
Reik, Theodor, 275-76
Reilly, Edward, 5, 19, 290, 293, 381, 385, 918
Reimer, Lennard, 603
Reiter, Franz Richard, 713
Restagno, Enzo, 31
Reuter, Evelyn, 891
Revers, Peter, 5, 8, 19, 575-76, 813, 994
Rexroth, Dieter, 10, 864
Richolson-Sollitt, Edna, 814
Richter, Ludwig, 553
Rickett, Richard, 454, 456
Rieger, Eva, 505
Riehn, Rainer, 861
Riesemann, Oskar von, 315
Rilke, Rainer Maria, 532
Ringel, Erwin, 713
Ringer, Alexander, 136
Ringger, Rolf Urs, 14
Ritter, William, 6, 13, 367, 692-94
Rivier, David, 726
Robijns, J., 26
Rock, Christa Maria, 175
Röllecke, Heinz, 543
Rognoni, Luigi, 2, 32, 339, 714, 1044
Rohland, Tyll, 17
Rolland, Romain, 342
Roller, Alfred, 1, 13, 16, 22, 201, 567
Roman, Zoltan, 8, 189, 381, 547, 779, 854-55, 860, 870, 892, 1047
Rosack, Henry Peter, 1026
Rosé, Alfred, 368
Rosenberg, Wolf, 10, 20, 195, 569
Rosenfeld, Paul, 176
Rosenheim, Richard, 416
Rosensaft, Menachem Z., 90
Rosenthal, Harold, 468
Rothmüller, Aron Marko, 137
Rottensteiner, Alois Franz, 428
Rottweiler, Hektor [pseud. of Theodor Adorno], 7, 703
see also: Adorno, Theodor Wiesengrund
Rousseau, Jacqueline, 3
Roy, Klaus George, 1027
Rozenblit, Marsha L., 98
Rozenshil'd, Konstantin Konstantinovich, 461, 682, 893
Rubin, Marcel, 715
Rüber, Christoph, 648
Rückert, Friedrich, 548
Rusk, J. Wayne, III, 815
Rutherford, Dolly, 315
Rutters, Herman, 241
Ruzicka, Peter, 17, 20, 1031
Rychetský, Jiři, 763

Sablich, Sergio, 483
Sachs, Carolyn, 592
Sachs, Edwin O., 200
Sachs, Joseph, 138
Sadie, Stanley, 29, 579, 585, 587, 589, 597, 603, 606
Sakata, Kenichi, 50
Salesky, Gdal, 139
Salten, Felix, 11, 695-96
Samaroff-Stokowski, Olga, 683
Samazeuilh, Gustave, 342
Sams, Eric, 544
Sandoval, Felipe Ximenez de, 204
Sargeant, Winthrop, 643
Scanzoni, Signe, 462
Schaal, Richard, 21, 325
Schaefer, Hans Joachim, 14, 410-11
Schäfer, Wolf-Dieter, 744
Schaefers, Anton, 745
Schalk, Franz, 343, 346
Schalk, Lili, 343
Scharberth, Irmgard, 424
Schenck, Rüdiger, 21
Schenk, Erich, 280
Schering, Arnold, 856
Scherliess, Volker, 1050

Index of Composers, Authors etc. 315

Schibler, Armin, 6, 816
Schiedermair, Ludwig, 316, 369, 801, 817-18
Schlechta, Karl, 537
Schleiden, Karl August, 536
Schlüter, Wolfgang, 697
Schmid, Leopold, 684
Schmidt, Heinrich, 177, 727
Schmitt, Theodor, 819
Schmitz, A., 984
Schmoll-Eisenwerth, Regina, 644
Schnapp, Friedrich, 336
Schnebel, Dieter, 7, 10, 20, 51, 927
Schneider, Gunter, 291
Schneider, Hans, 392
Schnitzler, Arthur, 344
Schnitzler, Heinrich, 344
Schoenberg, Arnold, 7, 78, 333, 345, 370, 728, 1015
Schönfeldt, Christl, 439
Schollum, Robert, 509, 645
Scholz, Gottfried, 195
Schonberg, Harold, 402
Schorske, Carl E., 5, 8, 74
Schreiber, Ulrich, 716
Schreiber, Wolfgang, 242
Schreinzer, Karl, 436
Schuh, Willi, 324, 336, 347
Schulik, Norbert, 700
Schultz, Klaus, 51
Schulze, Friedrich Karl Alfred, 419
Schumann, Karl, 780
Schumann, Otto, 178-79
Schuschitz, Elisabeth Desirée, 698
Schwartz, Rudolf, 788
Sebestyen, György, 501
Seckerson, Edward, 243
Seelig, Carl, 531
Seidl, Art[h]ur, 12, 15, 52, 403, 820
Seifert, Herbert, 481
Selden-Goth, Gisela [Tolney-Witt, Gisela?], 1028
Seligmann, A.F., 13
Seltsam, William, 53
Sendrey, Alfred, 140
Shanet, Howard, 500
Sharp, Geoffrey, 821
Shelley, Anne, 195
Sheratsky, Rodney, 927a
Shibata, Namio, 50
Shlifshtein, Natalya, 822
Silbermann, Alphons, 54
Simpson, Robert, 830
Sine, Nadine, 822a
Singer, Kurt, 699
Singer-Blaukopf, Herta, 19, 57, 194, 380-81, 385, 477, 857, 1039
Šip, Ladislav, 244
Sittard, Joseph, 1045
Slepnev, I., 634
Slezak, Leo, 13, 309, 317-18
Slonimskiy, Sergey Mikhaylovich, 894
Smith, Bradley F., 91
Smith, Warren Storey, 510, 646-47, 685, 729, 781
Smith, Willem, 545
Smoley, Lewis, 55
Smyth, Ethel Mary, 319
Soler, J., 3, 702
Sollertinskiy, Ivan Ivanovich, 245, 648
Sommerfeld, John, 331
Sondheimer, Robert, 978
Sonner, Rudolf, 180
Sopeña Ibáñez, Federico, 246, 649
Sorabji, Kaikhosru [Leon Dudley], 823, 973
Sorell, Walter, 511
Soublette, Luis Gaston, 1061
Specht, Richard, 11, 12, 13, 15, 16, 320-21, 371, 463, 700, 895, 907, 920, 928, 935, 960, 966, 979, 995, 1014
Spiel, Hilde, 75, 111, 195

Spielmann, Heinz, 524
Spiering, Theodor, 9
Spinnler, Burkhard, 21
Sponheuer, Bernd, 21, 824
Srbik, H. von, 432
Stadtlander, Karin, 514
Stahmer, Klaus Hinrich, 21, 650
Stauber, Paul, 464
Stefan[-Gruenfeldt], Paul, 1, 11-13, 15-16, 22, 23, 298, 322-23, 349, 465-67, 651-53, 825, 1037
Stehmann, Gerhard, 13
Stein, Erwin, 1, 23, 345, 468, 653, 936, 996, 1048
Stein, Leon, 141-42
Stein, Leonard, 370
Steinitzer, Max, 16, 22
Stekel, Eric-Paul, 629
Stengel, Theophil, 181
Stenzl, Jürg, 883
Stephan, Rudolf, 8, 19, 24, 56, 194, 381, 392, 782, 875, 921, 937-38, 967, 970, 1035
Stern, Julius, 469
Stevens, H.S., 137
Stiedry, Fritz, 470, 903, 916, 923, 932, 975, 989
Still, Robert, 277
Stockhausen, Karlheinz, 17
Stokes, Richard, 381
Stompor, Stephan, 404
Storck, Karl, 182, 202
Storjohann, Helmut, 14, 730
Stransky, Josef, 9, 372
Strauss, Gabriele, 348
Strauss, Richard, 324, 342, 346-48, 385, 432, 684
Stresemann, Ludwig, 349, 947
Strohm, Stefan, 970
Stuckenschmidt, Hans Heinz, 143
Subotnick, Rose Rosengard, 717

Swanson, Curtis, 247
Swarowsky, Hans, 826
Swift, Richard, 827
Szeps-Zuckerkandl, Berta, 331

Tancibudek, S., 764
Tarazona, Andrés Ruiz, 248
Taylor, Virginia Sue, 746
Teibler, Hermann, 801
Tenschert, Roland, 718
Tessmer, Hans, 699
Teweles, Heinrich, 980
Theurich, Jutta, 383
Tibbe, Monika, 20, 782
Tiedemann, Rolf, 3, 7, 702-03
Tietze, Hans, 37, 99
Timoshenkova, Galina Andreevna, 828-29
Tirso de Molina [pseud. of Gabriel Tellez], 557
Tischler, Hans, 654, 731-34, 896
Tolney-Witt, Gisela, see: Selden-Goth, Gisela
Toulmin, Stephen, 66
Tovey, Donald Francis, 939
Tramer, Hans, 144
Trenker, Marianna, 193
Trenner, Franz, 347-48
Trienes, Walter, 183
Trilling, Lionel, 307
Trunz, Erich, 534
Truscott, Harold, 830-31
Tsitsiklis, Michalis, 655
Tsukakoshi, Satoshi, 385
Türcke, Berthold, 292
Turner, J. Rigbie, 58

Uhlendorff, Franz, 411
Ullrich, Hermann, 18
Unterer, Verena, 471

Vartanyan, Z., 897
Velten, Klaus, 17
Vergo, Peter, 525
Vestdijk, Simon, 656, 832
Vetter, Walther, 765, 1013

Index of Composers, Authors etc. 317

Vignal, Marc, 3, 249
Vill, Susanne, 570
Vötterle, Karl, 590
Vogg, Herbert, 584
Voit-Hilmar, Renate, 657
Volbach, Fritz, 747
Volcani, Toni, 106
Volkmann, Richard von [pseud., Richard Leander], 558
Vondenhoff, Bruno, 59-60
Vondenhoff, Eleonore, 59-60
Vossler, Karl, 557

Wadmann, Anne, 545
Wältner, Ernst Ludwig, 862
Wagner, Cosima, 348
Wagner, Manfred, 8, 700
Wagner, Richard, 185
Wagner, Siegfried, 348
Waissenberger, Robert, 57, 76
Waldmann, Guido, 160
Waldstein, Wilhelm, 658
Walker, Frank, 44
Wallaschek, Richard, 472
Wallis, Alfons, 659
Walter, Bruno, 12-13, 16, 22, 33, 304, 325-26, 349, 373, 660, 771
Walter-Lindt, Lotte, 325, 349
Wandruszka, Adam, 701
Wanninger, Forrest, 766
Warrack, John, 661
Watkins, Geoffrey, 69, 189
Weber, Carl von, 566, 1046
Weber, Carl Maria von, 566-67
Weber, J.F., 61
Weigel, Hans, 77, 440
Weigl, Karl, 801
Weimar, Karl S., 127
Weingartner, Felix [von], 37, 327, 662
Weingartner-Studer, Carmen, 18

Weinheber, J., 432
Weinmann, Alexander, 585, 603, 605-06
Weisser, Albert, 145
Weissman, Adolf, 405
Wellesz, Egon, 328, 374-76, 473, 748-49, 833
Wellesz, Emmy, 328
Welter, Friedrich, 186
Weltsch, Felix, 107, 119
Wenig, Jan, 417
Wenk, Arthur, 551
Werba, Erik, 18
Werba, Robert, 441, 483-90
Werck, Isabelle, 929, 981
Werfel, Franz, 250, 502, 512-13, 533
Werker, Gerard, 982
Werner, Eric, 146
Werner, Heinrich, 352
Wessely, Othmar, 251, 1055
Wessem, Constant von, 252, 663, 834
Wessling, Berndt W., 253, 514
Weyer, Reinhold, 17
Whaples, Miriam, 1057
Whiteside, Andrew, 92
Wied, Martina, 37
Wiesmann, Sigrid, 195
Wildgans, Friedrich, 18
Wilkens, Sander, 948
Wilkins, Eithne, 345, 380
Williams, Jonathan, 1062
Williamson, John C., 783, 835, 930, 968-69, 983
Willnauer, Franz, 474-75
Winston, Clara, 312, 340
Winston, Richard, 312, 340
Winter, Josefine von, 329
Wiora, Walter, 712
Witeschnik, Alexander, 41, 442, 457, 476
Wittenberg, J.J., 395
Wörner, Karl Heinrich, 836
Wöss, Josef Venatius von, 898
Wolf, Hugo, 350-53
Wolff, Marguerite, 327

Wolfram, A., 432
Wood, Barry, 256
Woodrow, E.A.E., 200
Woolridge, David, 406
Worbs, Hans Christoph, 664
Wulf, Joseph, 187
Wunberg, Gotthard, 78

Xenakis, Françoise, 515

Zaccaro, Gianfranco, 254
Zahn, Leopold, 526
Zavadskaya, E., 552
Zelzer, Hugo, 233
Zeman, Zbynek A.E., 79
Zenck, Claudia Maurer, see:
   Maurer-Zenck, Claudia
Zenck, Martin, 767, 878,
   908, 1030
Zender, Hans, 20, 931
Zichy, Geza, 330
Ziegler, Hans Severus, 188
Zijkstra, Miep, 26
Zinn, E., 532
Zohn, Harry, 111, 119
Zweig, Stefan, 22, 80
Zychowicz, James, 940

SUBJECT INDEX

[All numbers are item numbers in the bibliography]

Adler, Guido, 290, 293, 310, 325, 374, 409, 1047
Albrecht, Hans, 811
Antisemitism, as political factor, 3, 81-92, 147-88
  Blessinger, Karl, as propagandist, 165, 177
  Brückner, Hans, as propagandist, 166
  Dreyfus, Alfred, as catalyst for work of Theodor Herzl, 66-68, 72, 74, 93, 99, 111, 688, 701
  Eichenauer, Richard, as propagandist, 134, 152, 159-60, 165, 186
  Gerigk, Herbert, as propagandist, 166
  Hitler, Adolf, and education in Vienna for later antisemitic policy of Third Reich, 75, 81, 85-86, 91, 156, 312
  Irkowsky, Rudolf, as propagandist, 147
  Jones, J. Sydney, on Hitler in Vienna, 260
  Louis, Rudolf, as propagandist of "racial" character in Mahler's music, 100, 131
  Lueger, Karl, antisemitic policy as Mayor of Vienna, 74, 81, 87, 89-91
  Moser, Hans Joachim, as propagandist, 152
  Müller-Blattau, Joseph, as propagandist, 152
  Rock, Christa Maria, as propagandist, 166
  Schönerer, Georg von, and antisemitic policy in Viennese politics, 74, 81, 89-90, 92
  Stengel, Theophil, as propagandist, 166
  Wagner, Richard, as propagandist,
      effect on antisemitic policies of Third Reich, 156, 161, 165, 178, 180, 182
      pro-semitic rebuttals to views of, 109, 124, 128, 135, 138, 142
  Wulf, Joseph, documentation of Nazi musical policy, 95, 173
Arnim, Ludwig Achim von, 6, 539-45
  see also Literary Sources and Influences (*Des Knaben Wunderhorn*)
Asher-Engel, Katherine, 1049

Bach, Johann Sebastian, 11, 120, 265, 282, 660, 704, 1047, 1049-50
    see also Mahler, Gustav, works (arrangements of works by other composers)
Bahr, Hermann, 69, 72, 75, 294-96, 312, 354-55, 696
Bahr-Mildenburg, Anna, 13, 22, 294, 297, 354, 468, 487
Banks, Paul, 27
Barford, Philip, 771
Bartos, Vydal Frantisek, 325
Batka, Richard, 12, 160, 356-57, 384
    see also Mahler, Gustav, correspondence, eyewitness accounts
Bauer-Lechner, Natalie,
    as writer, 12, 16, 298, 304
    position among other eyewitness accounts by Mahler's close associates, 19, 192, 282, 297, 310, 314, 325, 763, 921, 1047
    see also Mahler, Gustav, associates, eyewitness accounts
Bechstein, Ludwig, 553, 772
    see also Literary Sources and Influences (*Das klagende Lied*)
Beecham, Thomas, 623
Beethoven, Ludwig von, 45, 265, 282, 363, 426, 598, 712, 717, 927a
    influence on Mahler as composer in symphonic forms, 10-11, 23-24, 611, 613, 616, 658, 662
    Mahler as arranger of Beethoven's works, 23-24, 1048, 1051-53
    Mahler as conductor of Beethoven's works, 401, 413, 435
Behn, Hermann, 358, 381
Berg, Alban, 20, 191, 198, 328, 508, 631, 640, 722, 743
    eyewitness accounts of Mahler, 332-33
    conductor/editor of Mahler's works, 284, 1029
    Redlich, Hans, on position in musical history, 641
Besseler, Heinrich, 20, 954
Bethge, Hans, 549-52, 568, 881, 890
    see also Literary Sources and Influences (*Das Lied von der Erde*)
Bierbaum, Otto Julius, 69, 527, 529
    see also Mahler-Werfel, Alma, as composer (literary sources)
Blaukopf, Kurt, 892
Bote und Bock (music publisher), 572, 577-81
Brahms, Johannes, 191, 198, 427, 487, 568
Brentano, Clemens, 6, 539-45
    see also Literary Sources and Influences (*Des Knaben Wunderhorn*)
Bruckner, Anton, 17, 198, 265, 309, 373, 382, 425, 1034-35
    correspondence relating to Mahler, 334, 343
    influence on Mahler as composer in symphonic forms, 8, 613,

Subject Index 321

    629, 637, 646-47, 652
  Mahler as arranger of works of, 1054-55
  object of German nationalism assessed by followers of Wagner, 103, 154, 156, 170, 178, 180
  symphonies, analyses of form, harmony and orchestration, 725, 729, 732, 739, 744, 768, 774
  twin-status with Mahler, problems of, 224, 229, 233, 239, 251
Bülow, Hans von, 16, 335, 347, 361, 393, 1039
Busoni, Ferruccio Benvenuto, 336, 383, 654, 977

Cardus, Neville, 691, 793
Casella, Alfredo, 11, 688, 910
Clemenceau, Georges, 359
Clemenceau, Paul, 359

Damrosch, Walter, 300
Decsey, Ernst, 15
Dehmel, Richard, 69, 337, 528
  see also Mahler, Gustav, eyewitness accounts; Mahler-Werfel, Alma, as composer (literary sources)
Diepenbrock, Alphons (Alfons), 24, 338, 360, 391, 609, 792
  see also Mahler, Gustav, correspondence, eyewitness accounts
Diether, Jack, 273, 288
Disney, Walt, 1062
Doblinger, Ludwig (music publisher), 582-85

Ehlers, Paul, 156, 644, 690
  see also Empire, Austrian, antisemitism as political/cultural factor in; Holtzmann, Robert; Reception of Mahler's works (critical press)
Einstein, Albert, 65
Elvers, Rudolf, 392
Empire, Austrian,
  antisemitism as political/cultural factor in, 3, 81-92, 147-88
  history, cultural and intellectual, 62-80
    Kann, Robert, on, 84
  literati,
    Bloch, Josef, as publisher of *Österreichische Wochenschrift*, 87
    Kafka, Franz, 65, 119, 620
    Knab, Armin, 337
    Liliencron, Detlev von, 337
    Loerke, Oskar, 337
    Wittgenstein, Ludwig, 3, 66-67
    Zweig, Stefan, 75, 111, 337

minorities (including Jews), political and cultural influences, 93, 100-46
Morton, Frederic, on, 260
royal family,
   Franz Josef [Emperor of Austria], 3, 71, 468
   Rudolf [Archduke of Austria], 68
Schorske, Carl E., on, 199, 260
Engel, Gabriel, 844
Eulenberg, Ernst (music publisher), 571, 573, 586-87

Falke, Gustav, 337, 529
   see also Mahler-Werfel, Alma, as composer (literary sources)
Farrar, Geraldine, 301
Filler, Susan M., 5, 20
Foerster, Josef Bohuslav, 16, 302, 361, 409, 980
   see also Mahler, Gustav, associates, eyewitness accounts
Freud, Sigmund,
   as Viennese Jew, 65-68, 74, 99, 121
   work, 3, 8, 259, 261, 269, 271, 275-77, 307, 312
Furtwängler, Wilhelm, 623

Gabrilowitsch, Ossip, 9, 16, 299, 496
Goethe, Johann Wolfgang von, 294, 534, 718, 970
   see also Literary Sources and Influences (*Faust*)
Grimm, Jakob and Wilhelm, 554, 772
   see also Literary Sources and Influences (*Das klagende Lied*)
Gropius, Manon (daughter of Alma Mahler-Werfel), 504, 507-08, 512, 514, 519
   see also Mahler-Werfel, Alma, children
Gropius, Walter, 262, 501, 503a, 504-07, 511-12, 514-15, 519
   see also Mahler-Werfel, Alma, marriages
Grünfeld, Heinrich, 303
Gutheil-Schoder, Marie, 12-13, 305, 468

Hartleben, Otto Erich, 530
   see also Mahler-Werfel, Alma, as composer (literary sources)
Hauer, Josef Mathias, 198, 617
Hefling, Stephen, 912
Heine, Heinrich, 294, 563, 772
   see also Literary Sources and Influences
Herzfeld, Friedrich, 405
Heuberger, Richard, 362
Holtzmann, Robert, 644, 690
   see also Ehlers, Paul; Reception of Mahler's works (critical press)

Jews, 93, 100-46
   in music,

Subject Index 323

    composers,
      Bizet, Georges, 132, 688
      Bloch, Ernst, 120, 141
      Joachim, Joseph, 133
      Mendelssohn, Felix,
        antisemitic assessments, 149-50, 156, 158, 169, 177, 180, 184-85
        pro-semitic assessments, 109, 120, 133, 136-37, 141, 146
        psychology of composition, 265
      Offenbach, Jacques, 133, 478
      Rubinstein, Anton, 120, 133
      Sulzer, Salomon, 141
    historians,
      Berl, Heinrich, 128
      Brod, Max, 101, 119, 130, 136, 168, 278, 337
      Fischer, Theodor, 414
      Gradenwitz, Peter, 129, 168
      Grunberger, Richard, 188
      Kahan, Salomon, 658
      Karas, Joža, 119
      Mahler, Arnošt, 414
      Nadel, Arno, 101
      Nejedly, Zdenek, 414
      Sendrey, Alfred, 112, 116, 145
      Werner, Eric, 129, 131
        on Abraham and Moses Mendelssohn, 121, 146
Kahnt, Christian Friedrich (music publisher), 571-73, 588-90, 960
Kandinsky, Vasily (Wassily), 520
Karpath, Ludwig, 13, 308-09, 487
Keller, Otto, 52
Klemperer, Otto, 7, 188, 310
Klimt, Gustav, 8, 69, 74, 525
Klopstock, Friedrich Gottlieb, 536
  see also Literary Sources and Influences (Symphonies)
Kokoschka, Oskar, 74, 514, 522, 524-25
  see also Mahler-Werfel, Alma, sex life
Kretzschmar, Hermann, 921, 1047
Krisper, Anton, 285, 378, 407
Kurz-Halban, Selma, 13, 306

la Grange, Henry-Louis de, 235, 268, 279, 541, 549-52, 763
Langford, Samuel, 687
  see also reception of Mahler's works (critical press)
Leander, Richard, 558
  see also Literary Sources and Influences (Richard von Volk-

mann)
Literary Sources and Influences,
  da Ponte, Lorenzo, as librettist of *Don Giovanni*, and version of opera by Kalbeck, 477
  Dostoevskii, Fyodor, compared with Mahler, 8, 247
  Eichendorff, Joseph von, as forebear of Viennese literati of Mahler's time, 294
  Faust, in *Symphony no. 8*, 3, 534
  Heine, Heinrich,
    in works of Gustav Mahler, 563
    in works of Alma Mahler-Werfel, 563
  Das klagende Lied, 553-54
    see also Bechstein, Ludwig; Grimm, Jakob and Wilhelm
  Des Knaben Wunderhorn, 539-45
    see also Arnim, Ludwig Achim von; Brentano, Clemens
  Das Lied von der Erde (translations of Chinese poems by Hans Bethge), 549-52
    Hu Haiping, on original Chinese textual sources, 552
    Wenk, Arthur, on original Chinese textual sources, 552
  Mickiewicz, Adam, as author of *Todtenfeier*, and basis of first movement of *Symphony no. 2*, 912, 915
  Richter, Jean Paul, as author of *Titan*, and basis of *Symphony no. 1*, 772
  Rückert, Friedrich, as author of poems used in *Kindertotenlieder* and *Rückert Lieder*, 546-48
  Symphonies,
    Goethe, Johann Wolfgang von (use of *Faust* in *Symphony no. 8*), 3, 534
    Klopstock, Friedrich (use of *Auferstehungsode* in *Symphony no. 2*), 536
    Nietzsche, Friedrich (use of *Also sprach Zarathustra* and *Die fröhliche Wissenschaft* at composition of *Symphony no. 3*), 5, 537-38
    Nikkels, Eveline, on influence of Nietzsche, 537
  see also *Des Knaben Wunderhorn*
  Tellez, Gabriel (*pseud.*, Tirso de Molina), 557
  texts written by Mahler for own vocal works, 555-56, 559
    see also Mahler, Gustav, poems and vocal texts written by self
  Volkmann, Richard von (*pseud.*, Richard Leander), 558

Mahler, Alois (brother of Gustav Mahler), 262-64, 273-74, 389
Mahler, Anna Justina (daughter of Gustav Mahler), 332, 339, 344, 380, 504-05, 507, 514-15, 686
  see also Mahler, Gustav, family; Mahler-Werfel, Alma, children
Mahler, Bernhard (father of Gustav Mahler), 256, 262-64, 273-

Subject Index 325

74
  see also Mahler, Gustav, family
Mahler, Ernst (brother of Gustav Mahler), 262-64, 273-74, 277
  see also Mahler, Gustav, family
Mahler, Gustav,
  as conductor,
    Bad Hall, 11
    Budapest, 8, 13, 407-11
      and Sandor Erkel, 421
    Hamburg, 423-24
      and Bernhard Pollini, 423, 487
      Heinrich Chevalley on, 424
    Kassel, 14, 410-11
    Laibach (Ljubljana), 407
    Leipzig, 22, 418-19
      and Max Staegemann, 389, 418
    New York, 16, 491
      Metropolitan Opera, 492-97
        and Heinrich Conreid, 494
      New York Philharmonic Orchestra, 498-500
    Olmütz (Olomouč), 408-09
    Prague, 22, 409, 412-17
      and Angelo Neumann, 412
    Vienna, 16, 22, 425-27
      Hofoper, 443-90
        Franz von Dingelstedt as predecessor, 463
        Wilhelm Jahn as predecessor, 472, 487
        Herbert von Karajan as successor, 456, 476
      repertoire of Hofoper,
        Otto Erich Deutsch on repertoire, 959
        Leoncavallo, Ruggiero, 308, 362, 425, 481
        Mozart, Wolfgang Amadeus, 477, 479, 483-86, 488-90
          Rosa Papier-Paumgartner in cast, 487
          Robert Werba on productions, 479
        Wagner, Richard, 480
      Wiener Philharmoniker, 428-42
        Josef Hellmesberger, as conductor of, 427, 430
        Herbert von Karajan, as conductor of, 439
        Hans Richter, as conductor of, 308, 393, 406, 425, 431
        Robert Werba on Mozart repertoire, 441
        Alexander Witeschnik, on history of orchestra, 429
  associates ("Mahler Circle"), 1, 3, 8, 10, 16-18, 278-91
    Foerster, Josef Bohuslav, 409, 980
    Fried, Oskar, 381
    Graf, Max, 484-86, 921

Hauptmann, Gerhard, 312
Horwitz, Karl, 24
Krzyzanowski, Heinrich, 278
Krzyzanowski, Rudolf, 278, 389, 1035
Kurz-Halban, Selma, 306
Lehmann, Lilli, 479
Loewe, Carl, 978
Moser, Koloman, 69
Poisl, Josephine, 772, 847
Roller, Alfred, 447, 453, 455, 465, 477, 480, 525
Szeps-Clemenceau, Sophie, 359
Weber, Marion [Mathilde] von, 319, 1036-37
Weidig, F., 575-76
Weis-Ostborn, Julius, 880
compositional style,
  folk and nature influences on works, 2-3, 14, 17, 750-51, 754, 756-59, 762-64, 766-67
  formal style, 1, 3, 5, 17, 719, 721-27, 729-30, 732-34
    Agawu, Victor Kofi, on, 724
    Bekker, Paul, on, 101, 188, 564
    Cooke, Deryck, on, 5, 613, 676, 770, 810-11, 827
    Grant, [William] Parks, on, 793
    Nodnagel, Ernst Otto, on, 8, 13, 793
    Ratz, Erwin, on, 24, 726, 793
    Redlich, Hans, on, 24, 27, 172
    Schmidt, Heinrich, on, 730
    Tischler, Hans, on, 730
  literary influences on works, 3, 5-7, 534-70
    see also Literary Sources and Influences
  melodic/harmonic style, 3, 5, 17, 720, 727-28, 731-32, 734
    evaluation with techniques developed by Heinrich Schenker, 838, 943, 1011
  orchestration, 1, 735-49
  programs, 5, 750, 752-53, 755, 760-61, 765-66
  status in history of music, 1, 5, 8, 10-12, 16, 18-20, 23-24, 607-64
    vis-à-vis predecessors,
      Berlioz, Hector, 16, 265, 417, 621, 688, 743, 766, 841, 882
      Brahms, Johannes, 632, 645, 647, 650, 652, 722, 725, 849
      Chopin, Frédéric, 417, 974
      Couperin, François, 663
      Gluck, Christoph Willibald von, 659
      Handel, George Frederick, 265, 1047

Subject Index 327

Haydn, Franz Josef, 265, 363, 744
Heller, Stephen, 774
Liszt, Ferencz (Franz), 154, 309, 417, 588, 621, 766, 807, 835, 349, 882
Lully, Jean-Baptiste, 634
Meyerbeer, Giacomo, 109, 120, 149-50, 177, 185, 265, 1039, 1041, 1043a
Mozart, Wolfgang Amadeus, 610, 636, 648, 660, 744
Schütz, Heinrich, 970, 1047
Schumann, Robert, 4, 14, 23-24, 265, 282, 628, 1048, 1058
Strauss, Johann, the Younger, 659
Verdi, Giuseppe, 521
Wagner, Richard, 613, 616, 638, 646, 652
vis-à-vis contemporaries,
Bittner, Julius, 652
Charpentier, Gustave, 417, 688
Debussy, Claude, 663, 688, 722, 743
Delius, Frederick, 613, 841
Dvořák, Antonin, 19, 650
Elgar, Edward, 614, 774
Fauré, Gabriel, 774
Goldmark, Karl, 309
Grieg, Edvard, 417
Ives, Charles, 5, 20, 631, 635
  Robert Morgan on, 5
Janáček, Leos, 19, 29
Marx, Joseph, 652
Mascagni, Pietro, 308
Pierné, Gabriel, 688
Puccini, Giacomo, 308, 362, 481, 639
Reger, Max, 265, 308, 653, 717, 768, 848
Schreker, Franz, 617, 629
Sibelius, Jan, 29, 841
Smetana, Bedrich, 19, 393, 413, 425
Strauss, Richard, 625, 638, 647, 653
Tchaikovsky, Pyotr Ilyich, 17, 417, 425, 618
vis-à-vis successors,
Albeniz, Isaac, 774
Bartók, Béla, 39, 654
Berio, Luciano, 5, 535
Blacher, Boris, 704
Boulez, Pierre, 5
Britten, Benjamin, 23
Cage, John, 20, 631
Cerha, Friedrich, 645
Chavez, Carlos, 120

Dallapiccola, Luigi, 766
Einem, Gottfried von, 700
Hindemith, Paul, 156, 180, 188, 598
Korngold, Erich Wolfgang, 652
Krenek, Ernst, 188, 1000, 1029
Landré, [Guillaume], 609
Milhaud, Darius, 633
Orff, Carl, 180, 535
Pijper, Willem, 609
Prokofiev, Sergei, 634
Schmidt, Franz, 629
Shostakovich, Dmitri, 10, 648, 828
Steiner, Max, 686
Stravinsky, Igor, 20, 226, 265, 615, 624, 631, 643, 654, 797, 836
Webern, Anton [von], 3, 17-18, 191, 198, 547, 657, 722
correspondence, 2, 12, 14, 16, 377-95
   with Laura Hilgerman, 857
   with Ed. von Mihalovich, 377
   with Herwarth Walden, 392
   joint correspondence of Johannes Messchaert, 391
   Klemm, Eberhardt, on, 596, 948
eyewitness accounts,
   biographies and autobiographies of associates, 293-331
     Brahms, Johannes, 308-09
     Schoenberg, Arnold, 328
     Strauss, Richard, 309, 324
   letters, 22, 332-53
     of Thomas Mann, 337, 340
     of Hans Pfitzner, 341
     of Arnold Schoenberg, 333, 345
     of Paul Stefan-[Gruenfeldt], 349
     of Richard Strauss, 335, 342, 346-48
     of Cosima Wagner, 348
     of Bruno Walter, 349
     of Hugo Wolf, to Oskar Grohe, 352
     of Hugo Wolf, to Melanie Köchert, 351
     of Hugo Wolf, to Heinrich Potpeschnigg, 350, 352
   essays, 7, 11-13, 15-16, 22, 354-76
   see also Mahler, Gustav, associates
family,
   children, 339, 380, 504-05, 507, 514-15
   see also Mahler, Anna Justina; Mahler, Maria Anna
   marriage, 339, 380, 501, 503a, 504-07, 511, 514-15
   Moll, Carl (stepfater-in-law), 69
   parents, 256, 262-64, 273-74

see also Mahler, Bernhard; Mahler, Marie
Rosé, Arnold (brother-in-law), 374, 487
siblings, 262-64, 273-74
   see also Mahler, Alois; Mahler, Ernst; Mahler, Otto;
      Mahler-Rosé, Justine
see also Mahler-Werfel, Alma, children, marriages
medical/psychiatric assessments, 3, 5, 8, 255-77, 307
   of George Baehr, 270
   of Nicholas and Beverly Christy and Barry Wood, 266-68, 270
   of Joseph Fränkel [physician], 270
   of Ernest Jones, referencing work of Sigmund Freud, 3, 275
   of Edward Kravitt, 262
   of David Levy, 266
      referencing work of Emanuel Libman, 270
   of Theodor Reik, 3, 131, 1027
poems and vocal texts written by self, 12, 20, 378, 555-56, 871, 881
portraits, 189, 201-02
   by Otto Böhler, silhouette, 637
   by Auguste Rodin, bust, 359
works,
   arrangements of works by other composers, 8, 23-24, 1039-58
      Bach, Johann Sebastian, 1047, 1049-50
      Beethoven, Ludwig von, 23-24, 1048, 1051-53
      Bruckner, Anton, 1054-55
      Schubert, Franz, 8, 23, 1048, 1056-57
      Schumann, Robert, 23, 1048, 1058
      Weber, Carl Maria von, 567, 1039-56
         Heusgen, Birgit, on *Die drei Pintos*, 1043a
   songs, 2-3, 7, 15-16, 18, 560-61, 565, 768-71, 774-83, 837-56
      Lieder eines fahrenden Gesellen, 14, 857-62
      Des Knaben Wunderhorn, 6, 540-45, 863-64
      Rückert settings, 546-47, 865-70
      Das Lied von der Erde, 5, 550-52, 879-98
         Zoltan Roman on, 363, 857
   symphonies, 2-3, 6-7, 16, 768-836, 899-1030
      Symphony no. 1, 17, 21, 899-908
      Symphony no. 2, 19, 909-21
      Symphony no. 3, 5, 10, 20, 922-31
         Filler, Susan M., on, 922, 927, 930, 940
         Franklin, Peter, on, 930, 940
      Symphony no. 4, 8, 23-24, 932-40
      Symphony no. 5, 941-48

Symphony no. 6, 7, 20, 24, 949-60
Symphony no. 7, 5, 20, 961-69
Symphony no. 8, 970-83
Symphony no. 9, 7, 10, 21, 23, 984-96
Symphony no. 10, 5, 17, 24, 997-1030
  Bergquist, Peter, on, 997, 1011
  Filler, Susan M., on, 1000, 1010, 1029
  Maurer-Zenck, Claudia, on, 1010, 1012
  Ratz, Erwin, on, 1008, 1021
  version of Friedrich (Frederick) Block, 1022
  version of Clinton Carpenter, 5
  version of Deryck Cooke, 1000, 1008-09, 1012, 1018-20, 1024-25
  version of Remo Mazzetti, 5
  version of Joseph Wheeler, 5, 1022
  version of Hans Wollschläger, 5
works not otherwise classified above, 20, 771-72, 776, 871-78, 1031-38
Symphonic Prelude, believed to be by Mahler, proved spurious,
  Albrecht Gürsching as orchestrator, 1034-35
  Paul Banks on, 1034-35
  Donald Mitchell on, 1034-35
Mahler, Maria Anna (daughter of Gustav Mahler), 339, 380, 504-05, 507, 514-15
see also Mahler, Gustav, family; Mahler-Werfel, Alma, children
Mahler, Marie (mother of Gustav Mahler), 256, 262-64, 273-74
see also Mahler, Gustav, family
Mahler, Otto (brother of Gustav Mahler), 262-64, 273-74, 389
see also Mahler, Gustav, family
Mahler-Rosé, Justine (sister of Gustav Mahler), 262-64, 273-74, 368, 381, 389
see also Mahler, Gustav, family
Mahler-Werfel, Alma,
  as composer,
    analyses of works, 502-03, 509-10
    literary sources, 502-03, 509-10
      Bierbaum, Otto Julius, 527, 529
      Dehmel, Richard, 528
      Falke, Gustav, 529
      Hartleben, Otto Erich, 530
      Novalis (pseud. of Friedrich von Hardenberg), 531
      Rilke, Rainer Maria, 532
      Werfel, Franz, 502, 504, 509, 533
    see also Literary Sources and Influences
  publishers of works,

Universal Edition, 503, 509-10
Josef Weinberger, 502
children,
Gropius, Manon, 504, 507-08, 512, 514, 519
Mahler, Anna Justina, 339, 380, 504-05, 507, 514-15
Mahler, Maria Anna, 339, 380, 504-05, 507, 514-15
Werfel, Martin, 504, 507, 514, 519
marriages,
to Gustav Mahler, 339, 380, 501, 503a, 504-07, 511, 514-15
to Walter Gropius, 501, 503a, 504-07, 511-12, 514-15, 519
to Franz Werfel, 501-04, 506-08, 511-18, 520, 523, 526
sex life, 501, 503a, 504-07, 511, 514-15, 518-20, 522, 524-25
Mann, Thomas, 312, 523, 564
see also Mahler, Gustav, eyewitness accounts; Mahler-Werfel, Alma, sex life
Martner, Knud, 282, 413, 529, 699, 940
Masel, F. Lev Abramovich, 634
Mellers, Wilfrid, 691
Mengelberg, [Curt] Rudolf, 292, 993
Mengelberg, Willem, 11, 24, 280, 289, 292, 609, 683, 804, 948
Edna Richolson-Sollitt as publisher of verbal remarks of, on Mahler, 814
reported by Paul Stefan-[Gruenfeldt] to have seen early symphonies composed by Mahler at Conservatory in Vienna, 1037
writings on Mahler and correspondence with Mahler, 313, 387, 391, 984
Mitchell, Donald, 27, 241, 279, 541, 549-52, 676, 770, 857, 940, 961, 1054
Monnikendam, Marius, 609

Neitzel, Otto, 16
Nettl, Paul, 128, 1047
Newlin, Dika, 109a, 263, 619, 732, 927a
Nietzsche, Friedrich, 5, 138, 537-38, 564, 711
see also Literary Sources and Influences
Nikisch, Artur, 393, 403, 506
Novalis (*pseud.* of Friedrich von Hardenberg), 531
see also Mahler-Werfel, Alma, as composer (literary sources)

Palm, Albert, 967
Pamer, Fritz Egon, 541, 565, 845, 847
Perger, Richard von, 425
Peters, C.F. (music publisher), 571-74, 591-97

Hinrichsen, Henri, and negotiations with Mahler for *Symphony no. 5*, 592-93
Hinrichsen, Walter, second son of preceding, and establishment of American office of firm after World War II, 592
Lindlar, Heinrich, as chronicler of history of firm, 595-96
Pachnicke, Bernd, as chronicler of history of firm, 596
Pfitzner, Hans Erich, 20, 365, 482, 574, 631, 768, 841, 848, 1058
Pfohl, Ferdinand, 302, 314
Plato, 294
Pringsheim, Klaus, 366
Publishers of music, 571-76
  Bote und Bock (Berlin), 577-81
    Max Kuhn and Karl Lauterbach as predecessor in history of publication of *Symphony no. 7*, 580
  Doblinger, Ludwig (Vienna), 582-83
    Bernhard Herzmansky as founder of firm, 583
  Eulenberg, Ernst (Leipzig and Vienna, later London and Zürich), 586-87
    Redlich, Hans, as editor of Mahler works in, 586-87
  Kahnt, C.F. (Leipzig, later Lindau/Wasserburg), 588-90
  Peters, C.F. (Leipzig, later Frankfurt, London and New York), 591-97
  Rättig, Theodor (Vienna), 1054
  B. Schotts Söhne (Mainz), 598-601
  Universal Edition (Vienna), 602-05
    as publisher of works of Gustav Mahler, 42, 56, 602
    as publisher of works of Alma Mahler-Werfel, 503, 509-10
  Weinberger, Josef (Vienna, later London), 606
    as publisher of works of Gustav Mahler, 858-60
    as publisher of works of Alma Mahler-Werfel, 502

Quoika, Rudolf, 414

Rachmaninoff, Sergei, 315
Ratz, Erwin, 950, 953, 985
Reception of Mahler's works,
  critical press, 6, 8, 687-701
    Bienenfeld, Elsa, 489
    Hanslick, Eduard, 357
    Hevesi, Ludwig, 483
    Hirschfeld, Robert, 464, 484-85
    Kalbeck, Max, 479, 485-86, 488
    Korngold, Julius, 357, 479, 485-86, 488, 700-01
    Krehbiel, Henry Edward, 16, 299
    Sorabji, Kaikhosru [Leon Dudley], 691, 793

Subject Index 333

    Wagner, Manfred, as archivist of critical history, 690
    Wallaschek, Richard, 484-85
historiography, 1, 3, 6, 8, 10-11, 13, 17-20, 24, 665-86
    Adkins, Cecil and Alis Dickinson, 724, 752, 815, 824, 868
    Barsova, Inna, 310
    Blume, Friedrich, 603
    Namenwirth, Simon Michael [Misha], 644, 725, 755, 868
    Smoley, Lewis, 38
    Vondenhoff, Bruno and Eleonore, 49, 725, 755, 801, 868
    Weber, J.F., 38, 667
philosophical views, 2-3, 7-8, 10, 16-17, 20, 702-18
    Adorno, Theodor Wiesengrund, 564, 649, 717, 908, 985, 1030
    Greene, David, 705, 1027
        Heidegger, Martin, cited by, 706
        Sartre, Jean-Paul, cited by, 407
        Schopenhauer, Arthur, cited by, 564, 711
    Holbrook, David, 705
Redlich, Hans Ferdinand, 953
Reeser, Eduard, 360
Reilly, Edward, 940
Reznicek, Emil Nikolaus von, 16
Riedel, Johannes, 690
Rilke, Rainer Maria, 69, 532
    see also Mahler-Werfel, Alma, as composer (literary sources)
Ritter, William, 6, 13, 311, 367, 688, 692-94, 784a
    see also Mahler, Gustav, correspondence, eyewitness accounts; Reception of Mahler's works (critical press)
Rognoni, Luigi, 562
Rolland, Romain, 342
Rosé, Alfred, 368
Rosenthal, Moriz, 364
Rott, Hans, 278-79
    see also Mahler, Gustav, associates
Rückert, Friedrich, 17, 546-48, 568, 775, 783, 804, 842, 852, 865-70
    see also Literary Sources and Influences
Ruhnke, Martin, 482

Salten, Felix, 11, 75, 695-96
    see also Reception of Mahler's works (critical press)
Schaefers, Anton, 730
Schalk, Franz, 343, 346, 463, 1029
Scherchen, Hermann, 967
Scheu, Josef, 337, 967
Schiedermair, Ludwig, 8, 316, 369, 668, 793, 801, 817-18

see also Mahler, Gustav, eyewitness accounts, works
Schiele, Egon, 525
Schnitzler, Arthur, 72, 74-75, 111, 344
Schoenberg, Arnold, 3, 10, 23-24, 265, 286, 714, 797, 833
 as subject of pro-semitic/antisemitic debate,
  antisemitic views, 156, 180, 185, 188
  pro-semitic views, 113, 120-21, 123, 128, 132, 136-37, 141
 as supporter of performances of Mahler's music, 292, 861
 historical importance in music, 610, 619, 629, 640, 643, 652-54
 Egon Wellesz on, 374-76
 style influenced by Mahler, 233, 288, 717, 722, 732, 743, 841, 882, 1023
 Vienna and, 74-75, 198, 426
 writings on Mahler, 7, 78, 333, 370, 728, 1015
Schotts Söhne, B. (music publisher), 598-601
 correspondence between Mahler and Ludwig Strecker, 386
Schubert, Franz, 8, 23, 265, 282, 645, 844, 952, 1048, 1056-57
 see also Mahler, Gustav, works (arrangements of works by other composers)
Schuh, Willi, 883
Schumann, Robert, 4, 14, 23-24, 265, 282, 628, 1048, 1058
 see also Mahler, Gustav, works (arrangements of works by other composers)
Seidl, Art[h]ur, 12, 15, 52, 403, 820
 see also Mahler, Gustav, as conductor, eyewitness accounts
Selden-Goth, Gisela [Tolney-Witt, Gisela?], 390
Sievers, Heinrich, 864
Singer, Kurt, 122, 699
 see also Empire, Austrian, minorities (including Jews), political and cultural influences; Reception of Mahler's works (critical press); Tessmer, Hans
Slezak, Leo, 13, 309, 317-18, 381, 468
Smith, Warren Storey, 503
Smyth, Ethel Mary, 319
Sopeña-Ibáñez, Federico, 204, 248
Specht, Richard, 8, 131, 463, 466, 700, 793
 analyses of Mahler works, 895, 907, 920, 928, 935, 960-61, 966, 979, 995, 1014
 as literatus, nonmusical writings, 75
 eyewitness accounts of Mahler, 11-13, 15-16, 320-21, 371
 see also Mahler, Gustav, eyewitness accounts, works
Stefan-[Gruenfeldt], Paul, 14, 23, 119, 465-67, 651-53
 analyses of Mahler works, 825, 1036-37
 eyewitness accounts of Mahler, 1, 11-13, 15-16, 22, 298,

Subject Index

322-23
Stehmann, Gerhard, 13
Stein, Erwin, 1058
Steinitzer, Max, 16, 22
Stokowski, Leopold, 9, 979
Stransky, Josef, 9, 372
Strauss, Richard, 16, 23, 29, 39, 41, 198, 224, 369, 574, 977
  as conductor, 403, 406
      Hofoper/Staatsoper (Vienna), 457, 462-63, 476
      Wiener Philharmoniker, 425-27, 432
  as subject of pro-semitic/antisemitic debate, 103, 147, 154, 156, 178, 180
  correspondence, 385, 1039
  twin-status with Mahler, problems of, 684, 723, 743-44, 773-74, 807, 841, 848
Swarowsky, Hans, 967
Szeps-Zuckerkandl, Berta, 73, 331, 359, 483

Tessmer, Hans, 699
  see also Reception of Mahler's works (critical press); Singer, Kurt
Teweles, Heinrich, 119
Tirso de Molina (*pseud*. of Gabriel Tellez), 557
  see also Literary Sources and Influences (Gabriel Tellez)
Toscanini, Arturo, 494

Universal Edition (music publisher), 42, 56, 503, 509-10, 602-05
  as publisher of works of Gustav Mahler, 42, 56, 602
  as publisher of works of Alma Mahler-Werfel, 503, 509-10
  correspondence between Emil Hertzka (founder of firm) and Mahler, 388

Visconti, Luchino, 246

Wagner, Cosima, 381, 505
Wagner, Otto, 74
Wagner, Richard, 3, 11-12, 265, 309, 401, 417, 564, 598, 1052
  and Brahms, factional controversy in Mahler's generation of composers, 154, 265, 393, 717
  compositional influence on successors, 229, 702, 711, 717, 722, 738, 807, 877, 974
  Mahler as conductor of operas of, 357, 371, 413, 470
Walter, Bruno, 33, 564, 644, 660, 700, 771, 881, 948
  as conductor,
      Hofoper/Staatsoper, 41
      Wiener Philharmoniker, 437

correspondence of Mahler with, 192-93
eyewitness accounts, 12-13, 16, 22, 283, 297, 304, 306,
   310, 325-26, 373
Weber, Carl von, 319
Weber, Carl Maria von, 44, 282, 347, 417, 555
   performing version of *Die drei Pintos* by Mahler, 562, 566-
      67, 588, 661, 1039-46
Weill, Kurt, 188
Weinberger, Josef (music publisher), 502, 606, 858-60, 907
   as publisher of works of Gustav Mahler, 858-60
   as publisher of works of Alma Mahler-Werfel, 502
Weingartner, Felix [von], 18, 37, 327, 465, 662, 921, 1052
   see also Mahler, Gustav, associates, eyewitness accounts,
   compositional style
Wellesz, Egon, 1, 75, 291, 328, 374-76, 473
   on Mahler's compositional style, 617, 728, 738, 748-49, 833
Werfel, Franz, 75, 96, 119, 250, 312, 331-32, 340, 344, 349
   marriage to Alma Mahler-Werfel, 501-04, 506-09, 511-18,
      520-23, 526
   poetical stimulus for composition of Alma Mahler-Werfel, 533
Werfel, Martin (son of Alma Mahler-Werfel), 504, 507, 514, 519
Wessely, Othmar, 481
Wessling, Berndt W., 503a, 515
Williamson, John C., 922, 940-41, 961
Winter, Josefine von, 329
Wolf, Hugo, 191, 198, 265, 309, 394, 555, 840-41, 848-49
   eyewitness account of Mahler, in correspondence, 350-53
   relations with Mahler during classes at Conservatory in
      Vienna, 278, 287
women in music,
   Barbi, Alice, 427
   Berg, Helene, as editor of writings of Alban Berg, 508, 641
   Mahler-Werfel, Alma,
      profiled by Karen Monson, 503, 503a, 515
      profiled by Patrick Mahony, 515
      profiled by Walter Sorell, 515
   Mendelssohn-Hensel, Fanny, 505
   Schumann, Clara Wieck, see: Wieck-Schumann, Clara
   Wellesz, Emmy, as joint biographer of Egon Wellesz, 291
   Wieck-Schumann, Clara, 505

Zemlinsky, Alexander [von], 198, 286, 374, 394, 630, 652, 841,
   847. 1029
Zichy, Geza, 330, 421
Zinne, Wilhelm, 334

REFERENCE

ELIHU BURRITT LIBRARY
CENTRAL CONNECTICUT STATE UNIVERSITY
NEW BRITAIN, CONNECTICUT 06050